THAILAND

T R A V B U G S
TRAVEL GUIDES

Project Editor:	A. Lau
Editorial Coordination:	Sun Tree Publishing Ltd
Design & DTP:	Sun Tree Publishing
Layout:	Eric Yeo
Desktop Assistant:	Sares Kanapathy
Cover & Illustrations:	Susan Harmer
Maps:	Eric Yeo
	Bangkok map (Macmillan/Sun Tree
	Map of Thailand)
Consultants:	C. Chatri
	Vira Aroonvatanaporn
	L. Anchulee

© 1992
Co-Published by MPH Publishing (S) Pte Ltd
and Sun Tree Publishing Ltd

Copyrights
English, Japanese, Thai – MPH Publishing Ltd
Chinese – Sun Tree Publishing Ltd/MPH Publishing Ltd
All other languages – Sun Tree Publishing Ltd

Marketing & Sales
International Sales & Foreign Rights:
Sun Tree Publishing
Block 6, Level 3, 152 Tagore Lane
off Upper Thomson Road
Singapore 2678
Tel: (65) 452 2677
Fax: (65) 455 3758

Singapore & Malaysia Sales
MPH Distributors (S) Pte Ltd
Pan-I Complex #03-07
601 Sims Drive
Singapore 1438
Tel: (65) 747 5050
Fax: (65) 744 0620

ISBN: 981 00 2687 0
Printed in Singapore

THAILAND

Text by Keith Mundy

*With contributions from
Kelvin Rugg
Colin Piprell*

Editor
A. Lau

MPH Publishing (S) Pte Ltd

Sun Tree Publishing Ltd

CONTENTS

INTRODUCTION

Land of Smiles 1

PAST AND PRESENT

A trek through Thailand's colourful history to its current affairs.

History 7
From the bronze age to the arrival of the Thais.

History 8
Sukhothai – Ayutthaya – Chakri Dynasty – European Influence – Modern History.

Government 21
Civil Service – Military.

Economy 27
Agriculture – Industry & Commerce – Mining – Handicrafts.

ACROSS THE COUNTRY

Thailand's natural features.

Geography 33
The country and its climate.

Flora & Fauna 37
A look at natural habitats, wildlife, and vegetation.

BANGKOK

Discovering the metropolis.
City of Angels 47
Flavours and favours of Bangkok.

Sights to See 59
Places of Interest with practical information.

Shopping 79
What to Buy and Where to Shop.

CONTENTS

River & Klong Life 93
Exploring Venice of the East and life on the waterways.

Nights in Bangkok 105
The evening scene at discos, jazz bars, restaurants, cultural shows, cruises, Patpong and night markets.

REGIONS OF THAILAND

Follow that Bug.

Central Plains 117
The rice–bowl of Asia and cradle of Thai history.
Ayutthaya – Lopburi – Ang Thong – Saraburi – Suphanburi – Nakhon Pathom – Kanchanaburi.

The North 145
Hill tribes and trekking.
Chiang Mai – Lamphun – Nakhon Sawan – Phitsanulok – Sukhothai – Tak – Lampang – Mae Hong Son – Chiang Rai – Phrae – Nan.

North-east, Isan 175
Harsh and almost isolated terrain.
Nakhon Ratchisma – Buriram – Rot Et – Udon Thani – Nong Khai – Loei – Nakhon Phanom – Sakhon Nakhon – Yasothon – Ubon Ratchathani – Surin.

The East 195
Sun, sea and the Gulf.
Pattaya – Chonburi – Bang Saen – Rayong – Chantaburi – Trat.

The South 209
Andaman idylls and more of the Gulf.
Phetburi – Prachuap Khiri Khan – Chumphon – Ranong – Phuket – Surat Thani – Nakhon Si Thammarat – Phattalung – Songkhla – Phangnga – Krabi – Trang – Satun – Yala – Narathiwat – Hat Yai.

LIFESTYLE – FESTIVALS – CRAFTS

Ways of the Thai.

People 243
The Thais and their ethnic background.

CONTENTS

Religion 257
The dominance of Buddhism, the belief in spirits and superstitions, and other faiths.

Culture 267
A cultural tapestry of religious art, decoration and ornamentation, temple and palace architecture, traditional houses, literature, drama, dance, music, painting and modern art forms.

Fabulous Festivals 291
There's always something happening – throughout the country and all year round.

Handicrafts 311
From tribal wares to modern goods, where to buy and what to buy.

WHAT TO DO...WHERE TO GO

Sports & Recreation 323
Diving – Fishing – Waterskiing – Parasailing – Boating – Trekking – Golf – Tennis – Jogging.

Eating Out 345
Tasty recommendations. Follow that bug to restaurants in Bangkok, Chiang Mai, Pattaya & Phuket.

Off the Beaten Track 369
Going your own way.

BEYOND THAILAND...LAOS

Laos 375
A visit with the neighbour, a look at Vientiane and Luang Prabang.

EASY REFERENCE

Trav' Tips 399
All that you need to know but may forget to ask!

Directory 409
Quick lead to people and places.

Index 431
A quick find.

Photo Credits 446

v

Thailand, a land of people and their diverse ethnic

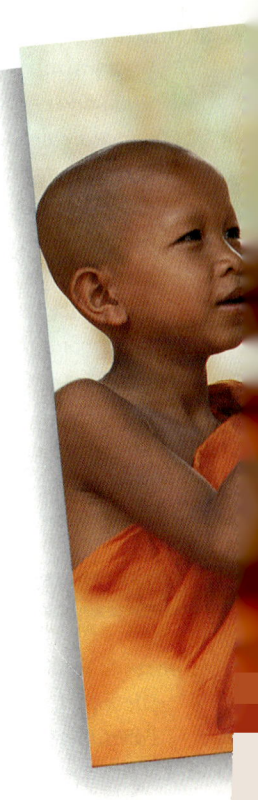

background, religions, beliefs and activities. Thailand, also a land of ready smiles.

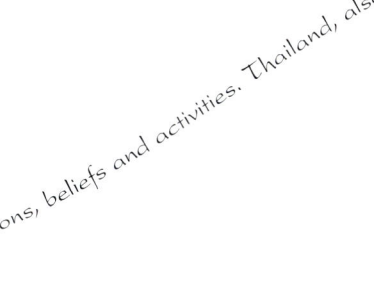

A land of serenity, awash with generous rivers  *which flow from mountains to the seas. A land*

images everywhere,

of peace so often watched over by Buddha

Rooftops that shelter millions of souls, their beliefs and culture, are also

details or mere simple, rustic covers.

a wonderment of architectural

Imaging is a major Thai preoccupation reflecting cultural and religious beliefs. Carving or sculpturing can

xii

be found on wood, stone, vegetable, fruits, candle-wax...

Introduction

In Thailand, you will hear much of the "Thai way", a phrase used to explain what might otherwise be inexplicable. If you are bewildered by some phenomenon or some action, the explanation is "That's the Thai way". If you get into the spirit of the place, you will react with a smile rather than a quizzical frown. The Thais themselves are given to taking life lightly rather than pondering it deeply, enjoying the moment and not dwelling on it too much.

That warm and friendly Thai smile.

Thailand is different - not just different from Europe or America but different from its next-door neighbours too. In a region of conflict and post-colonial divisiveness, Thailand stands alone as culturally and politically unified. It avoided European colonisation, uniquely in the region, and Indochinese communism halted at its borders. The Thai-Buddhist culture evolved over the course of a thousand years and survived not only such 19th and 20th century threats but also the annihilation of its great capital city, Ayutthaya, by the invading Burmese in the 18th century.

Monkhood is a common practice for Buddhists, many entering it during their youth.

Migrating from southern China a thousand years ago and dominating the current territory by the 15th century, ethnic Thais form around 85% of the population (Chinese making up most of the rest). For Southeast Asia, this is a high proportion for a dominant group and gives rise to a remarkably homogeneous and stable culture. There are naturally regional variations - the relative volatility of southerners, "hot hearts", or the serenity of northerners, "cool hearts", for example - but broadly a Thai is a Thai is a Thai. You have only

to contrast the racial divisions of Malaysia or the cultural diversity of Indonesia to see how integrated Thailand is.

What is a Thai? He may be a rice farmer (most likely) of the flat river-filled Central Plains or a sea-going fisherman of the monsoon-swept southern peninsula, a limousine-borne banker caught in a Bangkok traffic jam or a monk meditating in a northern forest monastery. She may be a housewife or a mother or a market vendor, and most likely all three together, a factory worker assembling televisions for a Japanese company or a Bangkok secretary spending eight hours in the office and another four commuting.

Whatever the profession, the status, the gender or the location, a Thai is a Buddhist and a monarchist and these allegiances form the cement that binds the Thai nation. The monarchy has a 700-year history through several dynasties and rarely has a king completely lost the faith of the people. Reigning King Bhumiphol is one of the most respected sovereigns in that whole history, representing the stable and conscientious eye of the politico-military storm that sometimes is Thai government.

One of the king's titles is Upholder of Religion, not only as protector of the Buddhist faith but as guarantor of freedom of religious belief. Buddhism is tolerant, or should be, and the Thai people exemplify that virtue.

One of the most common Thai phrases is *"mai pen rai"* meaning "It doesn't matter" or "Never mind". It expresses Thai-Buddhist culture in its willingness to forgive, its not dwelling upon a transient mistake or deficiency, and its urge not to upset the smooth passage of life.

This spirit of conciliation and consideration gives rise to Thai hospitality. It is a Thai article of faith to make the visitor feel comfortable and at ease. This ancient home custom has translated itself in the tourism age into a graciousness of service in hotels, restaurants and shops which is unequalled in the world. Not only that, the presentation is often superb – the welcome with a flower garland, the universal smiles.

Thailand is often called the Land of Smiles but this doesn't mean that everybody is always happy and pleased to see you. Though the Thais are a relatively contented and very easy-going people, the smiles have many purposes – a serene front to a challenging world, a smooth response to the unalterable vagaries of life, and yes, friendliness, for the Thais are certainly a friendly people.

Modern life is taking some toll on Thai tolerance: the nation of nearly 60 million souls is being propelled headlong towards industrialisation and some nerves are getting frayed in the process, notably in Bangkok. The environment is also suffering all the way from urban pollution to rural deforestation. The reverse side of the tolerance coin is indiscipline, a true Achilles heel in modern technological society.

Nevertheless, Thailand remains for the most part a place of frequent beauty and widespread charm – from glistening temples to aquamarine seas, from graceful women to

Songkran – time for a friendly douse and lots of "sanuk".

saffron-clad monks, from dense rainforests to mighty muddy rivers, from ancient ruins to holy caves. For the visitor, these sights are made easily accessible by a comprehensive and comfortable public transport system, ubiquitous accommodation, fine food for fuel and very reasonable prices.

Thailand is one of the world's best travel bargains and this guide, with all its information, illustrations and essays, is designed to help you get into it and get the most out of a visit to Thailand.

A key word in the Thai vocabulary is *sanuk*, or fun. Life has its problems and its obligations but its main objective is *sanuk*, having a good time. Since Buddhism says life is suffering, the Thais have decided to make sure they have a good time as often as possible, and they do their best to help visitors to have one too.

So enjoy yourself in Thailand – it's the Thai way!

PAST AND PRESENT

History

Most nation-states are the outcome of long processes of migration and assimilation, and Thailand is no exception. Their history is always complex, but can often be reduced to a simple essence. Thus, the Thais are a Chinese tribe who migrated southward one thousand years ago, encountered and adopted much Indian culture, especially the Buddhist religion, and developed a powerful and prosperous kingdom centred in the valley of the Chao Phraya River which is now rapidly industrialising.

Lotus-shaped offerings at the statue of King Ramkhamhaeng.

PRE-HISTORY

National history is the chronicle of the convergence of peoples and territory, and territory comes first. As long as 40,000 years ago, the Southeast Asian forests were inhabited by hunters and gatherers using wooden and stone tools and living in relatively permanent sites. From 20,000 to 10,000 years ago, they began to cul

tivate peas and beans and domesticate animals such as the chicken. Only around 10,000 years ago did individual cultures start to differentiate from this common background.

Around 7,000 to 6,000 years ago, metallurgy had been established, as evidenced by the bronze technology of Ban Chiang in northeast Thailand, a site of great significance in Asian pre-history. Little is known of the prehistoric people of Ban Chiang, east of Udon Thani, but it is guessed that this was a major burial ground of a regional culture which produced distinctive bronzeware and pottery. By about 3,000 years ago, iron was being worked in the region.

From about 2,000 years ago, tribal chiefdoms dominated the north-east and central regions. They practised rice cultivation and engaged in some trade between tribes. It was only in the 5th century A.D. that more evidence of historical record appeared, with the discovery of Mon remains at Nakhon Pathom in the west of the lower Chao Phraya valley.

The Mons

The Mon people, of uncertain origin, established a scattering of kingdoms across the central plains from the 6th to the 11th centuries. Known as Dvaravati, this civilisation was Indianised through contact with merchants and monks from the sub-continent. Besides Nakhon Pathom in the west, there were important centres at Lopburi (Lavo) in the centre and even as far north as Lamphun (Haripunchai). The Mon came increasingly under the influence of the Khmer kingdom of Funan to the east. It was at this point, towards the end of the first millennium A.D., that the migrating Thais began to arrive from the north and to encounter the strong Mon-Khmer Buddhist civilisation. Out of this meeting came Thailand, for this confluence of peoples and cultures brought about successive Thai states that led directly to today's nation.

The T'ai

From the history of the territory, it would be good to go back to pick up the story of the people. Ethnically, the Thais are one of a group of people called T'ai whose origins were in southern China, and possibly even further north. The T'ai peoples began migrating southwards in the first millenium, probably under pressure from the growing Han Chinese majority. From the kingdom of Nanchao (now Yunnan), they filtered down through the mountains of the north into what is now north-eastern Burma (the Shan people), northern Laos (the Lao Loum people), and northern Thailand (the Thai people).

By the 11th century, there was most probably a substantial Thai-speaking population in the Mon-Khmer kingdoms of the central plains as well as in Haripunchai in the north. A Thai king-

King Chulalongkorn (Rama V) and his family.

dom was established at Payao in the far north in 1096. Quite probably in the 12th century, the Thais outnumbered the Mons and Khmers in these areas and by the 13th century they had established principalities from Chiang Saen in the far north right down to Nakhon Sri Thammarat in the southern peninsula. At this time, the Mongols conquered China and accelerated the flight southwards of the T'ai peoples, enhancing the resources of the northern Thai kingdoms in particular. The most important of these were Lanna Thai and Sukhothai.

Lanna Thai

Lanna Thai was founded by **Mengrai**, a Thai chieftain from Chiang Saen who conquered the ancient Mon state of Haripunchai, centred on Lamphun, and then amalgamated it with his northern fiefs. He established a new capital at Chiang Mai and called his kingdom "A Million Thai Ricefields", Lanna Thai. Chiang Mai, completed in 1296, was to outlast other northern rivals and to become the stronghold of conservative Thai traditions.

Sukhothai

At the same time, further to the south, Sukhothai rose to pre-eminence under **King Ramkhamhaeng** as the overlord of much of the Chao Phraya valley. He ruled from 1279-99 and is credited with inventing the Thai writing system. Under his rule, a magnificent temple city arose with satellites at Si Satchanalai and Kamphaeng Phet; Lanna Thai was an ally rather than a rival. Under the influence of the Mons and Khmers whom they were supplanting, the Thais took up Theravada Buddhism in the Sri Lankan tradition. Though Sukhothai's supremacy lasted only a century, it is regarded as the cradle of Thai nationhood.

Ayutthaya

Ramkhamhaeng's successors were not of the calibre to maintain Sukhothai's hegemony; besides, the budding nation's centre of gravity was shifting south. By the mid-fourteenth century, the **Prince of U Thong** in the southern central plains had risen to overlordship. It was logical that the immense rice-growing wealth of the lower plains should give rise to military strength as the Thais continued to pour south and the weakened Khmers withdrew. This Prince, calling himself **King Ramathibodi** and setting up his capital at Ayutthaya on the lower Chao Phraya River, established in 1350 a realm that was to dominate the region for four centuries.

The kingdom of Ayutthaya spread all across the central plains and up to the borders of the Chiang Mai realm. It pushed the Khmers out of Angkor and extended itself down the Malay Peninsula. It established the forms and customs which characterise the Thai nation. In kingly rule, it moved from the paternalism of Sukhothai to Khmer-style autocracy: the king was divine, the Lord of Life.

This lord created four Great Officers of State: called Khun Muang, Khun Wang, Khun Klang and Khun Na. They controlled respectively Local Government, the Royal Household, the Treasury and Agriculture. Under continuing Mon and Khmer influence, Sri Lankan Buddhism and Brahman ritual became integral to both court and common life.

Ayutthayan power and tradition were significantly reinforced by the scholarly and astute **King Trailok** (1448-88) who followed. One century into Ayutthaya's dominance, the court and the national administration were centralised and re-organised in a sophisticated hierarchy, while Trailok's patronage of the arts stimulated literature in particular.

By the 16th century, Ayutthaya was an established regional power and attracted the interest of the newly arriving Europeans. A Portuguese armada bent on trade rather than conquest introduced fire-arm technology to Siam, as the kingdom had become known to foreigners. This was convenient in the light of growing Burmese aggression, a factor which was to dominate Thai history for the next two centuries, but it still did not enable the Siamese to prevent the sacking of Ayutthaya in 1569. The boy Crown

King Ramkhamhaeng

Third king of Sukhothai, reigned 1279-99.

Every nation has a founding hero – real or invented. Some are complete myth, like the Romulus and Remus of the Romans, and some are quite close to reality, like the George Washington of American schoolbooks. Most are a mix of the two.

Thailand's founding father is King Ramkhamhaeng of Sukhothai, monarch of an idyllic kingdom where everyone was well-fed and cared for and could bring their troubles to the king, who always lent a sympathetic ear. His name means 'Rama the Bold', for at only 19 he won an important battle on elephant-back. As third king of the new Thai state, he defended the people from enemies and extended the realm far and wide. Ramkhamhaeng built cities of great temples and encouraged a culture of great artistic achievement.

More than this, the king was a great scholar who devised an alphabet and writing system for the Thai language and himself wrote the first and most famous Thai manuscript, on stone. On a siltstone obelisk, in his new script, he described the conditions of his kingdom: abundance, free trade, justice. "There is fish in the water and rice in the fields...The lord of the realm does not levy toll on his subjects...He has hung a bell in the opening of the gate – if any commoner has a grievance, he goes and strikes the bell; the King hears the call, examines the case, and decides it justly... So the people of Sukhothai praise him".

And so the people of modern Thailand praise him, ever since King Mongkut discovered this stone himself on a visit to Sukhothai's ruins and proclaimed it to the nation. King Ramkhamhaeng's inscription has become a kind of manifesto of the Thai polity, an ideal Thailand of plenty and freedom and fairness. The king himself has come to represent an ideal of leadership – just, brave, devout and scholarly.

All this is too good to be true, of course, and there is growing debate as to whether Ramkhamhaeng devised the Thai script or even wrote the famous tablet. Some experts suspect that King Mongkut himself made it, others that it was a late Sukhothai artefact harking back to an imagined golden age, hoping to recreate it as the state declined before the rising power of Ayutthaya.

Whatever the truth on this score, the national feeling of reverence and gratitude towards King Ramkhamhaeng reflects a reality. He was the consolidator of the first strong Thai state. He ensured the creation of Thai-Buddhist culture. He facilitated the development of the finest Thai art – Sukhothai bronze sculpture.

Whether he wrote the script or not, the tablet represents an ongoing truth about the Thai nation. Thais still eat well, avoid paying taxes, and rush off with their problems, not to the palace, but to ring the Prime Minister's bell at Government House in Bangkok.

Prince Naresuan was taken as hostage to Burma.

Released at the age of 15, Naresuan used the knowledge he had gained of Burmese military matters to organise effective defences against future attacks from the rival Buddhist kingdom to the west. Crowned king in 1590, **Naresuan the Great** took Ayutthaya into the 17th century as a further strengthened and prosperous power.

The kingdom of Ayutthaya in the mid-16th century extended from Korat and Chanthaburi in the east, across to the Andaman seaboard as far north as Moulmein; from muslim Pattani in the south to as far north as Sukhothai. If Ayutthaya had managed to push the Khmers back and out of Angkor, it did not yet have the strength to oust Lane

Xang from Isan nor to annexe Lanna Thai, which became a Burmese vassal instead.

Though Chiang Mai had developed a rich culture with a city full of fine temples, particularly under **King Tilokaraj** (who ruled between 1447-89), it could not resist Burmese pressure and from 1557 it entered a long period of decline. Caught between Burma, Lane Xang and Ayutthaya, it suffered frequent wars, depopulation of towns, deportation of peoples, and conscription into armies.

A rapid increase in foreign trade, particularly with Europe, Japan and China, marked the kingdom of Ayutthaya in the 17th century. The Dutch, the English, and the French sent diplomatic and trade missions. The Dutch arrived in 1608, and soon eclipsed the Portuguese and went on to dominate trade, not without the occasional use of military threats from a well-armed navy.

The reign of **King Narai**, (1656-88), marked the high point of Ayutthayan internationalism. It was in this period that Louis XIV of France sent a grand ambassadorial entourage to the Siamese court which was mightily impressed with the great walled city of canals, temples and palaces, set on an island ringed by channels of the Chao Phraya River.

The French were assisted in their commercial and territorial designs by a Greek, **Phaulkon**, who had gained high position at the Siamese court. Phaulkon's influence and the French military pres-

ence were resented by powerful courtiers. When Narai fell ill in 1688, they assassinated the Greek; upon his death the regime reduced its European contacts.

The last great Ayutthayan reign was that of **King Boromakot**, (1733-58), under whom arts and letters flourished, and peace prevailed, only to be shattered with renewed Burmese aggression. As Boromakot was succeeded by the dissolute **Ekatat**, so Burma was galvanized by an upstart militarist called **Alaungpaya**. His designs spilled over into Siam and eventually, in 1767, after a year's siege, Ayutthaya fell to his son's armies.

King Mongkut (Rama IV) so credited for his foreign policies at the Court of Siam, receiving French emissaries.

The Sacking of Ayutthaya

It was a catastrophe for Thai civilisation, akin to a nuclear holocaust. After everything of value had been looted, the whole city was burned and razed to the ground. Not only were gold, jewellery and the like carted off, but also 90,000 people as slave labour. The rest of the city's estimated one million population either fled or were slaughtered. Since the historical records and a great deal of art were not considered valuable, they went up in smoke. All of the physical cultural heritage of Ayutthaya was obliterated in one savage stroke.

It says much for the resilience of the Thai people that they did not take long to bounce back from this incomparable trauma. All they needed was someone worth rallying round and the man of the moment was a general named **Phya Taksin**. He and his band bravely broke through the Burmese siege with the express purpose of rallying outside help. They regrouped at Chantaburi on the far east-coast close to Cambodia and mustered an army and a navy.

Sufficiently strong seven months after Ayutthaya's fall, they set sail for the ruined capital and overthrew the

Burmese occupation force. Seeing the extent of the devastation, Taksin decided on both logistical and mystical grounds to relocate the capital downriver. It was believed that such ruination meant Ayutthaya was no longer an auspicious site and it was decided that a location nearer the river mouth would be both easier to provision and to withdraw from if necessary.

Thonburi

Thonburi on the west bank was the chosen site. From this base, Taksin's armies achieved the astonishing feat of not only repelling all further Burmese attacks, but of freeing Chiang Mai from their yoke and of taking a good deal of Lao territory. One of the principal generals was **Chao Phya Chakri**; it was he who took the Emerald Buddha from Vientiane in 1779, symbolising new Thai strength.

Chakri dynasty

The strain of these years took their toll on Taksin's mental health, to the extent of paranoid megalomania. He thought himself to have attained Buddhahood, and abused everyone from monks to his own children. He was deposed and ritually clubbed to death in 1782; Chao Phya Chakri took the throne as **Rama I** and established his capital on the opposite bank at a trading post named Bangkok.

Rattanakosin era

The year 1782 was a watershed for the Thai nation. Today's Thailand descends directly from then - the same capital, the same dynasty, and broadly the same national territory. It is known as the Rattanakosin Era or the Bangkok Period. The Chakri dynasty takes its royal name from Rama, the mythical hero of the Hindu Ramayana epic whose Thai version is called the Ramakien, set to verse by Rama I and his courtiers.

King Rama I chose Bangkok to site his capital because its position on the east bank of a westward bend in the Chao Phraya River resembled that of Ayutthaya and could be similarly insulated by the digging of a channel to the east. Thus was Rattanakosin Island created upon which he began to build the Temple of the Emerald Buddha as his royal chapel with an adjacent complex of royal residences and official buildings for the governance of the nation.

Besides the physical recreation of

Emerald Buddha and its eminent trail

Buddha images vary in value according to many criteria, amongst which are age, beauty, material, history, and magical power. Such facets combine to give spiritual power and no image in Thai history has surpassed the Emerald Buddha which now resides in the temple of the same name, Wat Phra Kaew, the royal chapel of the Grand Palace.

So highly prized, it has led a very peripatetic life. Legend has it that it was carved in Palibutr in India and then went to Ceylon. From there it made its way to the Khmers of Angkor, so they say. What is sure is that it revealed itself in Chiang Rai in the 1430s, emerging from under plaster and gold leaf.

There are two stories to choose from here: either it cracked open while being transported or it was struck by lightning and revealed itself. Either way, it was immediately thought to possess particularly potent spirituality.

Thus began its coveting by kings. The King of Chiang Mai wanted it brought to his palace but the chosen carrier elephant refused to go all the way, stopping in Lampang. The image resided there in the first of many Temples of the Emerald Buddha for some 30 years before eventually reaching Chiang Mai.

In 1551, the powerful King of Lane Xang conquered Chiang Mai and took the prized image back to his capital of Luang Prabang on the upper Mekong. When his Kingdom of a Million Elephants moved capital to Vientiane a few years later, the Emerald Buddha went too and gained pride of place in the royal chapel, naturally named Wat Phra Kaew.

After the fall of Ayutthaya, the resurgent Siamese expelled the Burmese and went on to invade Laos in 1778 under Chao Phya Chakri. This great general naturally seized the Emerald Buddha from Vientiane and took it back to King Taksin in Thonburi, who set it up in his royal chapel, the Temple of the Dawn.

Upon the dethroning and execution of the mad Taksin in 1782, General Chakri became King Rama I, set up his capital across the river at Bangkok, began the present Wat Phra Kaew, and ceremonially transferred the Emerald Buddha. Ever since, this temple has been the principal royal chapel of the Chakri dynasty and three times each year, the King goes to change the image's gold robes.

The Emerald Buddha is made of translucent green jasper and is a sitting image 75 cm in height. It is raised on an 11 metre high altar and crowned by a nine-tiered umbrella. Its three raiments are all made of gold. The hot season robe resembles that of a monk, the robe for the rainy season is an arrangement of breastplate, belts and bands, whilst the cool season covering is an intricate chain-link cloak.

The three raiment changes are performed by the king in ceremonies attended by high ecclesiastical, court and government officials at the official commencement of each season.

If ever the Emerald Buddha changes place rather than just clothing again, this will surely be a sign of some major upheaval in Thai history.

Siam's power centre, Rama I united as much as possible of the cultural heritage and ritual practices of Ayutthaya in his re-establishment of Thai tradition, and this renewal of the nation was consolidated by his successors **Rama II** (1809-24) and **Rama III** (1824-51). A noted artist, Rama II's chief legacies to the nation are Thonburi's extraordinary Temple of the Dawn and his devoted re-establishment of the classical dance-drama tradition.

Under his rule, Western powers were again allowed permanent trade and

Historical Gallery of Thailand

c.40,000 BC	Hunter-gatherer peoples present.
c.20-10,000 BC	Agriculture and husbandry in practice.
c.4000 BC	Ban Chiang bronze culture in the north-east.
c.1000 BC	Ironworking culture in existence.
6th-11th centuries AD	Dvaravati civilisation of Central Plains.
c.900	T'ai tribes begin arriving from southern China.
1096	Thai kingdom proclaimed at Payao in north.
12th century	Thai kingdoms established from Chiang Saen in the far north to Nakhon Si Thammarat in southern peninsula.
1220	Coronation of the first King of Sukhothai.
late 13th century	King Mengrai unites the upper north as Lanna Thai.
1279-99	King Ramkhamhaeng rules Sukhothai and gains hegemony over much of present-day Thailand.
1296	King Mengrai establishes Chiang Mai as capital of Lanna Thai.
1350	Coronation of the first King of Ayutthaya; Ayutthaya soon becomes pre-eminent.
14th century	Decline of Khmer power, rise of Thais to regional power.
1448-88	King Trailok of Ayutthaya creates a centralised and hierarchical administration.
16th century	Burmese armies threaten, European traders arrive, firearms are introduced. Ayutthaya controls territory from Sukhothai to Pattani, from Mergui to Korat.
1557	Lanna Thai comes under Burmese control.
1569	Burmese sack Ayutthaya.
1590-1605	King Naresuan strengthens Ayutthayan power.
17th century	Increase in foreign trade and European influence.
1656-88	King Narai reigns and receives important French ambassadorial missions.
1688	Narai dies and the regime severely restricts foreign access to Siam.

1733-58	*Ayutthayan arts and letters flourish under King Boromakot.*
1767	*Burmese sack and destroy Ayutthaya.*
1768-82	*King Taksin expels the Burmese and sets up capital at Thonburi.*
1782	*King Rama I sets up capital at Bangkok. Beginning of Chakri dynasty and Bangkok period.*
1809-51	*Reigns of Rama II and III: Bangkok grows rapidly, Siam eclipses Laos and controls Isan and Lanna Thai, the classical heritage is re-established, foreign traders regain access.*
1851-68	*King Mongkut (Rama IV) reigns, begins modernisation of the state, negotiates with Western powers.*
1868-1910	*King Chulalongkorn (Rama V) expands the reform process, introduces Western technology and keeps Siam independent.*
1932	*Constitutional monarchy declared, subsequent rise of military in politics.*
1942-5	*Under pressure, Thailand allies with Japan in World War II.*
1945 onwards	*Growing United States influence; US base in Thailand during the Vietnam War.*
1960 onwards	*Rapid economic growth and industrialization.*

diplomatic facilities, and increasingly under his successor. By the time of Rama III's accession in 1824, the Burmese threat had disappeared and Bangkok was a sizeable city commanding a large and prosperous nation covering broadly its present boundaries and holding sway over both Laos and Cambodia. However, the Western imperialists were looming with growing British influence in Burma and Malaya and French influence in Vietnam. It fell to **King Rama IV**, ruling from 1851 to 1868, to deal with this threat.

Mongkut

King Mongkut, as he is usually known, had the wisdom to foresee that Siam could only forestall Western colonisation by a dual policy of modernisation and accommodation. A monk for 27 years before accession to the throne in 1851, he astutely negotiated a series of trade treaties with powers such as Britain, France and the USA which allowed privileges whilst preserving Siam's independence and territorial integrity.

At the same time, he instituted reforms in the military, the bureaucracy and in education.

Chulalongkorn

This policy was inherited and extended by his son, **King Chulalongkorn**, who expanded the reform process, abolished slavery and introduced modern infrastructure such as railways and telegraphs. His astute employment of foreign advisers helped meet the imperial challenges of France and Britain, whilst his flexibility in ceding some Laotian territory to the French and some Malay land to the British helped keep them at bay.

Rama IV and V were much respected monarchs who brought Thailand into the modern age but their reforms ironically did much to bring about the end of the absolute monarchy.

Increased contact with the West, experienced in particular by those members of the elite educated abroad for the purpose of modernisation, encouraged a consciousness that the levers of power lay in the hands of too few people, largely aristocrats. In 1932, this frustration culminated in a coup by middle-ranking officials and officers called the Promoters who demanded a constitutional monarchy.

Such a constitution was promulgated in December, 1932, and **King Rama VII** abdicated in 1935 despairing of politicians. Thailand thus entered the political era which continues to this day: theoretically a parliamentary democracy but in practice a regime in which the military, the bureaucracy and perhaps the wealthy exert strong influences in the systems.

Present-Day Thailand

In the Second World War, Thailand attempted to stay neutral with Japan. In the post-war years, it became increasingly close to the triumphant USA for whose air force it became a forward base during the Vietnam War. The American-born **King Bhumibol** took the throne in 1946. Under a combination of military-backed authoritarian rule and skilled technocratic administration, rapid economic development has ensued, significantly since 1960 and most notably from the mid-1980s, fuelled by massive Japanese investment in manufacturing.

The 1980s brought boom times, at least to Bangkok and some other urban centres, with the mid-80s marking a watershed in Thai history. Both the economy and government underwent a change. Massive Japanese investment arrived, particularly in manufacturing, and Thai leaders began seriously to look forward to Newly Industrialised Country status.

Thailand in the 1990s is an increasingly urban, pluralist and technological society that still operates largely on a feudalistic patron-client basis. It re-

H M King Bhumiphol blesses his people.

mains to be seen how far the country's significant economic progress can be matched by genuine democratic advance.

Notwithstanding the coup of 1991 which replaced a democratically elected parliamentarian, it would seem that Thailand's successful industrialised status is not to be marred.

Government

The most important element in the Thai state is the king. Though the mid-century period after the declaration of a constitutional monarchy in 1932 saw an eclipse of royal influence while new political forces jockeyed for power, the monarchy has since regained enormous prestige, putting King Bhumiphol on a par with the greats of Thai history.

King Bhumiphol salutes at the Trooping of Colours.

Its function is nevertheless different from that in the past. Previously the king was ruler, embodiment of the nation and upholder of religion. He is no longer an absolute ruler – he makes no policies and gives no orders – but he is the guiding light by moral example and the arbiter of any political conflict which threatens national stability. In brief, he is the cement of a sometimes fractious governing system.

That system is theoretically a parliamentary democracy based on universal suffrage. There are two legislative chambers, the Parliament elected by the people and the Senate appointed by the king (on cabinet advice). Numerous political parties stand for election so that governments are usually coalitions of several parties. Their cabinets control the national administration through ministries. The Ministry of

Trooping the colours outside the old National Assembly, Royal Plaza, Bangkok.

Trooping the colours, an event to mark the King's birthday.

the Interior appoints all the provincial governors.

Thus far, it incorporates a structure similar to the British system with Dutch and French undertones, with elected Members of Parliament and a cabinet. Power is not always centred in the cabinet. It is a parliamentary system with some compromises in which the armed forces, the monied classes, and high officials wield considerable influence.

Hence a fractious body politic of factionalism and continual jockeying for power and influence, but tempered by Buddhism's moderation and the king's moral authority should things get out of hand. In 1973 and 1976, when there were violent upheavals involving a swing to the left then to the right, and in 1981 and 1985, when there were attempted military coups, the king's intervention each time was crucial in limiting damage and encouraging reconciliation.

Thailand entered the 1990s with a roaring economy. At the same time, political awareness has developed rapidly, notably amongst the burgeoning urban middle class, whose growing influence is leading the country towards greater democratisation.

The Thai people give their faith and respect to the monarchy. King Bhumiphol is a sovereign perceived as truly concerned with their welfare, particularly that of the poor rural majority for whom he has instituted numerous development projects on which he spends a good deal of his time touring the country to monitor their progress.

It is as much from this as from tradition that he gains his moral authority, and thus it is that the monarchy remains the cement of the Thai nation. It is the so-far essential upholder and central focus of a state of contentious power centres.

Economy

From rice to chips – microchips, that is – is the story of Thailand's economic transformation in the late 20th century. From an overwhelmingly agricultural base just a decade or so ago, the nation is now chasing NIC (Newly Industrialised Country) status to join other East Asian economic tigers such as South Korea, Taiwan, Hong Kong and Singapore.

The process originated roughly in the 1960s but really gathered pace in the 1980s. The Thai economy boomed in the late 1980s averaging 10% GNP growth per annum, much due to massive – particularly Japanese – investment in the industrial sector.

In the 1990s, with slightly slower growth, the proportion of the working population engaged in agriculture continues to shrink towards below half, down from 80% in the 1970s, whilst manufacturing employees are rising beyond 10%. Commerce and services account for most of the rest.

Threshing rice in the north-east

Agriculture

More Thai workers grow rice than do any other activity, and in that at least Thai

Working at a salt farm.

land is as ever. During some years tapioca may have earned more foreign exchange but working the ricefields is the core of rural life in most provinces. Sugar, maize and pineapple are major crops too, whilst fish farming produces significant amounts of shrimp and prawn.

By some counts, Thailand has the largest fishing fleet in the world. Sea fishing is most important in the south with squid and tuna being the major catches. The south is also noted for its rubber plantations from which major exports of rubber are made.

Mineral resources are varied. In the south, Thailand has large tin deposits, for example, around Phuket and also significant natural gas fields in the Gulf. There are some oil wells, notably in Kamphaeng Phet province in the lower north. Last but not least, precious stones are mined, particularly sapphires and rubies in eastern Chanthaburi province and western Kanchanaburi province. Thailand is reputedly the second largest gems and jewelry centre in the world.

Electronics is second in importance: Thailand produces anything from television sets to transistors, from disk-drives to microchips. A top item is integrated circuits, with nearly 20 billion baht worth of exports in 1988.

Tourism

Nevertheless, the big daddy of them all in the Thai foreign exchange economy is tourism. Visitor arrivals have soared from under two million at the beginning of the 1980s to well over five million in the early 90s. In 1988, tourist expenditure almost topped 80 billion baht, giving tourism a clear lead over textiles and more than double the export earnings from rice.

All this phenomenal growth and radical transformation may unfortunately not have been matched by corresponding and rapid improvements in the infrastructure. Highways and railways nationwide are possibly inadequate and transport in Bangkok can at times be a nightmare, with too many vehicles, not enough roads, and in sufficient mass public transit. The telephone system has had its weakness, with far too few lines in an overloaded situation. However the government recognises the importance of improvements to the entire infrastructure and steps have been taken for major improvements.

Thailand will undoubtedly continue to prosper in the '90s and be an impressive economic leader in South-east Asia.

Manufacturing

In the manufacturing industry, most of which is light, by far the most important area is textiles and garments, with exports totalling nearly 60 billion baht in 1988, compared to nearly 35 billion baht for rice. Thai-made clothes are exported world-wide and a large number of world-famous designer names produce their garments here, benefitting from high-quality and low cost in both local materials and labour.

Oil exploration at Songkhla, in the Gulf of Thailand.

ECONOMY

Fishing fleet at Hua Hin.

A tin mine on Phuket Island.

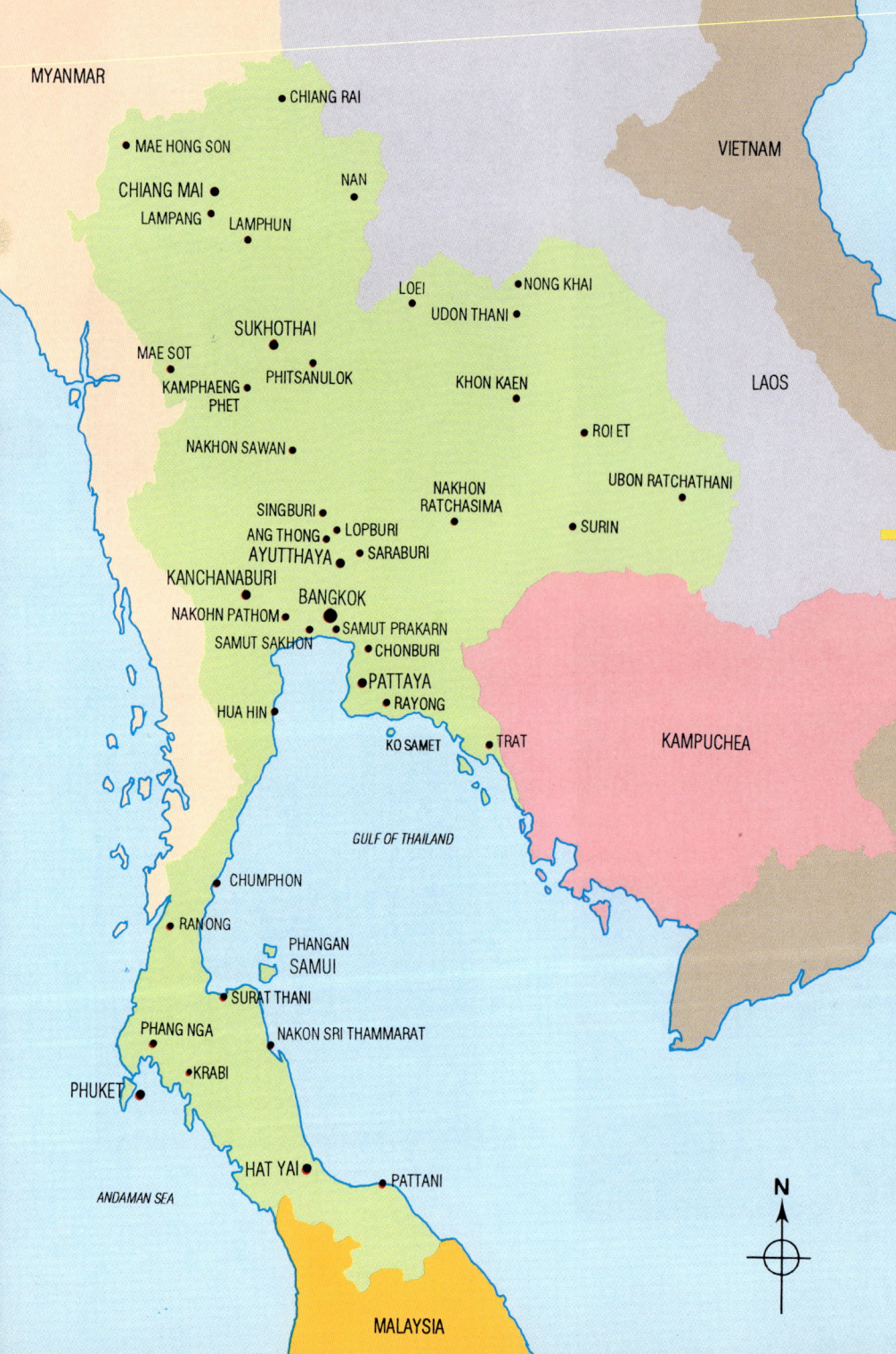

Geography

Thais, with their age-old reverence for the elephant, symbol of Siam, like to say their country is shaped like an elephant's head. They mean in profile, thus Isan is the ear, the north is the dome of the head, Bangkok is the mouth, and the south is the trunk. If you look at the map and include Burma's southern extension (it was once part of Siam), the amusing analogy is quite convincing.

From top of the dome to the tip of the trunk, Chiang Saen in the Golden Triangle to Songai Golok on the Malaysian border, the distance is around 1800 km, which is a little more than the vertical length of the British Isles. From top of the trunk (west) to tip of the ear (east), the widest distance is roughly 800 km, from Three Pagodas Pass in the Burmese border mountains to the River Mekong at Ubon Ratchathani.

The area is 514,000 sq km, about equivalent to the size of France or that of Texas. Despite its odd shape, the country has a clear and constant centre of gravity in the great rice-growing plains along the Chao Phraya River and her sisters. These waters flow principally

from the north, the elephant's dome, a region of forested mountains and fertile valleys centred upon Chiang Mai.

They also flow from the mountains in the north-east which mark off the elephant's ear. This would be the great plateau of Isan, 300 metres above sea level, sparsely vegetated and poor in soil. Beyond Isan lies Laos, separated by the broad Mekong River. To its south lies Cambodia, over the low Dong Rak mountains. The eastern seaboard and interior is flat and agricultural.

The rivers of the Central Plains also flow from the western mountains that form the divide with Burma; this is a region of great timber and wildlife resources, which unfortunately may be under threat of depletion or extinction at this time.

Southern Thailand is likened to the elephant's trunk. The Burmese border mountains, averaging around 1000 metres in height, is thought to run south of this 'trunk' to Chumphon and Ranong, around 500 km from Bangkok, at which point the true south begins. This is a region of rubber and coconut plantations, of coastal fishing and interior mountains and forests, the latter especially near the Malaysian border.

CLIMATE

Most of Thailand has three distinct seasons which shade into one another. These are the rainy season, the cool dry season, and the hot dry season.

The lushness of the vegetation is accounted for by the rainy season which normally begins in May and gets into full swing in July, climaxes in September or October, and then peters out in November. Just because it is called the rainy season, does not mean it rains all the time, nor even every day. What it does mean is that it rains heavily on many days, most often in the afternoon, but rarely for more than an hour or two.

In Bangkok and the Central Plains, rain averages about 200mm monthly from May to October, and temperatures average 24°C to 32°C, from night to day. In Chiang Mai in the same period, rain averages 160mm monthly and temperatures range from 23°C to 31°C. The north-east falls roughly into the same weather pattern, with a shorter and lighter rainy season.

The cool dry season from late November to February is Thailand's most

Some of the spectacular limestone caves found in Thailand.

pleasant. Temperatures drop in the Central Plains just enough to make all the difference, with an average minimum temperature of 21°C, whilst Chiang Mai goes down to 14°C on average.

The most unpleasant time is the hot dry season from late February to early May, when temperatures are usually in the upper 30s in the daytime and the will to do anything at all evaporates. Most Thais take their holidays in April (if they have them) and the long university and school vacations wisely extend through this period. The north-east areas experience the hottest weather at this time.

These patterns prevail except in the south, where there is less seasonal variation and more constant distribution of rainfall and temperature. Since this peninsular region receives two monsoons, rain falls in December and January too.

Flora and Fauna

Two eternal symbols of Thailand are teak and elephants, the latter working the former, the noble beast shoving and dragging the great tree trunks. This still happens in northern Thailand; in fact, an "Elephants at Work" show is a highlight of every tourist's trip to Chiang Mai.

But Thailand today is a highly domesticated – and partially devastated - country. Over the centuries, almost all flat land has been progressively cleared of forest and replaced by crops – rice and maize, sugar cane and tapioca, tobacco and rubber. In recent decades, much of the upland forest cover has been cut away for timber.

The result is a land of cultivated fields and denuded hillsides, with some remaining pockets of forests. Ricefields and the buffalo represent the real Thailand, whilst teak forests and elephants are more of a romantic vision. That said, the land still offers magnificent natural scenery and significant reserves of wildlife.

The slithering reptile, a significant member of Thai wildlife.

FLORA

The amount of forest remaining

is forever in dispute, but would seem to be between 10% and 20% of the national territory; it falls into several types, according to climate and elevation.

In the south, where rain falls most of the year, there are evergreen rainforests with vegetation of tremendous variety. The tree canopy rises up to 30 metres and is pursued by lianas, whilst ferns carpet the forest floor. The densest type is cloud forest, found above 1800 metres, for, as its name implies, it is almost always moist, encouraging prolific growth. Astonishingly, a small tropical cloud forest is likely to contain more native species of flora and fauna than a whole European country.

In central, northern and north-eastern Thailand, rain is seasonal and the forests are of a type sometimes called 'monsoon'. Trees turn autumnal and shed their leaves in the dry season, though not all at once, and regrowth is immediate; another name for this type is therefore 'semi-deciduous'. Teak and bamboo are notable trees of these forests; most of Thailand's remaining teak stands in the northern and western lower mountains, whilst bamboo thrives more in the valleys. At greater heights there is oak and pine.

In the dry north-east plateau, acacias are common amidst thornbush savannahs, though for periods during the rains this can turn to swamp forest. Around parts of the coastline spread mangrove forests, though these are rapidly decreasing in favour of shrimp and prawn farming, for which the swampy land is suitable. The majority of the coastline, particularly in the south, is lined with coconut and nipa palms.

Flowering Trees

Thailand is rich in flowering trees such as the frangipani and flamboyant and colourful shrubs such as rhododendron, whilst hundreds of varieties of orchid thrive in the forests. Another eternal Thai symbol, the lotus, spreads across ponds and lakes.

FAUNA

Thailand's wildlife is much reduced from what it used to be in living memory, yet there still are magnificent beasts such as the Asian elephant and the tiger, and just possibly the Sumatran rhinoceros, roaming some remaining forest areas. Most notable of these is the mountainous western border region of Kanchanaburi and Tak provinces. There a dedicated tracker would encounter both elephant and tiger as well as the rhinoceros if very lucky. In other words,

Chameleons are particularly fascinating to observe as they change their tones ..... if one spots them.

The poppy flower, common in northern Thailand.

Orchids

Orchids abound in Thailand both in the forests and the florist's. Over one thousand varieties flourish in the wild and many people cultivate them commercially.

Most varieties are found in the north and the most common genus is *Dendrobium*, flamboyant and fragrant and found in colours all the way from white through gold and orange to violet. Conversely, the *Vanda cerulea* is very rare, the only blue Vanda in the world.

Orchids are epiphytes, having a fleshy root system which grips tree bark and ingests water and minerals from its environment. Orchid flowers comprise three petals and three sepals, the oft-found large lower lip giving a distinctive and somewhat sensual look.

Few homes in Thailand are not in some way decorated with them – why not when an orchid plant can be bought for as little as 5 baht! On the other hand, a very special variety can cost 2000 baht and orchids are thus big business in Thailand, with exports of both blooms and plants totalling around US$25 million annually.

The blooms are packed with each stem in its own water reservoir and flown out. They last about two weeks and their value soars almost with every mile they fly. Visitors are thus advised to buy before they leave, even in Bangkok Airport departure lounge which does a thriving trade in them.

Plants are also exported, especially to Italy, Germany, Japan and North America.

Besides Dendrobium and Vanda, Cattleya, Phalaenopsis and Paphiopedilum are preferred varieties. Cattleya are large and showy with broad leaves. Phalaenopsis bear white, pink or yellow flowers with different coloured lips. Paphiopedilum, "Lady's Slipper", has the expected orchid shape with the sensual lower lip.

The wild flowers may be spotted in forest walks but the surest way to see them in profusion is to visit a Bangkok nursery, many of which congregate out towards the airport. The best of both worlds is to be had by strolling in the forest orchids gardens of Kanchanaburi or Chiang Mai provinces, such as in the latter's Mae Rim Valley.

The Thai love for the flower is demonstrated by the national custom of presenting orchids on special occasions, sometimes hung up as a blessing over a new venture, frequently offered in leis as special gifts. Its status within Thailand is further shown by names such as the Royal Orchid Sheraton, a Bangkok luxury class hotel, and the Royal Orchid Holidays offered by Thai Airways International. Above all, the purple and pink symbol of the national airline, sported on every aircraft tail, is directly inspired by the Thai orchid.

Thailand's vast terrain and dense foliage host a huge variety of birds.

these animals are now rare and tourists are unlikely ever to see them in the wild. The chances are a little better for seeing other large mammals such as tapir, leopard, bear and boar.

On the other hand, the chances of seeing deer and monkeys are pretty high if you go in certain national parks, of which Khao Yai to the north-east of Bangkok is a good example. Thai deer range from the large sambar to the diminutive mouse deer, which is no more than 20 cm tall. Wild cattle like the banteng and kating are also relatively common. Amongst monkeys, gibbons and macaques are most frequently seen.

Also up there in the trees are flying squirrels and lemurs, flying lizards and frogs, whilst birdlife is prolific, from

The ever-present water lily is to be found in parks, gardens, farms, klongs, etc, and like the lotus, is often depicted in Thai decorative art forms.

FLORA AND FAUNA

Crocodiles are no longer to be found in estuarine areas but many are reared to support not a few fashion industries these days.

parakeets to carrion crows, from mynahs to magpies. Water birds are particularly common, with kingfishers, egrets and herons found along river banks, such as the River Kwai, and many migratory fowl found particularly in the south, such as at Thale Noi near Phattalung.

Crocodiles used to be found in the estuarine rivers, but no longer, perhaps happily, since not a few Thais passed to the next life via those reptiles in past times. Sea turtles come ashore at Phuket once a year to lay eggs. Tortoises, lizards and snakes could be common.

Even though there are 10-metre re-

Siamese Fighting Fish

Thais are inveterate gamblers and especially enjoy betting on fights, whether between boxers, bulls, cocks, snakes and mongooses, or fish. Yes, fish, for Thais breed fighting fish – small, savage and beautiful.

The Siamese Fighting Fish has prettily mottled colours, like a tachiste painting, and disproportionately large fins, as if waving wispy fans from its back, belly and tail. It is about 7 cm long. Only the males fight, coloured blue, red and purple.

Breeders meet with their best fighters in glass jars, bringing them face to face and testing the reaction. Upon this showing, wagers are made and the two fish are placed together in a glass tank.

They attack. Fins, scales and tails are savaged off, flesh gouged out, jaws locked together. It is a fight to the death, often quick, occasionally prolonged.

They can be seen in many aquaria, such as at Bangkok's Weekend Market. The thoroughbred type is called *lukmoh*, specially bred for battle; a type called *pah* abounds in the canals but they do not last for long in fights.

Siamese fighting fish flare at being placed face-to-face.

ticulated pythons slithering about in some parts and king cobras and banded kraits too, they are rarely seen and would rather avoid humans anyway if at all possible. Lizards, by contrast, are ubiquitous and extremely handy, especially in the case of the house gecko which eats mosquitos.

BANGKOK

City of Angels

Bangkok is a mess, there is no doubt about it – ugly, noisy, polluted, congested and chaotic – yet it inspires affection in a great many people, both visitors who don't have to cope with it for long and residents who must. How does it do it? What is its secret?

In a word, Thainess. The people of Bangkok, what they do, and the way they do it, are the key to the city's character. They spend a lot of their time making sure that, whatever their job or position, whatever their duties and responsibilities, life is a pleasurable business whenever and wherever possible. The happy-go-lucky hit song "Don't Worry, Be Happy" struck a strong chord here; it was almost made for Thailand.

Thais are not much given to organisation and planning, regulation and coordination: it goes against the grain. Life is a passing show whose acts and scenes are a matter of karma, chance and luck. If so, why take a lot of trouble trying to organise the future and control the present? Hence a capital city full of generally carefree citizens, and hence a lot of visitors who fall under its spell.

But if the quality of personal interaction is the

Street hawkers near the Grand Palace.

city's primary asset, and its environmental disorder a drawback, there are nevertheless a great many things to see and do in Bangkok which are, at the very least, fascinating and in many cases quite unique. And it has all sprung up in the last 200 years!

History

The Thais as a people date back several millennia, most likely to origins in China, but their residence in what is now Thailand is only about a thousand years long. The city of Bangkok is far younger still, dating almost completely from the late eighteenth century. In the seventeenth century, the site was a port for trading ships with a few houses, some Chinese merchants and a couple of forts. Upon the razing of the great capital of Ayutthaya by the invading Burmese in 1767, the Thais regrouped under General Taksin whose forces drove back the Burmese marauders. He then made himself king and set up his capital at Thonburi some 80 km further south down the Chao Phraya River.

Krungthep

There he established a riverside residence with Wat Arun as his royal chapel, but under the strain of continual warfare he developed paranoid delusions which brought about his execution. He was succeeded by Phya Chakri, who became King Rama I and set up his capital on the opposite bank at Bang Kok, "the village of hog plums". This not being a very exalted name for a capital city, the first king of the Chakri dynasty that still reigns today proclaimed the official name to be Krungthep Mahanakorn Bovorn Rattanakosin Mahainthara Ayutthaya Mahadilokob Noparathathani Burirom Udomrajanivej Mahasathani Ampornpiman Avararnsathit Sakkatattiya Avisnukamprasit. Fortunately for everyone, the first two syllables were considered sufficient to identify it, and thus the city is known to Thais as *Krungthep*, the City of Angels. Only foreigners demean it with the name "Bangkok"!

This spot is a bulge of land around which the Chao Phraya curls on the west, and thus it resembles the site of Ayutthaya, the great fallen capital. This appealed to Rama I both for sentimental and strategic reasons; it offered historical continuity and the opportunity to dig defensive moats to the east creating an artificial island. Klong Lawd was the first of these to be dug, resulting in **Rattanakosin Island**, the city's historic heart.

Resting Place of the Emerald Buddha

In the centre of this new island, on April 21st, 1782, Rama I erected the City Pillar, *Lak Muang*, as the foundation and then he consciously set about restoring

Wat Arun, Temple of the Dawn.

Siamese nationhood with the construction of a great religious and royal compound – the Temple of the Emerald Buddha and the Grand Palace. Late in 1784, with great ceremony, the Emerald Buddha image was brought across from Wat Arun in Thonburi to symbolise Bangkok's supremacy (Rattanakosin means 'Resting Place of the Emerald Buddha') and as the great complex arose, so Siamese national pride was reborn.

A further defensive moat, called Klong Banglamphu in the north and Klong Ong Ang in the southern section, was built to encompass the rapidly growing city, and along it a city wall with 14 regularly-spaced forts and just one bridge; such was the fear of further attack. Both for continuity and convenience, much of the brickwork for the royal works was brought downriver from the ruins of Ayutthaya.

One of the first new temples to arise was Wat Suthat, in 1784, built for the Brahmin priests who determined court ritual at a central point between the inner and outer moats. In front of it arose the Giant Swing essential to their festival of Shiva. The city's main thoroughfare led from the palace via the Giant Swing to the city wall; it is now called Bamrungmuang Road. Outside the wall, the main thoroughfare was a waterway, Klong Mahanak, which ran directly east through orchards and ricefields.

However, even in the early nineteenth century, the city was spreading beyond its walls. Many commuters lived outside and came in daily for work and business; the Chinese merchants had set up home in the riverside area outside the southern defenses. By mid-century, many immigrant communities existed, sheltering Cambodians and Vietnamese, Mons and Muslims; Bangkok's cosmopolitanism had already begun.

Within and without the walls, trade quarters sprang up, specialising in bronzeware and pottery, in ironwork and fireworks, in woodwork and waxware. Only one of these, Ban Baht still exists. This village is known for making monks' alms bowls and lies just outside the city wall beyond the Giant Swing. Today, Ban Baht still reverberates to the tapping of metal. In the nineteenth century, much of the city moved to the rhythm of ancient trades and crafts.

Golden Mount

The first large structure outside the city defenses was to be one of Bangkok's greatest landmark, the Golden Mount.

Bangkok

Index — Bangkok

Selected Hotels

Ambassador	40	C3	Siam	46	D3
Asia	15	B3	Siam Intercontinental	30	C3
Bangkok Centre	17	B3	Silom Plaza	58	B4
Bangkok Palace	27	C3	Tawana Ramada	22	B3
Central Plaza	1	C1	Thai	5	B2
Century	9	C2	The Menam	61	B4
Continental	8	C2	The Oriental	59	B4
Dusit Thani	45	C3	The Regal Landmark	42	C3
Federal	38	C3	The Regent Bangkok	32	C3
Florida	25	C3	Tower Inn	55	B4
Fortuna	37	C3	Victory	57	B2
Golden Horse	13	B3	Viengtai	11	B3
Grace	36	C3	Windsor	44	C3
Hilton International	28	C3	World Hotel	47	D3
Impala	63	C4	YMCA (Collin's House)	62	C4
Imperial	33	C3			
Indra Regent	24	B3	**Embassies**		
Le Meridien President	31	C3	Argentina	1	D3
Liberty	7	C2	Australia	2	C4
Mahohra	50	B4	Austria	3	C4
Majestic	12	B3	Bangladesh	4	D4
Mandarin	20	B3	Belgium	5	B4
Manhattan	41	C3	Brazil	6	C3
Miami	43	C3	Brunei	7	C3
Mido	6	C2	Burma	8	B4
Ma-ana	14	B3	Canada	9	B4
Montein	34	C3	Chile	10	D4
Morakot	48	D2	China	11	C2/D2
Nana	35	C3	Czechoslovakia	12	C3
Narai	54	B4	Denmark	13	C4
New Empire	16	B3	Egypt	14	C3
New Fuji	53	B4	Finland	15	C3
New Peninsula	51	B4	France	16	B4
New Trocadero	52	B4	Germany	17	C4
Park	39	C3	Hungary	18	D4
Parliament	4	B2	India	19	C3
Plaza	26	C3	Indonesia	20	C3
Prince	29	C3	Iran	21	D3
Ra-jah	23	C3	Iraq	22	C1/C2
Rama Tower (Holiday Inn)	56	B4	Israel	23	C3
Ramada	49	B4	Italy	24	C4
Rex	64	C4	Japan	25	C3
Riverside Plaza	3	A1	Korea, S	26	C3
Rose	23	B4	Laos	27	B4
Royal	10	A3	Malaysia	28	C4
Royal Orchid Sheraton	18	B3	Nepal	29	D4
Royal Plaza	19	B3	Netherlands	30	C3
Royal River	2	A2	New Zealand	31	C3
Shangri-La	60	B4	Norway	32	D3

Pakistan	33	C3
Philippines	34	D4
Poland	35	C3
Portugal	36	B3/B4
Romania	37	C3
Saudi Arabia	38	B4
Singapore	39	C4
Spain	40	C3
Sri Lanka	41	B3
Sweden	42	B4
Switzerland	43	C3
Turkey	44	C3
United Kingdom	45	C3
United States	46	C3
U.S.S.R.	47	B4
Vietnam	48	C3
Yugoslavia	49	D4

Places of Interest

Chatuchak Park		C1
Chinatown (Yaowarat)		B3
Chitlada Palace		B2
Dusit Zoo		B2
Erawan Shrine		C3
Giant Swing		B3
Grand Palace		A3
Jim Thompson's House		C3
Kamthieng House		D3
Lakmuang Shrine		A3
Lumphini Boxing Stadium		C4
Lumphini Park		C3
Nakorn Kasem		B3
National Gallery		A3
National Museum		A3
National Theatre		A3
Ratchadamnoen Boxing Stadium		B2
Royal Barges		A3
Sanam Luang		A3
Snake Farm (Pasteur Institute)		C3
Suan Pakkard Palace		C2
Thailand Cultural Centre		D2
Winanmek Palace		B2

Shopping Centres

Amarin Plaza		C3
Asean		D4
Bai Yoke		C3
Bangkok Doll		C3

Central		B4
Central		A4
Daimaru		C3
Mah Boon Krong		B3
Merry King		C2
New World		B4
Oriental Plaza		B4
Pata		A3
Rajdamri Arcade		C3
River City		B4
Robinson		C3
Robinson		C2
Siam Centre		C3
Siam Acco		D2
Siam Square		C3
Silom Plaza		B4

Selected Wats

Golden Mount (Wat Saket)		B3
Wat Arun (Temple of Dawn)		A3
Wat Benchamabophit (Marble Temple)		B2
Wat Bowonniwet		B3
Wat Kanlayanimit		A3
Wat Mahathau		A3
Wat Pho		A3
Wat Phra Kaeo		A3
Wat Rajabophit		A3
Wat Rajanada		B3
Wat Suthat		A3
Wat Suwannaram		A2
Wat Traimit		B4
Wat Yannawa		B4

Selected Markets

Atok Market		C1
Bangrak Market		B4
Khlong Toey Market		C4
Pratunam Market		C3
Weekend Market		C1

Selected Roads

Arun Amarin Road		A3
Bamrung Muang Road		B3
Bandinso Road		B3
Bang Kruay Road		B3
Bang Kruey-pang Bua Thong Road		A1
Bang Kruay-Sai Noi Road		A1, A2
Bangkok Noi-Nakhon Chaisri Road		A2
Benhat Thong Road		B3
Chakkrawat Road		A3-B2
Chakraphong Road		A3
Chan Road		B4-C4
Charan Saninvong Road		A1-B3
Charoen Krung Road (New Road)		B3-B4
Chatcern Nakhon Road		A4-B4
Din Daeng Road		C2
Intraphithak Road		A4
Isarephep Road		A3
Kamphaeng Phet Road		C1
Kasem Rat Road		C4
Krung Kasem Road		B2
Krung Thonburi		A4-B4
Lanluang Road		B3
Latphrao Road		C1-D2
Latphrao 53 Road		D1
Latya Road		A4-B4
Maha Phru Tharam Road		B3
Mahachai Road		B3
Mahai Sawan Road		A4
Mahorat Road		A3
Nang Linchi Road		B2
New Phetchaburi Road		C4
Phahon Yothin Road		C1-C2
Phayathai Road		C3
Phetchakasem Road		A4
Phetchakasem Road		A4
Phibunsongkhram Road		B1
Phloen Chit Road		C3
Phra Samen Road		B2-B3
Phran Nok Road		A3
Pracha Thipok Road		A3-A4
Prachanat Road		B1
Pracharat I Road		B1
Pracharat II Road		B1-C1
Pradiphat Road		C2
Prapinklao Road		A3
Rama I Road		B3-C3

Rama III Road		B4-C4
Rama IV Road		B3-D4
Rama VI Road		B2
Rama VI Road		B1-C2
Rama IX Road		D3
Ratcha Damri Road		C3
Ratchada Phisek Road		C3-C4
Ratchadamnoen Road		B2-B3
Ratchadamnoen Klang Road		A3-B3
Ratchadaphinek Road		C3-D1
Ratchaprarop Road		C2-C3
Ratchawithi Road		B2
Samsen Road		B1-B2
Son Phawut Road		D5
Sanam Chai Road		A3
Sawankhalok Road		B2-B3
Si Ayutthaya Road		B2-C3
Silom Road		B4-C4
Siphaya Road		B3
Soi 21 Asok Road		C3
Soi 63 Ekamai Road		D3
Soi 71 Phra Khanong Khlong Tan Road		D3-D4
Soi Atthakan Prasit		D5
Soi Suan Phlu		C4
Somdet Chao Phraya Road		B3
Sukhumvit Road		C3-D4
Surawong Road		B4
Suthisan Winitchai Road		C2-D2
Techa Wanit Road		B1-C1
Tha Phra-Taksin Road		A4
Thahan Road		B1
Thang Rothaikao Sai Paknom Road		B2
Thred Thai Road		A4
Thoot Damri Road		C1-C2
Tri Phet Road		B3
Vibhavadi Rongsit Road		A3
Wang Doem Road		B2-B3
Wisutkasat Road		B2-B3
Witthaya Road		B3
Wongsawong Road		B1
Worachak Road		B3
Wutthakat Road		A4
Yaowarat Road		B3
Yen Akat Road		C4

The Golden Mount, one of Bangkok's greatest landmarks, against a typical temple roof.

There had been a Golden Mount at Ayutthaya beside Klong Mahanak and King Rama III decided that he wanted to recreate it in the new capital. Accordingly, a site was chosen just north of Ban Baht and below Bangkok's Klong Mahanak; labourers set about piling up the city's one and only hill, but the soft earth kept subsiding. Eventually, King Rama IV completed the structure in 1863 with the aid of a thousand teak logs as piles. Eighty metres from foot to tip, it was crowned with a golden *chedi* and became the popular place of pilgrimage and sightseeing that Rama III had intended.

From the Golden Mount could be seen a garden city spread out along canals, upon which much of the populace lived in raft-houses. Eighty temples shimmered among the trees and glinted off the waters. A few muddy paths carried pony and elephant traffic; most transport was by water. The upper classes lived in teak houses amidst gardens.

Though there was much commerce, Westerners were rarely seen, having been effectively banished from the kingdom in the late seventeenth century for political interference.

Something had to give in this time-honoured pattern; the industrial revolution in the West and consequent European power were beginning to affect the whole world. The Thai monarchy was wise to this and King Mongkut with wisdom and foresight instituted modernisation in Thailand. It was he who built Bangkok's first paved way, New Road, in 1863. King Chulalongkorn who reigned between 1868-1910, built city roads, tramlines, a railway and a hospital and generally continued his father's modernisation schemes. Grand European-style ministries arose, while merchants began stringing concrete shophouses along new streets. New Road ran down to the Oriental Hotel and the burgeoning European quarter of embassies and trading houses. The upper classes and foreigners travelled by horse and carriage wherever possible, such as along the new Silom and Sathorn Roads.

By the end of the century, electricity had arrived and the city's population had reached around half a million. This was only half that of Ayutthaya in its prime but nevertheless constituted a major city at least ten times larger than any other in the land.

In the early twentieth century, as the modern international trading community expanded to the south-east around New Road, the aristocrats moved out of the old city towards the north-east. The grand Rajdamnern Avenue led from the Grand Palace to the new Dusit district, dominated by the Capitol-like Ananta Samakom Throne Hall with the huge grounds of the new Chitrlada Palace and the imposing Marble Temple nearby.

This whole upper class suburb was

Young monks at the Golden Mount.

Life in Thonburi, across the river, remains rural and suburban.

laid out with elegant tree-lined streets in the European manner and remains so today.

Upon the revolution of 1932 during which a constitutional monarchy was installed, the grand throne hall became the National Assembly and the Prime Minister resided in nearby Government House, making Dusit the centre of government, as it remains today.

The Thirties were also a significant turning point in transport, the first bridge spanned the Chao Phraya in 1932; the new Memorial Bridge connected the southern old city near Chinatown with Thonburi and thus spurred the expansion of the west bank and the development of commerce and industry.

From Klongs to Concrete Carpet

In 1942 the city was occupied by the Japanese. In the forties, Bangkok was still a canal and garden city, thriving yet leisurely, but the process of filling in the *klong* and laying down roads was gathering pace. As the automobile gained favour over boats, so the waterways gave way to concrete and tarmac thoroughfares and the city fundamentally changed character. In the fifties and sixties, Sukhumvit and Petchburi Roads laid concrete carpets to the east and new commercial districts rapidly arose, spurred on mightily by the sudden influx of massive US funds in support of the Vietnam War. Silom Road, suitably located between the old and new commercial districts, sprouted highrise office blocks and hotels and became the top business and banking district.

While the Thonburi side remained essentially a garden and canal suburb behind a few major roads and commercial developments, Bangkok's concrete jungle spread far to the east and north, eventually harbouring six million souls in the late 1980s.

MODERN BANGKOK

Bangkok today is a sprawling metropolis of probably seven million souls that is reckoned by some observers to reach ten million during the post-rice harvest months when rural labourers flock into town in search of temporary work. It is about 50 times bigger than any other Thai city. Its suburbs spread around 20 kilometres to the north, east and south, rather haphazardly, and it has an official area of 1,537 square kilometeres. The national economy has averaged growth of almost 10% per annum since the late eighties and that boom is heavily weighted towards the capital. Hundreds of new vehicles are registered daily and roll out onto an already grossly inadequate road system.

Whatever the figures, what you see is what you get: a very large splodge of

Unworldly monks in quiet abode at Thonburi.

Bangkok – modern metropolis.

concrete and brick jammed with traffic and animated by a teeming citizenry both energetic and laid back. A typical Bangkok vision is a motorcyclist speeding crazily, ear-shatteringly and smokily through heavy traffic past high-rise office blocks with an expression of complete serenity on his face. The bus passengers, stuck in a jam, moving maybe one kilometre an hour, asphyxiated by carbon monoxide fumes, deafened by "Bus Radio", simply go to sleep. Black-booted, khaki-uniformed policemen and blue-uniformed security guards whistle frantically to no apparent purpose or tune, but it is rumoured that they are controlling the traffic. All around, pneumatic drills and wrecking balls rip up the old and pile-drivers and sky-high cranes construct the new. As the city sinks into the mud, descending little by little each year towards sea level, so at the same time it reaches for the sky.

But behind all this there is another

Bangkok, the city of grace and peace, the City of Angels indeed, for it does exist. Step into any establishment – shop, office, hotel, restaurant – and the chances are you will be treated with a degree of charm and grace unknown in the rest of the world. Walk down a side street and off into a lane and you will quite likely find yourself in a peaceful tree-shaded village. Enter a restaurant and experience heavenly tastes at down-to-earth prices.

The angels are still here – it is just that they are part-time ones! Bangkok is now big business, Thailand's industrial and commercial centre and increasingly an international hub of commerce and communications, of finance and diplomacy.

The temples of trading overshadow those of contemplation, the traffic is nearing gridlock, the air is usually poisonous, but Bangkokians survive smiling, most of the time anyway.

BANGKOK

Sights To See

There is only one absolute must-see in Bangkok: the **Grand Palace Complex**, the spiritual heart of the Thai capital and one of the world's great architectural spectacles. Its magnificence was a deliberate act of national renewal after the annihilation of the former capital, Ayutthaya, by the Burmese in 1767. Bangkok is the phoenix that arose from that holocaust and the **Grand Palace** and the **Temple of the Emerald Buddha** are its finest plumage. The compound which they share is roughly rectangular and is bounded by a whitewashed, battlemented wall almost two kilometres long. The complex lies alongside the Chao Phya River; the temple is on the side of the city, whilst the Palace grounds abut the riverside. Building began in 1782, the year that Bangkok was declared capital and the Chakri dynasty took power under Rama I.

Wat Phra Kaew, the Temple of the Emerald Buddha, is a large religious compound decked with a great variety of extraordinary structures. Seen from outside across the open field of Sanam Luang, it is a stunning tableau of jostling,

Wat Phra Kaew and the Grand Palace Complex.

Richly gilded works adorn the Temple of the Emerald Buddha within the Grand Palace compound.

multi-coloured spires and roofs. Inside, the visitor walks trance-like through a kaleidoscope of astonishing forms and colours.

All these have meaning. The chief building is the **Chapel Royal**, the King's place of worship, built in 1784 to house the kingdom's most sacred Buddha image, the Emerald Buddha. Actually made of translucent green jasper and only 75cm tall, its pre-eminence rests in the Thai belief dating back 500 years that its spirituality is the most potent in the region. Captured by conquering kings over the centuries, it has rested in Bangkok since 1778 and symbolised the city's supremacy and the reign of the Chakri dynasty.

Raised on a tall pedestal and seated below a nine-tiered umbrella, the Emerald Buddha wears three changes of orange raiment according to the season. It is the King's sacred duty to perform the changing ceremony at the start of the cool, hot and rainy seasons.

The chapel's murals have suffered the effects of time and climate but were substantially restored in 1982 for the capital's bicentenary celebrations. Both to the left and right over the entrance are depicted scenes from the Buddha's life, while the universe is portrayed on the back wall in Buddhist astrological terms. The *Ramakien* story is told on the doors and window panels.

Giant demons, called *yak,* guard most chapels and pavilions from evil spirits. One such, **Prasad Phra Thep-**

important state ceremonies and receptions. Unfortunately, the magnificent throne room is forbidden to visitors, who are only allowed into duller anterooms.

Just to the west is the **Dusit Maha Prasad**, a pure Thai-style pavilion with a cross-shaped ground-plan, tall white stucco walls, four-tiered roofs and a soaring golden spire. Formerly an audience hall, it is now used for the lying-in-state of deceased kings. Just outside this lies a smaller pavilion, **Aporn Phimok Prasat**, where kings alighted from their palanquin before entering the audience hall.

The Grand Palace Complex is accessed on the Sanam Luang side; open daily 9am-5pm, last tickets at 4pm, fee 100 baht (includes entry to Vimarnmek Palace on the same day).

idon or the Royal Pantheon, located by the northern wall, houses statues of the first eight Chakri kings. (The reigning king is the ninth.) Nearby is the **Library** containing the *tripatka*, or holy scriptures. The cloister walls around the complex tell in murals the story of the *Ramakien*, the Thai adaptation of the Hindu 'Ramayana', mixing myth, Buddhism, legend and social history.

The **Chakri Maha Prasad** dominates the royal residential compound known as the Grand Palace. Completed in 1882 by King Chulalongkorn, this Italianate palace was the finishing touch, suitably majestic and crowned by three Thai-style tiered roofs with soaring spires. The royal residence up till 1946, it now serves as the setting for

Elaborate roofs, intricate mosaics drench the structures and statuary in this magnificent compound.

The complex lies alongside the Chao Phya River on **Rattanokosin Island**, the historic heart of Bangkok bounded by the river to the west and Klong Lawd to the east. North from the Grand Palace is the racetrack-shaped open field called **Sanam Luang** or **Pramane Ground**, which, while serving usually as a public park and a favourite kite-flying spot in the windy February to April months, is highly significant as the setting for great occasions like royal cremations and the annual Ploughing Ceremony held each May.

At cremations, enormous and elaborate wooden pavilions are erected for the performance of the ritual and the shelter of dignitaries.

Sanam Luang is bounded to the west by several important national institutions. From south to north, these are **Silpakorn University**, the top fine arts academy where Thai contemporary art exhibitions can often be viewed, **Wat Mahathat**, containing Mahachulalongkorn Buddhist University, one of the top two monks' colleges, and **Thammasat University**, the nation's second-ranking university which specialises in social sciences and has a reputation for political radicalism. At least 200 students were massacred here in 1976 in a right-wing backlash, bringing to an end the turbulent democratic period that the country experienced in the mid-70s.

Then comes the **National Museum** housing the nation's most comprehensive collection of classical Thai art objects together with a large collection of South-east Asian art (open 9-12noon and 1-4pm except Mondays and Fridays, fee 20 baht; Western volunteer guides offer free tours in English on different themes on Tuesdays [Thai Art and Culture], Wednesdays [Buddhism], and Thursdays [Pre-Thai and Thai Art] at 9.30am).

Lastly, on the corner, there's the **National Theatre**, a great concrete hangar now infrequently used since the opening of the new Thailand Cultural Centre across town; and over the road, the **National Gallery**, which regularly presents exhibitions of the work of contemporary Thai artists, and sometimes foreign ones. (Open same hours as National Museum; fee 10 baht).

In this area, the place most popular with Bangkokians is the **City Pillar** or **Lak Muang**, Bangkok's foundation stone and home of its guardian spirit to which citizens flock to make wishes for good luck and success. Located just to the north-east of Wat Phra Kaew, it swarms with supplicants on lottery result days (open daily 7am-4.30pm).

Wat Po, to the south of Wat Phra

Wat Po Temple, Bangkok's oldest, Thailand's largest.

Keaw, is Bangkok's oldest and Thailand's largest temple. Often called the **Temple of the Reclining Buddha** and officially known as **Wat Phra Jetuphon**, it is a bewildering maze of chapels and pavilions, statues and spires, covering almost eight hectares. It grew to this size because it was in past times the city's premier educational institute and today it is still famed for its traditional medicine, particularly herbal brews and 'ancient massage'. Visitors may sample the latter, performed mostly by strong, skilled women practitioners for 120 baht per hour, a good way to smooth out the aches and pains of a sightseeing day. For tourists, the top attraction is undoubtedly the enormous Reclining Buddha which represents the Buddha at the moment he entered Nirvana. 46 metres long and 15 metres high and covered with gold leaf, it is the largest reclining Buddha image in the country. (Open daily 8am-5pm; fee 10 baht).

Within The City Wall

Most of Bangkok's growth has been westward from Rattanakosin Island, right from the early days, so that to the west beyond Klong Lawd several historic sites can be found. Completed early last century, **Wat Suthat** on Bamrungmuang Road features Bangkok's tallest *viharn* housing an eight-metre tall 14th century bronze Buddha barged down from the ancient capital of Sukhothai in the north.

On a square outside stands one of Bangkok's historical oddities, the **Giant Swing.** Two towering red poles with a carved crossbeam atop, it – until the 1930s – served to enable young men to swing up to 20 metres in the air trying to grab a bag of gold from atop a pole. The consequent death toll brought about the abolition of this annual Brahmin feat of daring.

A little further westward and north of Bamrungmuang Road lies Bangkok's highest hill, but even so, it's a man-made one, planned in the last century by King Rama III to outdo one that was raised in the previous capital, Ayutthaya. The new **Golden Mount** proved intractable, collapsing several times until a thousand teak logs were pile-driven in to reinforce the soft earth. Finally in 1863 a square concrete crown arose on top with a great golden *chedi*, reached by climbing 318 spiralling steps. This structure houses important Buddhist relics from India.

From here, the view of Bangkok's historic heart is panoramic, there being no interfering high-rise buildings in this district. Each November, the city's premier temple fair is held in the grounds below, with everything from vending stalls to ferris wheels to monkey theatre.

The Giant Swing

In Bangkok's old city, Wat Suthat is the Buddhist temple of the royal Brahmin priests, performers of important court rituals. In the square fronting it stands a strange, very tall, bright red arch made from two colossal teak trunks. This is the Giant Swing, centrepiece of a Brahmin ceremony discontinued owing to its danger.

Up till 1935, Bangkok Brahmins gathered here each year on the fifth day of the second lunar month (usually in January) to welcome the god Shiva on his annual visit to Earth. A high court official, usually the Minister of Rice, would represent Shiva and would preside over the ceremony as Lord of the Swing.

His entertainment was provided by teams of young men swinging high in the air from the Giant Swing. They did so in longways manner on a board, like swingboats at English fairs, with two men in the middle doing the swinging and one in the prow ready to do the main business.

As the board swung higher and higher, so it came nearer and nearer the top of a 25-metre pole holding a bag of silver coins, and so the front man leaned far forward to snatch the bag, not with his hands but with his teeth!

It was a death-defying feat and young men regularly fell to earth with rather less grace than Shiva, never to perform anything again, eventually incurring the ceremony's abandonment.

Other parts of the ceremony still take place in reduced form within Wat Suthat but the swinging stopped in 1935. Let's hope Shiva enjoyed it while it lasted.

Continuing to the north, walkers will find a restored section of the old city wall, whitewashed and crenellated, complete with a small fort at the junction with Ratchadamnoen Klang, a formal avenue lined with uniform brick buildings laid out in the 1930s in one of Bangkok's intermittent bouts of town planning. To the left at its head is the newly-restored **Lohaprasad**. This great salmon-pink pyramid surrounded by tiers of white spires is a recent revelation that popped up, to the delight of Bangkokians, when a cinema in front got demolished in 1989. The Metal Mansion, for that is the meaning of its name, had been obscured for decades; now this imitation of an ancient Sri Lankan monastery is a prominent feature of the old city. A monument to the Buddhist faith, only its spires are metallic, the structure being of stucco on brick. Nevertheless, in form it is now unique in the world.

Halfway down broad Rajadamnoen Klang sprouts a brutishly pompous monument to democracy. In a good cause ill-served, **Democracy Monument** shoots four concrete pillars skyward and forms a large roundabout. Better to turn right and amble up to Banglampoo, one of the capital's more lively quarters and especially good for clothes-shopping. Here can be found a most pleasant and well-kept temple, **Wat Bovornives**, whose abbots have a long history of adherence to fundamental Buddhist principles. King Mongkut (Rama IV) was abbot here for many of his 27 years as a monk and the present king was ordained here. Its spiritual reputation has led to the founding of an international Buddhist institute within the crowded grounds, which feature many turtle-filled canals and a chapel with superbly original murals.

DUSIT

From the fort near the Golden Mount, another ceremonial avenue leads northwards to the Parliament. This road, Rajadamnoen Nok, sports Thailand's premier boxing venue, **Rajadamnoen Stadium.** It was here just over 40 years ago that Thai boxing entered the modern era of purpose-built stadiums, professionalism and official regulation.

This grand avenue, unique in the city, leads to the select Dusit district, location of government and royal residences. Rajadamnoen Nok sweeps up to the elegant **National Assembly**, a Capitol-like structure in white marble completed in 1916 as the Ananta Samakom Throne Hall; it became the national political seat in 1933 upon the inauguration of the constitutional monarchy and parliament. Since the politicians moved to a modern assembly building some years ago, it is now ghostly, but can be entered by arrangement (contact the Tourist Authority of Thailand).

Behind the National Assembly lies **Vimarnmek Palace**, built as a country retreat by King Chulalongkorn but now virtually in downtown Bangkok. Nevertheless, this golden teak structure, said to be the world's largest, retains, within its spacious lotus-pond laced grounds, a wonderful period charm. Indicative of this, its name means Celestial Residence. Still fully furnished in a melange of Victorian and traditional Thai styles, it is probably the best representative extant of nineteenth century royal living. (Open Wednesdays to Sundays, 9.30-4.00, 50 baht fee which includes guided tour).

To its east is Bangkok's most pleasant public park (there's not much competition), **Dusit Zoo**. For the price of 10 baht, visitors can roam the tree-lined paths, skirt the numerous ornamental lakes, go boating, feed the huge carp, eat at open-air cafes, and even ride on merry-go-rounds, besides inspecting a wide and motley selection of caged animals, not just from Thailand or Southeast Asia but from all over the world.

To its east lies **Chitrlada Palace**, the residence of King Bhumiphol whose grounds occupy one large city block. A conscientious monarch who has devoted much time to the affairs of the poor rural majority, he has given over much of this space for the agricultural experimentation in which he takes much in-

Thai Boxing

Thai boxing is an ancient martial art that has become the nation's number one spectator sport. Any Sunday afternoon will see half the male populace glued to the TV screen gasping and grunting at a fierce flurry of fists and feet.

Thai boxers have ten weapons – their fists, elbows, knees, shins and feet. All are permitted for use in attack, while only the groin is off-limits as a target. Other prohibitions are the same as in straight international-style boxing – no head-butting or biting, no hitting a man when he's down, and so on.

Other things are pretty international too – ring, gloves and shorts – but no boots are worn. Bouts are shorter and breaks longer – five three-minute rounds with two-minute breaks between. The main differences are in weaponry, as detailed, and atmosphere.

Muay Thai, its local name, features fascinating warm-up rituals to the eerie sound of traditional music. Fighters pay homage to the Buddha and their trainer, amongst other things, by individual ritual dances wearing a special stiff headband with a long rear tassle.

Before the fight, frantic betting takes place among the spectators. During the fight, the music reflects the battle, sometimes rising to a frenzy in sympathy with the boxers' flying fists and feet.

Top stadiums in Bangkok are Rajdamnern and Lumpini; a top boxer of the moment is Saengtien-Noi, "The Deadly Kisser", who cheekily gives his opponent a peck before socking him a knockout.

---

terest. Here also live the white elephants, actually pinky-grey rather than completely albino. Any such animal found in the kingdom must be offered to the sovereign, by ancient tradition. King Bhumibol has accepted a dozen white elephants during his reign.

Chitrlada Palace and grounds cannot be entered but can be seen behind their protective moat and railings. This is actually a pleasant part of town to stroll around, with many tree-lined streets and little commercial activity.

To the south of the zoo lies **Wat Benjamabopit**, better known as the **Marble Temple**, one of Bangkok's royal temples. Designed by King Chulalongkorn's half-brother, construction began in 1899 and was completed in 1910. Its walls are lined with white Italian marble. Its design is unique, with many-tiered roofs stepping up on each side towards the central chapel; this gives it unusual breadth and symmetry. These aspects and the relative austerity of its decoration render the Marble Temple particularly attractive to European taste, which tends to become bewildered by the Thai penchant for decorating every temple surface. (Open daily till 5pm; fee 10 baht).

Over the river - THONBURI

Only two of Bangkok's major attractions lie on the west side of the Chao Phraya River, which was until recently a separate municipality known as Thonburi and is where the whole metropolis originated.

Upon the destruction of Ayutthaya

Wat Benjamabopit, the Marble Temple, displays unusual symmetry mostly set in Italian marble.

in 1767, King Taksin first relocated the capital to Thonburi and by the riverside built **Wat Arun** as his royal chapel. Better known as the **Temple of the Dawn**, it is famed for its unique formation of spires soaring above the river. An 86-metre tall central *prang*, or spire, is ringed by four smaller *prang,* all of them encrusted with a kaleidoscope of Chinese porcelain fragments. The central *prang* represents Mount Meru, the centre of the universe, while the smaller ones symbolise the oceans of the world. The group of spires silhouetted against the rising sun forms a favourite Thai image which features in the logo of the Tourist Authority of Thailand.

At the riverfront, a paved and gardened plaza separates the towers from the water. Here stand bearded Chinese stone guardians and delicate topiary, a porcelain-speckled rock garden and tiled pavilions.

Wat Arun is a many-facetted spectacle besides being one of the city's royal temples. That status endows it with the honour of its monks being presented with new robes by the King each October at the end of Buddhist Lent. Though, as its name suggests, it would be a wonderful sight to behold at dawn hours, Wat Arun also makes a great silhouette against the sunset. (Open daily, 9am-5pm; fee 5 baht).

Royal Barge Procession

Traditionally, the King travelled to the temple in the magnificent Royal Barge Procession, but this has become rare in modern times. In a custom dating back at least 600 years, up to 51 long, slim, ornately-carved barges are rowed downriver by red-and-gold-garbed oarsmen to the eerie sound of deep horn-blasts. It is one of the world's most spectacularly atmospheric ceremonies, sadly performed only three times in the last half-century, in 1959, 1982 and 1987. The most important barges can be seen, however, at the **Royal Barge Museum**, on the bank of Klong Bangkok Noi in Thonburi, hard by the Chao Phraya next to Bangkok Noi Railway Station. Here one may marvel at the 44-metre long *Sri Suphannahongse,* the King's barge with a prow protuding a long-beaked bird's head, as befits its name, that of a mythical swan. Another barge, the *Anantanagaraj,* has a prow in the form of the seven-headed *naga* serpent. (Open daily, 8am-6pm).

Jim Thompson House

If Vimarnmek Palace is the best peek at royal living, three other houses in Bangkok provide the visitor with a glimpse at the best of traditional Thai interiors. Most famous is **Jim Thompson's House**, actually several old teak houses moved and reassembled into one by the American celebrated for reviving the Thai silk industry. His love of things Thai led him to create his home thus (Soi Kasemsan 2, off Rama I Road), and to furnish and decorate it with a fabulous collection of Thai, Khmer and other Asian antiques and artifacts, plus the best of local handicrafts. (Open Monday to Saturday, 9am-4pm, 100 baht with guided tour).

Suan Pakkad

Suan Pakkad is a collection of five traditional teak houses transported from the north by a prince in the 1920s to become his residence. Located at 352 Sri Ayutthaya Road, its glory is the Lacquer

Initiation ceremony at the Marble Temple.

The Jim Thompson house continues to draw many visitors to his personal collection of Thai, Khmer, and Asian objets d'art.

Pavilion whose walls are covered with black and gold tableaux of the Buddha's life intermingled with historical figures and social scenes out of the Thai past. Other pavilions contain priceless antique cabinets and neolithic Ban Chiang pottery. Upon lawned gardens, pelicans strut. These interconnected teak houses cluster quietly on a klong on the one side, amidst an artfully arranged garden. The entire house and its contents are virtually preserved as is since the mysterious disappearance of Jim Thompson while on holiday in the Cameron Highlands in Malaysia. (Open Monday to Saturday, 9am-4pm, 50 baht).

Kamthieng House

The Siam Society is Thailand's premier private institute devoted to research into Thai history in all its aspects: social, architectural, folkloric, ethnic, and so on. An extensive library for Thai and Asian studies is housed here. In its grounds at 131 Soi Asoke, there is a fine example of a 200-year-old Northern Thai house which serves as an ethnological museum. **Kamthieng House** contains all sorts of local craftwork from pottery to fish-traps, with ox-carts and herb gardens outside. It speaks volumes for Thai folk artistry. (Open Tuesday to

Saturday, 9-12am and 1-5pm, 20 baht).

These three houses are found in the part of the city that has sprouted in the last 50 years or so, west from the old heart.

Erawan Shrine

Mid-to-late twentieth century Bangkok is generally not a pretty sight, yet there are jewels amongst the dross. One such is the **Erawan Shrine**, located on the corner of Ploenchit and Rajdamri Roads, outside the new Hyatt Erawan Hotel. Almost every Thai building has a spirit house somewhere in its grounds where the local spirits disturbed or displaced by the construction are given a nice home to keep them benevolent, hopefully. Hotels are no exception to this rule; indeed some of the most elaborate spirit houses of all are to be seen by Bangkok's luxury establishments.

When the original Erawan Hotel was being built in 1956, a series of nasty accidents prompted the owners to hurriedly install a shrine to Brahma, whereupon all went smoothly. The shrine quickly gained fame amongst Bangkokians as one of particular potency, likely to bring success and good fortune to all who paid respect to it. Ever since, it has been the city's foremost spirit shrine, swarming from early morning to late night with devotees offering garlands, incense, candles, gold leaf, wooden elephants, etc, and making their wishes.

For much of the day, a troupe of four female classical dancers and a small traditional orchestra are on hand to perform, for a fee, in the god's honour. (Open daily, 7am-11pm).

Lumpini Park

Bangkok's principal park, indeed almost its only one and certainly the largest, is **Lumpini Park** on Rama IV Road. It is also the only large public space in the whole downtown area and thus prized by Bangkokians as a respite from the concrete jungle all around. It contains a large boating lake, an ornamental lake, and many tree-shaded paths threading through its grassy expanse. In early morning and late afternoon, joggers and other exercisers abound, getting fit before and after work in the nearby Silom Road business dis-

The Erawan Shrine

The Kamthieng House grounds contain an assembly of Thai ethnic architectural styles; also located here is The Siam Society, an institute dedicated to the research and preservation of Thailand's social and cultural heritage.

trict. Chinese shadow-boxers stroke the early air while weight-lifters favour afternoons, but most people most of the day just laze by the lakeside. In the north-western corner lies an open-air cafe-restaurant with a good selection of reasonably-priced food. (Park open daily, 5am-9pm).

Snake Farm

A little further west along Rama IV Road lies a top tourist attraction, the **Snake Farm**. This is part of the Pasteur Institute run by the Thai Red Cross; it produces anti-snakebite serum for hospitals nationwide and abroad by "milking" snakes of their venom and injecting it into horses whose blood then produces an antidote. Visitors witness the venom extraction process and see the snake pits and cages containing cobras, vipers and banded kraits. Pythons are also on display. (Open Monday to Friday, 10am-4.30pm; shows at 10.30am and 1.30pm. Saturday and Sunday, 8-12am; show at 10.30. 40 baht including show).

Chulalongkorn University

Around the corner up Phyathai Road is the imposing main entrance to **Chulalongkorn University**, the nation's premier educational institution and its first secular university, founded by King Rama V in 1910. Beyond an ornamental pond and extensive playing fields rises the steep-roofed traditional facade of the Auditorium, where the monarch annually dispenses degrees to new graduates. The grounds are spacious, and students are always to be seen at wooden and concrete benches outside, eating or chatting, drinking or thinking, and even studying. Theoretically, all students must wear white shirts or blouses and black trousers or skirts of regulation design, but the limits are continually being tested by today's more individualistic youth. Blue denim skirts are one ploy. (Though it is not actually a public place, discreet visitors are unlikely to be turned away).

Golden Buddha at Wat Traimitr

About a kilometre further west along Rama IV Road lies Bangkok's rail terminus, **Hua Lampong Station**, a distinctive curved-roofed building set back behind a plaza dotted with food vendors and rural migrants wondering where to go in the big city. A little further on over the canal bridge and down Traimitr Street is **Wat Traimitr**, an unremarkable temple with an extraordinary Buddha image, known as the **Golden Buddha**. Thailand is full of golden Buddhas but very few are made of real solid gold and none such as big as this one – 3 metres tall and weighing 5-1/2 tons. On top of this, it was discovered entirely by accident in 1957. An old stucco Buddha kept in a storeroom was damaged on being craned elsewhere, and the plaster fell away to reveal the golden wonder, a Sukhothai-style sitting Buddha. It had probably been stuccoed 200 years previously to hide it from the rampaging Burmese. (Open daily, 9am-5pm).

Chinatown

Wat Traimitr lies at the western entrance to **Chinatown**. In a recent book about Chinatowns worldwide, an overseas Chinese writer rated Bangkok's her favourite, citing not just its size and variety but its vitality and authenticity. This Chinatown is not one prettified for tourist consumption such as London's or San Francisco's; it is a vibrant hive of commercial activity, a warren of shophouse-lined streets where Bangkok's traditional Chinese community plies multifarious trades, from coffin-making to chick-breeding, from printing to motor mechanics, from gold-trading to candle-making, all of them clearly visible from the sidewalk, indeed, many trades spill out onto the pavement.

One of the major trades is in cloth, centred along **Sampeng Lane**, which is where the first Chinese set up some 200 years ago, and which ends up at **Pahurat Market**, the Indian cloth-trading area. Another famed market is the **Thieves' Market**, or Talad Nakhon Kasem, which used to be just that, a selling-place for stolen goods, but which now features a number of specialisations such as antiques, musical instruments, brassware and electric motors. Rather than a street market, it is actually a grid of narrow shophouse streets.

To tell the truth, Chinatown does not really have any must-see sights; it is a place to wander round, despite the high level of air and noise pollution emanating from its clogged traffic. Wandering, the visitor comes upon dragon-adorned temples and clan-houses, chemists' shops lined with jars of herbs and potions, restaurants offering crocodile, lizard and python meat, and pawnshops and goldshops galore – see which are doing best and you will know how business is. While most of Bangkok's Chinese are upwardly mobile and live elsewhere in the city, the core of the Chinese community remains and still thrives in Chinatown.

Chinatown's two principal arteries, Yaowaraj and Charoen Krung converge to the south-east and head down by the riverside to the original European trading and diplomatic quarter along **New Road**. Here is where the Portuguese and the French built their embassies, where the Danes erected the grand East Asiatic Company complex, and most famously where the original Oriental Hotel hosted the writers Joseph Conrad and Somerset Maugham. The Oriental, now vastly expanded, largely high-rise, and frequently rated the world's best, treasures its still extant original building. A white stucco villa set amongst gardens at the riverside, its internal courtyard has become a bamboo-shaded atrium serving as an Edwardian tearoom called the Authors' Lounge.

Markets

Markets abound in Bangkok, where housewives favour fresh food daily. There are many specialist markets too, and one is found just beyond Oriental Lane along New Road. **Bangrak Market's** frontage is a flower market specialising in elaborate wreaths and garlands. Elsewhere, **Pratunam Market** deals in clothes and the **Weekend Market** in just about everything. (These two are described in the Shopping section).

Tewes Market, upriver east of Dusit district, deals in plants and flowers, notably orchids. To experience the city's wholesale fruit, vegetable and flower market, go to **Pak Klong Market** by the river next to Memorial Bridge. This teeming and odour-filled central market is of the kind now banished from Western capitals, such as London's former Covent Garden and Paris's Les Halles.

Amulets and Charms

A Bangkok speciality is amulet markets. Two famed ones are in the compound of **Wat Rajanada** off Rajadamnoen Klang Road and at **Maharat Pier** on the river next to Thammasat

Flower Garlands

The delicate art of garland-making and the custom of garland-offering is ubiquitous and distinctive of Thai culture, today as ever. Flower garlands are in the forefront of the image of charm and beauty that Thailand presents to the world and that so impresses the visitor from more mundane cultures.

It is naturally a feminine art. Traditionally, mothers teach their daughters the *puang malai* craft, cultivating the patience and delicacy required of a Thai woman. The apogee of the art occurs in the Grand Palace where highly-skilled practitioners make floral decorations for royal functions.

Garland-making can be seen widely on the streets of Bangkok near popular shrines and temples, notably the Erawan Shrine. Women and girls spend their days sitting at sidewalk tables threading jasmine buds, petals of jasmine, red roses, purple orchids and a kind of marigold. The brilliant and sweet-scented creations are purchased by devotees about to visit the places of worship.

Religiously, garlands are offered in homage to the Buddha, to Brahma, and to the nature spirits.

Secularly, they may be presented in welcome or in congratulation, or as a sign of appreciation as for a performing artist. From temple to nightclub, from palace to spirit house, *puang malai* are a constant and colourful feature of Thai life.

A garland stall.

University. Here stallholders display all kinds of lucky charms to be worn round the neck, usually Buddha images. Those regarded as particularly powerful are extremely expensive, even running to thousands of dollars.

ENVIRONS OF BANGKOK

There are several purpose-built tourist attractions located within easy reach of the city in surrounding provinces. In a garden setting, they present aspects of Thai tradition or animal life, or both. They are all designed for day-trips or half-day trips from Bangkok.

Ancient City

The most erudite of these attractions is **Ancient City**, or *Muang Boran* in Thai. This is a park spreading over 200 acres in the elephant-head shape of Thailand. In their correct geographic position, replicas of all the country's most historically significant structures have been erected, some full-size but most scaled down. All have been accurately and meticulously recreated. Some buildings are even genuine, moved here for preservation.

Other genuine buildings have been transported to recreate traditional scenes of Thai life, such as The Market of Yesteryear, the Floating Market and the Northern Thai Hamlet.

Another facet of Ancient City is the beautiful gardens, some of them portraying Thai legends with bronze horses flying over waterfalls and suchlike.

Ancient City is located 33km southeast of Bangkok near the end of the No.8 and No.11 air-conditioned bus routes at Samut Prakarn. Most tour operators arrange trips there. (Open daily 8am-5pm, fee 50 baht adults, 25 baht children. On Saturdays, Sundays and holidays, a coach service with guide leaves Ancient City's Bangkok office near Democracy Monument at 9am, arriving back at 4pm; fee 250 baht adults, 125 baht children).

Crocodile Farm

On the same bus routes just before Samut Prakarn lies the **Crocodile Farm**, said to be the world's largest with over 30,000 denizens. Crocodiles used to inhabit the canals of Thailand, causing great fear and loathing, but have now been eradicated from the natural environment. Those at the farm perform the dual function of providing skin for fancy leather goods and giving regular shows in which trainers wrestle with the beasts and stick their heads in the reptiles' mouths. (Open daily 8am-6pm, fee 80 baht).

Rose Garden & Parks

32km west of town lies the **Rose Garden**, offering various entertainments

Lumpini Park, Bangkok's principal park and restful respite.

amidst extensive tropical gardens. On offer are traditional dances, elephant shows and rides, Thai boxing bouts and sword-fights, traditional wedding and monk's ordination ceremonies, craft-making demonstrations, and so on. Set beside a river, the grounds include a bungalow resort and golf course. (Open daily, 8am-6pm; shows in the afternoon; fee 140 baht, including shows).

There are several historical sites around Bangkok that are commonly visited on day-trips, notably the ruins of the former capital at Ayutthaya, the royal summer palace of Bang Pa-In, the ancient city of Nakhon Pathom, and the River Kwai Bridge at Kanchanaburi. These are dealt with in the Central Plains chapter of **THE REGIONS OF THAILAND**.

Visitors, especially children, who just wish to escape Bangkok's urban pressures may visit two large amusement parks on the outskirts. **Magic Land**, is located in the northern suburbs on Phaholyothin Road beyond Central Plaza shopping mall. It features mostly mechanical rides, such as a ferris wheel and a big dipper. **Siam Park**, is situated on the northeastern outskirts towards Minburi. It offers spacious grounds with large expanses of swimming pools with fantasy islands, convoluted water-chutes and even artificial waves. Other mechanical rides include back-breaking high-speed loop-the-loop, shows like the Wall of Death and visiting circuses and ice-shows.(Siam Park open daily, 10am-6pm weekdays, 9am-7pm weekends and holidays; fee 80 baht, children 50 baht).

Further out in Minburi, **Safari World** is an extensive safari park containing Asian and African wildlife plus a dolphin show.

Shopping

Paradise is an overworked word in the tourism business but Bangkok comes pretty close to being a paradise for shoppers. It is doubtful that there is anywhere else in the world which offers an equivalent combination of variety, quality and price. You will find a wider range in London or New York, better fashions in Paris or Milan, and much cheaper electrical goods in Hong Kong and Singapore, but across the board, all the bills totted up, Bangkok gives the best value. While quite a lot of imported goods are available at affordable prices, it is the cheapness and acceptable quality of the huge range of locally-made goods that give Bangkok the edge.

Thai silk, available in traditional and modern designs, still sold in yardage.

Clothing & Fabrics

Textiles and garments have become Thailand's leading exports, edging in front of the age-old rice trade, on account of their extremely competitive combination of quality and price. Thus it is that most tourists find Thai clothing and fabrics difficult to resist.

A department store of Thai silk and cotton products built in traditional style, along Silom Road.

The speciality is Thai silk, most of which is coarser than the Chinese or Indian product but consequently more practical and to many eyes more attractive too. Available in every colour and also in prints, it can be bought by the yard, tailored into suits, shirts and dresses, or purchased ready-made as clothing such as blouses and shirts, accessories such as handkerchiefs and ties, and even handbags and wallets. One noted form of silk is *mudmee*, whose thread is tie-dyed first and then woven into intricate patterns.

Bangkok is probably now the best place in the world for inexpensive tailoring. Since Thais still prefer to go to a tailor for their best clothes, or even most of their clothes in the case of women, suiting for men and dressmaking for women are available throughout the city at all levels of price and quality.

Ready-made clothing of good quality and very reasonable price is sold everywhere in the city, particularly in and around department stores and markets. Materials range from 100% local cotton to mixtures and to completely man-made fabrics. Brand–names may be local or international; if the latter, the clothes will most likely be made in Thailand to international standards yet sold considerably cheaper than in the industrialised countries. Fake designer clothes are touted on the streets, especially in tourist areas, but are unlikely to be encountered in better stores. Local brands are often of equal quality to well-known international names.

A wide range of leather goods is on sale, from handbags to belts, shoes to briefcases. Besides the more normal cowhide and buffalo-hide, there is a good deal of crocodile and snake-skin, and even elephant hide.

Metalware

To begin at the expensive end, **gold** is to be found all over the city – not, unfortunately, on the pavement, though many provincial people do still think Bangkok's streets are paved with it, but in the ubiquitous gold shops, which are still where most Bangkokians go to invest surplus cash. After all the philosophy is, that banks just take your money and hide it away, and who knows if they will ever give it back? But with gold jewellery one can see and keep and, above all, other people can then see what one is worth.

So Thais are avid buyers of **gold** chains, necklaces, bracelets, bangles, rings, brooches, earrings and whatever else the precious metal can be worked into for personal ornamentation, and there are gold-sellers throughout the city ready to cater to this demand. Almost always distinguished by scarlet-painted frontages and glass showcases, often open to the street rather than air-conditioned, they sell jewellery by weight unless the piece is of exceptional craftsmanship. Prices are government-regulated and very good value compared with most other countries; because goldshops function as a form of bank for so many local people, they are officially controlled and visitors need not fear rip-offs.

Silver jewellery, though not nearly so popular, may be bought in the same shops, while elsewhere silverware is available in the form of boxes, cases, tea-sets, statuettes and the like. Particularly well-worked are pieces from Chiang Mai in the north, which specialises in silverwork, while the most unusual pieces are made by the northern hilltribe people, many of whom favour great displays of silver jewellery and have developed distinctive styles.

Pewterware is widely available at reasonable prices on account of Thailand being a major producer of tin, its prime constituent. Tankards, plates, vases and hip-flasks are just some of the many products available.

Also very reasonable are **bronze** in the form of bowls, gongs, trays and such like and **brass** lanterns, cabinets and so on.

A unique local craft is **nielloware**, the etching and filling of silver with black metals; it is favoured for such objects as jewel boxes, lockets, trays and vases.

Precious Stones And Ivory

Thailand is increasingly renowned for its gemstones, chief amongst them **sapphires** and **rubies**. The kingdom possesses large quantities of both gems and skilled cutters who are adept at fashioning the blue, green and yellow sapphires and the rubies of varying depths of red. In jewellery, both traditional and modern designs are available.

Fine cultured **pearls** from Phuket Island in the south are widely available in necklaces, earrings, brooches and the like.

Jade is imported from Burma and fashioned into rings, bracelets and pendants, as well as ornamental dishes, ashtrays, and so on. It comes not only in the widely-known translucent green shade but also in yellow, brown, red, orange and purple.

Carved **ivory** is widely sold; if it is not fake, it comes largely from the endangered African elephant rather than the indigenous breed.

Ceramics, Glassware, Lacquerware

Celadon pottery is a local speciality; this stoneware of a high sheen in light green and brown shades is a popular choice for tableware.

Two forms of fine porcelain are widely available, the Chinese **blue and white** style which is a favourite for crockery, and the indigenous **Bencharong** which appears in the same five colours – red, green, blue, yellow and white – usually as delicate ornamental jars and bowls.

Decorative **glassware** animals are widely sold.

Lacquerware, sometimes inlaid with **mother-of-pearl**, is another quality craft most often seen in the form of boxes and bowls, usually black or red.

Theatrical & Musical Items

Theatrical costumes and props can be bought at souvenir and specialist shops. The vivid and grotesque masks of the traditional *khon* dance-drama,

elaborate court dancers' head-pieces, shadow puppets of buffalo hide, and finely-dressed and expressive Burmese marionettes are especially interesting purchases.

Musical instruments, both traditional and Western, are particularly good value. Xylophones and gongs, flutes and lutes, bells and drums are just some of the many traditional instruments that can be bought; quality ranges from shoddy to superb – it is up you to tell the difference. Thais also manufacture many sorts of Western instruments ranging from electric guitars to Latin percussion. Both fibre-glass and wooden bongos and congas are much cheaper than in the West and quite serviceable.

Art & Antiques

There is a thriving antiques trade in Bangkok, not just in Thai items but also in Burmese and, to a rather lesser extent, Cambodian, Chinese and European pieces. Porcelain, wood and stone items are the most common; Thai Buddha images are forbidden for export whilst Burmese ones are freely exportable; fakes abound but they are usually declared as such.

Modern Thai art is available in galleries around town; pretty landscapes and folk scenes predominate and several shops do portrait painting while you wait. Most serious artists produce abstracts or Buddhism-inspired works (best seen at Visual Dhamma Gallery, Soi Asoke).

There is an abundance of craftwork sold for decorative purposes: hand-painted waxed-paper umbrellas, exquisitely-dressed dolls, woodcarvings of anything from Buddhas to elephants, hilltribe weaving and embroidery,

Bangkok's market places sell anything to everything from livestock to finished goods.

framed beetles and butterflies, Burmese *kalaga* tapestries, etc.

Basketware

Excellent basketware of widely varying texture is made in Thailand. All sorts and sizes of bags, baskets, mats, lampshades, fans and the like are on sale, as well as purely decorative items in the shape of fish, birds, elephants, houses, and so on. Older traditional pieces tend to be more expensive and, as its popularity among visitors increase, these antique pieces will be scarcer in the shops. Modern weaves are plentiful but as Thailand mechanizes and industrialises futher, one wonders about the eventual natural passing of these crafts, handed down through the generations.

Furniture & Woodwork

Two furniture specialities are rattan and teak. There are teak armchairs and tables that are elaborately carved with rural scenes and a wide variety of well-made rattan items ranging from tables to sofas, from bookcases to bar-stools.

Practical woodwork items include salad bowls and ashtrays, coasters and breadboards, pen holders and serviette rings. Ornamental wood carving are exquisite, plentiful and relatively inexpensive.

Other Handicrafts

There are many practical and decorative items fashioned out of materials such as paper, cloth, plaster and *papier-mache*. These include paper flowers, plaster animals, cloth dolls and *papier-mache* money-boxes. Thais produce a myriad of such items ranging from tiny glass insects to huge plaster giraffes, from exquisite cloth bouquets to gaudy plaster fruit, from painted paper umbrellas to lacquered fans.

At street-stalls and even in shops, all is not what it seems. Fakery abounds in Bangkok but the price will immediately tell you whether you are perusing a real Rolex watch or not, whether the Lacoste sports shirt is what it claims to be, or if the Gucci bag really is such. The imitations are often ingenious and the quality sometimes quite good, but if you do buy, the customs officer at your home airport may have a few words to say.

WHERE TO SHOP

Bangkok seems to be a city of shopkeepers; just about everywhere you go there is somebody selling something. Even at the end of the most obscure suburban lane, somebody will be hawking brushes or fruit or icecream. Equally, there is no main shopping district, no predominant street such as London's Oxford Street or Singapore's Orchard Road. Shopping goes on everywhere.

Breakfasting at a market place in busy Chinatown.

That said, there are several districts where shops cluster especially close together, usually around the magnet of a department store, and these areas offer most of the goods that tourists seek. The most convenient place to shop for local crafts and clothing, which are the most popular purchases, is in department stores, for several reasons: they are all air-conditioned, the displays are usually extensive, and the prices are fixed at a reasonable level. Even if you prefer to try your hand at bargaining in individual shops or at street stalls, it is still advisable to visit department stores first to get an idea of the right price for whatever item you want to buy.

Hereafter follows a rundown of Bangkok's main shopping areas and what you can expect to find there.

The greatest agglomeration of stores lies along the north-south axis of Rajdamri and Rajaprarop Roads right smack in the middle of town. Beginning at the north end, at the Indra Hotel, there is the **Indra Arcade**, a somewhat dated indoor shopping complex offering clothes and crafts amongst other goods. Immediately south is the vast **Pratunam Market**, one of the city's top draws for cheap clothing. It is basically a wholesale market supplying the whole city but, unlike in London's or New York's garment district, retail buyers are perfectly welcome to feel the cloth and inquire the price. It is especially good for cheap shirts, blouses, skirts and dresses. If you so desire, you can buy exotica such as go-go dancing bikinis and erotic underwear. Though Pratunam means "watergate", you need not fear any chicanery here; you can see what you are getting and you can always get a reasonable price for it.

The southern side of Pratunam Market fronts on Petchburi Road, which also has cheap clothing stores and shoeshops and, further west on the opposite side, **Pantip Plaza**, a mall specialising in computer goods. If you do not object to buying pirated computer software, this is the place for you.

Over the Petchburi intersection along Rajdamri Road on the east side, lies Bangkok's biggest concentration of department stores comprising **Thai Daimaru**, **The Mall**, and **Robinson**, along with **Rajdamri Arcade**. These emporia offer the full range of consumer goods at very attractive prices, except for the imported electrical and luxury items. Considerable savings may be made on household goods like kitchenware and tableware, for example. Stalls selling cheap yet quite well-made clothing proliferate in the streets between these stores.

A little further south along Rajdamri Road, the shops become more upmarket.

This area around the crossroads of Rajdamri and Ploenchit is known as Gaysorn and is dotted with some of the best shops in town. Newest is the **World Trade Center** containing **Zen** department store and a considerable collection of international designer boutiques. Down Rajdamri between the Erawan and Regent Hotels lies Bangkok's most elegant mall, **Peninsula Plaza**; indeed, it's the only one which is a credit to its architect and a pleasure just to look at. About a third of it is a Galeries Lafayette store, the remainder is tiers of high-class fashion outlets and cafes, plus a very good bookshop.

Amarin Plaza, on Ploenchit Road just behind the Erawan Shrine, is one of Bangkok's exercises in wedding-cake neo-classicism. Behind its kitsch Greek facade lie a Sogo department store and four floors of clothing and shoe boutiques, restaurants, an art gallery, luxury electronics dealers, and the like.

Opposite, by Le Meridien President Hotel, is a collection of expensive clothing shops, while a little further east is

A great variety of masks are sold in markets.

Bangkok's Chinatown that never stops.

Central Department Store (Chidlom), the flagship outlet of Thailand's premier store chain, the most spacious and best arranged of all Bangkok's department stores.

Further east along Ploenchit Road on the other side is the **TAT Duty Free Store** containing all the luxury consumer goods that one expects. If you shop here, you pick up your purchases in the airport departure lounge as you leave the country. The advantage is that the selection is wider than at the airport itself and you have plenty of time to browse; the disadvantage is that the goods may still be cheaper in your home country, and certainly are in Hong Kong or Singapore or Abu Dhabi.

Ploenchit Road continues east and becomes Sukhumvit Road shortly after

the expressway flyover. **Sukhumvit** is the most Westernised part of Bangkok on account of its large expatriate population and concentration of tourist hotels. It is therefore lined with clothing and souvenir shops and cluttered with street vendors touting clothes. Since these shops are aimed at foreigners and there is a widely-held belief that they are all rich, bargains are less easy to come by along Sukhumvit than in less touristy parts of town.

Back west, Sukhumvit Road becomes Ploenchit Road again, then Rama I Road after the Gaysorn intersection, and soon it reaches **Siam Square** on the left. This is a grid of private streets with several blocks of ground floor arcades specialising in youth fashion. Weekends and weekdays, after school and

Products from the outer regions of Thailand are sold in Bangkok.

work hours, see this area flooded with shoppers going after chic new shirt and skirt styles, original belts, bags and accessories, and so on. Prices are very reasonable, generally in line with the quality of the cloth and cut. For young fashion, there is no better value nor wider variety in the whole city, unless it be at Chatuchak Park (see later).

Across Rama I Road from Siam Square is **Siam Center**, a four-storey mall that is also filled with youth fashion boutiques.

Rajdamri Road leads south into Silom Road, the city's main business and banking district. **Silom** is also lined with shops, many of them dealing in souvenirs and local crafts ranging from silk to woodcarving, from jewelry to hilltribe crafts. Silom Village, a quaint mini-mall, is especially pleasant for this kind of shopping. Silom also hosts two department stores, Robinson located at the north end and Central towards the bottom end.

Silom Road ends up near the river at New Road. To the right along New Road there are several souvenir, craft and antique shops, especially in the lane leading to the Oriental Hotel. As befits the district, quality and prices tend to be high here. **Oriental Plaza** is the leading emporium. Further north beyond the Royal Orchid Sheraton Hotel, beside the river, lies **River City**, a huge luxury mall specialising in antiques and art. This is the place to go for the widest variety of good quality Thai antiques, as well as a substantial amount of Burmese and other regional pieces.

New Road (Charoen Krung) runs on up into **Chinatown**, and Chinatown is all about trade. If you so wish, you can purchase the traditional items of Chinese ritual, from spirit altars to massive joss-sticks to elaborate coffins, but most visitors are more likely to look for the fabric bargains in **Sampeng Lane** and **Paruhat Market** or the porcelain and lacquerware, the traditional furniture and musical instruments that abound in the **Thieves' Market**, or **Nakhon Kasem**.

Cheap Clothes

Another terrific district for cheap local clothes is **Banglampoo**, north of Rajadamnoen Klang Avenue and Sanam Luang, not far from the Grand Palace. Stretching between Wat Bovornives and the New World Department Store, this market district is full of locally-made clothes at low prices sold both at street stalls and in countless shops.

Weekend Market

The grand-daddy of all markets in Bangkok is the **Weekend Market** at Chatuchak Park in the northern suburbs opposite the Northern Bus Terminal on Phaholyothin Road. It originated at Sanam Luang in the historic heart of the city but transferred here in 1982 to a purpose-built site, and a whole book has been written about it alone. As its name implies, the stall-holders set up only on Saturdays and Sundays, and they vend just about anything you can put in a three-by-two metre space, which is a stall's typical extent: clothing, books, kitchenware, antiques, pets, plants, leather goods, plasticware, pickled fruit, pirate tapes, hilltribe crafts, posters, earthenware, songbirds, toys, furniture – you name it. Whether you are looking for a king cobra or a Burmese manuscript, a unique T-shirt or a rare orchid, or just a plastic washing bowl, it is all here and it can be haggled over. Mornings are better than afternoons, both because it gets hot later in the day and because some stall-keepers pack up early.

Chicks awaiting new owners.

River & Klong Life

Water has long ruled the life of the Central Plains of Thailand. Its abundance created the great rice-growing culture and its channels became the roads. Houses clustered along canals and rivers and people moved about by boat. Not only this, they drank the water, cooked with it, washed in it and flushed away waste in it, as well as just frolicked in it for fun. There was a great folk tradition of singing boat songs, *pleng rua*. Such was the extent that the people of the rice-growing heartland lived upon the waters that some early European visitors actually believed the Siamese to be semi-aquatic.

Mother river Chao Phraya washes through Bangkok.

Multi-purpose Waterways

The river first attracted the city of Bangkok, and its waters became its thoroughfares, just as they were in rural areas. As soon as construction of the Grand Palace was begun, so were defensive canals to its east, creating an artificial island but also waterways for transport. As the city expanded eastward so did the canal system, some of it already in place

Fully laden with coconuts, small boats make their way through the water hyacinths in the Rangsit Canal.

amongst ricefields, but much of it new. The *klong* were the city's roads, marketplaces, bathrooms and rubbish tips.

So they remained for a century and a half, earning Bangkok the soubriquet of 'Venice of the East', until modernisation mania hit the city roughly forty years ago. Cars and trucks increasingly displaced boats and barges and within remarkably few years water was dethroned by concrete. Progressively, canals were filled-in to make roads, until Bangkok was a concrete jungle with just the odd fetid *klong* here and there, trying to survive the abuse heaped upon it.

Things went better on the Thonburi side. Saved from most heavy development by being "on the wrong side of the tracks" with few connecting bridges to Bangkok proper, at least until very recently, Thonburi has retained a substantial network of canals and a considerable amount of traditional *klong* life. The Chao Phraya River too, separating the twin cities, is still a major waterway and a hive of riverine life. Thus it is this that river and canal tours offer today's visitors – fascinating views of Bangkok's traditional ways. Though there are not many boat songs to be heard now, boating through Bangkok provides insights which you would otherwise miss.

Exploring the Chao Phraya River

The river remains the vital artery of

A lattice-work of teakwood is rafted down the Chao Phraya.

the city and is characterised by a constant flow of upstream and downstream traffic and a perpetual criss-crossing of boats from bank to bank. Most of the cross-river traffic is passenger boats, either slowly chugging ferries or rip-roaring long-tail canal buses. Downstream come heavily-laden rice barges in long stately trains and sometimes rafts of teak logs. Upstream go oil tanker barges and either way there are naval and harbour patrol boats, sand barges, luxury speedboats, even simple sampans, and a full gamut of passenger and tourist vehicles ranging from the river bus through cruise barges to sleek motor yachts.

There are several ways to sightsee by river, the cheapest being the river bus known as the Express Boat (*rua duan*). This plies between Krung Thep Bridge in the south and Nonthaburi in the north for a maximum fare of 7 baht from 6am-6pm. Noisy, smelly, crowded and infrequent it may be, but it does provide a very cheap and flexible mode of seeing river life. If you spot something worth inspecting further, you could simply get off at the next stop. Most of the stops are on the Bangkok side though it does occasionally pull in to the Thonburi bank.

The favourite starting point for a river bus trip is beside the Oriental Hotel at Oriental Pier and it is best to sit or stand on the right side for the most

Not too far from Bangkok city is Klong Damnoensaduak, known for its floating market.

RIVER & KLONG LIFE

97

A mosque on the banks of a klong.

interesting sights. The boat immediately passes the old wing of the Oriental Hotel which a century ago welcomed the greatest novelist of seafaring life, a sea captain himself, Joseph Conrad.

This part of the river bank is the most rapidly changing of all, and the one with most contrasts. This is where the European community first set up shop and there are several reminders of this period – in sequence, the East Asiatic trading company, the Oriental old wing, the French Embassy, the old customs house, the Portuguese Embassy and the Holy Rosary Church – all of them cowering beneath the towering luxury hotels and malls that now throng the riverside.

After the twin spans of Memorial Bridge, the city's wholesale fresh produce market, Pak Klong, appears bustling on the east bank with Santa Cruz church opposite representing the remains of the old Portuguese quarter. Then comes the river's supreme landmark and the sight that catches every eye, the glittering spires of the Temple of the Dawn, Wat Arun.

Next, it's eyes right for the panoply of temple roofs, golden *chedi* and palace walls that Wat Po and the Grand Palace present to the river. After Phra Pinklao Bridge, the most notable sights, again on the right bank, are Phra Sumane Fort, part of the old city's defences, the royal barges in the Royal Boat House, and Tewes plant and flower market, but the urban Chao Phrya is always presenting interesting sights. There are tumbledown warehouses and Muslim mosques, stilt-house communities and gingerbread mansions, barge-dwellers and sampan commuters, shimmering temples and tantalising glimpses up canals, and all the time the passing and criss-crossing traffic of other river users.

The river bus eventually, after some 30 minutes, reaches rural territory, with the orchards of Thonburi on the west bank, where the boat makes two stops and a country stroll can be taken. Finally it passes the great long wooden facade of the old provincial hall and docks on the east bank at Nonthaburi.

Old rice barges converted to comfortable cruise boats also offer tours along the river and around the canals of Thonburi. Morning, afternoon and evening "dinner" cruises are available. These excursions can be booked with any travel agent. Alternatively, you can hire a boat yourself and be in control of your trip.

Touring Thonburi's Klongs

There are regular boat-bus services along Thonburi's main canals which cost a few odd baht and depart from Tha Chang Pier, just north of the Grand Palace at the end of Na Phralan Road. Most boats for hire also start from Tha Chang, or from Tha Orienten, adjacent to the Oriental Hotel. A sedate motor launch, *rua mai,* is preferable to a roaring long-tail boat, *rua hang yao,* and the price should be bargained down to 200 baht an hour. Though hiring a boat for exclusive use is considerably more expensive, it gives the huge advantages of being able to go wherever you wish and take whatever time suits you.

Your first destination will most likely be the Temple of the Dawn, Wat Arun, (see Sights To See), an old temple which King Taksin took as his royal chapel when he founded the new capital at Thonburi in 1767. Downstream a short distance, you pass the old royal palace of King Taksin, now a naval station, and reach **Klong Bangkok Yai**. Of interest on the right side at the klong's mouth are the remains of an old Ayutthaya period fort, Vichai Prasit Fort, once garrisoned by Louis XIV's soldiers when the French traded with King Narai, and later part of the city defenses.

The banks of Klong Bangkok Yai are studded with temples. The first of interest on the right side is Wat Sangkrajai, an old temple restored by King Rama I's queen in the early Bangkok period. She rebuilt the attractive *ubosot* (ordination hall) with its murals depicting the three worlds of Buddhist cosmology, heaven, earth and hell.

A little further on the opposite bank is Wat Inthararam, an old temple restored by King Taksin. The warrior king used to come here to meditate in solitude.

The *ubosot* contains a fine sitting Buddha image of the Sukhothai period. Two *chedi* contain the ashes of King Taksin and his queen; the king's statue stands in the temple and his bed is

The smaller the craft, the easier to manoeuvre in the klongs.

preserved as a memorial. King Taksin's father was Chinese, thus this temple is an important site for Bangkok's Chinese community.

Next comes the confluence of **Klong Sanam Chai** and **Klong Phasi Jaroen** with the main canal, on the south side, and there wedged between the two tributaries is the grand Wat Pak Nam, a well-endowed and famous temple which possesses an important monks' college and meditation centre. Many Western Buddhists study here.

Turning down Klong Sanam Chai, also known as **Klong Dan**, you see Wat Nang Chi, the Nun's Temple, on the right. It owes its name to the legend of a young nun who was so pure that her corpse would not decay. It is actually mummified and kept in a glass case for the curious to to observe and the superstitious to approach for winning lottery numbers. The *ubosot*'s murals are interesting, as are the *viharn*'s wall motifs.

Further on on the right side lies Wat Raja Orot, built by King Rama III in the early 19th century. Tree-shaded and Chinese-styled, the temple has a *bot* with somewhat battered Chinese ceramic guardians at the entrance. The *viharn* is decorated with rich painting, while the wall and pillar murals have been washed over. The buildings were restored by the Royal Fine Arts Department in 1977-8.

Just a little further south at the junction with **Klong Bangkhunthien** is where a Floating Market takes place in the early morning.

Returning up to Klong Bangkok Yai and proceeding west, and rounding to

Klongs, like ordinary streets, are lined with lamp-posts, telephone & electricity wires, and at times some form of traffic order is observed.

the north, you come into more rural territory and the canal changes name to **Klong Bang Khun Si**. The charm of a *klong* trip is as much in the glimpses of everyday life and typical scenery as in the famous temples, the scenes of riverborne monks gathering alms at dawn, of the fruit-sellers hawking their produce by boat, of the postman paddling about on his rounds, of sprucely-uniformed children being ferried to school.

In the late afternoon when the light is often golden and the time has come to wind down the day, klong-dwellers bathe artfully inside their sarongs, children frolic in the water, women prepare the evening meal at the waterside.

For these homely scenes and for the greenery of the orchards of Thonburi, it is best to explore off to the west along tributary canals or up to the north along **Klong Bangkok Noi**, which Klong Bang Khun Si flows into. If you have no time, then your boat can swing round south down Klong Bangkok Noi and meet the Chao Phraya River with the Royal Barge Museum (see Sights To See) on the left. Just before this on the right stands Wat Suwannaram, dating from the early Bangkok period. The *bot*, with its fine proportions, elegant roofs, sober stucco and carved wooden decoration, is a good example of the transition from Ayutthaya to Rattanakosin architecture. The interior is entirely covered with frescoes regarded as some of the finest in the city. The front wall depicts the victory of the Buddha over Mara while the back wall shows the Buddha coming down from heaven.

Those with the inclination can truly spend days roaming the *klong* network seeking and soaking up its diverse charms.

Up & Down River

Trips out of town can be enjoyed on both the canals and the river. Long-tail boats ply many of the canals that stretch out through the surrounding ricefields and some are available for hire. Connections westwards can be made from the Thonburi urban boat services; to the east, canal services can be reached by taking the Chachoengsao line train from Hua Lampong Station and getting out after 40 or 50 minutes when you see a canal near a station.

The most popular and grandest trips out of town are upriver to the royal summer palace of Bang Pa-in and the ruined city of Ayutthaya (see the Central Plains chapter for details).

Several well-appointed motor cruisers ply this route, namely the Oriental Queen I and II, the Ayutthaya Princess and the River Sun.

The tours begin around 8am and return to town at around 6pm. Since a round trip cruise tour cannot be done in a day, travellers are given the choice of going up by boat and back by coach, or vice-versa. Buffet lunch is included. Besides giving tourists access to two of the central region's prime attractions, these cruises offer the chance to witness up-country riverine life and scenery in comfort and style. Top price is 900 baht per person.

On a Rice Barge

Even more stylish and relaxed is the overnight trip offered on the Mekhala, an old teak rice barge converted to floating hotel. This docks for the night on the way up, and similarly coming downriver. Prices for these trips begin at around 3000 baht.

Another boat tour goes only to Bang Sai, near Bang Pa-in, to a handicraft centre under royal patronage, and stops downriver at Wat Phai Lom, a temple noted as a nesting-place for a rare stork between December and June. Since the boat is an express, it offers a complete day trip beginning at 8am and returning towards sundown.

To go downriver, hire a longtail boat from one of the landings, such as Oriental Pier, at about 200 baht an hour. In roughly two hours this will take you past Thailand's major port of Klong Toey, the import/export hub of the nation's trade, complete with swinging cranes and blasting horns, great freighters in dock and at anchor. Further downwards, winding past industrial and rural scenes to Pak Nam, the river mouth, where the great Mae Nam, "Mother Water", sweeps muddily out into the the Gulf of Thailand. If you want, it is possible to return to town by regular air-conditioned bus (No.8 & 11 to Sukhumvit Road and Siam Square).

BANGKOK

Nights in Bangkok

Bangkok nightlife is famous worldwide yet largely unknown to foreigners. This paradox arises from the fact that there are yet dozens of dancehalls, hundreds of Thai–style nightclubs and thousands of neighbourhood restaurants which tourists never go to. Bangkokians are indefatigable *sanuk*–seekers and there are a myriad of places catering solely to Thai tastes.

A local songstress entertains with Thai 'pop' melodies.

Boundaries break down in the area of discotheques, restaurants, massage parlours and jazz bars, which appeal to Thais and foreigners alike, whilst some areas are heavily tourist–orientated, notably go–go bars and traditional dancing shows.

Bangkok nightlife is not noted for its intellectual quality: you will find very little thought–provoking artistic culture, quality cinema, modern dance, satirical cabaret and so on. Thais must stand accused of taking their pleasures below the belt: eating, dancing and making love, to be precise. Most Bangkok entertainment is in these areas, so when in

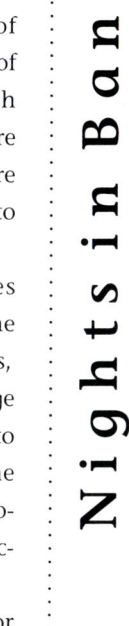

Night life and Patpong are almost synonymous.

Rome, do as the Romans do. What else?

Evening Cultural Entertainment

If there is a regular entertainment of some artistic standing, it is the dinner shows of traditional Thai dance offered at several restaurants around town.

The most scenic of these are at the *Sala Rim Naam*, a traditional Thai teak structure on the river bank opposite the Oriental Hotel, of which it is part; and the Thai Night at the Thai Village of the Siam Inter–continental Hotel, where both dances and martial arts are performed. The latter takes place by a handicraft bazaar and mini floating market in the hotel's extensive gardens.

Other restaurants offering dinner with classical and folk dance performances are *Ruen Thep* at Silom Village on Silom Road, *Baan Thai* in Sukhumvit Soi 32, *Piman* in Sukhumvit Soi 49, *Maneeya Lotus Room* off Ploenchit Road,

and handicrafts, plus pirate audio and video tapes. You will find them clustered in areas frequented by tourists.

Silom Road

The longest strips of night markets are along Silom Road near Patpong and in Patpong itself. Here you will find shirts and jeans, skirts and T-shirts, belts and bags, fake watches and pirated tapes, hilltribe crafts, Burmese wall-hangings and puppets, bronzeware and silverware, and more clothes, many bearing designer name logos. "Designer wear" of these markets are unbelievably blatant fakes. This night bazaar goes on from about 7pm to 1am.

At Silom Village further down Silom Road towards the river, the night market takes place from 4–10pm.

Street Stalls

The other main drag of street stalls trading at night is along both sides of Sukhumvit Road roughly from the Ambassador Hotel around Soi 13 to the flyover at Soi 1. Here, under the expressway going south, there is the Bangkok Night Bazaar trading in much the same things as does Patpong, including clothes, hilltribe crafts, woodcarving, lacquerware and silverware. It is open until 10pm.

Additionally, the daytime markets of Pratunam and Banglampoo (see the Shopping chapter in this section) selling

and *Sala Thai* at the Indra Regent Hotel.

For entry it will be best to make a reservation at these hotels or check with their desks for more information.

Night Markets

If you have not had enough of shopping in the daytime, or if you prefer to devote the day hours for sightseeing, then the night markets are for you. They all concentrate on clothes, souvenirs

Dancers at the Erawan Shrine.

the same wares stay open until about 9pm.

Dinner Cruises

Dinner cruises on converted rice barges are a cool, relaxing and scenic way to pass an evening. They mostly all offer Thai food and meander up and down the Chao Phraya River in the central section of the city, affording twinkling night-time views of riverside life. The barges usually have a beautiful teak superstructure and traditional decor, and the staff offer gracious Thai service in traditional clothing.

The *Tasaneeya Nava* departs from the Si Phya Pier next to The Royal Orchid Sheraton Hotel and makes two trips nightly, 6–8pm and 8–10pm, at 700 baht per head.

The *Wan Fah* departs from River City nightly for a two-hour cruise from 7 to 9pm; it offers a Thai menu at 550 baht or a seafood menu at 600 baht and a girl plays traditional violin music for accompaniment.

Baan Khun Luang, a top Thai restaurant located just north of Krungthon Bridge, offers a nightly cruise from 8 to 10pm. You may board the boat at its mooring from 7pm and order a *la carte*; alternatively, there's a set menu at 150 baht. Either way, you pay 50 baht per person for the boat trip. Called *Sakorn Sin*, this barge is favoured by Thais and is undoubtedly excellent value.

Disco Scene

The disco boom of the '80s spattered the city with electronic dancefloors. The apotheosis arrived in the mid–eighties, *Nasa Spacedrome*, billed as the biggest discotheque in the world and you can well believe it. Inside you find yourself on the set of 'Metropolis', all gleaming bare steel with tiers of balconies of tubular railings and a sky–high roof; around midnight you get 'Close Encounters of the Third Kind' as a spaceship descends from the heights above the dancefloor and hovers over the bobbing heads.

Another mega–disco is *The Palace*, located in Din Daeng at the beginning of the Superhighway to the airport.

Otherwise the discos are relatively small and range from the high class *Diana's* at Oriental Plaza to the earthy teenage *The Theque* at Victory Monument. The veteran *Bubbles* at the Dusit Thani Hotel has been transformed into a videotheque. The Ambassador Hotel offers the *Flamingo*, popular with the young, and the Montien Hotel has *Casablanca*.

At Silom Plaza on Silom Road, *Freak Out* and *Freak In* videotheques cater to a young rich clientele. The *Rome Club* in Patpong 3 is more adventurous than most discos, with a massive video screen and midnight gay cabaret.

Patpong 1 has several discos catering to Western tastes rather than Thai, for instance the New York–designed *Mars Party House* and the *Superstar* which was the first and remains the biggest. There are also two discos much frequented by bargirls which really warm up at bar closing time (2am), *King's Lounge* and the *Peppermint Bistro*.

Patpong & Her Sisters (& Brothers)

Bangkok has achieved worldwide fame on account of a couple of little streets named Patpong, which have done much to make the city's name synonymous with sex. Thus, seeing it for the first time, most people are some-

Traditional Thai dancing performed at dinner shows.

Neon leads the way.

what disconcerted to find themselves in a brightly–lit clothes market. In recent years, come sundown, the main drag, Patpong 1 Road, has become completely jammed with stalls selling garments, tapes and souvenirs, obscuring the renowned raunch and sleaze.

Like red light districts everywhere, Patpong inspires fascination and fear, curiosity and disgust, as well as plain old lust, according to a person's principles and predilections, but most people when they get there find it at least interesting, for Patpong has something for everybody. You do not even have to go in a go–go bar, let alone a sex show bar, for its streets and surroundings contain numerous discos, restaurants, piano bars, cocktail lounges, besides late–night shops and street markets. Dancing, eating, music listening and shopping are as much a part of Patpong these days as boozing and ogling.

But girlie bars are still what Patpong is really about, the core activity, and the core ranges from very soft to extremely hard. The prices vary too, but not much, unless you step into certain nefarious establishments expressly designed to rip off unsuspecting tourists. Relative to most such districts in the world, say London's Soho or Paris's Pigalle, there is very little overcharging and most bars are remarkably honest, while all are comparatively pretty cheap.

The typical bar is an arrangement of barstools and soft seating around a central bar and stage on which scantily clad young women dance to disco music. Customers must buy one drink each for around 60 baht and they can make it last almost as long as they like. Girls usually cajole customers to buy little glasses of soft drinks for them, for which they get a 15 or 20 baht commission, but you are by no means obliged to buy "lady drinks", which vary in price from 40 to 70 baht. For paying, the standard procedure is that a bill for each order of drinks is put in a cup on your table as the drinks arrive. You can then check immediately what you are being charged. You pay when you leave. A trick is occasionally practised on the unwary, usually drunks, who while in their cups inspire the more ruthless bargirls to order drinks for themselves without permission, resulting in a well-stuffed bill cup, but this is comparatively rare.

Going Upstairs

Besides avoiding unwitting generosity, there is really just one simple rule to follow to avert financial disaster in Patpong: do not go in any upstairs bar in the central blocks between Patpong 1 and Patpong 2 Roads. Almost all these upstairs bars, especially round the Bookseller bookshop, slap huge "entertainment charges" on your bill when you leave and threaten violence when you refuse to pay. If you still inadvertently stray into one of these gouging bars and are faced with an outrageous bill, first threaten to go to the Tourist Police. If this does not work, do not be heroic, for the barmen can be really violent. It would be best to simply pay up, then go immediately to the Tourist Police at the top of Silom Road in front of Lumpini Park and report the matter. They will accompany you back to the bar and get retribution for you.

All the upstairs bars are hard core in some way or other, usually presenting bizarre vaginal stunts with ping-pong balls, cigarettes, etc., sexual coupling and nude dancing. The south side of Patpong 1 is the best place for these, with the star acts undoubtedly being at *Supergirls*, featuring solo sex in a telephone booth, coupling on a massive motorbike, and bubble-bathing in a huge cocktail glass. Similar but less stylish are *Lipstick, Pussy Galore/Alive, Firecat and Queen's Castle*, all of them upstairs.

Core activities.

Drinks tend to be about 10 baht pricier in these "sexotic" bars.

In downstairs bars, the format is almost universally straight go–go dancing in bikinis and swimsuits, with occasional bare breasts and even bottoms in some bars, and maybe body–painting, snake–charming or drag shows. These bars vary from sedate and conservative, like *Butterfly* or *Grand Prix*, to raunchy get–up–and–dance joints like *Goldfingers* and *Thigh Bar*, from huge music machines like *King's Corner* and *Superstar* to tight–packed glamour parades like *King's Castle 1*, from the friendly funky *Safari* to the cool swish *Limelight*.

Just take your pick – the music, the prices, the drinks and the costumes are pretty uniform in these downstairs go–go bars, but there are definite differences in ambience.

The third category of Patpong bar is the cocktail lounge and piano bar, catering to customers who prefer a quieter and more respectable time. If you look into a place and all the women are in dresses, you are there. A concentration of them is found on Patpong 2 terrace, upstairs near Suriwong Road. Some feature Filipino pianists playing and singing American standards.

Now the inevitable male question: "What if you want to do more than look at the girls?" In the upstairs bars, the girls will most likely tell you in graphic details what they will offer in the back room and for how much. Little is negotiable in these places and value for money is poor. Elsewhere, and with some

Patpong punk.

girls upstairs, the form is this: you ask the girl if she wants to come out with you, or she may ask you. In either case, you have to pay a "bar fine" of 300–350 baht to secure her release from work for the night and from there on all is negotiable. You can wait till closing time, 2am, to avoid the bar fine, but a surprising number of girls would rather just go home then.

Patpong is not the only go–go area in town: there are lesser ones at *Nana Plaza* on Sukhumvit Soi 4 and at *Soi Cowboy* between Sukhumvit Soi 21 and 23. *Soi Cowboy* is named after an ex–GI who opened the first bar there at the end

popular with young 'straights' of both sexes. Further up Silom down an alley just before Robinson Department Store is the long standing gay rendezvous, *Harrie's Bar*, featuring a drag cabaret and muscle man show. Transvestite reviews are a Thai speciality, with numerous troupes doing true–to–life Diana Ross and Shirley Bassey melodramatics. The main venue is *Calypso Cabaret* on Sukhumvit Road between Soi 24 and 26, while many troupes just pop up in go–go bars and discos around midnight. The *Pink Panther* in Patpong 2, *Midnite Bar* in Soi Cowboy, and the *Rome Club* in Patpong 3 are examples.

Finally, here's an oddity for the ladies – *King's Hawaii* Cabaret on Suriwong Road near Patpong, which bills itself as "a perfect place for ballroom dancing – ladies can select your own dancing partners".

of the Vietnam War; it is rather smaller, slightly cheaper and somewhat sleazier than Patpong, though it is more and more imitating its big sister. *Nana Plaza* is terraces of go–go bars around an open courtyard, plus a snooker hall for sporting respite.

One note of caution for visitors from South Asia, the Middle East and Africa. Many places in Patpong and Soi Cowboy operate a colour bar.

Patpong has a gay brother just a little further up Silom Road: it's a cul–de–sac known as Patpong 3 which features almost exclusively gay bars and a gay disco, the *Rome Club*, which is also

Jazz Clubs & Rock Pubs

Jazz bars have bloomed all over Bangkok. Most of them do not actually play live jazz, or even any sort at all, so do not be fooled by the signs: "jazz" seems to be the code for "fashionable". But some most certainly do.

Doyen of them all is *Brown Sugar*, located next to Lumpini Park on Soi Sarasin. This place set the trend: nightly mainstream jazz, occasional black American singers, informal atmosphere, good vibes. The musicians change frequently, the style very little. Somebody is usually doing 'Satin Doll' and 'One Note Samba', and maybe 'Kansas City'.

Brown Sugar is not a big place and soon others took up the tune and eased the crush. A string of music pubs sprang up alongside offering anything from blues to country and western. Just round the corner in Soi Langsuan: *Round Midnight*, with a terrific moody jazz mural on the side wall. Lately its jazz has pretty well been supplanted by pop/rock/soul, drawing tablefuls of young Thais. More roomy than Brown Sugar, it also spreads onto the sidewalk. Speciality: Round Midnight cocktail, tells Pina Colada where to get off.

For a lot more space and upmarket ambience, Sukhumvit is the locale. On Soi 53, *Blues Jazz Pub* offers the most professional of performances. Nightly except Sunday, the six-piece Bangkok Connection shakes the walls with a tight-reined ride across the jazz-rock range. Drinks start at 90 baht.

Similarly priced and billed as a "modern-day Victorian Pub", the *Witch's Tavern* is way out front architecturally, a classy piece of London on Soi 55. A slightly shaky modern jazz quartet weaves from Art Blakey to bossa nova, standards all the way. Specialities: British food and "Thailand's biggest selection of Scotch whisky".

Around the corner on Soi Charoen Suk lies *Dixieland Jazz Club* which does not play New Orleans jazz. Instead, the Rolls Royce Band purrs along very nicely in a soul groove. They play Monday-Saturday, with the more jazzy Xanadu on Sunday. This place is no snip at 200 baht a drink, but there does seem to be almost one server per customer, usually a hostess in hotpants or miniskirt.

Off Soi 23, way past the go-go raunch of Soi Cowboy, *Black Scene*, all dark glass, lurks behind palms. Styled 'Pub & Restaurant Parisien', this is French-run and movie-themed. It has an excellent selection of jazz videos; live, there's a jazz singer early and a relaxed Latin jazz combo later in the evening.

Go out at the weekend for the best jazz and the best musician: Tewan Sapsanyakorn. a virtuoso multi-instrumentalist on tenor, alto and soprano sax, flute and electric flute, plus violin. On Fridays at Brown Sugar and Sundays at *Blue Moon*, he whips up creative fusion jazz in a four-man combo. On Saturdays at Blue Moon, he fronts Infinity, a larger mainstream jazz-rock outfit. Blue Moon is above the Moon Shadow by Le Meridien President Hotel.

Last but not least, *Saxophone*. Located at Victory Monument, this enormous barn is a student and artists' favourite, bohemian and eccentric, with walls covered by old horns – that's trumpets and antlers! Catch what you can – tuneless folk, wailing blues, doodling new age, rabid rock, laid-back fusion, hot soul, cool swing.

Watch that word "jazz", it'll take you strange places in Bangkok! The time is always 10 pm to 1 am, and maybe even 9 pm to 2 am. Round midnight, indeed.

The jazz scene, Round Midnight, offers more sophisticated entertainment.

REGIONS OF THAILAND

Central Plains

The Central Plains are the heart and the lifeblood of Thailand. Spread out in a fan around Bangkok, they contain both the nation's capital and its granary. Its flat and fertile fields are watered by ample rainfall and rivers flowing down from the western, northern and northeastern highlands. It grows a high proportion of the country's rice and contributes mightily to Thailand's status as one of the top rice exporters in the world. Just about wherever and whenever you go in this region, you will see farmers either planting, tending or gathering the crop. Indeed this has to be the rice-bowl of Asia, at least.

Waterways host many a floating market in the Central Plains.

At the beginning of the rainy season in May to July, bright green seedlings will predominate across watery expanses. Late in the rainy season, great green oceans of paddy sway in the breeze, then towards November the rains cease and the grain turns golden. The fields become filled with harvesters and threshers, and then for the rest of the dry season brown stalks poke from the land or are rapidly burnt to ash. By April, the hottest month, the ground is parched and cracked. And then the farmers get to work

once more, breaking and turning the earth with buffalo or tractor-drawn ploughs, and getting the seedlings ready for the rainy season.

These scenes are timeless – apart from the recent introduction of machinery, chemical fertilisers and herbicides, the pattern is more than a millenium old. Mon and Khmer peoples preceded the Thais, whose kingdom of Ayutthaya came and went and was replaced by brash young Bangkok, but the ricefields go on forever.

Or almost. For increasing urbanisation and industrialisation is eating away the fields around Bangkok and in many other parts too, as houses, shops and factories spring up and country resorts and golf courses spread to feed the tastes of the newly affluent. Nevertheless both rich and poor, both the growing industrialised minority and the traditional farming majority, need to eat and nowhere in Thailand is better for producing the staple. Rice will assuredly remain the mainstay of the Central Plains.

NAKHON PATHOM

The town of Nakhon Pathom is famed for its enormous stupa and is reckoned to be Thailand's longest continuous settlement. It may have been visited by Indian Buddhists spreading the faith over two thousand years ago and it was certainly the centre of the Dvaravati kingdom of the 6th to 11th centuries.

Its bustling central street leading from the railway station over a canal to the great *chedi* gives a strong feeling of ancient tradition, a market of a millenium or more old, no matter that none of its buildings are more than a few decades old. A 10-minute walk would take in all this.

Tallest in the world

Phra Pathom Chedi, reputed to be the tallest in the Buddhist world, was founded in the 6th century and, after successive over-building and ruination

Rice The Life-Giver

Without rice, it will be a different Thailand. Eaten at every meal, grown by half the population, a major export, it supports the nation and conditions its life. As the basis of existence, its growth cycles are integral with the traditional pattern of life and rice-eating is a standard topic of conversation.

The concept 'eat' in the Thai language is expressed *gin khao* or *thaan khao,* meaning 'eat rice', the word *khao* (rice) being used much more often than *ahaan* (food). A common polite interpolation in conversation is *thaan khao laew ru yang?* – "have you eaten (rice) yet?" – used in the way that English people say "It's a nice day today, isn't it?" or some such trivial oiling of the social wheels. In both cases, the phrases reveal national preoccupations, the English with the weather and the Thais with rice.

The rice-planting season begins in May and the start is grandly symbolised by the Royal Ploughing Ceremony at Bangkok's Sanam Luang (see Fabulous Festivals). Farming families nationwide work as one to prepare their land, ploughing with water buffalos, planting rice seedlings and flooding the fields by irrigation. As the rains return and increase, all across the country peasants bend double in flooded fields further transplanting seedlings in the rich mud.

As the rains fall off in November, the rice becomes ripe enough to be harvested. Families join up to slash the crop down with sickles, lay it to dry for a few days, then thresh and winnow it to extract the prized golden grain, age-old staff of life. Another revealing Thai phrase is *tham ngaan*, literally "make a party", meaning "work". Thais are very group-conscious people and work is traditionally a group activity, not an act of individual endeavour. "Pull together and enjoy it" is the Thai way of work.

Except in the south where monsoons arrive later, harvesting usually ends in January or February. The farming cycle is complete and the grain goes to the middleman for milling and marketing. Mostly ending as polished white rice, it goes on the market, whether in Lopburi or London, Bangkok or Buenos Aires, Surat Thani or Sydney. Thailand is one of the world's biggest rice exporters.

At home, its varieties are many and its uses are endless. It may be sticky or straight, (*khao nio* or *khao suay*) and of several types and grades. It may be processed into noodles fat or thin, distilled into whisky or *lao khao,* compressed into sweet delicacies, or most likely served up good and plain, the foundation of every good meal. Whichever, the cultivation and the consumption of rice form a central pillar of Thai life.

Rice, bounty rising from the muddy fields, the staple of Thai life, next to religion.

in the course of history, rose in 1860 to be a great bronze-glazed stupa 127 metres high, which is its current condition.

By far the most pleasant way to visit Nakhon Pathom is by train out of Bangkok's Hua Lampong Station. It gets you there in about an hour and soon gets you out of the city, passing through quiet rural communities and fields.

Floating Market

Around 50 km south of Nakhon Pathom town lies another ancient market tradition, the water market whose current best example is reckoned to be at Damnoen Saduak. Better known as the Floating Market, this is an early morning press of women paddling sampans loaded with fruit and vegetables which they hawk on the town's central canal. It's traditional, colourful and at times over-run with tourists.

KANCHANABURI

Kanchanaburi province, while officially categorised as part of the central region, is mostly not plains country but wild and mountainous. Close to Bangkok yet far from following the tame rice-growing life of adjacent provinces, it is Thailand's wild west, largely a forested frontier land bordering Burma with mountain ranges and surging rivers, some dammed to form large lakes.

Nevertheless, the province's most famed sight is not natural but a product of man's inhumanity to man, the Bridge over the River Kwai. Located just outside Kanchanaburi town, 130 km west of Bangkok, this is not the elegant bamboo structure that many visitors expect from familiarity with the film that made it famous, but a construction of steel girders and concrete pillars. Neither does it span a ravine amongst dense jungle as in the film (known to be shot in Sri Lanka), but rather a broad lazy river flanked by farmland on the far bank and restaurants and souvenir shops on

Bridge over the River Kwai, a landmark in World War 2 history.

the town side.

Still, looking across to it is pleasant enough, as the stately brown waters flow past. There are also floating restaurants from which to view it, and to note how the central spans are of a different shape from the outer ones. This is because the British eventually managed to bomb the middle section near the end of the war, after which the Japanese replaced the missing spans as a postwar act of friendship. Thus a peacetime railway runs to this day along these tracks built for war. The movie of course brought this tract not a little fame.

Bright red and black examples of the bombs stand vertically in emplacements at the head of the bridge, like tin sentries. Locals use the bridge as a foot and bike crossing, for it has wooden planking as well as rails, and so may tourists tread the planks across the river too. On the near side there are also two well-kept examples of the steam engines that once plied the route.

Death Railway

It is called the Death Railway, on

River Kwai Bridge/Death Railway/Three Pagodas Pass

DEATH RAILWAY BY THE RIVER KWAI.

Thailand's wild western mountain country provides a natural border that has separated it from successive Burmese states for a thousand years, yet has only hindered rather than prevented the aggressive ambitions of Burmese kings. The most direct route from power centre to power centre was, and still is, the Three Pagodas Pass through the Tenasserim Mountains in upper Kanchanaburi province.

Today it is an official frontier post marked by three white stupas, hence its name, and through it thunder Thai logging trucks importing their plunder from the Burmese teak forests. Here, Mon people predominate over ethnic Thais or Burmese. In past times, invading kings on elephant-back led great armies to conquer Thai territory, most devastatingly of all in 1767 when they destroyed great Ayutthaya.

From the pass, there is a drop as you enter the upper valley of the River Kwai Noi – in English, the lesser River Kwai, a name redolent with recent history and the brutality of World War II. For the Japanese also found this route to be the most convenient for their imperial ambitions. Having subordinated Thailand and conquered Burma from the British, they wished to build a strategic railway connecting the two national systems and, by extension, the subcontinent with Indochina.

They were in a hurry and wanted it done quickly, so they imported hundreds of thousands of impressed Asian labourers and tens of thousands of Allied prisoners-of-war, railroaded up in cattle trucks from Malaya, then route-marched up the jungle valley. Kept in disease-ridden and insanitary jungle camps, ill-fed and grossly overworked, they died like flies.

A job which would normally have taken several years was rammed through in just one, 1942-3, and such was the inhumanity of the Japanese overseers that some 100,000 Asians (Tamil, Burmese, Chinese, Malay, Javanese) and 16,000 Westerners (mostly British, Australian and Dutch) died. So it is called the Death Railway.

Not far from the bridge in Kanchanaburi town are grim reminders of this atrocity, the Kanchanaburi and Chong-Kai War Cemeteries where some 9000 Allied servicemen lie buried, and the JEATH Museum, a reconstruction of the appalling prison camp conditions with photos and pictures by taken inmates. These places serve both to commemorate the dead and to warn of the horrors of war.

Something more cheerful has come of it though, for today visitors can take the exciting ride along the railway, which is still in daily use up to the village of Nam Tok, some 60km onward from Kanchanaburi. It runs through farmland and forest with mountain and river views while, in one dramatic place, the train trundles upon great wooden trestles alongside a cliff high above the river. It slows to a crawl for this seemingly perilous transit, all the better for taking in the view and appreciating the work and hardship that went into its making.

Beyond Nam Tok, the line is abandoned. The jungle and the mountains have taken it back.

The railway viaduct through what used to be frontierland.

account of the tens of thousands of forced labourers who died in its construction. The Japanese had it built to connect the conquered Burma with Bangkok and thus Indochina and through to the Malay Peninsula. It was logical, and the methods used had an inhuman logic too – the impressing of hundreds of thousands of prisoners of war and conquered civilians to get the job done within one year, 1942-3.

Conditions were appalling in the jungle and mountain camps and an estimated 100,000 Asians and 16,000 Westerners died as a result. Two cemeteries and the JEATH Museum in Kanchanaburi town commemorate the lives and the suffering of the Western victims.

Some good came out of all this, however, for the railway now provides a twice-daily link to the interior of the province for local people and at times

Sai Yok Yai Falls, a popular picnic spot for locals.

spectacular ride for tourists. About an hour beyond the bridge, the train suddenly slows to a crawl and begins to trundle along a great wooden viaduct built against a cliff almost perpendicular to the water, over the River Kwai (or Kwae Noi in Thai). The view is spectacular and the experience a little frightening. Those who have had enough or alternatively want more, can alight at the next stop and come back to stay in riverside bungalows or floating rafthouses on offer at this point.

Falls

The train eventually halts at Nam

The glory of Ayutthaya.

Tok, which appropriately means 'Waterfall'. Nearby are the Sai Yok Noi Falls, a popular picnic spot for locals. Here the mountain territory begins and the tracks onward to Burma were long ago ripped up. Onward travel is now best by boat. At the nearby river landing, longtail boats are for hire at around 1000 baht the trip winding way upriver to Sai Yok Yai Falls.

On the way through this forested and mountainous country there is a stop-off at a large cavern, Lawa Cave, where one may catch glimpses of herons, kingfishers and watering buffalos, and floating hotel resorts. The round trip is about four hours long, and at the falls which cascade from the north bank direct into the river, there are further floating hotels and restaurants.

Erawan Falls

Northeast of this area, but reached direct from Kanchanaburi by bus, is Thailand's most famous waterfall and a favourite weekend destination for Bangkokians, Erawan Falls. Set in a national park, this is a liquid stairway of white cataracts and turquoise pools extending quite a distance. Paths run alongside.

A similar series of falls is to be found at Huay Khamin further north beside Sri Nakharin Lake. Also a nicely laid-out national park and located on the west side of the lake formed by Sri Nakharin Dam, Huay Khamin is reached by hiring a longtail boat from a village on the the lake's east side.

There are bungalows to rent both inside and outside Erawan Park and bungalows and raft-houses to rent on the east side of Sri Nakharin Lake.

Ayutthaya

The most historic site in the whole Central Plains region is Ayutthaya, capital of the Kingdom of Siam for four centuries and at its height reckoned to have harboured more than a million souls and been bigger than any contemporary European city. It represented the great power of the Siamese state within the Indochinese region of the time. All this ended in the conflagration of 1767 when the Burmese enemy sacked the great capital and razed it to the ground.

This stunning act of vindictiveness destroyed a vast city of palaces, canals, temples and wooden houses, and with it, most of Siam's most precious cultural artifacts. Much of the remains were then transported downriver to Bangkok to build the new capital. What is left requires today's visitor to engage in imaginative reconstruction in order to realise the full glory of Ayutthaya. If one had time it would be extremely interesting to delve into the historical archives.

A Museum Guide

There are three museums to help in

Wat Raj Burana Ayutthaya.

this. The older ones are the Chao Sam Phraya Museum on the corner of Rotchana and Sanphet Roads in the centre of the old city, and Chan Kasem Palace in the northeast corner near the river and boat pier. The best and newest one, also on Rotchana Road and opened in 1990, is the Ayutthaya Historical Study Centre, a grand Japanese-financed research and educational facility with excellent museum facilities including audio-visual presentations.

The museum has five distinct themes:

1) Ayutthaya as the royal capital, with models of it at its height.

2) Ayutthaya as a port city, presenting its commercial history and wide foreign trade.

3) Ayutthaya as administrative cen-

A European-style pavilion at Bang Pa-In for royal variety.

ings were lavishly adorned with gold leaf and decorative stucco, where stonemasons and woodcarvers added their fine craftsmanship, and expert painters expressed their art through murals within the temples. Imagine also the canals teeming with boats, the ceremonial ways trod by elephants, the saffron-robed monks of several hundred temples, the markets selling the abundance of the surrounding fields and orchards, and a million people living their lives. Then you have an historic city before your eyes.

Ayutthaya can also be viewed on longtail boat trips (hired near Chandrakasem Palace at about 200 baht an hour) around the rivers which form its moat. Though none of these defences prevented the Burmese from eventually annihilating the city, it was also encircled by battlemented walls and periodic forts, the best example extant being Phom Phet Fortress in the south-eastern corner where the Pasak River meets the Chao Phraya.

Elephants were important in defence too, being a mainstay of Ayutthayan armies as well as used in heavy land transport and jungle clearance. They were kept and trained in kraals, a kind of stockade of which a restored example can be seen 5 km north of the old city. (See Box story on

Elephants in Flora and Fauna chapter).

Ayutthaya is 85 km north of Bangkok and is served from the capital by tour and hire boats, all north-bound and north-east-bound trains, frequent buses from the Northern Terminal, and Highway 1 running into Highway 32 at Bang Pa-In.

BANG PA-IN

Some 20 km downstream from Ayutthaya and 60 km upriver from Bangkok lies Bang Pa-In Palace. Unique in Thailand, it is an eclectic collection of mansions and pavilions in European, Chinese and Thai styles. Set amid ornamental lakes right beside the Chao Phraya, it was created by King Chulalongkorn in the late 19th century as a summer retreat, on the site of one used by the Ayutthayan kings until destroyed by the Burmese (at the same time as the old capital).

Aisawan Tiphaya-art

Greeting the visitor at the main entrance, a broad and straight watercourse flanked by avenues of trees runs up to a neo-classical bridge complete with Carrara marble statuary. Beyond this in the middle of a wider pool stands a small yet elaborate Thai-style pavilion, the Phra Thinang (Royal Residence) Aisawan Tiphaya-art, much photographed and regarded as a classic of Rattanakosin architecture.

The Divine Seat of Personal Freedom, for such is the meaning of Aisawan Thiphya-art, is a cruciform open-sided pavilion with four-tiered roof and a tall central spire. Elaborately gilded, it is a copy of the Aphonphimok Prasat in Bangkok's Grand Palace and is named after a previous pavilion built by the Ayutthayan founder of Wang Bang Pa-In, King Prasat Thong (1629-56). It now houses a bronze statue of King Chulalongkorn in Field Marshal's uniform, set up by his son and heir. Thus the Thai monarchy reinforces its continuity.

To the right of the bridge a gazebo

Phra Thinang (Royal Residence) Aisawan Tiphaya-art, an open-sided pavilion, regarded as a classic of Rattanakosin architecture.

Neo-classic at Bang Pa-In.

juts into the lake. It was favoured by King Rama VI for his writing. To the left, between lake and river, stands the European elegance of Phra Thinang Warophat Piman, a Renaissance style mansion in ochre-and-white stucco, used as a throne hall.

Inner Palace

This is the extent of the Outer Palace consisting of buildings for public and ceremonial purposes. Just past the gazebo, a footbridge leads across a moat to the Inner Palace, reserved for the King and his immediate family.

The first building is the Phra Thinang Uthayan Phumisathian, Royal Residence of the Garden of the Secured Land and the one favoured by King Chulalongkorn himself. This is a stunning 1990 recreation of the original building burnt down in 1938. It is a rambling two-storey hybrid of Swiss chalet and Chekhovian dacha, its horizontal boarding painted in alternately deep and light turquoise. There is also a water tank disguised as a crenellated tower.

To the north on an island formed by a channel running round its back stands a Chinese-style mansion where King Rama V and his court generally resided during the rainy and cool seasons. Phra Tinang Wehat Chamrun, the Royal Residence of Heavenly Light, donated by the Chinese business community, is the only building that can be entered. It contains some fine Chinese porcelain, furniture and screens, with a Chinese-style throne on the ground floor. This mansion was the favoured lodging of King Rama VI (1910-25).

There is also a curious observation tower that looks like a cross between a lighthouse and a Chinese pagoda. This is the Ho Withun Thasana, the Sage's Lookout Tower, built for viewing the surrounding countryside.

Another curiosity stands on the island in the Chao Phraya to the park's west – a Buddhist temple built in Victorian Gothic style, Wat Nivet Dhammaprawat. This charming complex has been renovated and now features a beautiful little museum of decorative art, mostly European. Strange indeed is the method of crossing the river channel, a kind of cable car that swings across powered by a monk!

Bang Pa-In Palace underwent substantial renovation in 1990-91 and is possibly now in better condition than ever in its history. It is open daily 8.30 to 5.00, with the Inner Palace grounds and Chinese mansion closing at 3.30.

Bang Sai Folk Arts & Crafts Centre

In Bang Sai district near Bang Pa-In is located the Bang Sai Folk Arts and Crafts Centre, where provincial people are trained in handicrafts and demonstrate them too. Products manufactured include fern vine basketry, woven basketry, artificial flowers, woven silks and cottons, dyed silks, woodcarvings, Thai dolls and furniture. The centre is under the Queen's patronage.

LOPBURI

Lopburi, 155 km north of Bangkok and 70 km north of Ayutthaya, has a very long history. Many neolithic and bronze age artifacts have been unearthed here; it was an important centre of the Dvaravati kingdom from the 6th to the 10th centuries, when it came under the control of the Khmer empire of Angkor. In the 13th century, the Thais arrived from the north and took it. With the ensuing establishment of the Thai capital at Ayutthaya just 70 km to the south, it lost its importance but regained it in the 17th century as King Narai's second capital and the site of his extensive palace, Phra Narai Raja Nivet.

17th-Century Diplomacy

The palace grounds are still intact, though none of the buildings have survived in original form. The site is a walled and well-kept garden containing ruins of varying completeness with a museum housed in two restored throne halls, Chanthara Phisan and Phiman Mongkut (the latter being a 19th century creation of King Mongkut). The king engaged French as well as Thai architects in the palace's construction from 1666 onwards, and the result was an interesting hybrid.

The Chinese pavilion at the summer palace.

The French and Persians

King Narai was the sovereign who received the emissaries of the Sun King, Louis XIV of France, Europe's dominant power, and those late 17th century envoys were mightily impressed with his court and his capital, Ayutthaya. The Dusit Sawan Thanya Maha Prasat Hall, Lopburi Palace's most intact original building, was constructed for the reception of high-ranking envoys such as the French mission in 1685. It had a Hall Of Mirrors in imitation of Versailles'; the emplacements are still visible.

There is further evidence of Siam's growing international relations in the Royal Banquet Hall, which has Islamic-styled windows and doorways to please Persian envoys.

To the left of the entrance on Sorasak Road stand the remains of the royal elephant and horse stables extending in a line east to west, and in the right quadrant stand the reception hall, various pavilions, the concubines' quarters, etc. A model of the intact palace is on show and a guide book is on sale at the museum (open Wednesday to Sunday, 9-12 noon and 1-4 pm).

The Khmers

North from the palace entrance on Sorasak Road at the junction with Wichayen Road stands a Khmer sanctuary, Prang Khaek, dedicated to the Hindu god, Shiva. Another grander monument with three *prang*, or stupas, lies off to the right. Prang Sam Yod is in classic Khmer-

Lopburi style and is widely known because its image decorates the back of the old 500 baht note.

The three stupas were raised to Brahma, Vishnu and Shiva and later rededicated to the Buddha. Most of the best Khmer architecture remaining in Thailand is found near the Cambodian border; Lopburi's buildings are the exception – there are no other buildings of this quality as far west of Cambodia.

A Hindu God

Just to the east of Prang Sam Yod over the railway line is a hillock inside a roundabout. It is a shrine to Kala, Hindu god of time and death, entwined with banyan trees and infested with monkeys.

A Greek

Back west along Wichayen Road, before the end on the right, stand the remains of Constantine Phaulkon's mansion, Chao Phraya Wichayen Residence. The wily Phaulkon, a Greek, ingratiated himself into becoming King Narai's chief adviser on foreign affairs and a powerful *eminence grise* in the late 17th century court. The grounds contain a Catholic church and the premises were also used to house European ambassadors to the court.

A short walk north brings you to a river bridge and an island with the modern temple, Wat Mani Cholakhan. From around here there are taxi-boats that ply the disparate channels of the Lopburi River along which many people live in stilt-houses.

The principal ancient temple of Lopburi is Wat Phra Si Ratana Mahathat, opposite the railway station. It is a 12th century Khmer complex featuring many *chedi* and *prang*, including one very tall laterite *prang*, some carved lintels and decorative stucco. A chapel was added by King Narai.

Shrine of the Holy Footprint

About 20 km southeast of Lopburi along Highway 1 to Saraburi lies the Shrine of the Holy Footprint, Phra Putthabat. This is a beautiful sanctuary of labyrinthine complexity nestled under a limestone outcrop that juts from the flat plains.

A hunter in the 16th century is said to have stumbled upon a pool with miraculous healing properties; the king subsequently declared the water-filled depression to be a footprint of the Buddha and built a shrine over it, which was later destroyed by the invading Burmese.

The present complex with its multiple spires and crowning gold-and-blue mosaic pavilion dates from the 19th and 20th centuries.

In February and July there are colourful merit-making festivals here that attract folk from all around and feature long processions of monks climbing the steep stairway to the Holy Footprint.

NAKHON NAYOK

South of Saraburi and east of Ayutthaya lies Nakhon Nayok province, noted for its natural beauty on the slopes of the grand Khao Yai National Park. East of Nakhon Nayok town can be found the nine-level Sarika Waterfall, the multi-level Nangrong Waterfall and the high falls of Heo Narok. They are wonderful sights to behold.

In the same area are several orchard gardens open to the public – the 200 Rai Suan Sida with streams and pools, the 20 Rai Suan Kong Kaew, and the 1400 Rai Wang Takrai Botanical Garden. All of these gardens have bungalow and camping accommodation.

Khao Yai National Park

Khao Yai National Park extends over 2168 sq km of forested and mountainous land at the point where the Central Plains meet the Northeastern plateau 100 km directly northeast of Bangkok. It harbours a wide variety of wildlife including elephants and tigers, bears and boars, deer and monkeys, porcupines and mongooses, and many more. Bird and butterfly life is also prolific, and, on the downside, watch out for leeches in boggy and wet areas. Of

Parking on the banks of Kwai Noi, one of the many rivers which flow through the Central Plains.

the larger animals, you are most likely to see deer, whilst elephant droppings and tiger roars are probably the closest you will get to the most exciting animals.

The park has several trails which are unfortunately poorly marked, and the free trail map is none too accurate either. Hiring a guide is advised for anything bar the short walks near the park headquarters.

For motorists, there is a road through the centre of the park from north (Pak Chong) to south (Nakhon Nayok), with a branch to the east ending up at the popular Heo Suwat Waterfall, which gushes down a 15-metre drop.

There is a pleasant walk upstream where the water ripples over rocks in

between overhanging trees.

There are over 20 waterfalls in the park which features rolling savannah as well as forested mountains, the highest of which is Khao Laem, 1351 m.

Park Amenties

For golf enthusiasts there is an 18-hole golf course with bungalow accommodation, which is best booked ahead. The park also provides camping facilities and a restaurant, all of these situated around a pond next to the headquarters in the middle.

There is also a motel down at Pak Chong with a variety of accommodation, including dormitories.

The Rest of the Central Plains

Thailand's ricebowl can seem somewhat like America's breadbasket, the Midwest – flat, prosperous and dull – but something of interest can usually be found even in the plainest provinces.

Nakhon Sawan is an important commercial town with a large Chinese merchant population grown prosperous from trade in the rice-growing heartland – panoramic views from Wat Chom Khiri Nak Phrot on a hilltop. Chainat provincial capital also boasts a hilltop temple with a splendid view – Wat Thammamum.

Suphanburi province is notable historically as the site of the U Thong principality of the 14th century whose ruler established the kingdom of Ayutthaya – Suphanburi town has an enormous seated Buddha of that period in Wat Palelai. Nearby Don Chedi is the site of a great 16th century elephant-back battle between Ayutthaya's King Naresuan and the Prince of Burma, who lost, re-enacted each late January in the Don Chedi Memorial Fair and represented permanently by a monumental statue.

Little Ang Thong province has a 22-metre long reclining Buddha of the 15th century at Wat Pa Mok and drum-making at Ban Phae. Ratchburi province is famed for the colourful Damnoen Saduak floating market, held early each morning and thronged with tourists.

The Central Plains, rice bowl of Asia, a lattice-work of rice fields, rivers and complex irrigation systems.

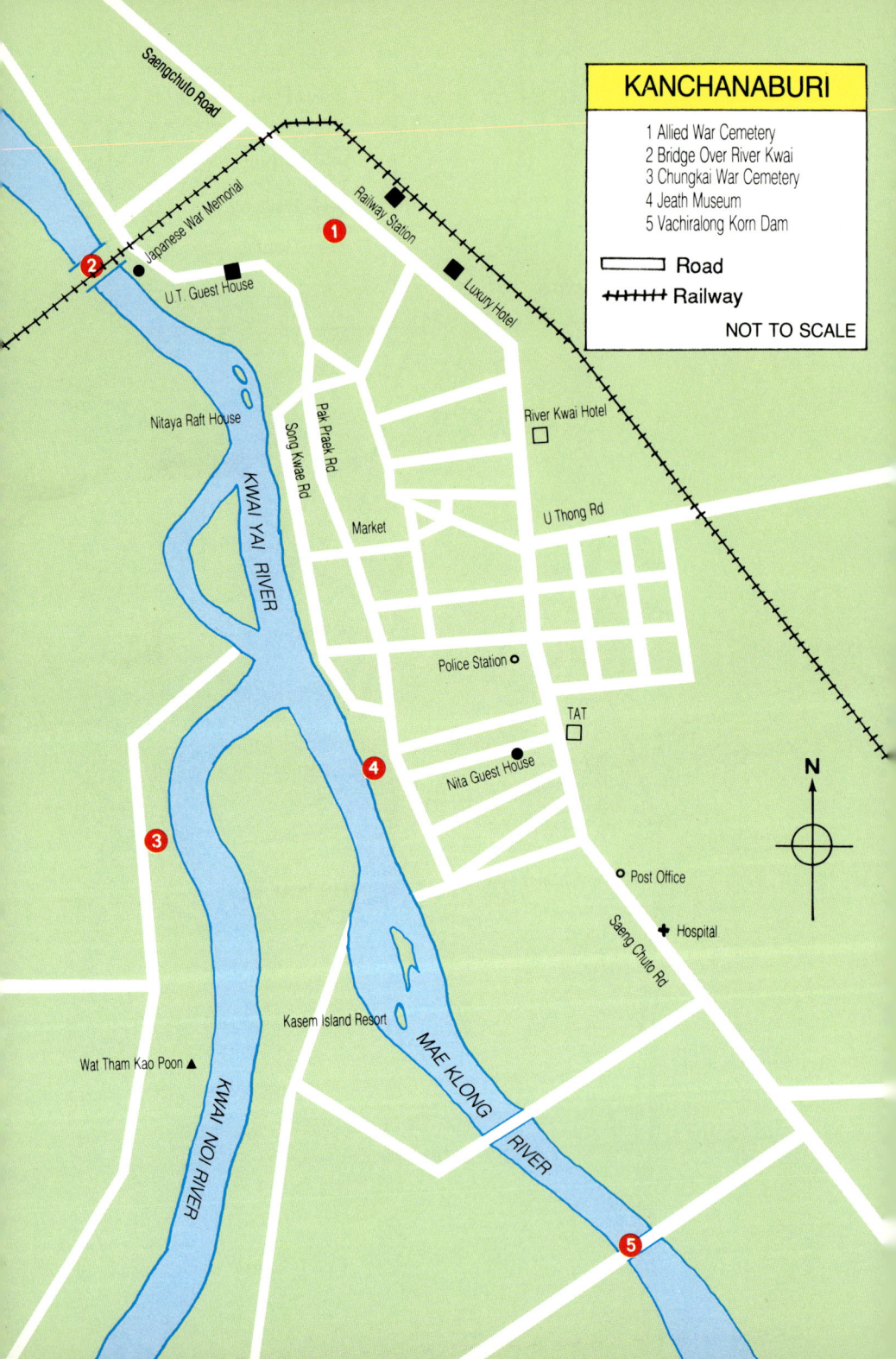

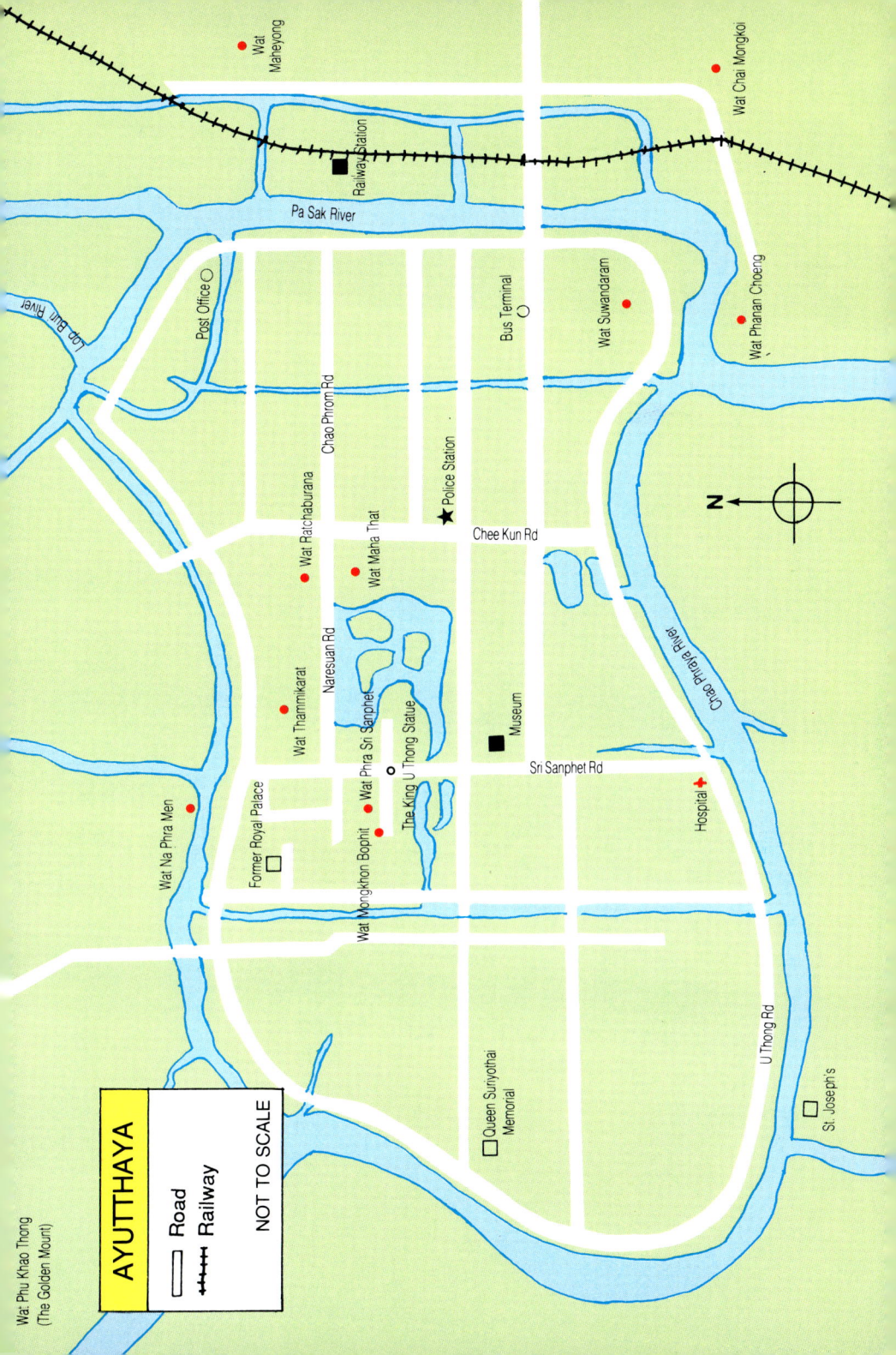

REGIONS OF THAILAND

The North

Northern Thailand was the cradle of Thai-Buddhist civilisation and its rich history, from whence came Thai art, culture and tradition. From the 11th to the 14th centuries it nurtured principalities and kingdoms which laid the foundations of modern Thai society. From Chiang Rai to Kamphaeng Phet, and most notably at Lamphun, Sukhothai and Chiang Mai, important political centres arose and fell, gaining regional power and then giving way to a successor. In these fiefs there developed the royal, religious and social customs which, further refined at Ayutthaya and Bangkok, persist to this day.

Sukhothai, once a centre of Buddhist civilization with its distinct sculptural style, reclaimed from the jungle as recently as 1950s.

HARIPUNCHAI

The first kingdom of the north was established by the Mons at Lamphun, then called Haripunchai. In 897 AD, the Mons began building the great *chedi* of

Wat Phrathat Haripunchai, to this very day the north's greatest temple. From around that time, Thai tribal groups migrated down from south western China in increasing numbers. In 1096, a Thai principality was declared at Phayao, and others followed at Chiang Saen and Chiang Rai; all were in the far north of present-day Thailand.

Sukhothai

In 1238, the Thai kingdom of Sukhothai was established considerably further south. By the end of the 13th century, King Ramkhamhaeng had raised it to hegemony over the whole north and to the status of cultural leader Lanna Thai.

At the same time, King Mengrai of Chiang Rai captured Haripunchai and united the upper north under his rule, founding a new capital at Chiang Mai in 1296. He called his kingdom Lan Na Thai, 'A Million Thai Ricefields', perhaps as a celebration of moving down from the hill country to a well-watered valley.

While Sukhothai was a shooting star, declining rapidly through the 14th century and falling under the sway of the powerful new state of Ayutthaya in the Central Plains, its ally Lanna Thai continued prosperous and independent, only falling to Burmese control during the mid-16th to mid-18th centuries.

Modern Thais still look to the north as the guardian of conservative tradition, which they still call Lanna Thai culture. They look particularly to the one city which remained powerful from medieval times almost to the Bangkok period, and which is now the big, bustling capital of the north – Chiang Mai.

Chiang Mai

Chiang Mai is the capital of the north's most populous and prosperous province. Located in a broad, flat valley of the Ping River, it has long been supported by the great expanse of ricefields around about, particularly to the south and east. To the west, it is overlooked by the bulk of Doi Suthep, a wooded mountain, beyond which extend forested mountains all the way through into Burma. The city is about 300 metres above sea level.

Old Section

Seven hundred years old, Chiang Mai was originally a square site bounded by ramparts and a moat. The moat still exists, together with parts of the wall, within which there now stands a network of relatively quiet, mostly residential streets bejewelled with many fine old temples.

New Town Centre

The old town spread out towards

Town transportation in Chiang Mai.

the river long ago, and this area is now the commercial centre of the city, indeed, the whole north. It harbours department stores, office blocks, the central market and night market, big hotels, nightclubs, and so on, and it is growing fast, mostly upwards.

Even so, the mega-growth in Chiang Mai city is along the road out towards Doi Suthep, in the Huay Kaew area. Here every succeeding year brings a new luxury hotel or condominium, and before too long a huge new commercial complex will have arisen.

Chiang Mai is a boom city, benefitting investment-wise from the overheating of Bangkok as well as the continuing tourist expansion. Many local people fear for its future, foreseeing a little Bangkok-in-the-hills instead of the old laid back Chiang Mai.

The city is now reckoned to have about 200,000 inhabitants, which makes it Thailand's second largest city, whilst the province as a whole has 1.3 million. Many local people have Chinese, Burmese and Laotian blood, whilst the uplands host tens of thousands of Sino-Tibetan and Austro-Asiatic hill tribes. Handicrafts, cotton and tourism are major industries.

King Mengrai founded Chiang Mai, meaning 'New City', in 1296, and since then the city grew in splendour towards a golden age under King Tilokaraj (1447-89). This period saw the building of some great temples which remain in some shape or form to this day.

Inside the viharn of Wat Chiang Man, Chiang Mai.

Exquisite Temples

The first was Wat Chiang Man (northeast part of the old city), most likely Mengrai's royal chapel. The main hall and the library behind it demonstrate the skill of the northern woodcarver. Its Burmese-influenced stupa is approached by a steep stairway flanked

to make rain if you pour water over it.

Dating from 1345, Wat Phra Singh (western part of the old city) has a large compound and houses the highly revered Buddha Phra Singh. Said to have come from Sri Lanka and to be 1700 years old, it was a palladium of the Lanna dynasty and often carried away in conquest, so that temples in both Bangkok and Nakhon Sri Thammarat claim also to possess the real thing. This Phra Singh rests in a beautiful hall called Viharn Laikam; its walls display paintings executed a century ago which give an intriguing account of 19th century northern life. These murals are the best preserved in the city.

Under an Old Gum Tree

Chiang Mai's most massive religious monument was and still is, despite its ruin, the Chedi Luang. The centrepiece of Wat Chedi Luang (centre of the old city), it towered 90 metres above medieval Chiang Mai. Begun in 1401 and later heightened by King Tilokaraja, it was visible for miles around. Then the 1545 earthquake toppled it and only now is it being restored.

The grounds also contain the city's 'foundation stone', the City Pillar, under a great old gum tree. Since the city's guardian spirit resides in the pillar and there is a belief that it will last only as long as the tree, the fate of Chiang Mai is very much bound up in this spot!

by large stone elephants. Two fairly recent *viharns* house a couple of interesting images: the Phra Setang Khamani, or Crystal Buddha, a tiny favourite of King Mengrai, and the Phra Sila, thought

Wat Suan Dok.

Indian Influences

Other notable temples are found outside the old walls and moat. One, Wat Chet Yod, stands beside a more recent marker of the city boundary, the Superhighway, which has itself been surpassed. Its name means 'seven *chedis*' and these stand together on a rectangular brick base in a vague echo of a famous Indian temple. The finest feature is the numerous stucco angels.

Wat Suan Dok, Flower Garden Temple, lies beyond the old city's western gate, also called Suan Dok. It has spacious grounds which were once enclosed by fortifications. Besides its great Sri Lankan influenced *chedi*, it is notable as the keeper of the ashes of the

Lanna royal family in a cluster of white stucco tombs of diverse shapes and sizes.

Wat Suan Dok is off Suthep Road to the left. Further out along Suthep Road and off to the left is a peaceful temple in the foothills of Doi Suthep, Wat Umong. It has large wooded grounds and is in fact a forest wat with connections to the famous radical abbot, Buddhadasa, of Suan Moke in Surat Thani province. It encourages creative art amongst its monks, some of whom are Westerners, and also philosophical comment: many of the trees sport signs with nuggets of wisdom in English or Thai.

A Place of Pilgrimage

If the temples of Chiang Mai had

The naga, highly featured at Wat Bupparam.

box offices, tops in receipts would be Wat Phrathat Doi Suthep. This golden temple perches on the side of forested Doi Suthep overlooking the city and is reached first by a steep, winding road, then by a *naga*-flanked 300-step stairway. King Keu Na interred a Buddha relic in a golden stupa here in 1383, and ever since it has been a place of pilgrimage. The whole platform is a riot of gold and scarlet, with four tall filigree umbrellas at the *chedi*'s corners. The temple's present form dates largely from the 15th century.

An Elephant Marks the Spot

Legend has it that King Keu Na placed the Buddha relic on a white elephant's back and followed its wanderings to this spot, where the beast trumpetted in indication of where the relic should rest. Today pilgrims make the same trip from all over the north and elsewhere in Thailand to pay homage and make merit, and they can even avoid the steep and endless steps by taking the little funicular railway from the car park at the head of the road to the lower platform of the temple. On the Buddhist holy days of Makha Bucha mid-February and Visakha Bucha in May, both lay people and monks throng the precinct. (See Fabulous Festivals chapter for more).

Meo Village

Also on Doi Suthep is a modern royal residence, Phuping Palace, more interesting for its flower gardens than its building, and a hilltribe village of the Hmong people, called Meo Village.

If buying hilltribe handicrafts, you are better advised to do it in Chiang Mai Night Market, where the selection is huge and the prices are as negotiable as anywhere. This is also the city's premier piece of nightlife, thronged with locals, Thai tourists and foreign visitors alike from nightfall to late. It's located on Chang Klan Road in the main commercial district amongst many restaurants and big hotels.

To the south of the old city on Thiparet Road lies the Chiang Mai Cultural Centre, a large compound noted for its traditional wooden buildings and evening hilltribe and folk dance performances.

Wat Bupparam, a many splendoured temple of exquisite ornamentation and elaborate nagas.

Mae Salong hills, bordering Burma.

Karen

Meo

Yao

The Hill Tribes

The hills of Thailand's north and western regions are the home of over half a million hill-tribe people, i.e. about 1% of the country's population. In the last two centuries, and particularly in recent decades, they have drifted in from China, Tibet, Burma and Laos to occupy upland territory that Thais traditionally shun. Thais are lowland farmers whereas these semi-nomadic Tibeto-Burman and Austro-Thai peoples are slash-and-burn hill farmers.

The colourful dress of the women and the cultivation of the poppy for opium have given the tribes a somewhat glamorous image but their lives are nevertheless those of simple farming folk, within distinct and complex cultures. Opium growing is now greatly reduced (and transplanted to Burma and Laos) on account of Thai governmental and royal projects and policies. Their main crops are now rice and maize. Gradually and painfully, they are becoming more integrated into Thai society; most children now speak some Thai.

The main tribes are these six:

Karen: the largest and longest-established people, comprising nearly half the hill-tribe population present and possibly lived in Thailand even before the Thais. They live at the lower levels, in valleys or even lowlands. The women are fine weavers and they wear kaftan-like woven dresses. The Karen are animists, with significant numbers of Christians and Buddhists. They live largely in the area west of Chiang Mai and down the western border to Kanchanaburi.

Hmong: the second largest group, comprising 15% of tribes and also known as *Meo*. They live largely to the north and west of Chiang Mai and near the Laotian border, inhabiting the hilltops. They used to be major opium-growers. They wear black or deep blue, the women in tunics and the men in broad flappy-legged trousers. Many Hmong migrated from Laos during and since the Vietnam War. There they were tough fighters; now they are more renowned as shrewd traders, to be seen selling their wares in the Chiang Mai Night Market and Bangkok's Silom Road and Weekend Market.

Yao: numbering around 35,000, the Yao demonstrate their Chinese origins in their Taoist beliefs, ancestor worship and ideographic writing. The women cut a stylish figure in distinctive black turbans with fluffy red neck surrounds. The Yao are found mostly in the Laotian border provinces, and are also called *Mien*.

Lahu: they comprise about 10% of the hill tribe population and inhabit high territory, mostly along the northern border with Burma. They are animists with a supreme deity. They were originally noted as hunters, hence their Thai name *'muser'*, but are now most famed for their woven shoulder bags.

Lisu: numbering over 20,000, the Lisu live at similar heights to the Lahu, largely to the north of Chiang Mai. Socially, they are noted for their relatively liberal sexual code, whilst sartorially the women are a riot of colour. More competitive than other tribes, many families have prospered.

Akha: numbering around 30,000, these are the least settled and generally poorest tribe, remnants of a Tibetan people once firmly established in southern China. They only arrived in Thailand in this century and live in hilltop villages, largely in Chiang Rai province. The women are distinctive in their black bonnets, thick black pleated knee-length skirts, pipe in mouth, and mounds of heavy silver jewellery. Despite this, they are the least economically successful tribe, much given to opium-smoking. The women are now often to be seen begging with children in Bangkok in small groups.

Lahu

Lisu

Akha

The Thai Elephant

Elephants are a Thai's second best friend after the water buffalo but sadly they are much depleted from their heyday. In the days when forest covered most of the land and motor vehicles were unknown, hundreds of thousands roamed the jungle or worked for their keep.

They were beasts of burden able to carry 300 kilos and log-draggers capable of hauling up to two tons; they led armies into battle. They worked especially in the north, sure-footed on mountain trails and hard-working in the teak forests.

Today there are just a few thousand domesticated beasts, largely in the northern and northeastern hardwood forests. They occasionally turn up in Bangkok where mahouts charge two baht for people to scramble under their belly for good luck.

In the wild, there are reckoned to be 2,000 to 3,000 remaining, and they are decreasing owing to forest destruction. They rarely show themselves but in sanctuaries such as Khao Yai National Park northeast of Bangkok, their dung is quite easily seen as evidence that they have at least recently lumbered that way.

The magnificent beast is classified as the Asian or Indian elephant, the only other species being the larger African.

The measure of its honoured status in Thailand was shown by its image on the national flag against a red background up until 1917, and today is indicated by one of the highest royal decorations, the Most Exalted Order of the White Elephant.

It is the tradition in Thailand that white (albino) elephants must be presented to the king. In fact the palace grounds house quite a few of them, presented to the king.

Working elephants at Chiang Dao.

Hill Tribe Handicraft

Handicrafts are a major industry of Chiang Mai province and some of the most interesting producing villages are found strung along the eastern road to San Kamphaeng. Bo Sang produces the famous painted paper umbrellas and San Kamphaeng is a cotton and silkweaving centre. Other places produce lacquerware, silverware, basketry, woodcarving and celadon. Many workshops can be visited; most have willing guides.

Elephant Camp

Another insight into traditional northern life is to watch elephants at work. North 13 km along Highway 107 to Mae Rim, then west a little way up the Mae Sa Valley brings you to the elephant camp which presents a daily morning show of pachyderms toting teak logs and getting bathed in a stream.

Trekking

One of the main attractions of a visit to Chiang Mai is to go trekking in the hills and stay in hill tribe villages. Twenty years ago such a trek was likely to fulfill your romantic vision; now, since widespread deforestation, the tourism boom and rampant commercialism, it's quite likely to be a bad dream. Most routes are over-trekked, most hills are denuded, and most hilltribe people just want your money. You need a good guide to get you a good trek, and the only way to find one is by word of mouth when you are in the city: ask people who have just trekked if they can recommend their guide.

CHIANG RAI

The secondary centre for trekking is Chiang Rai, just under 100 km northeast of Chiang Mai. This was King Mengrai's capital before he founded Chiang Mai. He eventually died in Chiang Mai at the age of 80. The king was enthroned at the age of 21 and glory is long gone; the much-coveted and consequently much-travelled Emerald Buddha once resided here in Wat Phra Kaew. Wat Phra That Doi Tung is one of the places to visit. The town stands on the Kok River; boats can be hired to starting points for one-day treks, if that is all you have time for.

Boats may be hired along River Kok for river cruises, or to reach starting points for treks.

Golden Triangle

Roads lead further north to Mae Sai and Chiang Saen. Mae Sai is Thailand's northernmost town, with a border crossing to Burma, and Chiang Saen was the site of one of the first Thai principalities in the 13th century. Some ruins remain. This area is the nominal heart of the infamous opium-growing Golden Triangle; actual production centres fluctuate with politics and war. The great majority of this raw material for heroin is currently grown not in Thailand but in Burma and Laos, whose borders meet Thailand's just north of Chiang Saen, at the confluence of the Sop Ruak and Mekong Rivers.

MAE HONG SON

Thailand's remotest province is Mae Hong Son, tucked away in the Shan Mountains of the far northwest. Close to Burma, its culture is Burmese-influenced. Half the province's population is Shan, or Thai Yai, the Thai ethnic group which predominates in the Shan States of Burma over the border. The town has rustic charm but is about to succumb to a tourist onslaught with the rapid increase in guest houses and hotels. Its most picturesque sight is the postcard image of white-washed Wat Jong Kham and Wat Jong Klang beside a large lotus-pond, and also numerous other temples and Lod Cave, many within 30 minutes drive south of Mae Hong Son.

In addition there are plenty of hill-trekking and trail-biking opportunities, plus raft trips down the Pai River and rip-off trips to see the Padaung giraffe-neck women.

LAMPHUN

The first kingdom in the north was created by the Mons at Lamphun, 25 km south of Chiang Mai. The great tall trees that line the connecting road today demonstrate the ancient links between the two cities. The Mon state was called Haripunchai. Its royal temple was begun in 897 AD and firmly established in 1044; it has remained of major sig-

Paduang hill tribeswoman.

A poppy harvest that propagates the dark fame of the Golden Triangle.

Farm folk near Chiang Rai.

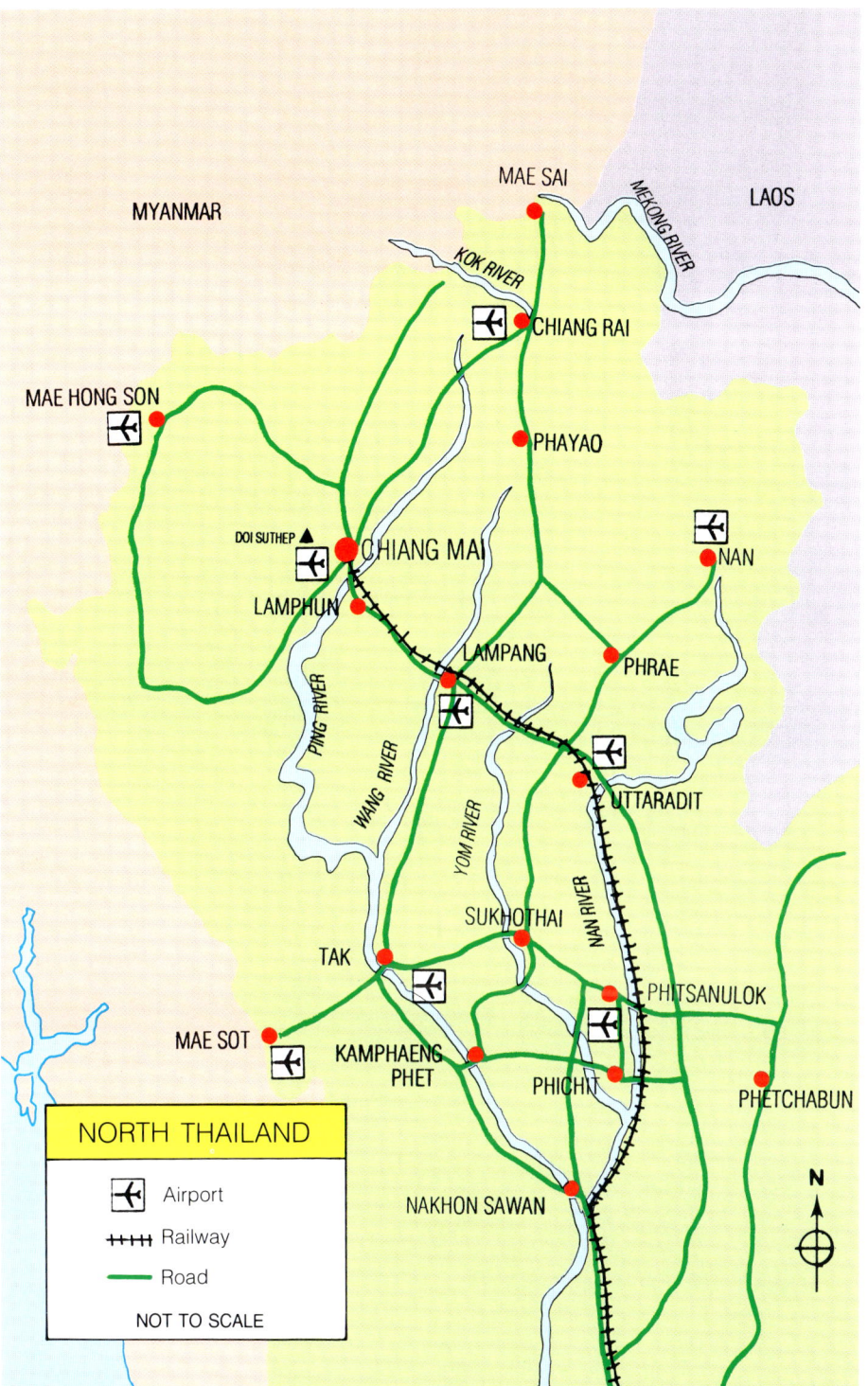

Mae Hong Son landscape.

nificance to this day – Wat Phrathat Haripunchai.

Wat Phrathat Haripunchai

By the Kuang River, the temple has a large precinct dominated by a tall *viharn* and a lofty golden *chedi,* whose walls are gaudily painted with modern murals of the Buddha's lives. A crimson-painted pavilion to the right supports a bronze gong claimed to be the world's largest. The glittering *chedi,* enlarged to a height of 50 metres over the centuries, is attended by tall golden filigree umbrellas at each corner of its surround of golden-railings.

The town retains its ancient moat; restored with railings, it sprouts lotus flowers and serves as a fishing pond for local urchins. Doi Khun Tan Park may be good to visit.

Lampang

Lampang (100 km southeast of Chiang Mai) is the second largest town of the north and conserves much Lanna tradition, particularly in its temples and festivals. It dates back to the Haripunchai period, about the 7th century. The town's claim to uniqueness is its horsedrawn carriages for hire.

Wat Phra Kaew Don Tao, the principal temple, was a religious centre in the 15th century and a resting place of the much-travelled Emerald Buddha.

Most of its current buildings are quite recent, only the *chedi* being of venerable age. The temple mixes Burmese and Lanna architecture. Then there is Wat Chedi Sao of 20 *chedis.*

Lampang has several strongly Burmese temples built by Burmese timber traders around the turn of the century. Wat Sri Chum is a charming example; it still houses Burmese monks. Wat Sri Rong Muang, the more colourful is more recent.

Lampang's finest temple, the finest in the north, is Wat Phrathat Lampang Luang, 20 km south of town. Part of a fortress in Haripunchai times, it has a *chedi* with more claim than most to containing a genuine Buddha relic. Many of the current buildings and temples like Wat Phra That Sadet and Wat Prakeu date from the 16th century. Harmonious proportions and exquisite interior decoration make this temple a premier example of northeren architecture.

Sukhothai

Sukhothai is the ruined site of the first large Thai kingdom and its name, meaning 'Dawn of Happiness', seems to signify awareness of a new and fruitful era for the Thai people. It was, however, not founded all of a sudden like Chiang Mai; rather, it was a takeover job.

In the first millennium AD, the Central Plains and the lower north were settled by Mon and Khmer peoples; the

Burmese and Lanna Thai architecture blend at Wat Haripunchai, Lamphun.

The ruins of Sri Satchanalai, sister city of Sukhothai.

city at Sukhothai was the northernmost stronghold of the Khmers. Towards the end of the millennium, Thai tribes started arriving in the area and in the course of time settled in substantial numbers amongst the Mons and Khmers.

A Thai Kingdom

With the decline of the Khmer empire of Angkor in the 13th century, the Thais took over the fiefdom and rapidly expanded Sukhothai to a kingdom holding sway over a large territory that included parts of Burma, Laos and the southern peninsula.

Fine Sculptures

Under King Ramkhamhaeng (1279-99, see box story, page 11) and his 14th century successors, Sukhothai became a centre of Buddhist civilisation and there developed a distinctive and graceful sculptural style that is now regarded as classic. Many great temples were built, some with huge Buddha images.

A City Abandoned

Sukhothai's glory did not last long; inheriting a complex Khmer irrigation

The glory that was Sukhothai, 'Dawn of Happiness', absorbed by Ayutthaya before final abandonment.

system, the Thais gradually lost control of it and the land suffered. In the early 15th century, the reduced kingdom was absorbed by Ayutthaya. Eventually, the city was abandoned and it was only reclaimed from the jungle in the 1950s and substantially restored in the 1980s.

An Historical Park

Today it is the Sukhothai Historical Park, spread over hundreds of hectares, divided into five zones with an entry fee of 20 baht each, open daily 6am-6pm. The best place to start is the Ramkhamhaeng National Museum, for its models and maps enable visitors both to visualise the original city and to plan their visit. Some fine sculpture can be seen there too. It is open daily, 9am-4pm, fee 20 baht.

Sukhothai's atmosphere is greater than the sum of its parts – not much majesty remains after the depredations of man and nature, though some ruins are impressive. Set in parkland amidst grass and trees, the place has a romantic aura, unfortunately somewhat diminished rather than enhanced by the recent restoration and landscaping.

Wat Mahathat was the principal and largest temple, built in the mid-13th century to represent Mount Meru, centre of the universe in Buddhist mythology. It includes nearly 200 *chedi*; the central one has a lotus-bud top, a Sukhothai creation.

Wat Sri Chum lies to the northwest of the main site and features the famous 15-metre tall sitting Buddha. The high enclosing wall is 3-metres thick and contains a decorated stairway to the top.

Wat Trapang Thong, east of the museum, is surrounded by a lotus-pond which is the original location of the Loy Krathong festival (see box story, page 307).

SRI SATCHANALAI

Sri Satchanalai, about 70 km north of Sukhothai on Highway 101, was a contemporary and sister city of Sukhothai. Its ruins are similar in style, less numerous and less widespread, and the setting is less developed. This makes for more charm and easier access, if less majesty, than Sukhothai. Sri Satchanalai Historical Park has an entry fee of 20 baht.

KAMPHAENG PHET

Meaning 'Diamond Walls', Kamphaeng Phet was once a Sukhothai fortress. Much of the earthen ramparts can still be seen, overgrown with bushes and trees, but little of the walls with their diamond-patterned bricks.

The road leading from Highway 1 (Bangkok-Chiang Mai) crosses the Ping River bridge and then the line of the old walls to lead straight up to the Provincial Hall. To the left is a branch of the

Weathered down by time, Buddha images at Kamphaeng Phet still remain, at times facelessly.

National Museum containing some fine sculpture, especially a striking standing bronze of Shiva called Phra Isawara Sumrit. The museum explains the significance of the ruins which spread northwards from here. The old city within the walls had a long rectangular shape north-south along the east bank of the Ping River. Apart from the southern tip, which is commercial and administrative, and includes the local jail, most of the area today is simply parkland or extensive banana plantations. Some of the most interesting ruins lie in the centre in a historical park. The greatest quantity of temple ruins lies outside the walls to the northeast in woodland.

Kamphaeng Phet has many surviving Buddha images so striking because of the way they have weathered. The less worn ones are rounded and resemble Bibendum the Michelin Man, with horizontal lines of mortar between laterite layers. Others are so worn, wasted and pitted that they are worthy of Giacometti, the Swiss modernist sculptor.

Wat Phra Kaew

The principal temple of medieval

Lovely ladies of the north during the Egg Banana Festival at Kamphaeng Phet.

Kamphaeng Phet was Wat Phra Kaew, the royal chapel situated by the vanished royal palace. It features a reclining Buddha with twin-sitting Buddhas behind and many little Giacometti Buddhas around the base. To its south stands the large laterite stupa of Wat Phrathat.

A road passes these temples and leads out towards the outer site, which is within walking distance (about one kilometre). The most famous temple is Wat Phra Si Iriyabot, whose tall sanctuary once housed four huge and complete Buddha images in reclining, sitting, standing and walking postures, facing the four directions from around a central wall. Now only the standing image is mostly intact, and, being colossal, it has become something of a symbol of this small town.

Close by, Wat Singh is the Michelin Man temple, with an eroded laterite Buddha of smooth round body and eerily featureless face. The other distinctive temple is the most northerly, Wat Chang Rop, whose ruined central *chedi* has a base buttressed by laterite elephants. These stucco figures, interspersed with demons and sacred bo trees, were a Sukhothai favourite, better preserved here than elsewhere.

Kamphaeng Phet is noted for its *kluai khai*, 'egg bananas', a short stubby variety that is extensively grown. Even within the old city. The height of the harvest is in late September, when the Egg Banana Festival (see Fabulous Festivals, page 291) is held.

The fabulous Buddha at Wat Mahathat, Phitsanulok.

The North ... a round-up

Many of the outer provinces of the North are remote and little populated – notably Mae Hong Son, Tak, Nan and Phrae. Forested and mountainous, they retain much of the wildness that until this century characterised all of the upper north, though deforestation is stretching its deadly tentacles everywhere now.

Mae Hong Son, among these northern towns, appears to be more rapidly developing. It has benefited from road development and investments in tourist amenities. It has at least one international chain hotel and several others of reasonable standard.

Nan and Phrae even harbour the hunter-gatherer Mrabri tribe – known as the Spirits of the Yellow Leaves on account of their regularly disappearing from their leaf-clad shelters when the covering turns yellow.

In the lower north, medieval cities flourished. While Sukhothai, Kamphaeng Phet and Sri Satchanalai left significant remains, the ceramic-making centre of Sawankhalok (see Celadon section in the Handicrafts chapter, page 318), now sports just a few ruined kilns as evidence of its former glory while the ancient city of Phitsanulok fell to a disastrous fire just a few decades ago. Fortunately, Wat Mahathat survived with its golden *prang* and great bronze Buddha of 14th century.

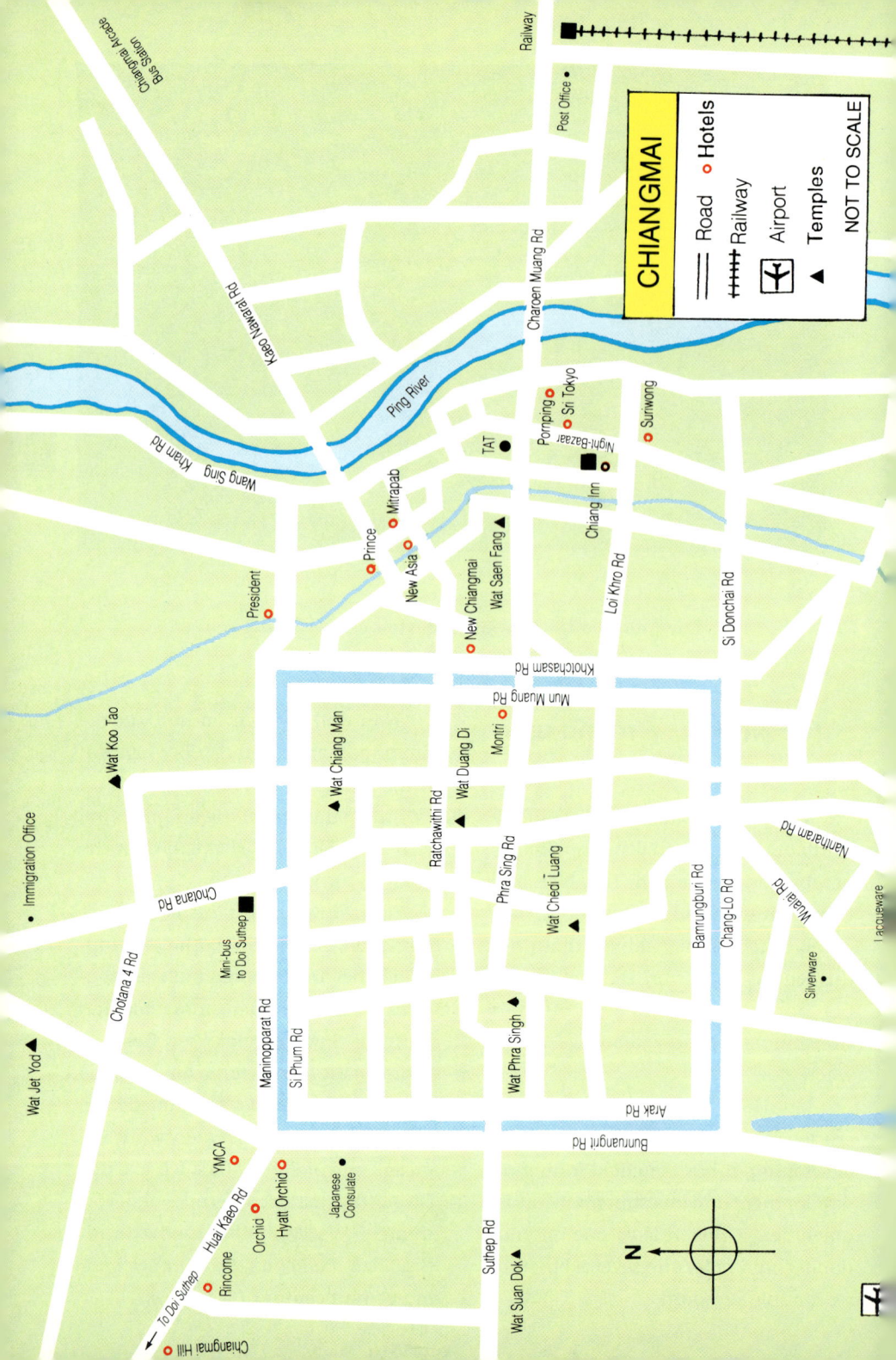

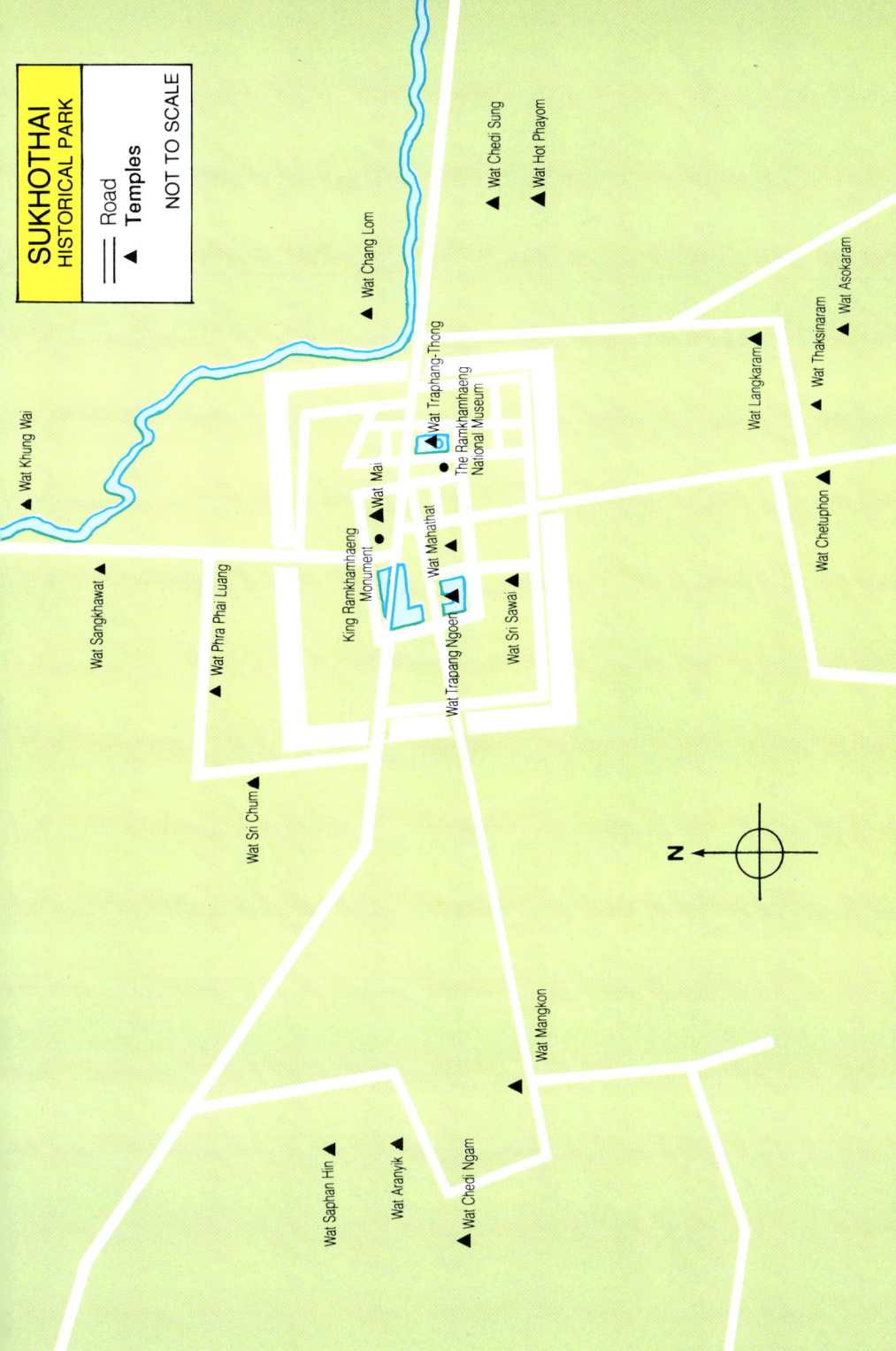

REGIONS OF THAILAND

The Northeast — Isan

The northeast region of Thailand is the only one which has a proper name, Isan, and perhaps this reflects the feeling of Thais from other parts that this is almost a country apart, with its own language, cuisine and music, a unique landscape, and people of distinctive features and customs. The name actually derives from Isana, a Mon-Khmer kingdom that dominated the area over one thousand years ago. Subsequently, the region fell under Khmer, then conflicting Siamese and Lao suzerainty, until it was fully absorbed by Siam only in the 19th century. The Lao influence is still dominant, particularly in speech.

Isan's culture remains underpinned by Buddhism throughout all the periods of Lao, Khmer and Hindu influences.

Isan is rich in people, around one third of the nation or 18 million, but poor in soil and prone to drought, all too often leaving a region of destitute farmers. As a result, the farmers leave the land. In Bangkok, where a huge proportion of Thailand's money resides, the construction sites and the maids' parlours, the taxi driving seats and the hostess bars are filled with north eastern Thais making a living where and how they can. There is also a great seasonal influx of Isan people after the rice harvest

Details at Prasat Phanom Rung reveal the Khmers to have been great sculptors, engineers and architects.

is in and they tend to remain until the new planting a few months later. Fortunately, this coincides with the dry season which is also the high tourist season and the best time for construction, from November to April, and so there are jobs to be had.

A Tough Terrain

There is little industry and even less tourism in the Northeast, so there is almost nothing within the region to complement the meager living from raking a parched land. Most of Isan is a sandstone plateau whose sandy soil mixed with clay yields poor harvests and whose rainy season is short and irregular. The typical Isan landscape is a domesticated savannah of flat dry fields with isolated trees.

It is bordered in the north and east by the River Mekong, beyond which lies Laos. To the south, its limit is the Dong Rek mountains which form the frontier with Cambodia. To the west and southwest, a range of highlands separates it from the northern, central and eastern regions.

Isan can be conveniently divided into four parts: the southern borderland near Cambodia; the Mekong river provinces to the east and north; the western highlands; and the great central plateau.

Along The Cambodian Border

This part of the northeast is easy to tour, having both a trunk road and railway line. The railway runs due east from Korat to Ubon Ratchathani whilst Highway 24 runs the same way about 50 km to the south and about the same distance from the Cambodian border.

Korat

Korat, officially known as Nakhon Ratchasima, is the main gateway to the northeast and one of Thailand's bigger cities. The main highway and the railway line from Bangkok pass through it. Its history as a single town goes back to the 17th century, before which it was two municipalities, Sema and Khorakhopura. both of which had ancient origins. It had rectangular ramparts but only the moat remains. Its latest period began in the 1960s with the establishment of a USAF bomber base for the pursuance of the Vietnam War, which brought considerable commercial expansion.

Its only significant sight is the pleasant paved area around a reconstructed city gate now in the middle of town, Chumphon Gate. It has a statue and shrine to Khunying Mo, alias Thao Suranari, a governor's wife who heroically defended the town against Laotian armies in the early 19th century.

Most visitors in fact use Korat purely as a staging post on the way to the sights of Isan, and particularly to the Khmer temple ruins found along the Cambodian border, of which the most accessible is Phimai.

Phimai

Just over 50 km northeast of Korat, there lies the little town of Phimai centred on an ancient Khmer city of the great Angkor period. It used to extend 1030 metres by 560; traces of its ramparts remain. It had four gateways and the southern one, Pratu Chai or Victory Gate, still stands imposingly at the end of the present town's main street. Eight hundred years ago a road led from the gate to the imperial capital, Angkor.

Prasat Hin Phimai

The point of a visit to Phimai is to witness the impressive sanctuary of Prasat Hin Phimai, one of the best examples of classical Khmer architecture of the 12th century, in the style of the world-famous Angkor Wat. Since Angkor Wat and other major Cambodian sites are out of bounds due to war and politics, and other significant Khmer ruins in Thailand are much more re-

Sophisticated Khmer architecture dating to the 11th century.

mote, Prasat Hin Phimai offers a unique opportunity to experience classic Khmer culture.

Prasat Hin Phimai was created by King Jayavarman VI before the building of Angkor Wat in the mid-12th century. Later additions were made by King Jayavarman VII who took the Khmer Empire to its greatest extent in the late 12th century and built widely, including roads and bridges still in use today. The temple is dedicated to Mahayana Buddhism and restored by the Royal Fine Arts Department.

The sanctuary is a walled quadrangle in which stands yet another walled, inner courtyard. In the courtyard, a central towered shrine stands. Fine stonecarving on interior lintels show scenes of the life of Buddha. Some stonework is preserved in a museum to the north of the sanctuary. Open daily 8.30am-4.30pm, the entrance fee is 20 baht, whilst the sanctuary is open daily 7.30am-5.00pm, entrance fee 20 baht.

Nearby, north-east of the town on an island in the Mun River, stands what is claimed to be Thailand's biggest banyan tree. It is a local picnic spot, with foodstalls on hand.

Prasat Phanom Rung

Another impressive ancient Khmer site is located to the southeast of Korat, about 130 km distant along Highway 24. Prasat Phanom Rung is reached

Who Were The Khmers?

The culture of Thailand's first kingdoms, particularly young Ayutthaya, was profoundly influenced by Khmer civilisation – religious practices, court rituals, the concept of kingship, art and dance, and so on. Impressive Khmer carved-stone architecture remains to this day in Isan and the Central Plains. Just who were the Khmers?

The Khmer people founded a kingdom called Chenla in the 6th century in the area of today's Isan and Cambodia. Much influenced by Indian culture, by the end of the 9th century there existed a highly organised state cloaked in Hinduism and divine kingship, while the people were Mahayana Buddhists. The city of Angkor was founded, irrigated by a remarkable system of canals and reservoirs.

The Khmer zenith came in the 12th century with the building of the magnificent structures of Angkor Wat and the Bayon. Khmer power extended from Cambodia over most of present-day Thailand and Laos, and parts of Burma and Vietnam.

King Suryavarman II (reigned c.1113-50) built Angkor Wat as the ritual centre of his kingdom to house the royal lingam, emblem of power. Covering over one kilometre square, its structures were covered in exquisite bas-reliefs of divine dancers, plants, birds, Hindu legends and so on. Khmer kings saw themselves as reincarnations of the Hindu god, Shiva.

His son, Jayavarman VII (reigned 1181-1219) embarked on an extensive building programme across the empire, the strain of which probably lead to popular revolt and the rapid decline of Khmer power, allowing the rise of the Thai kingdom of Ayutthaya in the 14th century.

The Khmers were great architects, engineers, sculptors and soldiers. Their legacy lives on in Thailand most notably in the temple ruins of Prasat Phanom Rung, Phimai and Lopburi.

more directly from Buri Ram, being about 50 km due south down Highway 219, just beyond the town of Prakhon Chai. Buri Ram is a provincial capital and a stop on the Ubon Ratchathani railway line.

A Little Closer to Angkor Wat

Both the site and the approach to Prasat Phanom Rung are splendid. It stands on the spur of a hill, actually an extinct volcano, overlooking broad flat country from which the Dong Rek

Khmer statuary testify to a glorious ancient civilization.

Temple beneath a cliff, Loei.

mountains rise in the south, beyond which lies Angkor, the former imperial capital. For access, it has a long paved avenue flanked by lotus-bud-topped pillars, leading to a monumental staircase split by landings and culminating in terraces decorated with five-headed *nagas*, mythological serpents.

The main sanctuary is surrounded by galleries on four sides and has a tower on a square base with antechambers at the entrances from the four compass points. It is one of the most perfect examples of Khmer art extant. The doorways have fine pediments and carved lintels while friezes decorate the walls and pillars. The inner eastern entranceway has a lintel depicting five hermits, which seems to support the theory that the sanctuary was built to commemorate a famous hermit.

A Little More Ancient Than Angkor

The bulk of Prasat Phanom Rung dates from the early 12th century, shortly before Angkor Wat, and though much smaller, it is on a par artistically. Construction on the site appears to have begun in the 10th century and lasted until the early 13th. Major restoration was carried out by the Royal Fine Arts Department from 1961-88. The site is open daily, at an entrance fee of 20 baht, and a 20 baht guidebook and negotiable English-speaking guides are available at the entrance. There is a small museum.

A little south, 5 km directly, is another Khmer site, Prasat Muang Tam. It predates its neighbour by over a century and its inner courtyard is in ruins but its quadrangle walls are in a good state of preservation and feature some fine carving.

Prasat Khao Phra Viharn

This is the most easterly of the three major ancient Khmer sites in Thailand, and only just, for the temple stands right on the border within Cambodia and only the access is from Thailand. Even then, at the time of writing it was still mined and off bounds as it had been for two decades as a result of the Cam-

Khmer sites in Isan are thought to predate those at Angkor in Cambodia.

A contented Buddha sits in the shade in Loei.

bodian conflict. However, hopeful noises about mine-clearing are being made in official quarters and this large and magnificent mountain-top sanctuary may soon re-open. It is directly accessible by Highway 221 from Si Sa Ket, exactly 100 km to the northwest, a provincial capital and railway stop, and by the same highway off Highway 24.

UBON RATCHATHANI

Ubon Ratchathani province occupies the far south-east corner of Isan where it meets both Cambodia and Laos. With nearly two million people, it is the northeast's most populous province, with its economy based on agriculture and some industry. It currently has many development plans on the drawing board, such as a hydro-electric dam on the Mun River and a bridge over the Mekong to Laos, or some plans in progress, such as new industrial estates and the upgrading of its airport to international status.

Meanwhile, the city of Ubon, the terminus of both the lower northeast railway and Highway 24 from Korat, belies its ancient origins with a hotchpotch of commercial buildings dating largely from the Vietnam War period when a USAF bomber base lay just outside town. Its touristic claim to fame is the grand annual Candle Festival each July.

Its most distinctive temples lie outside town. On the northern outskirts, Wat Nong Bua is notable for its double four-sided stupas, elegant stone structures modelled on the Mahabodhi of Bodh Gaya, India. Some 75 km north of town in Amnat Charoen district is the Buddha Uthayan, a park with a huge gold mosaic sitting Buddha, the Phra Mongkol Ming Muang.

Foreign Monks

In the other direction and in contrastingly ascetic mood are two forest monasteries. Wat Nong Pa Pong at Warin Chamrap is in the care of Ajarn Cha, known for his simple and direct teaching which has brought hundreds of Westerners to study here in recent decades. Nearby is Beung Wai International Forest Monastery where the abbot and monks are mostly foreign.

Waterfalls and Rapids

Ubon Ratchathani province's scenic attractions are mostly water-related: the Mekong and Mun Rivers, their rapids, the Sirindhorn Dam and some waterfalls. The dam lies some 70 km east of the city and forms an extensive lake. On the Mun River east of town are two rapids that are popular picnicking and wading spots in the dry season. At this time, the rocks of Kaeng Saphue and Kaeng Tana are high and the waters foaming. Some 9km from Kaeng Saphue

Ubon Ratchathani province has been blessed with many rivers and waterfalls.

is the five-metre drop of Tad Tone Waterfall.

As the Mun enters the Mekong, its relatively clear waters run alongside the richly muddy Mekong, creating the sight known as the Two-Colour River, once described as "where the blue Moon meets the brown Khong". Here at Khong Chiam are also to be found the strange mushroom-like rock formations of Sao Chaliang. Just a few kilometres north lies Ubon's most atmospheric attraction, Pha Taem. This cliff rises jagged above the Mekong flood plain and faces the river with prehistoric rock paintings extending over one-and-a-half kilometres.

Many of Isan's people live close to the Mekong.

Along the Mekong

From Ubon round to Loei, Isan borders the River Mekong with the People's Democratic Republic of Laos dozing across the water. Relations with Laos, drastically curtailed in 1975 after the communist takeover, are now warming up again since Laos's economic liberalisation in the late 1980s and the former Thai Prime Minister's 1988 promise to "turn the Indochinese battlefields into marketplaces".

This separation was always artificial and unpopular since the people of Isan have more in common racially, linguistically and by custom with the Lao than with other Thais. Indeed, many northeasterners call themselves "Lao".

Petty border trading continued across the Mekong all these years and is due for great expansion in the 1990s. There are official river crossings at several points along the Mekong, for example, at Mukdahan, That Phanom, Nakhon Phanom, Nong Khai and Chiang Khan. Thai and Laotian citizens are allowed to cross at all places on border passes, but at the time of writing, other nationals could only cross at Nong Khai with a visa obtained at a Laotian embassy.

The river is called *Mae Nam Khong* in Thai. The proper Romanised spelling is actually 'Mekhong', hence the name of Thailand's most popular rice whisky.

Nakhon Phanom

The province of Nakhon Phanom

Long stretches of the Mekong are shared between Thailand and Laos.

lies by the Mekong in the northeast's farthest reaches. Nakhon Phanom town has an atmospheric view, particularly at sunset, across the river to a jagged range of Laotian mountains. The province has significant Laotian, Vietnamese and Chinese populations, largely assimilated but giving a distinct character to the commercial districts and some architecture.

One of the nicest little towns along the Mekong is also Isan's principal place of pilgrimage. Located on the Mekong just 50 km south of Nakhon Phanom town, That Phanom has a *chedi* which is revered all over Thailand and regarded as a symbol of Isan. The original, fondly believed to be 1500 years old, collapsed in 1975 to the great consternation of the populace and was rapidly replaced with a somewhat flashy imitation. It is Lao-style, four-sided, 57 metres tall, in white stucco with gold embellishments. It is situated within Wat That Phanom set in a pleasant formal park.

The temple and the *chedi* look directly east down the town's main street to the river, at which there is a little customs post. Halfway along, marking the entrance to the main commercial streets, there stands a Lao-style archway. These streets contain some charmingly faded French-Indochinese architecture.

From Nakhon Phanom, Highway 212 meanders alongside the Mekong all round Isan's far northeast corner to Nong Khai. There is nothing outstanding to see but it's a pleasant off-the-beaten-track tour, with local bus connections all the way. Alternatively, Highway 22 cuts west to Udon Thani town, 250 km

Pre-historic pottery from Ban Chiang, a civilization now thought to date from the bronze-age.

away, with the major prehistoric site of Ban Chiang just 50 km before Udon.

Ban Chiang

It may well be that agrarian civilisation first developed not in Mesopotamia or in China but in Isan – that is the significance of the pottery and bronzeware finds at Ban Chiang in Udon Thani province. Since serious study began in 1966, many human and animal remains have been found and a great number of artifacts, notably bronze jewellery and pottery decorated in reddish-brown swirls. These pieces indicate a well-developed society in existence around 7,000 years ago. There is a museum displaying many of the finds. Ban Chiang remains important in the research on the origin of bronze in ancient civilisation.

Nong Khai

Nong Khai is a pleasant provincial capital strung along the Mekong. It is the terminus of the upper northeast railway line and Highway 2, the Friendship Highway built with US aid. The waterfront provides the principal river crossing to Laos and the only one usable by nationalities other than Thai and Laotian.

In the quiet meandering riverside streets and alleys, Laotian handicrafts are on sale. Another very welcome influence from over the river is the availability of fine French bread, usually in roll form. This is a distinct relief after the tissue-paper bread you get served in the rest of Thailand!

West from Nong Khai, a minor road winds along the course of the Mekong into Loei province. This pleasant route has small towns at regular intervals, the last of which, Chiang Khan, has the best views and the most accommodation.

Chiang Khan

Chiang Khan is a quiet town with wooden houses banked high above the Mekong, some of which are guest houses which afford great views of river life, the

Statuaryat Wat Khaek, Nong Khai

Distinct Hindu-influenced features at the Buddhist temples of Nong Khai.

green hills of Laos and some fine sunrises and sunsets. It is located in a cotton-growing area and many townswomen can be seen in their houses making cotton quilts, the local speciality. The town's temples offer a wide range of styles.

The local curiosity, located 25 km towards Nong Khai on the riverside road, is the great stone phallus of Ban Kok Lao, a penis-shaped boulder found in the river, hauled out, placed in an open-sided shed by the river, and worshipped as a fertility symbol by local women.

Phu Kradung National Park

Regarded by many as Isan's greatest natural sight, Phu Kradung is a lone

Long-boat racing at Sakhon Nakhon province.

flat-topped mountain reserved as a national park, one of Thailand's first and most beautiful. Rising to 1325 metres, it affords a panoramic view of the surrounding lowlands and the Phetchabun Mountains to the west. Temperate plant species thrive on the summit; wildlife there observed includes deer, tiger and, amazingly, elephant.

From its foot, a trail climbs steeply for the first kilometre and then eases off for three kilometres only to rise steeply again for the last kilometre. It emerges onto a grassland plateau studded with pine, oak and beech, amongst other trees, and wild flowers such as violets, orchids, rhododendrons and daisies.

Blooms are best in March and April, and the park is closed in the rainy season, mid-July to mid-October. Porters are available to carry gear up to the top, a climb of four hours. There are cabins and camping facilities on the plateau. Phu Kradung is some 70km south of Loei on Highway 201.

The Rest of Isan

West of Loei province, mountainous Petchabun rises to divide the northern and upper central regions. Central Isan – Khon Kaen, Kalasin, Maha Sarakham, Roi Et, Yasothon, Chaiyaphum – does not have sights of any particular note and thus little tourism.

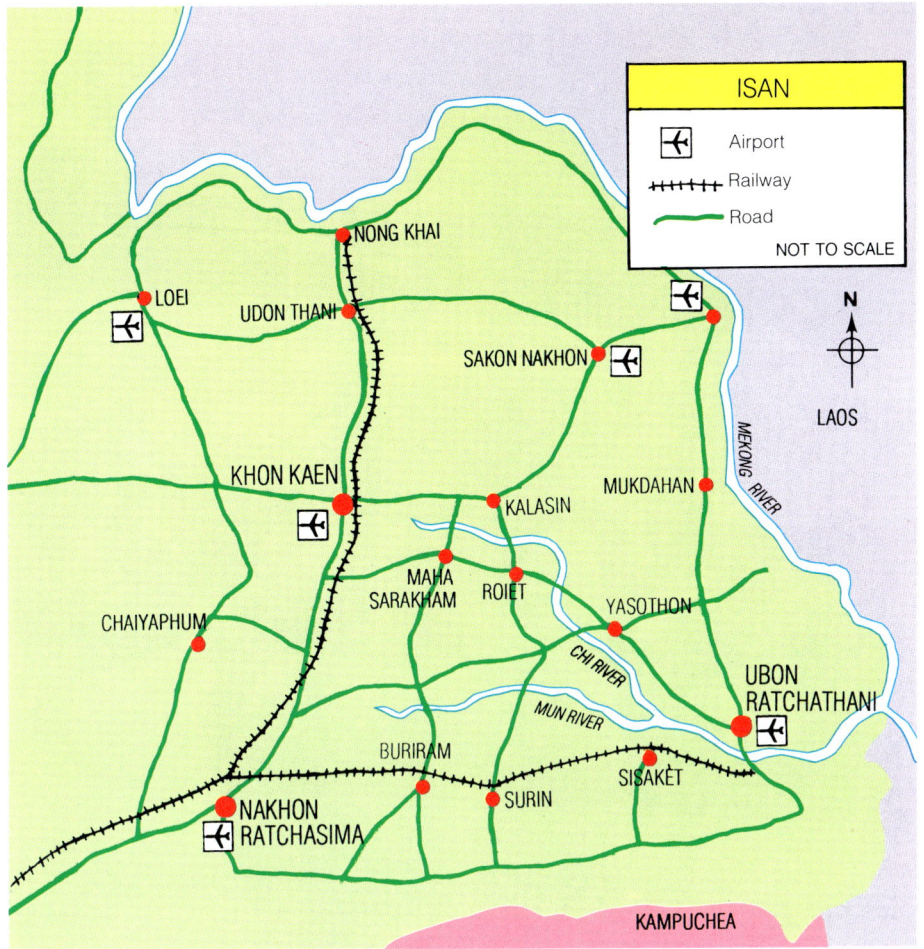

Khon Kaen, largest town in the Northeast, is a transport and commercial hub, and also a university town. There's little to see but plenty of Isan handicrafts to buy – silk, silver, basketry, triangular floor cushions. Roi Et is noted for producing the emblematic Isan instrument, the *khaen*, a large, almost metre-long, pan pipe. Yasothon is noted for the most ribald and boisterous of Isan Rocket Festivals, held in May.

Some parts of Isan defy the general flatness. The Phu Phaan Mountains separate Kalasin and Sakhon Nakhon provinces and contain Phu Phaan National Park, where deer and monkeys abound and elephants and tigers survive. In Phetchabun province, two north-south mountain ranges rising to 1500 metres divide Isan from the North.

Package tours to Isan are few or non-existent. Bus connections are available, however, you will have to create your own travel plan in your own time.

Yasothon is noted for the Isan rocket festival, an event of excitement and pageantry each May.

Owing to the harshness of the land, much of Isan still moves along at a retiring pace.

The East

The eastern region of Thailand is presently its major growth area. The government's Eastern Seaboard Project is rapidly developing the coast from Bangkok down to Rayong. There will be much new industry, including a deep-sea port at Laem Chabang, an upgraded international airport at U-Tapao, as well as a great increase in housing and commerce. The region is destined to divert a lot of future investment away from Greater Bangkok, which is vastly overdeveloped by comparison with the rest of the country. Indeed, some economists forecast that, as Bangkok progressively seizes up in the face of overdevelopment, commerce and development will just ooze down the east coast to make one great long megalopolis.

Meanwhile, this coast still presents a recreational face to the sea, most of the way from Bang Saen to Trat.

Access from Bangkok is by bus from the Eastern Bus Terminal on Sukhumvit Road near Soi 42. A bus ride to Bang Saen lasts about one and a half hours, or one could drive there from Bangkok in one and a quarter hours. Trat would be about a three-hour drive from Bang Saen.

Balmy breezes, calm waters and sandy beaches still make Pattaya a choice seaside retreat.

The shores of the East are enjoyed by Thais, as much by tourists.

Bang Saen

Bang Saen has long been the popular resort of Bangkokians, as Southend-on-sea to Londoners or Coney Island to New Yorkers. Some 100 km from the capital, it is a long stretch of scruffy sand at many points covered in beach umbrellas, deckchairs, foodstands and wall-to-wall trippers.

More interesting is the nearby Aquarium of the Scientific Marine Centre on the local university campus. For 40 baht you can see what is said to be Southeast Asia's best marine life collection.

For children of all ages, there is also Ocean World, a park of swimming pools with artificial waves and great waterchutes to delight them.

On the main highway, just past the turn-off to Bang Saen is Nong Mol, where at a cluster of shops one may find a variety of snacks, local desserts and delicacies. This is also known for dried seafood, dried as well as fresh fruits.

Koh Si Chang

About 15 km south is the fishing port of Si Racha, famous for its seafood and hot sauce. Offshore from here is the

Thai Rodeo – Buffalo Racing

The water buffalo is the Thai farmer's best friend, his compliant and docile workhorse, so massive and strong yet so easygoing that children are habitually put in charge of it. Seeing them trudging through the ricefields with ploughs or wallowing lazily in ponds and ditches, you would never imagine them racing, but that is exactly what the farmers of Chonburi do each year with their trusty beasts to celebrate the end of Buddhist Lent.

Coming in from their farms in this flat eastern seaboard province each October, the buffaloes are made to parade through town pulling huge red-wheeled carts, themselves very pretty in brilliant head-dresses and coats! After the procession, they get unhitched at the fairground ready for the serious business of racing.

Young farmers clamber bareback onto the broad beasts and charge off in a series of heats, armed merely with a long stick for whip and some red rope for reins. Thundering down the long straight dirt-track course, not a few riders and steeds get separated, the farmer falling to earth with a dusty thud, the buffalo galloping ever onward.

Eventually a winner emerges. In 1989, it was Red Dragon with a young sugarcane farmer atop who had prepared his beast with a 15-day herbal medicine course and a 25-egg breakfast. Less wise racers are known to ply their steeds with stimulant drinks and rice whisky, with wild results, like a buffalo in a china shop. All this for just a 5000 baht first prize? No – for the glory!

---

island, Koh Si Chang, which has a small town with three hotels. The island has some moderate beaches and the sea offers reasonable snorkelling. Of special interest are the remains of a summer palace built by King Chulalongkorn and also secluded hermitage in caves and huts for Buddhist monks.

Pattaya

Next down is possibly Asia's biggest beach resort, Pattaya. Once, only 30 years ago, this was a quiet fishing village set in a beautiful curving bay that looked out to scenic offshore islands across a crystal sea. Besides its proximity to Bangkok, there was its calm water and attractive sandy beaches that naturally taken up as a seaside retreat by some Bangkokians. It eventually sprouted hotels everywhere with the accompanying bars and discos but neglected to install long-term public utilities such as water supply and treatment systems or a safe public transport systems. However, the local administrative body set up by the government is taking positive steps to upgrade and refresh Pattaya with a shower of funds. The entire infrastructure of utilities and amenities will be spruced up, and when completed will have wonderfully redeeming effects on the tourist industry at Pattaya.

A hydrofoil service operates from Bangkok to Pattaya from the Menam Hotel on the Chao Phraya River taking roughly 2 1/2 hours. The fare is about

Pattaya Beach.

450 baht first class and 350 baht on second class. The hydrofoil also serves the journey from Pattaya to Cha-am at the same fares and taking about 2 1/2 hours as well. A more rapid service is offered by the Yellowbird seaplane which flies 6 times daily between Bangkok and Pattaya for 2100 baht return. The flight time is 30 minutes.

Koh Larn

The most popular excursion from Pattaya is to a group of offshore isles called Coral Islands, the largest of which is Koh Larn. The trip can be made in anything from speedboats to Chinese junks; the standard ferry boat takes 40

minutes and deposits you on a beach lined with souvenir sellers and foodstalls. You may possibly still be able to see some coral and tropical fish, either by snorkelling or going in a glass-bottom boat.

The only unfortunate thing is that Koh Larn has become somewhat over run with tourists.

Nevertheless, the view out to sea is still fine and if you want to party, to indulge in water sports, or just relax in the grounds of a well-appointed hotel, this is the place for you.

Pattaya abounds in resort hotels such as the Montien, the Royal Garden and the cream of the crop, the Royal Cliff Beach. It also offers the complete gamut of water sports from parasailing to scuba diving (round the offshore islands), from jet-skiing to windsurfing (Refer to Sports and Recreation chapter, page 323). A lot of the day and of course, for most of the night, the sex trade is in operation, with bargirls at open-air beer bars and go-go dancing bars, plus masseuses at their parlours. For something different one could watch transvestite shows. The weekends are especially crowded.

Rayong

This north-south coast reaches a point at the naval base of Sattahip and turns eastward towards Rayong, a province long noted for its durian and fish sauce, and increasingly now for its beaches. As Bang Saen became overpopulated and Pattaya overdeveloped, Bangkokians began discovering this quiet coast. Students in particular became enamoured of Koh Samet, led on by the renowned 19th century Thai poet, Sunthorn Pu, who eulogised it.

Koh Samet

Koh Samet is a triangular island with a very long southern end pointing down to the open sea. This gives it a lengthy shoreline for its small area of 130 sq km. The west side is great for rocky walks and diving; it is generally steep and forested and has hardly any

sand. By contrast, the east side sports a magnificent string of fine white sand coves. In many places this sand is so exquisite it feels like fresh snow under the feet. Reflecting its fineness, the most northerly beach is called Crystal Sand Beach.

This is the most frequented beach, being the closest to the main boat jetty and a favourite for camping students.

Pattaya is lined with resort hotels.

There are bungalow hotels all the way down this east shore and if you are not already booked in somewhere and you are not overloaded with bags, the best thing to do is just keep walking until you find something you like. Prices range from 50 baht to 500 baht and vary according to demand.

The price/quality ratio is definitely inferior to that of the southern Thai beaches but, on the other hand, if you cannot get down to the south, this is one of the very few substitutes. It is definitely to be avoided around New Year, however, since this is both a peak Thai and *farang* holiday time and bungalows become absolutely impossible to get. All the resorts have a number of restaurants and the quality varies, with Wong Deuan Beach being generally reliable –

Sunthorn Phu, Best Loved Poet

Thailand's best-loved poet is Sunthorn Phu, born in 1786 at Laem Mae Phim on the eastern coast near Koh Samet, which he adored and with which his name is much associated. His birthplace is commemorated by a park with a statue of him and well-known characters from his most famous poem, *Phra Aphaimani*. The eponymous hero plays a flute by a pond, enchanting the sea ogress Pi Sua Samut, from whose clutches he escaped with the aid of a gorgeous mermaid who reclines on a rock. Some of the setting for his poetical works is thought to be inspired by the beauty of the eastern coast.

Despite this extravagance of setting, Sunthorn Phu is renowned for his down-to-earth wisdom, the result of his humble rural background. As a youth, he went to study at a Thonburi temple and early on showed skill in all poetic forms, gaining himself a post as King Rama II's literary assistant. Sunthorn Phu cut a dashing figure at court: he was artistically gifted, very handsome and had an acid wit. He was also rather fond of women, who eagerly returned the compliment. When he fell out of favour at court in later life and escaped into monkhood, his vows did not hinder his love life, it seems. Under King Mongkut, he returned to court favour as poet laureate, dying in 1856 after a fruitful life of 70 years.

Thais still much appreciate his poetry for its refined and skillful expression of widely-held beliefs and everyday concerns. He was an artist who had the common touch and he continues to reach the Thai heart. There follow some examples of his verse, loosely translated. As with all poetry, much is lost in the translation in terms of both of meaning and rhythm, but a strong flavour remains.

Wealth stays for only a lifetime
At death you must leave it behind
But the merit you make in this lifespan
Will stay with you eternally.
from *Phra Aphaimani*

Never trust anybody completely
Another heart cannot be understood
See the vines all twisted in the forest
Then consider the human heartstrings
Now I tell you, they are more tangled.
from *Phra Aphaimani*

it is more upmarket than most.

Access is by boat from the fishing port of Ban Phe due north on the mainland. Passages are frequent and cost 20 baht, though you may find yourself sitting and waiting for the boat to fill up. Boats go to Samet's northern jetty, Na Dan, from where you can walk or take a pick-up bus along the island's one track that runs behind the beaches and along the central ridge. Alternatively, and more conveniently, there are direct boats to many of the eastern coves, such as Ao Cho, Ao Wong Deuan and Ao Wai.

Access from Bangkok is by air-conditioned coach direct to Ban Phe. There are also connections from Pattaya, by bus and by inclusive tour on either buses or boats.

There are also several bungalow resorts on the mainland near Ban Phe and further east, such as at Wang Kaew, and more are appearing all the time.

About 50 km east of Ban Phe and off the coastal highway to the north lies Khao Chamao National Park featuring forest and mountains, caves and cliffs, streams and waterfalls, and bungalows to rent. A short stay would allow a more leisurely exploration of the variety of landscape.

Chanthaburi

About 30 km further on and 350 km from Bangkok lies Chanthaburi town, capital of the eponymous province which is renowned for its gems, particularly sapphires. The town has much evidence of Vietnamese-French influence on account of the many Vietnamese Christians who fled here from persecution in Vietnam. There are a lot of Vietnamese-French style shophouses and a large cathedral dating from 1880, a unique sight in a Thai provincial town.

Rubies and Sapphires

Thailand is often associated with ruby and sapphire jewellery, but this does not mean that these precious stones are mined throughout the country. However it is here in this province that the main supply originates.

The principal business here is gem-polishing and trading, of interest to both the traders and the tourists. This can especially be observed in the Trok Chang quarter where heaps of blue sapphires and rich rubies are put to the lathe and energetically bargained over.

Tourists can go out to a nearby mine, Khao Ploi Waen or "Sapphire Ring Hill", and see the digging and sifting process. In addition, there are or-

Those two excerpts show the traditional wisdom that is couched in the fantastical tale, a combination characteristic of Thai literature. Sunthorn Phu was also a more direct moralist and wrote a well-known set of verses called 'Maxims for Women'. Here now, to ruin his reputation amongst feminists, is part of his homily to wives regarding husbands.

Tend to his needs, pander to his mood
What he doesn't like, you mustn't do;
Guard your tongue, rein your speech in,
Keep your counsel and your feelings within.

While distasteful to the modern mind, both Asian and Western, and certainly to today's young Thais, this reflects traditional Thai concepts of feminine conduct which are still propagated by the older generation and still condition the relative modesty of Thai women.

ganised mine-them-yourself tours on which you can keep what you find!

Fruits, Rice Noodles

Chanthaburi province is also famed for its high quality fruit, such as durian, rambutan, mangosteen and longan, and for its rice noodles which are of export quality.

In household goods, it is noted for the red reed matting produced by descendants of Vietnamese. The matting is made in sections joined by black tape and thus foldable; they are sold as both floormats and for the table.

One further curiosity is a legacy of French rule in the late 19th century when Chanthaburi was a part of colonial Cambodia. The French put troublesome locals in in the red-brick Khuk Khee Kai which had a slatted ceiling above which chickens were kept, hence the name Chickenshit Jail!

30 km to the north of town is Krating Waterfall in Kitchakut National Park. It tumbles spectacularly 400 metres over boulders. A trail runs alongside.

Further north is Khao Soi Dao Tai National Park, forested and centred round a 1670 metre peak, the highest in east Thailand. It is 745 sq km in extent and famed for its butterflies.

To the south of town about 15 km along the Trat road is Pliu Waterfall, which spills down a huge-rock face into a clear fish-filled pool. In the forest nearby, King Chulalongkorn built a pyramid for the ashes of a wife who drowned as well as a *chedi* in her memory. This spot was a favourite of hers.

Trat

The East's far outpost is Trat province, wedged between war-torn Cambodia and the waters of the Gulf. The boundaries are natural, for the Cambodian border is formed by a low mountain range. For tourists, the main interest lies in its beaches and islands, particularly Koh Chang, Thailand's largest after Phuket.

Koh Chang

The frontier nature of this province was highlighted in 1988 by the robbery murder of two Western tourists on Koh Chang, but this did bring about increased security consciousness as a benefit. The island hosts the headquarters of Mu Koh Chang National Park which encompasses 52 islands in total, one of which, Koh Kut, approaches Koh Chang in size.

There are now regular boat services to Koh Chang from the mainland port of Laem Ngop. The island is hilly and forested and has streams and waterfalls. The best beaches are on the western and southern shores, and most of them sport huts for rent, though none are very sophisticated yet. Koh Chang is still in the early stage of tourist develop-

A quick solution to the sweltering heat in the Chanthaburi area.

ment and should appeal to visitors who like to break new ground. A Bangkok developer plans to turn Koh Kradat into a massive resort comprising a 1300-room hotel, a marina, an ocean park, a health club and a golf course, with hydrofoil transport from the mainland.

There are also little-frequented beaches along the narrow spit of Thai territory that runs down the shoreline to Hat Lek, Little Beach, the eastern region's farthest point. One of them, Ban Cheun, has accommodation. This frontierland along Highway 318 is noted for its contraband trade with Cambodia, particularly at Khlong Yai, which appropriately can be translated as Big Channel.

The northern parts of Trat and Chanthaburi provinces along the Cambodian border are restricted for military reasons. The area is little inhabited until the border town of Aranyaprathet, over 200 km by road from Chanthaburi town.

There are several Cambodian refugee camps nearby, a sign of this region's recent unhappy history.

REGIONS OF THAILAND

The South

Southern Thailand is in many ways a world apart from the rest of the country. Geographically it is nigh on cut-off at Prachuab Khiri Khan where Burma almost reaches the Gulf of Thailand. From Chumphon downwards, Southern Thailand has a distinctive dialect and cuisine. The people are generally darker-skinned and influenced by long association and proximity with Malaya, Indonesia and India. In the very south, the population is largely Muslim and even speak a Malay dialect.

Andaman idyll, at Koh Phi-Phi, near Phuket.

Economically, rice-growing has minor importance whilst fishing, rubber production, coconut growing, tin mining and tourism are all major industries, giving a prosperity only second to Bangkok's. Tourism is growing rapidly on the strength of a wealth of fine beaches and beautiful waters, and skillful Thai hospitality, of course.

Climatically, the south is also unique in having two monsoons, with varying effects over the region. Thus Phuket is consistently stormy from July to October while Koh Samui's wet weather is from September to December.

The south is well served by public transport. There are buses to virtually everywhere and flights from Bangkok to

Koh Samui, Surat Thani, Phuket and Hat Yai are frequent. The railway goes from Bangkok all the way down the gulf coast with a branch that makes its way from Hat Yai to the Malaysian west coast.

Though officially the south begins at Chumphon, over 400 km south of Bangkok, for the purposes of this guide we start at the top of the peninsula, at Phetburi.

Phetburi

Phetburi is an old city which has played a strong part in Thailand's history. It was, for example, the end of a caravan route from India and derived much importance from that. It was a centre for the arts in the Ayutthaya period. In the 19th century, it became a favourite retreat of the modernising King Mongkut.

Phetburi means 'Diamond City', named after the gems found in the Phetburi River flowing through it. Though it contains its fair share of boring shophouses, there is still much charm in its meandering streets, along which can be found some interesting old houses and temples. Its main features are the river and the wooded mount on which perches Rama V's palace.

Khao Wang (Palace Mount) rises from the western edge of town. A winding cobbled path leads up through the frangipani trees; this used to afford horsedrawn access to the royal residence, known as Phra Nakhon Khiri, City on the Mount. Here King Mongkut, amateur scientist and astronomer, built not only a summer home but an observatory too. Today the Phetbumiroj Hall of the Khao Wang displays some of his scientific equipment and furniture.

Renovated in 1987 to a pristine white, the palace offers an intriguing array of neo-classical and traditional Thai architecture, connected by a fascinating maze of pathways, stairways and platforms around which to wander. It includes battlements, turrets and a large *chedi* atop the summit.

Annual Fair

In late January or early February at the annual fair, it becomes quite magical as the trees over the whole mount are laced with little golden lights; and a Sound and Light Show is performed dramatising its history. A traditional court orchestra, formed entirely of women, greets visitors at the stable by the cobbled pathway, while classical puppet shows are performed in an adjacent courtyard. At this same time, the frangipani trees are in bloom giving off their rich fragrance, while down below lies the bedlam of a temple fair, with its blaring music and bellowing hucksters.

On any clear day, fine views can be had of the town below and the sea beyond, while to the west limestone outcrops protrude incongruously from the ricefields. The mountains of the

Burmese border can be seen to rise in the distance.

Down in the town, the main sight is Wat Yai Suwannaram, across the river and beyond the market. It dates from the 17th century and its main chapel displays some of the oldest and best preserved murals in the country, featuring rows of praying saints. Around this is a cloister, and further outside a fishpond and a charming old wooden library.

Hotels in Phetburi are not at all fancy, in fact quite basic and inexpensive, rising only to about 200 baht a room, at the top end.

North of town about 3 km away lies Khao Luang Cave, where one can see a cavernful of magnificent stalactites and stalagmites and masses of much-worshipped Buddha images. A natural skylight in the high roof allows a brilliant shaft of light to beam down dramatically, especially around midday.

Some 13 km east of town is Hat Chao Samran, a beach lined with palm trees and fishing boats much favoured by local Thais.

Some 40 km southwest of town lies Kaeng Krachan Dam and National Park. The park spreads up to the Burmese border and, at nearly 3000 sq km, is Thailand's largest and actually covers almost half of the Phetburi Province. The reservoir within the dam has wooded islands, while the park features grasslands and forests, mountains and caves, rivers and waterfalls. It contains elephant, tiger, bear and boar, but a visitor is most likely only to see deer. Some Karen hilltribe people are known to live here too.

Cha-am

Cha-am is a long straight casuarina-lined beach favoured by Thais. It is some 30 km south of Phetburi. Delicious seafood is served at many places along this breezy beach and great black tractor-tyre inner tubes are for hire for lolling in the gently rolling waves. Big multi-coloured umbrellas provide shade on the sand, additionally furnished with deckchairs and tables, all at a price, which tourists should negotiate. There are several beach hotels charging from

The Royal family's waiting room at Hua Hin's train station.

"Far From Worries" Palace at Hua Hin.

150 baht (Arunthip) up to 1500 baht per day and more (Regent Cha-am).

A Hydrofoil service operates between Pattaya and Cha-am, costs about 450 baht first class, 350 baht second class and takes about 2 1/2 hours.

Hua Hin, A Royal Favourite

Some 30 km south of Cha-am, Hua Hin is Thailand's oldest beach resort, with royal origins, but it has got a long way to go before it attains the cachet or the look of Brighton or Deauville, two European beach resorts of somewhat similar origins. As the Prince Regent built a palace at Brighton in the early 19th century, so King Rama VI built one at Hua Hin in the early 20th century. Shortly after, in 1928, King Rama VII built his Klai Kangwon ("Far From Worries") Palace, which remains to this day an official royal residence. Lesser aristocrats took to building homes here and then the rising middle class began holidaying here, all of them finding it a pleasant and not-too-distant escape from Bangkok.

It developed in two ways; in the central cove as a fishing port built out on straggling wooden piers, and, to the south along a long, curving sandy bay as beachfront summer homes. It pretty much stayed that way until the late 1980s when the international tourist boom sent new hotels and guest houses springing up all over Hua Hin. Tall condominiums began to sprout along the crescent bay too.

Nevertheless, Hua Hin is no Pattaya, nor even a Phuket, as yet retaining its old world charm, though perhaps not for much longer. It still has children poking about amongst the rocks for shellfish and horse-rides along the beach; there are still far more local Thais than foreigners, frolicking or dozing, eating or drinking, chatting or contemplating, whichever is their wont, in the waves, on the sands, or under the parasols.

The trawler jetties are hives of activity from dawn to dusk and can be observed from several large waterfront seafood restaurants. This area is very pleasant for late afternoon strolls, with many old wooden houses along the seafront housing their obviously very relaxed inhabitants. Boats can be hired for trips across to Singtoh Island.

Accommodation goes from the simple guest house room at under 100 baht to around 2000 baht for one at the Hotel Sofitel Central, formerly the Railway Hotel and Hua Hin's *piece de resistance* since 1923. Located to the right of the main access road to the beach, Damnernkasem Road, this would seem like a scene out of Somerset Maugham polished up for the modern tourism age, with wooden panelling and brass fittings, and elegant topiary including elephant shapes in the forecourt.

Sports facilities at Hua Hin include golf, tennis, windsurfing, parasailing, sailing and horseriding, mostly developed by the Royal Garden Resort.

The Yellowbird seaplane service operates a twice daily flight to Hua Hin from Bangkok. (Check with your travel agent for more details.)

About 25 km further south lies the small town and fishing port of Pranburi which also sports the expensive Club Aldiana and Pranburi Beach Resort (1,400 baht per day upwards) and also the cheap Pransiri Hotel at a tenth the price.

Khao Sam Roi Yod

Just south of Pranburi lie the immense limestone outcrops of Khao Sam Roi Yod, which translated, means Three Hundred Peaks. This is a 98 sq km National Park, with mountains rising out of salt flats. It is spectacular just to ride around amongst these (motorbikes can be hired in Hua Hin at 200 baht a day), and climbing them gives terrific perspectives over this jagged mini-range, as it follows the curving bays of the coast. Towards the west one could over look the pineapple plantations all the way to the Burmese border mountains. Khao Krachom, one of the mountainous outcrops, rises 600 metres high and mountain goats known as *serow* live on these peaks, as well as porcupine and monkeys.

Thoroughly fabulous beaches at Hua Hin.

Limestone out-crops at Khao Sam Roi Yod (Three Hundred Peaks) National Park.

The park's most copious wildlife are birds, such as herons, egrets, kingfishers and sea-eagles. Most of the birdlife is migratory and at its height from November to January.

There are interesting caves near the fishing village of Bang Pu. Reached by boat, Phra Nakhon Cave is the favourite, especially since it was favoured by King Chulalongkorn as a resting place. Beams of light descend from holes in the roof.

Leaving the saltflats and winding in between some of the highest peaks, a river carries boatloads of trippers.

Accommodation: it is possible to stay in the park as there are a few bungalows for rent near the park headquarters.

Prachuap Khiri Khan

This is a fishing port set in a long and scenic bay. It almost has no rival in beauty on this whole coast. Curling from a Rock of Gibraltar-like headland in the south, Khao Lom Muak, it sweeps to an equally massive cape in the north. It is a magnificent sweep seen from any angle and particularly from the summit of Khao Chong Krajok, a steep conical hill by the sea. This has steps all the way to its summit and it is a stiff climb unless you take it slowly or are pretty fit. Mangy monkeys may pester you for food so it is best not to carry any; they are prone to snatch and grab. At the top sits Wat Thammikaram, nicely landscaped with

Prachuap Khiri Khan, stunning land and sea-scapes.

paths and steps, shrubs and *chedi*. There are great views all around – up an down the coast, round the bay to both headlands, out to sea and over the town, and all the way west to the blue Burmese mountains.

Fishing Port

Unfortunately for tourism development but fortunately for the continued naturalness of the place, the waters of Prachuap Bay are somewhat murky and unsuitable for bathing, so that only two sets of bungalows and one inexpensive concrete hotel front the beach. There is, however, plenty of fishing activity to observe at the pier where a constant stream of trawlers puts in and out and trucks trundle away the fruits of the sea. All along the seafront to the south, gutted fish are laid out to dry in the sun on basketwork trays.

Ao Noi, Little Bay

On the other hand, to the north of Prachuap Bay, turning left before the massive Khao Mong Rai headland, you come to Ao Noi, Little Bay, an exquisite sandy beach stretching from the great rock in the south (under which a fishing village shelters) to a conical hill at the north end. There is a small bungalow development here run by a German teacher; the accommodation is well-equipped with air-conditioning, and priced around 400 baht per day.

Islands

Boats can be hired from Prachuap Bay to venture around the islands near the southern headland and round to Ao Manao, Lime Bay, a good sandy beach to the south. This is difficult to reach by road along the seafront because of an intervening air base at which foreigners get turned back while local Thais wheel through!

Good seafood is to be had in Prachuap town and in the seafront restaurants and foodstalls.

Chumphon

Chumphon province, nearly 500 km south of Bangkok, is where the South really begins, ethnically and linguistically. From here on down, people tend to be darker-skinned and speak in a lilting and charming dialect.

Edible Bird's Nest

Chumphon town, 180 km south of Prachuap Khiri Khan, is unremarkable. The province's most notable features are the offshore islands where millions of swallows nest and provide high quality material for birds' nest soup. Indeed, Bangkok's pre-eminent Oriental Hotel uses Chumphon birds' nests in its Chinese restaurant as do many other Chinese restaurants in Thailand and all over the world.

Nest Hunters

Understandably, Ko Lang Kachiu, the most prolific isle, has restricted access, but visitors can go out in boats to watch the nest collectors scaling its pre-

Nest hunters scale precipitously for edible birds' nest in the cavernous islands near Chumphon.

cipitous cliffs in the mating season, January to September.

These islands are all reached from the port of Pak Nam (River Mouth) just 13 km from Chumphon town. To the north there are some good beaches – Ao Phanang Tak, Ao Thung Wua Laen, and Ao Baw Mao. Thung Wua Laen Beach hosts Chumphon Cabana Resort, with rooms costing 300-1000 baht per day and the area offers good diving opportunities from June to October.

Ranong

Ranong province lies to the west of Chumphon by the Andaman Sea and abuts the southernmost point of Burma. Thailand's west coast begins here.

There are some very good beaches in the province, although the area is largely mountainous and forested. In addition there are also many waterfalls and streams.

Verdant peaks soar from the Andaman waters at Phang-Nga.

Its foremost attraction is the hot springs of Wat Tapotharam, just outside Ranong town. There are three major sources which are called Father, Mother and Child Springs (Bo Paw, Bo Mae and Bo Luk), in family-conscious Thai style. The hot mineral water is piped from the temple to the Jansom Thara Hotel, where visitors can soak it up in a jacuzzi for 50 baht.

Phang-Nga

Phang-nga Bay is most people's vote for Thailand's most spectacular sight. Huge limestone outcrops jut jaggedly out of the water creating a unique seascape, given worldwide exposure and glamour by the James Bond film, 'The Man With The Golden Gun'.

The verdant peaks soar almost vertically and suddenly from turquoise waters, some 300 meters high and most of them honeycombed with caves and grottos. Few islands are inhabited but some host stilt-house communities of Muslim fisherfolk. Numerous operators offer tours of the bay with seafood lunches at a stilt village.

Phuket

Phuket Island hangs on the thread of the Sarasin Bridge from Phang-nga

Grotto-framed seascape at Pra Nang Beach.

province to the north. Some 50 km from top to bottom and averaging 10km in breadth, it is Thailand's largest island. Hilly and forested, it has a prosperous provincial capital grown wealthy on the proceeds of tin mining, rubber plantations and tourism.

Paradise Isle

Without a doubt, Phuket is about Thailand's premier beach resort destination. Blessed with several very fine bays on its west coast, it began to be frequented by independent travellers in the 1960s. Simple huts began to spring up along the beaches to accommmodate them and word started to spread about a new "tropical paradise". Phuket's major beaches are now lined with resort hotels.

Phuket now has an international airport capable of accommodating wide-bodied jets. It is positioned in the north–west of the island.

The most northerly beaches are quiet and little frequented. Mai Khao Beach is where sea turtles lumber ashore from November to February to lay their eggs, an event well worth watching. Further down, Nai Yang Beach is a long sweep of sand backed by casuarina trees with a fine coral reef about 1 km offshore. It is a national park with bungalows for rent, the standard being very

A southern boy shades from the sun at Patong Beach, Phuket.

basic. At the southern end, quietly setback in the trees, lies Pearl Village resort where a room costs about 1600 baht.

Further south is Bang Tao Bay, whose long sandy beach hosts the upmarket Dusit Laguna Resort. Then, round Son Cape along which the expensive and noted Pansea and Amanpuri hotels are located, comes Surin Beach. Swimming is not advised owing to an undertow but golf is available on a nine-hole public course. However Kamala Beach, further down, is safe for swimming at its nothern end.

Patong

The beach road cuts across a big headland and descends to Phuket's busiest bay, Patong. Sheltered by two massive capes and sporting a long flat sandy beach with a gentle shelf, Patong has inevitably become the most developed part of the island, with around fifty hotels of all grades. As well as all the usual hotel amenities, it offers a great variety of water sports from jet-skiing to windsurfing, from parasailing to scubadiving. At night, discos thud and bargirls yelp all around the central section – Patong has become a mini-Pattaya.

Clean Waters and Fine Coral

Over the southern headland lies little Relax Bay monopolised by Le

Ao Kata Beach at Phuket – clear, clean waters and fine sand.

Motor-cycles for hire at Patong Beach, Phuket.

Meridien Hotel; then, past another cape, comes the long straight stretch of Karon Bay and Kata Bay, interrupted only midway by a small promontory and the scenic and wooded Pu Island. At this point, there are fine corals in the clear waters, perfect for snorkelling. Snorkelling gear is available for rent from nearby bungalow resorts.

The accommodation on these beaches goes all the way from 70-baht per day huts up to the expensive all-in facilities of the Club Mediterranee.

At the southwestern tip of the island nestles Nai Harn Bay, Phuket's most picturesque in many eyes. Sheltered by extensive headlands and backed by sand dunes and a large freshwater lagoon, the beach shelves quite steeply and can be dangerous for swimming but is extremely scenic.

Accommodation ranges from 50-baht per day huts at the wooded southern end to 7000-baht per day suites at the Phuket Yacht Club, banked sensitively against the northern headland.

On the southeastern tip lies Rawai Beach, the first to be developed but now something of a backwater, not helped by its silty beach.

Best here are the diving opportunities offered by the offshore islands and Promthep Cape, Phuket's most southerly point.

Sea Gypsies

The east coast of the island is not noted for swimming beaches. Its main attractions are the Aquarium on Phanwa Cape and the sea gypsy village of Koh Siray. These previously nomadic fishing folk of Andaman Sea origins hold animistic beliefs and live in simple wooden houses. There is another village at Rawai Beach.

Old Elegance

Phuket town has more charm and elegance than the average Thai provincial city, featuring creditable Sino-Portuguese influences in shophouse, bank and hotel architecture in the town-centre and as well as in some fine mansions set behind large lawns in the northeast part. This elegance dates from the turn of the century and its early decades, when Phuket's star soared in successive tin and rubber booms.

Town Centre

Phuket town has about 50,000 inhabitants, around one third of the island's population, and for tourists it serves principally as a shopping and banking centre, with plenty of clothing bargains and money transfer facilities. It is also a transport interchange; twin bench pick-ups (*song thaew*) provide bus services to and from all points of the island. There is also the "baht-bus" but one should make clear before boarding that it is 1 baht.

The town has a night market, some cinemas and some *ramwong* Thai dancing nightclubs, but Phuket's nightlife centre is indubitably Patong Beach.

The interior offers Phra Taew National Park, some 20 km north of town. There are nice forest walks here and two waterfalls, Ton Sai and Bang Pae, most gushing in the rainy season from June to November.

The most scenic trips from Phuket, either day or overnight, are to Phangnga bay and Phi Phi Island (see Phangnga, page 231 and Krabi, page 226).

A sea gypsy plucking oysters at Ko Siray.

Back-to-back crescent beaches at Phi-Phi Island.

Krabi

Eastwards from Phuket across a gulf of the Andaman Sea lies Krabi province. Offering a wealth of fine beaches, rocky outcrops, offshore islands and water caves, Krabi has nevertheless only recently become developed as a tourism destination.

Phi-Phi Island

On the mainland, the main resort is Ao Nang, a beach to the west of Krabi town. The most famous island is Koh Phi Phi, a roughly H-shaped haven in the Andaman Sea celebrated for its back-to-back crescent beaches on a sandspit connecting the two mountainous land

Trang & Satun

The two most southerly provinces on the Andaman Sea are little visited by tourists. Trang is an ancient sea trading post and now a rubber-growing centre. Satun is 80% Muslim and offers Tarutao Marine National Park, a collection of remote islands of which Tarutao island is the largest. There is erratic boat access from Satun to several islands and accommodation may be found on some, including Tarutao. Not far south of Satun lies the Malaysian border.

Surat Thani Province

Surat Thani is Thailand's largest province but its main attraction lies offshore in the endless palm-fringed beaches of Koh Samui and neighbouring islands. The 30,000 people of Samui Island, Thailand's third largest, used to live almost entirely from coconut farming and sea fishing. Then in the 1970s international travellers began to discover its laid-back charms – the white sands, the warm sun, the crystal waters, the coral reefs, the tropical fish, the swaying palms, the forested hills – in other words, another veritable "tropical paradise"!

Koh Larn

The most popular excursion from Pattaya is to a group of offshore isles called Coral Islands, the largest of which

masses. The view from the heights of the western end, Koh Nok, is spectacular. Though there are no roads here, there is considerable boat traffic.

There is plenty of bungalow accommodation at both Ao Nang Beach and Koh Phi Phi.

Ferry connections to Phi Phi Island start from Krabi, Ao Nang and Phuket, taking from 1-1/2 to 3 hours.

is Koh Larn. The trip can be made in anything from speedboats to Chinese junks; the standard ferry boat takes 40 minutes and deposits you on a beach lined with souvenir sellers and foodstalls. You may possibly still be able to see some coral and tropical fish, either by snorkelling or going in a glass-bottom boat, but it's a long time since Koh Larn was worth the trip.

Koh Samui

Enterprising locals began to put up little thatched huts to shelter the visitors and make a little bit of extra cash. Now all the best beaches and most of the rest are lined with bungalow resorts offering anything from simple huts to elaborate villas, yet still single-storey. The island's low profile remains miraculously intact, probably by courtesy of a wise local administration.

Nevertheless, amenities become progressively more sophisticated year by year. Chaweng Beach on the southeast side has always led the way, being the first area to accommodate tourists and still having the longest spread of hotels. It is certainly Samui's grandest sweep of sand and features clear waters and some good snorkelling at the north end.

Over a headland to the south lies the second most popular beach, Lamai, straight and steep and interrupted in places by weathered boulders, most notably by the rock formation known as Grandmother and Grandfather Rocks on account of shapes somewhat similar to the female and male genitals.

The west coast is where all the ferries dock. The car ferry pulls into the almost deserted Thong Yang Beach. All the others dock at Na Thon, which is the main port and town.

All and sundry come to market here, locals for produce and tourists for clothes. It is a colourful market-place, in contrast to the laid-back beach life. Many cafes, banks, travel agents and second-hand bookshops provide additional business activity here.

The beaches tend to be silty on the north coast. The most developed are Mae Nam and Bo Phut. Near the north-eastern cape is a promontory on which sits the Big Buddha, a truly huge monument. In a secluded cove around this point lies Samui's most upmarket resort, Tongsai Bay.

Accommodation varies from huts as cheap as 30-baht per day to over 2,000-baht at the Imperial's premises.

Public transport around the island is provided by two *song thaew* routes, Na Thon-Lamai and Na Thon-Chaweng. If you want to go the short distance between Lamai and Chaweng, tough luck – the pick-up drivers operating may not allow it. However, jeeps, trailbikes, mopeds and bicycles are all available for rent at most beaches and in Na Thon.

Access by ferry is from three points on the mainland: Surat Thani, Donsak, and Khanom.

All operations have buses that pick

Village on stilts at Surat Thani.

Casting for fish at Koh Faan Bay, Samui Island.

Menam Beach, Samui.

up passengers at Surat Thani bus station, railway station and airport. Their touts will find you way before you find them, so all you have to do is pick your choice. The thing to avoid is the operators who pack you into a minibus and drive like maniacs to Donsak or Khanom over one hour away. Air-conditioned coach connections are the safest and Surat Thani port is the nearest. However, the port of departure can vary from hour to hour according to weather and tides, without passengers being warned. The car ferry, however, always goes from Donsak.

If you're in a hurry to get down to Samui from Bangkok, or vice-versa, there are several flights a day by Bangkok Airways in a 40-seater Dash 8. The airfield is near Big Buddha in the north-eastern corner.

To the west of Koh Samui lies the jagged shapes of the Ang Thong archipelago. This is a Marine National Park and can be visited in day tours offered by several operators.

Phangan Island

To the north of Samui lies Phangan Island (Koh Phangan), about two-thirds the size and far less developed. Their are fine beaches with hut accommodation on the south-eastern cape. Koh Phangan, though progressively developing, is extremely basic by comparison with Samui and attracts people who want as little commercialism as possible. Ferries leave from Na Thon.

Nakhon Si Thammarat

Nakhon Si Thammarat is the cultural centre of south Thailand with a history going back at least two millennia, though little of this is evident today. A city-state called Ligor existed then, the centre of the kingdom of Tambralinga and frequented by Chinese traders, who called it Tung Maling.

Srivijaya Empire

From the 7th to the 12th centuries, it was part, and some say the centre, of the Srivijaya Empire which encompassed the Malay Peninsula, Sumatra and Java. Srivijaya was a powerful Buddhist empire that controlled the trade of the crucial Straits of Malacca. It was Indian-influenced and friendly with China. Becoming a centre of Buddhist learning, with continual contact with Ceylon, the city was renamed Nagara Sri Dharmaraja, "City of the Sacred Dharma-King".

With the decline of Srivijaya, it became a local Malay-speaking principality and increasingly received Thai immigrants from the north. With the rise of Sukhothai to regional hegemony under King Ramkhamhaeng in the late 13th century, it came under Thai lordship and paid tribute to Sukhothai, and

Manohra & Nang Thalung

Two ancient Thai dramatic forms are now performed mostly only in the south, the shadow play and the *lakorn jatri*. Nakhon Si Thammarat is the centre of performance, being the southern city of leading cultural importance ever since Thais reached the southern peninsula around the 12th century.

Lakorn jatri is the oldest form of Thai theatre with origins in animistic rituals. *Jatri* means sorcerer and performers used always to be thought to possess magic power, particularly the troupe-master, who also presided over spirit ceremonies. Such was his reputation in the old days that young girls were forbidden to watch the plays lest they be bewitched into becoming one of his wives.

Over time, the rituals absorbed Indian influences to evolve into Hinduised dance drama portraying the Buddhist *jataka* tale called *Manohra*. Nowadays the southern form is always called *Manohra* rather than *lakorn jatri* and in its active and sometimes acrobatic movements we see something of the more energetic early Thai dance that existed before court refinements over the centuries.

The dancers wear brilliant bejewelled brocades and spired helmets. They used to perform the whole *Manohra* epic in episodes but now present only a greatly reduced and generalised version. In the old days too, a prime feature was improvisation in verse upon topical themes, and a troupe-master's reputation might rest on this ability. Troupes would even compete against each other. Today, popular *Manohra* often resembles *likay* in its contemporary recasting and impromptu versification.

The Manohra dance tells the story of a celestial being, the *kinnari,* half woman and half bird. *Manohra* (her name) is captured by a hunter while she and her handmaidens are bathing in a lake, by means of a noose provided by a *naga*, or mythical serpent. She is brought to Prince Suthon who falls in love with her, but war parts them. Suthon returns to find Manohra

Helmetted and bejewelled, the Manohra dancer performs movements inspired by ancient magical rituals.

has flown up to heaven. He sets out on an epic journey to win her back. Finally he succeeds and takes her back to earth.

This tale dates back at least to 3rd century India and interestingly appears to have universal currency: tales of swan-maidens are found in cultures from Japan to Persia to Scandinavia.

The southern shadow puppet form, similar to the Malay *wayang*, is called *nang thalung*. *Nang* means leather, of which they are made, and *thalung* comes from Phattalung, the southern town where it is still most often performed along with Nakhon Si Thammarat. The puppets are flat stencil figures cut from buffalo hide and held on sticks against a backlit screen. Translucent and smaller than their Malay counterparts, they portray the Ramakien.

Customarily, the shadow play was performed at temple fairs and festivals, but most often it was a paid performance at funerals, weddings and anniversaries. The troupe consists of puppeteers, singers, narrators and musicians. *Nang thalung* has naturally now been supplanted by cinema and TV as mass entertainment, but, revealingly, the Thai word for a movie is *nang*.

then from the late 14th century to the newly powerful Ayutthaya.

Cultural Centre of the South

Now known as Nakhon Si Thammarat, the city continues to be a religious, cultural and commercial centre, pre-eminent in the south. Whilst in recent decades it has been far outstripped commercially by Hat Yai, it remains the cultural centre of the south. It is especially known for two dramatic forms, the shadow-puppet play called *nang thalung*, and the variant of *lakorn* dance-drama known as *Manohra*, (see Box). Both of these are said to have originated in Nakhon, as the city is called locally.

Today, Nakhon Si Thammarat is somewhat of a backwater, the terminus of a branch line of the southern railway; it retains some of the dignity attached to its age while paradoxically at times being reputedly linked to gangsterism. The city lines a north-south main street, Rajadamnern Road, at the end of which is a National Museum. This displays a wide range of historical artifacts both from the provinces and from cultures with which it has associated in its long history, such as South India. (Open Wednesday-Sunday, 9am - 4pm; fee 10 baht). It is worth a visit.

Wat Phra Mahathat

The city's most sacred temple, Wat Phra Mahathat, is located a little north of the museum on the main street. It arose in the mid-13th century from earlier Srivijaya foundations and is one of Thailand's oldest. Its *chedi* is 77 metres tall and is topped by a great golden spire encrusted with precious stones. This stands within a tiled cloister and is surrounded by a gallery containing numerous Buddha images.

Also noteworthy is the temple museum inside Viharn Luang containing all the valuable objects donated by the pious, especially fine gold and silver pieces created by the town's skilled metalsmiths. Then there is the *bot* containing a Phra Singh Buddha, one of the three images contending to be authentic, the other two being in Chiang Mai and Bangkok.

Wat Phra Mahathat is a southern place of pilgrimage, particularly in October when the Chak Phra Festival takes place. Then there are performances of the shadow puppet theatre, *nang thalung*, and the dance-drama, *Manohra*, at the temple fair. On public holidays, many puppet theatres perform in front of the Boys' Secondary School.

Parts of the city's ancient earthed fortifications are still to be seen near Wat Maheyong. They originated in the 7th century, were renewed by Thai kings in the 15th and 17th centuries, and later topped by brick walls.

Handicrafts

Nakhon province is noted for its exquisite basketry made from the tough *yan lipao* climbing fern. Craftswomen produce truly excellent handbags, jewel boxes, trays and other objects in the fine tightly-knit weave. Nakhon Si Thammarat also specialises in nielloware, an inlaid silverwork craft, and the making of shadow puppets from buffalo hide.

Nielloware

Next to Wat Phra Mahathat there is a handicraft centre where a wide range of these craft products may be seen and purchased. Nielloware craftsmen can be seen at work in Chakrapetch Street where the craft began; in Nakhon In Tha Chang Road there are several arts and crafts shops.

Phattalung

Next south is Phattalung province, whose capital sits in the shadow of massive limestone mountains amidst luxuriant ricefields. It is also famed for its shadow puppet shows. There is a temple perched picturesquely at the northern end of Khao Ok Thalu, the great peak on the east side of the railway. Called Wat Tham Malai, it offers great views over the lush fields, forest clumps and rocky outcrops of Phattalung, and it also features a sacred cave.

Mieng Kham – A Taste Bomb

A short ride to the east of town brings you to the inland sea, Thale Luang, a great featureless expanse of water beside which locals are wont to loll and to snack on the delicious *mieng kham*, a wrap-it-yourself taste bomb. You get a plate with portions of peanuts, lime, toasted coconut, dried shrimp, chili, ginger and garlic, then you bundle up your choice in wild tea leaves, pop it in your mouth, and hope for the best. It usually tastes very good.

Some 30 km north-east of town lies

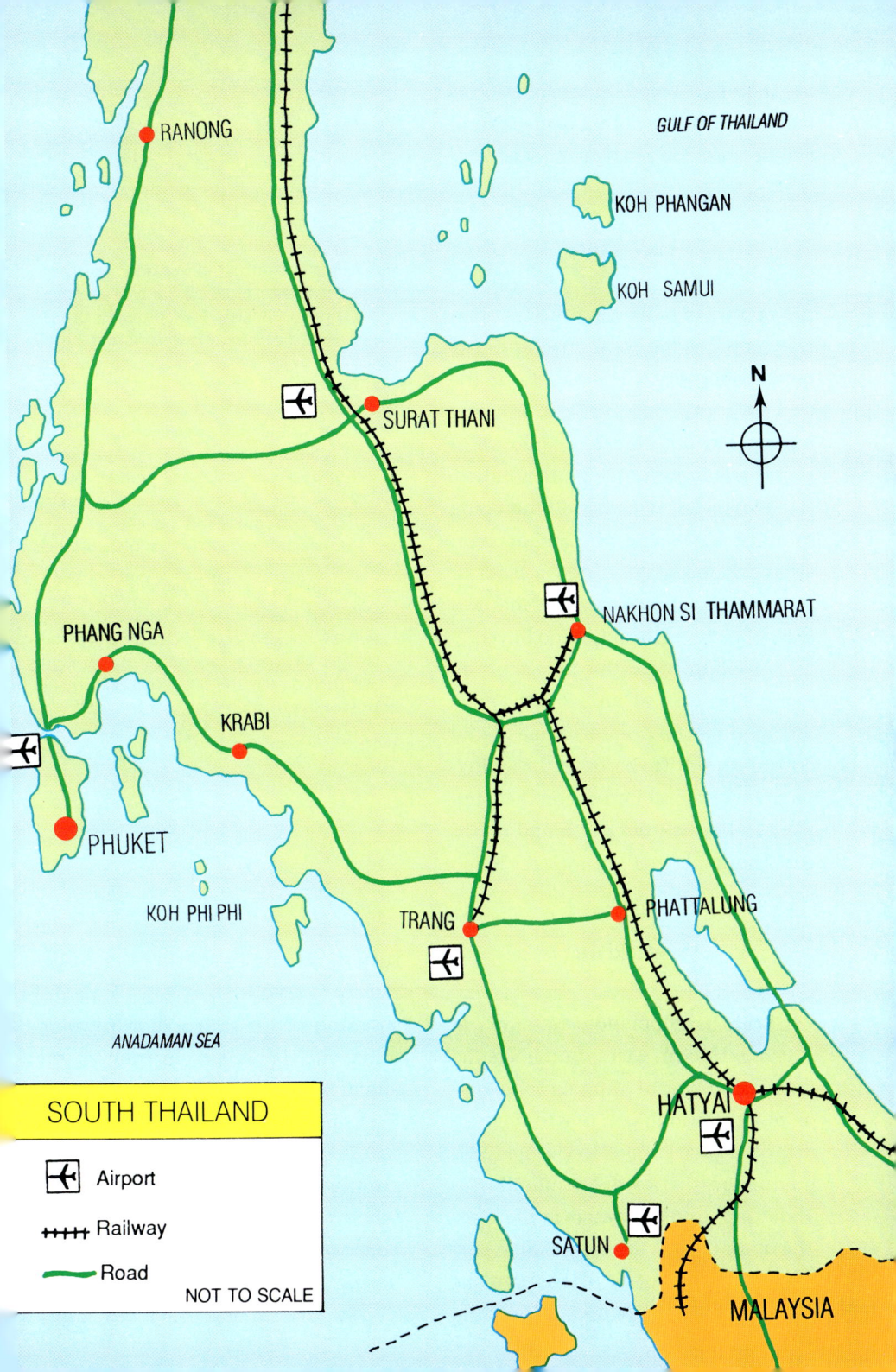

the Thale Noi Waterbird Sanctuary. This reedy lake shelters dozens of species and can be toured in passenger boats.

Hat Yai

Songkhla province is the commercial centre of the south, owing to the brash young city of Hat Yai, due to the trade in both goods and flesh, grown so especially with traffic from Malaysia, a short drive or train ride to the south.

Whether it is Thai clothing going south or Malaysian and Singaporean electrical goods going north, legal or smuggled, business is good and the town centre bustles with shops and buyers.

At night-time, the bars start to swing, the discos to blare and the massage parlours to give the come-on, and downtown Hat Yai becomes the Malaysians' favourite all-purpose brothel, supplied with girls from north and northeast Thailand.

Songkhla

With its population estimated at 130,000, Hat Yai well outnumbers the demure provincial capital, Songkhla, an ancient fishing port and former city of the Srivijaya Empire. It is located on a promontory between an inland sea, Thale Sap, and the waters of the Gulf. The inland side is the busy fishing port while the seafront is a long straight sandy beach, Hat Simila. Fringed by casuarinas and lined with a great variety of foodstalls, this is a walking and snacking beach rather than a swimming one; on a rock in front of the Simila Hotel there is a bronze mermaid, like Copenhagen's, with Cat Island (Koh Nu) chasing Mouse Island (Koh Meo) out to sea beyond. At this point, a hill (Khao Noi) rises to the west giving a panoramic view over the whole area from its top.

The inland waterside has many

Snake blood drinking

Hat Yai has become a Chinese gourmet mecca in the last decade, especially for bird's nest and shark's fin soup fanciers. Most bizarrely, the city has gained fame for snake blood drinking, largely performed by Malaysian and Singaporean tourists. These ethnic Chinese visitors relish cobra cocktails and numerous stalls and restaurants now cater for the gory predeliction.

The Chinese believe that drinking snake blood and eating snake gall bladder boosts virility, eases the circulation and enhances eyesight. The customer picks his choice of live serpent, which is promptly strangled, washed with water and white liquor, and slashed open lengthwise. The blood gushes out into a glass and the gall bladder is extracted.

Usually one cobra gives half a glass of blood, to which white liquor is added; the superstitious visitor then downs the brew and presumably hopes for the best.

Raging Bulls of the South

Bullfighting is a popular southern sport but you'll never see a toreador in the ring, for Thai bulls fight each other, charging, butting, locking horns and wearing each other down in trials of strength and courage that can last hours.

The animals are traditionally cart-pullers, ploughers, and log-haulers, and their owners have long been given to making wagers with each other over who had the stronger beast, the matter being settled in a makeshift ring. In time this has developed into a regular sport with permanent rings in such places as Hat Yai, Songkhla and Nakhon Si Thammarat.

The bulls are well-prepared for each fight, with uphill or mudtrack training runs, sparring partners, choice diets of young grass and plenty of eggs, and night-times in mosquito-proof pens, usually close to the arena for familiarisation.

On fight day, the animals are led into the ring in satin cloaks and colourful horncaps, decked with garlands and smeared with 'magic paste', such as scary hog badger fat. In the stands, frantic betting takes place and excitement mounts – it's a great day out for southern farming folk and gamblers of any ilk.

A gong sounds, the handlers turn the bulls face-to-face, and away they go. They charge, they butt, they withdraw, they butt again, they lock horns, they shove with all their might. This goes on until one animal concedes by turning away or falls down and does not get up, in which case the other is feted as winner. If they lock horns permanently, the fight is declared a draw.

Southerners enjoy this spectacle all the way from village skirmishes up to inter-provincial championships, paying up to 500 baht for all-day admission and betting thousands. Let's hope the bulls enjoy it too.

---

pleasant meandering streets with some interesting buildings showing evidence of Sino-Portuguese influence in architecture. The finest building in town, an old (1878) Chinese-style mansion, now serves as the National Museum and houses artifacts from several periods.

Pattani, Yala, Narathiwat

The three southernmost provinces of Pattani, Yala and Narathiwat are more Malay in character than Thai, and the majority of their inhabitants are Muslim. They used to form one independent principality.

The largest buildings in the towns are often mosques, while commerce is Chinese-dominated.

The coast features some good beaches and picturesque fishing villages. Not a south of Yala and Narathiwat lies the Malaysian border.

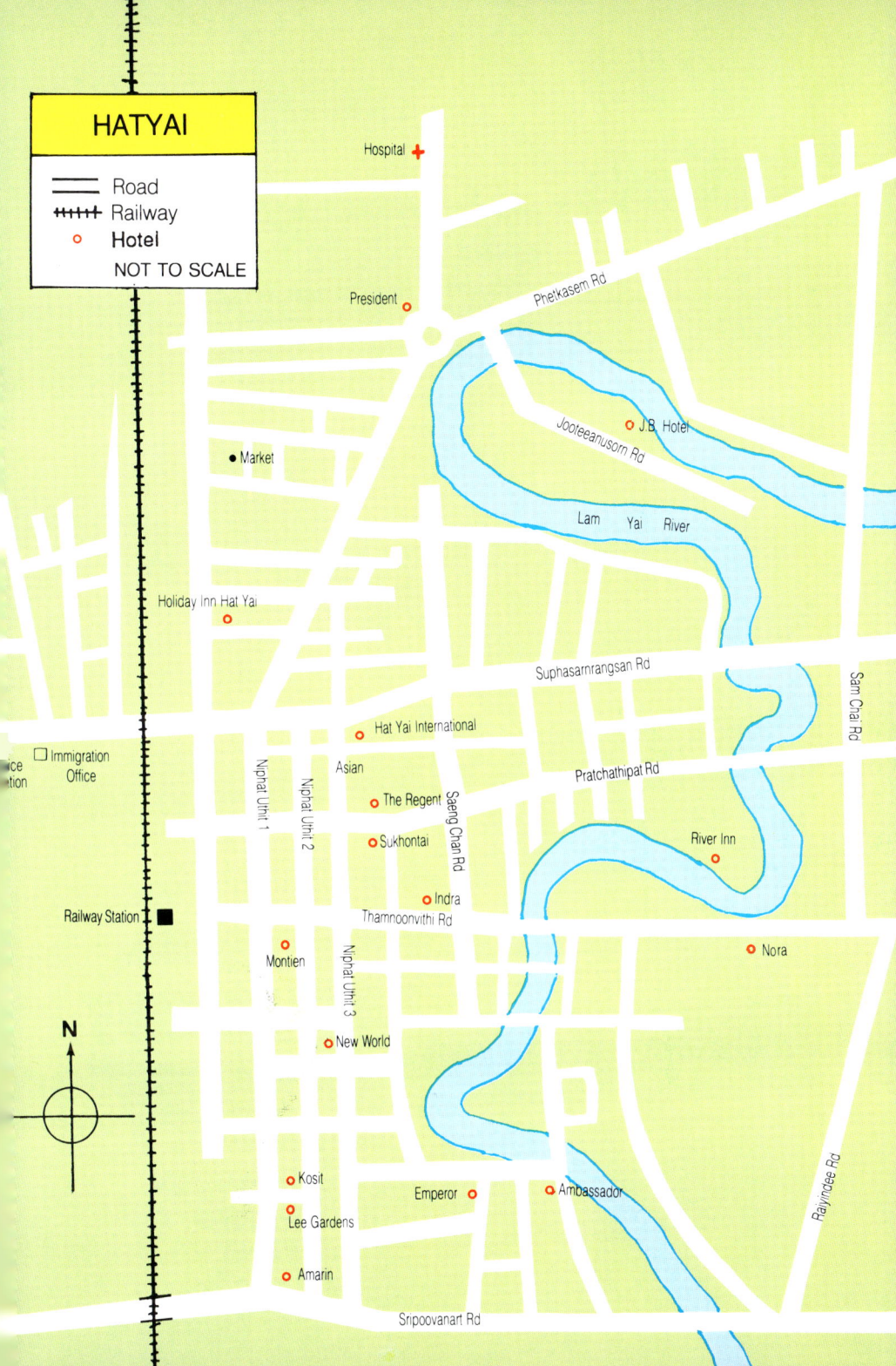

LIFESTYLE • FESTIVALS • CRAFTS

People

Thailand is a nation with a distinct and strong culture yet significant minority cultures thrive within it. The dividing line, in some cases blurred, is ethnicity.

Ethnic Thais actually form no more than 80% of the population, whilst over 10% is made up by Chinese. In the southern border regions, there is much Malay blood, whilst Vietnamese and Cambodians have entered in fair numbers in recent decades. Indian merchants can be seen to trade in the cities.

Thai school band boy.

Tribal Groups

In addition to these larger racial groups, Thailand is inhabited by tribal peoples too, notably the Karen, Hmong, Yao, Lisu, Akha and Lahu. Lastly, and almost forgotten are the remnants of the Mon people who predated the ethnic Thais in this territory.

Despite this diversity, Thailand is not a country characterised by racial or even cultural conflict. The largest minority, the Chinese, are well assimilated and all groups enjoy freedom of religious practice. Above

The Meo (Hmong), one of many hill-tribe folk in the north.

all, those categorised as ethnic Thai are nonetheless in large part an intermingling of Thai blood with all the other peoples who have found a home in this territory over the centuries – Mon, Khmer, Lao, Indian, Malay, Chinese, Burmese, Vietnamese.

Quite obviously though, the ethnic Thais are the flour of this rich cake. They are the central and dominant force that formed modern Thailand. Who are they? Where did they come from?

Chinese Influence

There is lively dispute over their early origins but what is certain is that they inhabited the part of south-west China now called Yunnan in the first millenium AD. Holding animist beliefs and organised under tribal chieftains, they came together in the seventh century in a kingdom called Nanchao. Much of the patterns of Thai family and farming life most likely originated in this early civilisation.

Intriguingly, tribal Thai groups still exist today, all across from Assam in northeastern India to Hainan Island off southeast China.

In north Laos and northwest Vietnam, for example, there are the Thai Dam (Black Thai), and in northeast Burma, the Thai Yai (Greater Thai). The Thais began migrating away from southwest China towards the end of the first millenium under pressure from the growing Han Chinese majority.

Lao Tribes

The major migration flow was down the Mekong valley and over into the Ping River valley, the area now forming northwestern Laos and northern Thailand. The Lao tribes eventually formed a kingdom centred on Luang Prabang in the 14th century, whilst the Thais formed kingdoms in the 13th century around Lamphun, Chiang Mai, and Sukhothai. Lesser principalities grew up at U-Thong in the central plains and Nakhon Si Thammarat in the southern peninsula. Soon after, in the 14th century, the central kingdom of Ayutthaya was established.

A charming Lisu, heavily laden with tribal neckwear.

Buddhist and Hindu Notions

All this brought the Thais into close contact with Mon and Khmer civilisation, which until then, were dominant in the area. Thai rulers adopted Buddhism and Hindu notions of kingship: Thai civilisation as we know it today emerged. The Indian cultural influence was reinforced by the frequent visits of merchants and monks from the subcontinent.

Ethnically and culturally, Thailand consolidated in the next centuries, to become a unique and powerful civilisation. Only in the nineteenth and twentieth centuries did major new influences arrive – huge Chinese immigration and considerable Westernisation. In recent decades, the Indochinese wars have caused massive displacement of Vietnamese, Laotians and Cambodians into Thai territory; most recently, Burmese have been fleeing their regime.

Amidst troubles all around, Thais have remained independent and become increasingly prosperous. The population is now reckoned to be 56 million and rising. To get a perspective on this, let us turn back to the year 1000 AD; the land is reckoned to have contained just 1 million people then. For 1500 AD it was reckoned at 2 million and in 1800 at 3 million. At the turn of this century, the figure was around 7 million, yet by 1950 it was 19 million and in 1975 there were 42 million Thais. Thailand's agricultural wealth had handled the growth so far but there was a limit to the numbers the land could comfortably sustain, and that limit was on the horizon.

Fortunately the authorities had become aware of the advisability of a national birth control programme if economic and environmental disaster from overpopulation were to be averted. From a 3% growth rate in the '60s, the rate was cut to 2.5% by 1980 and is now around 1.5%. This is a notable achievement and a tribute to the flexibility of Thai culture and its ability to modernise.

Population Control

No small credit either should go to a certain high official named Mechai who took to touring the city slums and rural villages blowing up condoms like balloons and distributing them to delighted children. The kids grew up with the idea of contraception and the parents took note of what he said about the economic advantages of smaller families. Today his name is immortalised: a condom is popularly called a "mechai"!

The population spread is strangely uneven. Whilst greater Bangkok has at least seven million souls (and some statisticians claim 10 million) and the rest of the Central Plains plus the eastern region has about 10 million people, Isan has almost 20 million. Yet Isan is the poorest region while the centre with Bangkok is the richest. Economically,

Chiang Mai girls, renown for their beauty, traditionally costumed for the Candle Dance.

the south follows closely, but it has only about 8 million people in its extensive length. The north is approaching 12 million.

Tribal Diversity of the North

The north is the most ethnically diverse region on account of the many hill tribes who occupy the forested mountains and practise slash-and-burn agriculture. These peoples have migrated southwards from southern China since the 19th century in a process akin to that of the Thais themselves one thousand years before.

There are estimated to be 550,000 hilltribe people in Thailand. About half of these are Karen who are widespread north and west of Chiang Mai and all the way down the Burmese border to Kanchanaburi. The Lisu, Lahu and Akha cluster near the northern border with Burma, whilst the Yao are found mostly in the area between Chiang Mai and the Mekong River. The second largest group, the Meo or Hmong numbering 80,000, are widespread throughout the upper northern provinces around Chiang Mai.

These are the most numerous tribes. They are all animists, practising nature worship; some tribes are also ancestor worshippers whilst some groups have adopted Buddhism or Christianity. The Karen are notable for the proportion of Christians. Each tribe has its own language, dress, customs and beliefs. Their most striking aspect is undoubtedly the

women's costumes which are colourful, even gorgeous in the case of the Lisu, or silver-laden as with the Akha. Many hill tribe groups earn high income by cultivating the opium poppy.

Lanna Thai

For all their fame, the hill tribes

School children making "wai", the traditional Thai greeting.

only account for 5% of the north's population. The majority people of Lanna Thai, as the northern region is still fondly called, after the ancient kingdom that flourished there from 700 years ago, are of a type that can be distinguished from other Thais. They are marked by an ivory skin colour and "Chinese" eyes, besides by their speaking the seven-toned northern dialect. Lanna Thai was long isolated. It only came under Siamese hegemony in the 19th century and even early in this century, travellers needed days of river and elephant-borne transport to reach it from Bangkok. The people have thus preserved ancient traditions and are particularly noted for the quality of their craftsmanship such as in wood and silver, basketry and lacquerware.

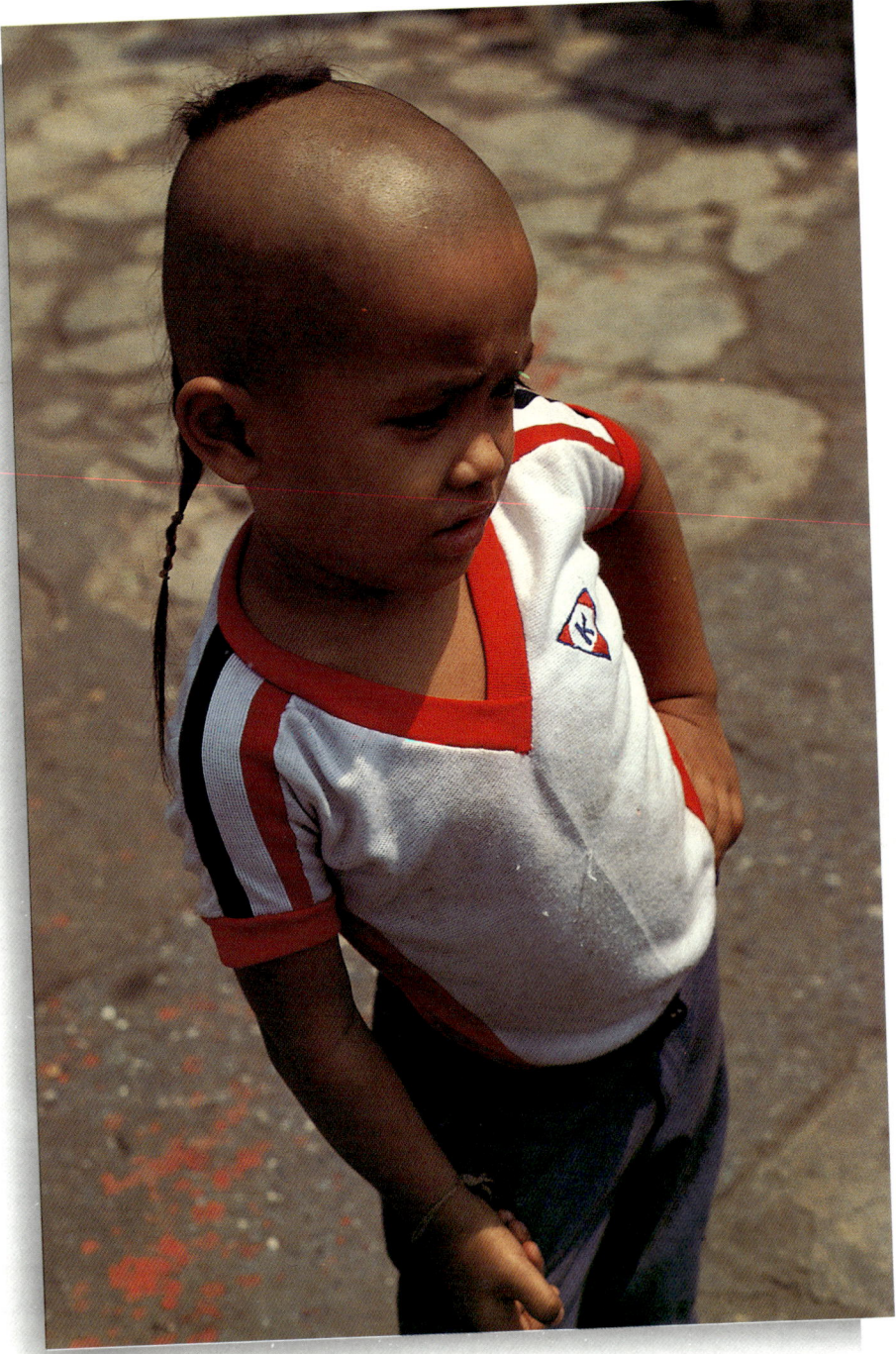

Young boys keep a strand of hair until the correct age for circumcision.

A toddler amuses himself.

Construction workers are vital to the building of the Bangkok high-rises.

Close Cousins

In the north-east, the vast majority of people are of Lao descent, speak Lao dialect, and actually call themselves Lao. The Isan region was populated by Lao people from the 14th century onwards as part of that southward migration of the Thai peoples – known as Tai to ethnologists – of whom the Lao are a major group. Isan was part of successive Lao kingdoms until the 19th century when Bangkok established control over the territory. The Lao are thus close cousins of the Thais and the two languages are quite similar.

Northeastern culture has distinct features besides the language, notably in music and food. The staple food is sticky rice and popular favourites are grilled peppered chicken, *gai yang*, and spicey papaya salad, *som tam*. Natives of a harsh, infertile land, they are also much given to finding their protein where they can, hence a popular predilection for fried grasshoppers and locusts.

Life may be tough, but it is also for living, and Isan people are very fond of a song and dance. The musical style is highly rhythmic, indeed hypnotic, with much playing of the *khaen*, a large pan-pipe made from bamboo. To go with it, as elsewhere in Thailand, there's rice whisky and *ramwong*, the graceful folk dance with delicate hand gestures.

Northeasterners themselves have

distinct features, typically snub noses, dark skins from working the fields (and some Khmer blood), and happy-go-lucky natures. Very many are to be found working elsewhere in Thailand, such is the dearth of well-paid work in Isan, especially since northeasterners constitute over a third of the national total. Bangkok is full of Isan *tuk-tuk* drivers and waitresses, ditch-diggers and maids.

The Chinese in Bangkok

The most noticeable thing about Bangkok in ethnic terms is the high proportion of Chinese, and not just in the traditional Chinatown. Chinese immigrants began arriving in significant numbers in the 19th century as the city constantly grew and needed both labourers and traders, and they only ceased coming when the creation of the People's Republic prevented it. They opened shops and restaurants, pawnshops and export-import businesses, and went on to create great corporations and major banks. Most of Thailand's biggest enterprises are Chinese-dominated, e.g. Siam Cement and the Bangkok Bank.

The same can be said of much of Southeast Asia, but it would be wrong to regard these Thai Chinese in the same way as those in, say, Malaysia or Singapore. They certainly don't see themselves as a distinct culture but more as a certain shade of Thai. Assimilation has been promoted both by official policy and by Thai culture. For example, Chinese language schools have long been strictly controlled by the government and all children must learn to read and write Thai in primary school. In addition, Thai Buddhist tradition is readily accepted by the Chinese and easily accommodates them in turn.

All this means that, though the Chinese may continue to look different and dominate business and commerce, they are culturally very much a part of the mainstream these days, with only some of the older people retaining clear cultural distinctness, such as the old ladies in bow-legged black pants who speak halting Thai and visit the clan-house daily. There is much inter-marriage with ethnic Thais, and has been for ages, so that probably most Bangkokians have Chinese blood these days. The king himself does. And most young Chinese today can neither read nor speak their ancestral language, nor think of themselves as Chinese unless prompted.

Bangkok is a Sino-Thai city and all of Thailand's towns contain significant numbers of Chinese businesses; whether the signs are in Chinese or Thai or English, most shopkeepers and restauranteurs have Chinese blood. Meanwhile, farming and government service is overwhelmingly ethnic Thai. For example, in the prosperous and fertile Central Plains, the ethnic Thai farmer sells his rice to an ethnic Chinese middleman but pays his taxes to an ethnic Thai official. Yet all are Buddhists and all speak Thai.

Some of these distinctions are breaking down: talented Thais, for example, are more and more taking to business as a respectable career and doing well at it, while the children of Chinese families are increasingly joining the professions and becoming government doctors, engineers and economists.

Thais in the South

Further south, however, the old pattern is very strong and many people are actually Malay. Virtually all business is in the hands of Chinese. These southern states, Yala, Pattani, Narathiwat and Satun were once Malay sultanates. These Thais stay largely in farming and fishing and leave commerce to the Chinese.

The people from Chumphon to Narathiwat are distinct in dialect and appearance. Farmers, fishermen, tin-miners and rubber planters, speak a quick sing-song Thai that is often amusing to the central Thai. Southerners, whose cultural centre is the ancient city of Nakhon Si Thammarat, are generally darker-skinned and have curly hair.

Language

Thailand is diverse in both people and speech but there is a consensus view on both. Whilst the women of the north are regarded as ideal in beauty, the dialect of the Central Plains is considered the standard. It is this brand of Thai

There are more than a million Muslims in Thailand mostly in the South.

which is taught in schools nationwide, which is used for nearly all printed materials, and which is spoken on television and radio (in the same sense as 'BBC English' in Britain).

Thai is one of the Sino-Tibetan languages which are spoken by peoples in a broad swathe from Tibet to Manchuria, and southwards in Burma, Thailand and Laos. It is monosyllabic in form and tonal in pronunciation. Words are integral and do not change form according to tense, gender, position or any other factor. The grammar is therefore fairly simple – the main problem for learners is pronunciation, for each syllable is composed of a sound spoken in a certain tone.

Thai is similar to Chinese, the prin-

A Sukhothai girl, costumed for the Loy Krathong festival.

cipal language of the Sino-Tibetan group, both functionally and in some vocabulary (such as numbers), but the encounter of the Thai people with Mon-Khmer civilisation and Buddhism introduced a considerable new vocabulary of largely polysyllabic words derived from Mon, Khmer, Pali and Sanskrit. These words tend to express more sophisticated concepts. The result today is that Thai academic and religious language is full of polysyllables whilst the speech of the ordinary people is much more monosyllabic.

In this, it can be compared to English: the more educated English speakers are, the more they use long French and Latin-derived words rather than succinct Anglo-Saxon terms. Historically too, Thai and English were transformed at roughly the same time, the European middle ages when Thai vocabulary was considerably Indianised as English was Latinised.

Nevertheless, most Thai words are short and sharp, with clipped endings, in contrast with English's elision, the running of one word into another. And Thai has endless possibilities for word-play, because so many words have the same sound at the end or, even better, are identical except in tone. This gives rise to the punning banter that Thais are so fond of, delighting in off-the-cuff word games of friendly abuse.

Thai is a poetic language too, not in the usual European sense of melodious sound, like Italian, but in the sense of the way that concepts are expressed, like Chinese.

The Thai writing system derives from the 13th century kingdom of Sukhothai and is credited to the inventiveness of King Ramkhamhaeng himself, the first great Thai monarch, though this is now in dispute. It is based on the Indian Devanagari system as adapted by the Khmers. It consists of 44 symbols plus 32 signs, and is thus not the kind of thing you can pick up in a weekend!

All Thais understand standard Central Thai and all the varied ethnic groups can speak Thai to some extent, from the total fluency of the Indian cloth merchants of Bangkok to the odd words of the hunter-gatherer "Spirits of the Yellow Leaf" people of remote northern Nan.

LIFESTYLE • FESTIVALS • CRAFTS

Religion

Thais are Buddhists, after their fashion. Well over 90% of the population profess the Buddhist religion yet a great deal of what they practise is superstition rather than spiritual enlightenment. Faith in Thailand is an agglomeration of beliefs and customs acquired through the millennia on the long road to modern nationhood. As such, whether it's called Buddhism or Brahminism or animism or just plain old wives' tales, the faith of the Thai people is the essential underpinning of the society.

Inside a viharn, a meditation hall and a place for preaching sermons to monks.

A typical day for a Bangkok housewife might go like this. Soon after getting up at dawn, she will wait in the street outside to give alms in the form of food to the monks from the local temple on their early rounds. Out shopping at midday, travelling in a bus in the main shopping district, she passes the renowned Erawan Shrine and does a respectful *wai* to it. Walking home later, she passes a sacred tree encircled with chiffon scarves which is known to harbour a good spirit; she offers it some food and asks it to tell her a winning lottery number. That

night, she goes to her local temple and shakes a holder full of wooden sticks; when one falls out, she checks its number, takes a corresponding slip and reads her fortune.

This Thai woman, all in one day, first made merit according to Buddhist tradition, then worshipped at a Brahmin shrine; thirdly she practised animism, and finally sheer superstition. None of these things took very long and none were exceptional, just part of the day's business between work and shopping and taking care of the family, eating, sleeping and having fun. Quite probably, she regards them all as Buddhism, no matter what a theologian may say. And she certainly could not imagine life without them. In Thailand life and faith are all one.

Thais swim in a rich soup of belief that permeates just about every activity. When a go-go girl in a Patpong bar mounts the stage to begin her dancing session, she will *wai* to the bar's spirit shrine, as will a factory worker starting the day's shift to the factory shrine. When a new massage parlour is opened, Buddhist monks will perform an inauguration ceremony, as they will for a new Thai Airways jumbo jet before its inaugural flight. A kick-boxer will perform elaborate rituals of respect and reverence to the Buddha and to his trainer before a fight; and fishermen will set off a load of firecrackers on the bows of their trawler to scare off evil spirits as they set sail.

But it is Karma in the End

All these rites ensure things will go as well as they possibly can, and if something goes wrong – a broken heel on the dance stage or an emergency landing by the jet – it's the result of *karma* and not your disrespect, for you have done the right thing, unless perhaps you performed the rite wrongly, in which case any trouble serves you right!

Charms May Help

The most ubiquitous expression of belief is the lucky charm, for just about everybody wears one. Men in particular are given to amulets that they wear around the neck, most often bearing the image of Buddha. They are reckoned to ward off evil – accidents, malicious spirits, whatever – or on the upside they may attract beautiful women. Be they of terra cotta or stone or silver, life would be too risky without them, and some command huge prices if they are reckoned to be especially high-powered. Another male predilection is for tattoos, especially up-country. Fishermen frequently sport full torsos of

Monks file through a padi field in Surin.

arcane symbols and scripts designed to ward off evil.

Spirit Houses

The most picturesque manifestation of animism is the spirit house. Spirits live everywhere, so most Thais believe, and they are the guardians of the land. If you want to build on the land, its spirits are inevitably going to be disturbed so they need a house of their own. A displaced spirit is an unhappy one and may cause mischief, so it should be placated with a nice new home. Not only that, the spirits should be fed daily!

Consequently, every home, office block, shop, school and so on has a spirit house in its grounds or, inside the building. The poorest people may only manage a little plywood affair, while the richest may erect grandiose marble shrines. Two conspicuous Bangkok spirit houses, actually Brahmin shrines, face each other at the Gaysorn intersection. Where Rajdamri Road meets Ploenchit Road is the huge World Trade Centre shrine, and diagonally opposite the Erawan Shrine.

Erawan Shrine

The Erawan Shrine is the country's most famous. It dates from the building of the old Erawan Hotel in 1956. A series of accidents occurred to workers so the owners hurriedly erected a spirit house on the corner of the site in the hope that the mischievous spirits would settle down and stop causing havoc. Sure enough, they did, and this mightily impressed Bangkok's populace. The Erawan Shrine must have special powers, they thought, and have done so ever since, so that the shrine is thronged with devotees from dawn till night, presenting flower garlands and burning incense, offering lighted candles and little wooden elephants – and making wishes for personal and family good fortune. Some worshippers have even donated massive two-metre tall teak elephants: several line the back wall. The Hindu god Brahma, you see, rides upon an elephant.

Worship and prayer are as old as human society: the forms change but the essence continues. The Thai people were animists until they migrated southwards out of China over a thousand years ago. Encountering Mon culture, particularly the Buddhist and Brahmin religions.

While animism had explained the forces of nature and protection against their harm, Brahminism offered formalised celebration of man as a higher being. It became particularly associated with the monarchy, governing court ritual and etiquette at least from the Sukhothai period, and it still touches every ordinary Thai through the traditional wedding ceremony and the countless Brahmin shrines around the country.

Buddhism is a profound and sophisticated faith, more a philosophy than a religion, and its adoption by the early Thai kingdoms was the single-most important event in Thai civilisation. It crowned the other beliefs with several supremely useful elements: it gave meaning to the individual, it explained existence, it provided order and direction in daily life, and it offered hope for a better future life.

Thai culture was ennobled by Buddhism and its guidance and its rituals have shaped both the inner and the outer life of the Thai people for nearly one thousand years. In their minds, the animist and Brahmin beliefs and all other superstitious practices such as astrology and fortune-telling are most certainly subordinated to – if not clearly distinguished from – the supreme role of the Lord Buddha.

Karma

Essentially, Buddhists believe that life does not begin with birth and end with death but that each human soul has a chain of lives. In each life, your deeds condition the kind of life you will have in the next rebirth; this is called 'karma'. Karma determines that selfishness and craving lead to suffering, whilst compassion and love bring about well-being and happiness. Therefore, to attain peace of mind, one must eliminate desire; ideally, following the Buddha's teaching, each soul eventually achieves enlightenment, or Nirvana, a state of complete equanimity and oneness with one's surroundings and the end of the cycle of rebirth.

This is the philosophical core of Buddhism, and it colours the aspirations of all Thai people, who know deep down that "whatsoever a man soweth, that shall he also reap" better than most Christians. (The Thais have a saying for it which translates "do good and get good, do bad and get bad".) In practice, for the Thais are nothing if not pragmatic, the central activity of the Thai Buddhist faithful, i.e. the great majority of citizens, is merit-making.

Merit-Making

Making merit is a formularised method of improving your karma. Most often it is an act of charity towards the monkhood – giving food in the early morning, presenting new robes, making donations to the temple; or it is an act of worship – offering flowers and incense, candles and gold leaf to a Buddha image. A popular, yet somewhat absurd, way of merit-making is to release caged birds to the sky or put captured fish and tortoises back in the temple pond – only for the vendors to go and catch the creatures again and resell them!

Entering Monkhood

The highest form of merit-making is ordination into monkhood, which every male should do at least once in his life, according to Thai tradition. This is the supreme act of merit-making, for both men and women; though a woman cannot enter monkhood (the order of nuns, *mae chi,* is not equivalent), the mother of a monk gains equal merit by her son's ordination. Entering monkhood is a public notice of a man's intention to follow the Buddha's teaching, but he need not stay all his life, neither is there stigma in returning to secular life.

Nevertheless, the traditional minimum period is three months, usually during the rains retreat, the high rainy season months from mid-July to mid-October. In the old days before paved roads, it was difficult to travel, so muddy were the tracks and paths, and so this period was appropriate for staying inside the temple precinct and concentrating on spiritual pursuits. The tradition survives, though without absolute confinement.

Within the monastery, men abide by strict monastic discipline, observing 227 rules of behaviour. If a monk breaks one of the four principal laws – against murder, theft, sexual relations or professing magical powers – he should be

TOD KATHIN ... something for the monks

At the end of Buddhist Lent each October, Thai people traditionally present gifts of new robes and personal necessities to the monkhood. Ceremonial presentations called *tod kathin* take place for the ensuing lunar month. The phrase means roughly 'laying offerings before all the monks in a temple'.

The practice varies in detail from place to place.

One interesting variety is that of Kamphaeng Phet town in the North where a grand *tod kathin* takes place in the grounds of the ruined Wat Phra Kaew. At Ok Phansa, several hundred monks from local monasteries sit at right in serried ranks at a ceremony attended by the provincial governor and hundreds of local people.

The people sit by little numbered trees with a candle atop and a pail of gifts and robes underneath. When the governor has completed his speech and the monks their chanting, each monk is allotted a number at random and goes to find the corresponding tree. After some inevitable confusion in the darkness, the monks all find their tree and receive respectful *wais*, new robes and a bucket of soap and tea, sugar and matches, condensed milk and detergent, daily necessities and little luxuries to use in their temple.

There are many kinds of *tod kathin* ceremonies but all serve to benefit the monkhood and bring merit to the donors and all take place between the 11th and 12th full moons. This is the end of the rains retreat and time for monks to get out and about again. What better time for new clothes?

Alms to monks at Kamphaeng Phet town in the north.

expelled from the order immediately. (Unfortunately for the devout, and to the surprise of those many Westerners who idealise Buddhism, monks are prone to human frailty and the Thai newspapers regularly regale their readers with juicy reports of gun-toting and embezzling abbots, Casanova *ajarns* [teacher-monks], and wizard-monks. The patriarchy sometimes seems unduly tolerant!)

Other important rules condemn lying and intoxication, but you will often see monks smoking cigarettes because tobacco was unknown at the formulation of the 227 precepts!

If a monk may be forgiven for not remembering all the 227 precepts he accepted at his ordination, he must surely keep in mind the Eightfold Path. If followed, this will put an end to suffering. It consists of right understanding, right thought, right speech, right conduct, right livelihood, right effort, right attentiveness, and right concentration.

A Social Structure

There are around 30,000 temples in Thailand and 200,000 monks, with over 100,000 novices or temple boys. The *dek wat*, temple boys, are the sons of poor families who live in the temple, wear saffron robes, do chores for the monks, and benefit by getting an education and getting well-fed. This is an excellent example of how Buddhism continues to serve social as well as spiritual needs. In the old days, a temple was not just a religious centre but an educational and social centre. The state school system has all but replaced the monkhood's role in secular education, but the *dek wat* tradition still provides a useful social service and village people still congregate at temples on many occasions, especially the temple fair and Buddhist holidays.

Despite the high profile of the Buddhist religion in Thailand – the ubiquity of Buddha images, temples and monks – Buddhism's most important contribution to Thai culture is invisible yet all-pervasive. The grace of manner and the tolerance so characteristic of the Thais is a direct outcome of Buddhist teaching,

A novice monk.

which stresses modesty and forbearance.

The faith is not without its problems as noted earlier. Amongst certain Thais, especially the middle class, there is growing concern over two major aspects of contemporary Thai Buddhism: the official emphasis on form rather than content, on ritual and ceremony more than the philosophy, and the presence of so many superstitious practices within the monkhood, such as abbots and senior monks who profess magic powers and temples which offer astrology and palmistry.

But these distinctions and concerns seem lost on the majority of Thais who, while taking the Buddhist view that the material world is an illusion and life a passing show, still wish to get as much pleasure out of it as possible – and if a lucky charm or a good spirit or a skillful astrologer can help, then why not?

Religious Minorities

Despite being overwhelmingly Theravada Buddhist, Thailand has significant religious minorities, by far the largest being Sunni Muslims. About one-and-a-half million followers of the Prophet Mohamed live in the southernmost provinces of Narathiwat, Pattani, Yala and Satun. They are largely of Malay descent and reflect their common cultural heritage with neighbouring Muslim Malaysia to which Islam was brought by Arab traders in the 13th century.

A significant number of Thailand's ethnic Chinese population, together with the Vietnamese, are Mahayana Buddhists. Bangkok in particular hosts many Mahayana temples and meeting-halls; the monks are orange-jacketed and trousered. The much smaller ethnic Indian population of around 20,000 people are either Hindus or Sikhs. Again, concentrated in Bangkok, they have temples in their business districts around lower Silom Road and Paruhat Market.

The half million hilltribe people in the north and western region are largely animist – nature spirit worshippers – though some are Buddhist or Christian. Christians form a total of about 200,000 Christianity is more notable in Thailand for its good works – schools, hospitals, development assistance – than for its converts.

A Muslim boy in the South.

Muslim women at prayer in Koh Pannyi in southern Thailand.

LIFESTYLE • FESTIVALS • CRAFTS

Culture

Thailand is at the crossroads of Southeast Asia and its culture is a melting pot of the East, the encounter of a Sinitic people with Hindu civilisation. The term Indochinese, though not normally used these days to refer to Thailand, is nevertheless highly appropriate.

As the Thais migrated from southwestern China in the 9th to 13th centuries, down the Mekong and Chao Phraya Valleys, they encountered the Dvaravati, Angkor and Srivijaya civilisations, all of them Hindu-Buddhist. In the new Thai kingdoms, Chinese and Indian culture coalesced under the guidance of Buddhism into Thai culture.

As elsewhere in the region, there was a division between the culture of the court and that of the people. Popular culture was that of crafts and festivals, and it thrives to this day. Court culture, so vibrant in the past, is now struggling to survive; it is the world of classical dance and music, drama and poetry.

A bridge between the two which has survived the ages is religious art: temple archi-

Khon, performed to the accompaniment of Thai musical instruments and operatic renditions of classical Thai verse. Actors in classical dance form and elaborate costumes. (See Ramakien, page 287).

tecture, sculpture, and painting. This meeting of high art and the common people in religious devotion is the age-old and still vital core of Thai art.

Nevertheless, as virtually everywhere in the world today, the most thriving cultural medium is television and the most popular form is the soap opera. Then comes pop music, with the cinema trailing. Most of today's popular culture is a Thai-Western hybrid.

If the culture of the common man is quite Westernised, it still retains a distinctly Thai stamp. Curiously, intellectual culture is much more Westernised, but this probably reflects the fact that it is a Western concept anyway to paint canvasses to hang on a wall, or to create dances to express modern life.

Fortunately, there is a growing movement particularly in painting and dance to find a synthesis of Western technique and Thai sensibility. This bodes well for the creation of a modern artistic culture to express contemporary Thai experience.

Buddha calms.

Court and temple art developed in several regions and during overlapping periods, whose styles are usually defined as follows:

Dvaravati (6th-11th centuries): the Theravada Buddhism-inspired art of the Mon culture of the Central Plains. Srivijaya (8th-13th centuries): the Hindu-influenced art of the Indonesian culture of the peninsula.

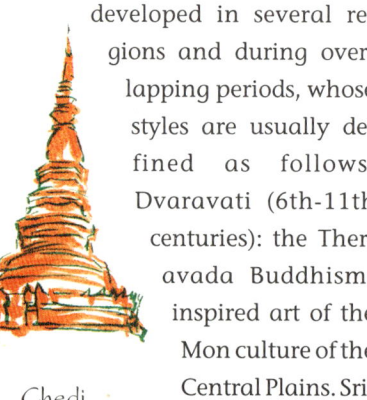

Chedi

Lopburi (11th-14th centuries): the Hindu-Buddhist art of the Khmer culture of the Central Plains, the east and Isan.

Chiang Saen (11th-13th centuries): the Burmese and Lao-influenced art of the first Thai kingdoms of the upper Mekong and Ping valleys, thus of Chiang Mai. Also called Lanna Thai.

Sukhothai (13th-15th centuries): the Buddhism-inspired art of the first great Thai state.

U Thong (12th-15th centuries): the Khmer-influenced art of the first Central Kingdom of Thailand.

Ayutthaya (14th-18th centuries): the classic period in which all threads

Seated Buddha from the Ayutthaya classical period.

came together in the greatest and longest-lived Thai state, in the Central Plains.

Bangkok (18th-20th centuries): the rehabilitation of Thai art after the destruction of Ayutthaya, characterised by increased elaboration and declining creativity.

SCULPTURE & THE BUDDHA IMAGE

Religion and art were inseparable in the early and classical periods of Thai culture. The image of the Buddha reigned supreme, whether in stone or bronze, wood or gold, and it was always executed according to certain rules and traditions inherited from India.

Interestingly, Buddha statuary first appeared in far northwest India about 2,000 years ago under the Greek influence of Alexander's descendants. Naturally, the Buddha himself had no wish to be deified or worshipped by way of image-making (or any other) but official religion almost always demands it.

By the 6th century AD, Indian Buddhists had elaborated a regulation image whose principal (and poetic) details were to be rigidly adhered to: eyebrows like drawn bows, nose like a parrot's beak, chin like a mango stone. There were 33 distinguishing marks, including smooth skin, tightly-curled hair, a bun-like topknot, and long earlobes (as befitted a prince who had worn heavy earrings).

Further to this, the Buddha was to be portrayed in four distinct postures: sitting, standing, reclining and walking. Good artists, even devout Buddhist ones, are never total conformists, and varying influences and interpretations over the years brought about dozens of styles and types of images.

The types are combinations of posture and gesture and there are forty that have been noted in different parts of Thailand. Common examples are: Buddha in meditation – sitting, legs crossed, hands in lap, palms upward; Buddha practising asceticism – sitting, legs crossed, hands crossed on chest; Buddha sleeping (attainment of Nirvana) – reclining on right side, head resting on right hand, left arm alongside body, feet together; Buddha calming quarrels – standing, right hand raised, left arm alongside body; Buddha calming the oceans – standing, forearms forward, hands upturned with palms outward; Buddha calling the earth to witness his enlightenment – sitting, left hand in lap with palm upward, right hand on knee with fingers pointing down.

The first specifically Thai style was that of the northern borderland kingdoms, named after the first influential one, Chiang Saen. The Buddhas of this style are usually seated cross-legged and have round or oval faces with wide open eyes. Thailand's most famous and most prized image, the Emerald Buddha, is attributed to this period.

The Sukhothai kingdom nurtured the most highly distinctive and exquisitely graceful of all Thai styles. Sukhothai Buddha sculpture is distinguished by its flowing lines, rounded form and a serenity of expression bordering on the sensual. It is epitomised in the walking Buddha whose sweeping grace expresses the irresistible progress of truth.

The later periods, Ayutthaya and Bangkok, did not improve on the spirituality and finesse of the Sukhothai style. Though often technically fine, their Buddha images lost strength as they gained elaboration. This reflected the adoption of the concept of semi-divine kingship and, later, the decline of traditional culture.

ARCHITECTURE

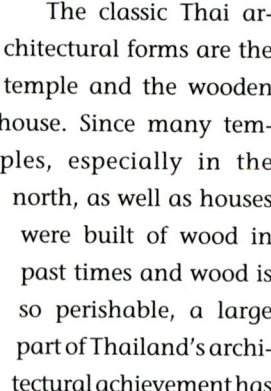

The classic Thai architectural forms are the temple and the wooden house. Since many temples, especially in the north, as well as houses were built of wood in past times and wood is so perishable, a large part of Thailand's architectural achievement has disappeared in the course of time. Further vast inroads into the heritage occurred with the sacking of Ayutthaya when every single building was at the least badly damaged; most were destroyed.

Nevertheless, a wide range of temples from past periods still exist around the country; if not complete, the remains allow us to get a fair idea of their original state, as at Sukhothai or Lopburi. From the 13th century onward, except in Lanna Thai where wood predominated, most important temples were constructed of laterite brick with stucco facing. The characteristic sharply-tilted, multi-tiered roof developed and later centuries saw the increasing use of decoration with multi-coloured tiling and glass mosaic.

A Thai temple is almost invariably a walled compound within which stands

The sacred naga on a temple roof.

Chiang Mai temple with strong Burmese influences.

a variety of buildings with specific functions.

They include: *bot*, the main chapel, the most sacred building, the repository of the principal Buddha image. Religious ceremonies take place in it, including ordinations; it should be large enough to shelter at least 21 monks, the minimum number required for certain rituals. It is usually rectangular, tall, and steeply roofed. *Viharn*: the monastic meeting place, meditation hall and place for preaching sermons to monks. It contains lesser Buddha images and looks similar to the *bot*. *Sala*: pavilion for meditation classes and funeral rites; communal meeting place where monks may preach to the people; a resting and sleeping place for pilgrims. It is open-sided, usually wooden, often raised on stilts. *Chedi*: a solid tapering tower, usually round and broad-based, rising to a point. A principal *chedi* normally enshrines relics of the Buddha, a saint, or royalty. Lesser ones serve as tombstones for ordinary people. The form is said to come from a wish of the Buddha that his ashes be buried in a mound shaped like a heap of rice. Most stupas are of laterite faced with stucco, but some are bronze or gold-faced, as at Doi Suthep above Chiang Mai city or Wat Phra Kaew in Bangkok. The world's largest, at Nakhon Pathom, is tiled. *Prang*: a tapering tower,

Mongkut

Carved teakwood door of a temple.

ang Mai, Lopburi, Ayutthaya, Thonburi and Bangkok. The obvious contemporary culmination is the Temple of the Emerald Buddha in Bangkok.

Temples continue to be built nationwide since, and by tradition, the funders gain great merit. The style is conformist in the extreme and few modern temples have any claim to beauty, much less creativity. Meanwhile, many fine old temples fall into disrepair because the funding of renovation gains less merit.

Palace architecture is the second form in importance but little survives from past ages, the most extensive ruins being those of King Narai's palace at Lopburi (see Central Plains, page 135). Of the Bangkok period, the grandest examples are Bang Pa-in Summer Palace, (Central Plains), Vimarnmek Palace (Bangkok) and, of course, the Grand Palace (Bangkok).

four-sided and round-topped. It may be solid, as at Wat Arun in Bangkok, or contain a chamber, as in the Khmer *prang* of Lopburi. *Mondop*: a square building, with multi-stepped, pyramid-like roof culminating in a spire, often mosaic-adorned. It houses a relic. Phra Buddhabat shrine in Saraburi is a fine example. *Hotrai*: a small square pavilion housing the library of holy scriptures (*tripitaka*). *Horankang*: the belfry, an open-sided pavilion housing the gong that regulates the monks' activities. *Kuti*: monks' living quarters. This may be anything from a little wooden hut to a huge dormitory building.

Temple architecture has long been on a grand scale in important royal and religious places, through the ages, such as at Nakhon Pathom, Sukhothai, Chi-

House-building in Thailand was until very recently nearly always in wood. Given the previous abundance of wood, notably fine hardwood in the north, wooden housing was universal and the teak houses of royalty and the rich attained levels of great artistry. (See box story).

Most of the country's current structures date from the last 50 years. Secular architecture of minimal quality abounds. Change is rapid, almost at break-neck pace: central Bangkok went from low-rise to high-rise in the space of the 1980s. Materials for major construction are steel, glass and concrete, and

Kinnaree, the mythical half-bird, half-woman commonly seen in all temples.

The Grand Palace, Bangkok (19th century). Palace architecture, second only to temple architecture, is still grandly elaborate.

the style international. The current fad is for neo-classicism and Bangkok continually sprouts wedding-cake townhouses and cocktail lounges, and even neo-Gothic apartment blocks. Kitsch rules!

PAINTING

Traditional painting in Thailand is synonymous with murals. Temple mural painting developed to a high degree from the belief that walls should enhance the beauty of the religious objects they surrounded.

The classic style used neither perspective nor relative proportion nor shadowing. It depicted legends of the Buddha and Buddhist mythology, often intermingled with scenes of Thai royal and common life. The result at times is flat human and mythical figures of varying size according to status, set against vague or fantastical backdrops.

The tropical climate and widespread neglect has ravaged most early murals and only a few pre-18th century ones remain. The few surviving examples show earthy colours and natural pigments. Painters were anonymous devotees whose work was sacred. They developed conventions of portrayal in which the Buddha, celestial beings and royalty were always serene and gestures were formalised

Sema

to express defined emotions and meanings, as in the *khon* masked drama.

Murals adorned *bot* and *viharn* interiors, quite often from floor to ceiling of all four walls. External galleries might also be decorated. Almost all the mural painting extant dates from the 19th and 20th centuries. Fine examples are those of Wat Phra Kaew and Wat Suthat in Bangkok and Wat Suvarnaram in Thonburi.

Most recent examples are sometimes gaudy and graphic, but they do have the advantage of clarity and drama, performing the task of vivid story-telling that is one of the traditional Thai mural's principal functions. An extensive example is that of the *viharn* of Wat Phrathat Haripunchai at Lamphun in the north.

Such modern murals have more in common stylistically with movie advertising than with the old temple tradition, and nowadays the painting that most Thais encounter most often is indeed that of movie posters, whether in print form or in huge original hoardings which tower luridly over city streets. This popular commercial art, though in decline along with the Thai film industry, is a vivid component of the urban scene.

Chofa

There is, however, a serious contemporary art scene in Thailand modelled on Western tradition, with galleries and museums. This interest grew in the 20th century.

One who especially influenced and helped to promote this appreciation in the local art scene was an Italian artist and teacher who became both Buddhist and a Thai citizen, Professor Silpa Bhirasri (taking a Thai name). He taught at the premier fine arts academy, Silpakorn University, at Sanam Luang, Bangkok.

Most of this art was in borrowed modernist Western styles and themes until a movement gathered strength in the 1970s to create truly Thai contemporary painting, a synthesis of Western materials and technique with Thai technique and sensibility. The upshot in the 1990s is that many Thai painters now express the Buddhist faith through the refracting prism of modern life, producing paintings for sale to the private collector.

Three of the most interesting of these Buddhism-inspired contemporary painters are Panya Vijinthanasarn, Chalermchai Kositpipat and Sompop Budtarad. They are especially interesting because they have together executed a huge contemporary-style temple mural, but not in Thailand. The mural is at Wimbledon, London Wat Buddhapadipa.

There are frequent shows of contemporary art in Bangkok at such places as Silpakorn University and the Na-

Mural depicting battle scenes at a temple in Thonburi.

18th century frescoes at Wat Intharam, Chonburi.

tional Gallery, both at Sanam Luang near the Grand Palace, as well as at private galleries.

DANCE DRAMA

In common with other dramatic traditions of Southeast Asia, notably the Cambodian, Javanese and Balinese, dance and drama are all of a piece in Thailand's classical tradition, and music is inseparable from them. All these traditions descend from Indian temple dance; the high Thai form is called *khon*.

Khon is masked dance-drama that was refined in the Ayutthaya period to tell the Ramakien story, the Thai version of the Indian Ramayana legend. Since the whole saga takes 720 hours, it was performed in different parts, but even these were extremely long – 20 hours – so that they had to be spread over two days. Evidently, it was the kind of performance at which one dropped into for a while now and then, rather than sitting through the entire drama.

If it made demands on the audience, then those on the actors were much more strenuous, for the story is expressed by every minute movement of the body, especially the limbs, in combination with the music, whilst a chorus at the side recites and sings narrative verses. Actors were court retainers and they performed in palace halls and courtyards, often by torchlight.

These performances could involve 200 characters at once in a battle scene, most of them mercifully static, for the *khon* is highly formalised. The principal characters, however, act out vigorous and often contorted gestures; these are Prince Rama, his brother Lakshman, his beloved Princess Sita, his ally the monkey-king Hanuman, and his deadly rival the demon king Ravana. Because of the energy required, it is quite likely that a series of actors donned the same mask and costume to perform each major role.

Each mask typifies the personality of its character, exaggerated, lacquered, gilded and bejewelled. Costumes are rich brocades adorned with sparkling gems, similar to the apparel of royalty and celestial beings in classical murals.

Lakorn is a closely related dramatical form which is more fluid and less formal. It portrays the Ramakien, the Jataka Buddhist tales, and folk stories. Characters other than gods and animals do not wear masks, but still a chorus tells the narrative. Its simplest type is the *lakorn jatri,* and this is what is performed for patrons at shrines such as Bangkok's City Pillar and Erawan Shrine.

These somewhat tired and degenerate displays are nevertheless the most thriving form of the classical dance today. Tourist dinner-dance shows also portray bits of *lakorn* and *khon,* a little

That

Door guards at Wat Dusit Daram, Thonburi.

Another Khon scene from Ramakien. It is common to find women playing male roles.

Likay

The most popular form of Thai drama is *likay*, a gaudy, bawdy travelling show mixing traditional tales with topical comment, ancient wisdom and current jokes, all-singing, all-dancing and all-sparkling. *Likay* is not what it was – cinema, TV and modern ways have seen to that – but it is alive and kicking and still pulling 'em in at country fairs and festivals.

Likay's origins are obscure yet recent: it appears to be an amalgam of Malay, Indian and Thai traditions over the past 100 years. Originally telling folk tales in vulgar adaptations of classical dance clothes with a small *piphat* band in accompaniment, it has evolved into pantomine-like music-hall entertainment with heroines in full-length low-cut European ballgowns.

The pantomine connection would be very clear to European spectators: the male leads often resemble Harlequin, coincidentally or not, with their pointed hats, baggy knee breeches, and white stockings, and the women seem to be fairy queens. Then there is the fairy-tale plot, the topical comments, the pop songs, and the bawdy jokes.

It all takes place on a travelling stage set up in a field or compound, acted against a brightly-painted backdrop of a palace interior. The male costumes are brilliantly sequinned satin and velvet creations with some relation to the classical *khon* and *lakorn* clothes. The actors are heavily made up and are fine troupers who mostly just joined up one day to get off the farm. They all need to be good at ready wit and repartee, for improvisation is the essence of the fun. Whatever the story, which usually involves princes, beautiful maidens, love and tribulation, there is always a hero, a heroine, a villain and a clown.

The show alternates between tragedy and farce, savagery and sentimentality, singing and dancing, ballet and buffoonery. Traditionally, gong, flute and drum play on the left of the stage and the audience is dominated by grandmothers and kids. The whole troupe may number 30 members and it typically gets 10,000 baht for a temple fair performance, which may last from 8pm way into the night.

Some say *likay* is on its last legs, being ousted not just by TV but by the rival travelling *luk tung* show (see page 288). But some *likay* troupes are meeting the challenge by bringing on synthesisers, drumkits and more pop songs. Let's hope they make it.

more enthusiastically. Occasionally, there are professional performances of *khon* lasting about 3 hours at Bangkok's National Theatre or Thailand Cultural Centre.

Also on its last legs but rather more common is *likay*, the folk theatre which still 'pulls 'em in' at upcountry fairs. It's a descendent of *lakorn* and a counterpart of English pantomine, with lots of action, colour and bawdy humour, and a love story, naturally. Musicians plink and plonk at the side but these troupers speak or shriek their own lines, embellished with local and topical references. (See box story, page 282).

There is also a puppet-play tradition in Thailand, with two branches. The shadow play in its classic form is called *nang yai*. In this, large filigree cowhide figures are manipulated behind backlit white screens, accompanied by music and singing. *Nang yai* is sometimes performed in Bangkok, but the southern version called *nang talung*, more agile and fast-moving, is more alive, performed at some southern festivals. (See box story – Regions/South).

The other branch is marionettes, the classical version being called *hoon*, manipulated from below and seldom seen now. A more popular version, *hoon krabok,* is sometimes performed at fairs or in Bangkok theatres; correctly, it is performed in a puppet theatre like Punch and Judy, but sometimes it takes off with the puppeteers charging about on stage holding the large hand puppets.

Thailand has Western-style theatre and dance too, though not much of it. There is a 20th century tradition of boulevard theatre, alive and kicking today at the Montientong Theatre in the Montien Hotel, Bangkok. The plays are usually comedies, Thai adaptations of Western playwrights such as Neil Simon and Noel Coward. More serious and experimental works, also often adapted and acculturated from the West, are occasionally presented by students such as those of Chulalongkorn University's Drama Department.

There is also a modern dance movement of some vitality but infrequent performances. In a similar way to artists and actors, dancers are searching for and experimenting with forms and styles that can express contemporary Thai experience while drawing on both Thai and Western tradition. TAM Dance Company is a leader.

MUSIC

Thai traditional music has a seven-tone scale with no semi-tones, and is influenced by that of nearby Burma, Malaya and Java, and is thought to be descended from that of China, India and Cambodia. The instrumentation includes xylophones, flutes, oboes, gongs,

Prasat

metallophones, stringed instruments, drums and cymbals. Written music is not often used; playing is usually by memory with frequent improvisation. The melodic line is predetermined and usually played by one instrument, the *khong wong yai*, a circular frame on which hang small gongs of different timbres with which the other instruments combine through variations, rhythms, repetition, and so on.

Traditionally, Thai music accompanied court and temple ceremonies, classical and popular drama, sporting events, fairs and festivals, weddings and funerals – just about anything. It still does, when not supplanted by Western-style music. It is played today mostly in ensembles based on percussion, the *piphat*, or on strings, the *mahori*, either in their smaller form of five to six instruments or in orchestra form of around twenty instruments.

The easiest way to hear one live, albeit a none too skilful one, is at the Erawan Shrine in Bangkok where musicians play daily by paid request from early morning till late evenings.

There is an interesting contemporary movement to fuse Thai classical music with jazz. (Jazz has a long tradition and elevated status in Thailand: the King is a skilled saxophonist who used to lead a band at the palace in a weekly radio show!) The leading lights are virtuoso jazz multi-instrumentalist Tewan Sapsanyakorn and master classical flautist Jamnian Srithaipahan who together guide Kangdadan, "The Cresecent Moon Orchestra", performing on an occasional basis in Bangkok and abroad.

While serious artists, actors, dancers and musicians have been striving for a contemporary Thai mode of expression, pop musicians have done it without even thinking. Thai pop music covers a broad spectrum from pure folk tradition to total Western imitation, but the bulk of it has a flavour that is both clearly modern and unmistakably Thai. With contemporary lyrics and cross-cultural rhythm, pop music is the most successful synthesis in the Thai arts today. Turn on the radio and spin the dial and you will catch the whole spectrum, in Bangkok at least.

LITERATURE

Classical Thai literature is dominated by the Ramakien, the Thai version of the Hindu Ramayana epic, with a supporting cast of folk tales and court poetry. The Ramakien is the central Thai myth and figures in drama, dance, painting and sculpture as well as on the written page (see box story, page 287).

Little pre-Bangkok literature survived the fall of Ayutthaya. The Ramakien verse epic had to be recomposed in the early 19th century by those who

Prang

Thai Musical Instruments

Thai musical instruments, like so much of Thai culture, reflect influences from Cambodia, India and China, plus Burma, Malaya and Java. They may be indigenous in type or introduced from abroad. Some were named after the sound they made, like *ching* for the small cymbal, and others after their shape, position or origin.

They are played in ensembles of which the two most common types are the *piphat* based on percussion and the *mahori* based on strings. They range from small groups of five or six players to orchestras of twenty or more musicians. Thai music accompanies all kinds of traditional dance and drama – *khon, lakorn, Manohra, likay, nang thalung*, and so on. Players perform at funerals and weddings, boxing matches and Brahman shrines, and all sorts of customary ceremonies.

The *piphat* consists of wooden xylophones *(ranat)*, metallophones *(khong wong yai)*, drums *(taphon* and *klong)*, gongs *(khong)* and the quadruple reed oboe *(pinai)*. The *ranat* has an elegant bowed shape, curving down in the middle, the keys made from either seasoned hardwood or special types of bamboo. They are played with wooden beaters. The *khong wong yai* is an almost circular framework of 15 horizontal gongs; the musician sits in the middle and plays them with hide-tipped beaters.

The *mahori* is a combination of the *piphat* with the *kruang sai*, the string ensemble. It adds bowed and plucked string instruments, plus flutes.

In all, there are about 50 types of Thai musical instruments, including many local versions of flutes, strings and gongs used at festivals, ordinations, lovers' serenades, social evenings and similar rites and diversions.

The Ramakien

Drama, dance, poetry, painting – the legend of the Ramakien is central to them all. This ancient story adapted from the Hindu Ramayana epic is the central legend of Thai culture. It is the sole play of the highest drama form, *khon*, it is the most prominent plot in *lakorn* and *nang thalung*, it forms classic Thai verse as learnt in schools and it features prominently in temple murals, notably at the Temple of the Reclining Buddha, Wat Po, Bangkok.

The Ramakien tells the story of the royal birth of Rama in the kingdom of Ayodhya (from which Ayutthaya took its name); of Rama's marriage to King Janaka's daughter Sita; of Sita's abduction by the demon king Totsakan to Longka (present-day Sri Lanka); of Rama's long struggle against Totsakan to rescue Sita, aided by his brother Laksana; of Totsakan's eventual defeat; and of Rama's return with Sita to claim his throne.

The Ramakien falls into three main sections totalling 138 episodes. The most popular and most represented section is the second which concerns the struggle to regain Sita. The brothers Rama and Laksana form an army and gain allies in Kings Sugripa and Thao Mahajambhu, plus the monkey-god Hanuman. They march to southern India opposite Longka and there acquire the help of Totsakan's banished brother, Piphek, who is an excellent astrologer.

Crossing the straits, the armies lay siege to the city of Longka; after a long series of battles with the demons of Longka, Rama takes the city, kills Totsakan and rescues Sita. The deities thus down the devils: good triumphs over evil.

Ramakien theatre performed against the Ayutthayan ruins.

Luk Tung – Song Of The Fields

Most Thai people live in the country and their favourite music is *luk tung*. More than a music, *luk tung* is a great travelling show of star singer, back-up singers, dancing girls and showband that tours the Thai provinces, has adoring fans and gangster enemies.

Setting up stage at temple fairs and provincial showgrounds, the *luk tung* show is a vibrant, vivid, sometimes shambolic, sometimes expert, non-stop flow of sound and colour. The lead singer croons to the adulation of the crowd, who ring his neck with flower garlands till he almost chokes. The big band playing Western dance-band instruments blasts and wails behind. In between a dozen girls do shakily choreographed chorus dancing and singing, dressed like anything from the Sugar Plum Fairy to Supergirl.

The songs are usually made up from folk tunes or some old Thai melody, with Western pop influences. The big stars are mostly male, patriarchs of the troupe, but many women rise to fame this way too. It's a great aspiration of young rural Thais and the songs very much reflect the rural perception of the world. Most of the lyrics are about real life and real events that have happened, rather than about imaginary things or dreams. As one *luk tung* superstar, Surachai Sumbatcharon, said: "When country people listen to *luk tung*, they feel they are experiencing their own lives through our music."

Some songs reflect rural poverty and the vagaries of nature, like this lyric:

This year it's very cold and the rice has failed.
The rice is dead and there is no rain.
The sky is red like a fever, my love, you must be crying, and so am I. You starve for rice and the buffalo starves for grass. There is no money to spend, I have to leave you now.
It is as if the sky intends to make us sad.

Others reflect separation, the boy gone to the city, the girl pining back on the farm:

The golden heads of rice in the fields are waiting to be reaped.
And I am also waiting.
The girl in the fields is still waiting for you.
Come back from the city, my love,
Or I shall come and join you there.

By contrast, some show the frustration of rural girls and the urge to flee to a better and freer life:

Tomorrow I shall be a lady, not a child any more..
I'm telling you, tomorrow I'm going on a bus,
Tomorrow I may lose it, and you won't find it any more.

Not all songs are melancholy – some may be self-mocking as in superstar Surachai's lament:

I was born a Superman with special powers
But I'm afraid of those girls with sharp tongues and itchy fingers,
Those girls who cry: "He's magical!"

Thus amusing the upcountry folk, expressing their everyday emotions and ringing profound chords within them, *luk tung* is Thailand's great contemporary popular art.

---

could remember the old texts. Folk tales were told and handed down in verse; they are both didactic and entertaining. The court poetry was highly complex and reached its zenith with Sunthorn Phu in the 19th century (see Regions/East, page 202). Thai writers and their audience (for literature was heard rather than read) were much given to the magical, the marvellous and the extraordinary, though the folk stories nevertheless often related to the lives of the villagers, featuring tales of official duplicity and peasant guile, with much bawdiness. Things have not changed all that much upcountry, and these stories are still told when the TV is not on.

Prose literature is a 20th century phenomenon. Most writing is in sentimental novelette form written by and

Festivals, pageantry, reenactment of history are all very much a part of its culture.

for women. Notable exceptions are the novels of the aristocrat MR Kukrit Pramoj, dealing with historical and contemporary issues, and the novels and short stories of the northeasterner Pira Sudham, treating the life and troubles of Isan's poor, including their encounters with the big city.

CINEMA & TV

The Thai film industry used to churn out hundreds of features every year. With the rise of television, movies have declined greatly in quantity; in quality, some might consider that they had no further to fall.

Perhaps that is a little unfair – what Thai film-makers do, they do well technically, but the plots and characters are so stereotyped that no Thai film has ever had the remotest sniff at an Oscar. Rags-to-riches, country boy goes to the city, cops and robbers (cops always win), gory ghost stories, all with lots of sentiment and slapstick – would be the standard menu. One fine exception was a screen version of the novel *Luk Isan: Child of the Northeast*, about the drought-stricken lives of poor northeasterners in the 1940s. It was movingly filmed in the early '80s.

Television is now the supreme cultural medium in Thailand, as in most countries today. On five channels, it screens a hotch-potch of soap operas, game shows, talk shows, popular music, children's programmes, traditional culture, sport and news.

The coverage of news reporting and documentary filming is rapidly improving. An international news network is also received via satellite.

LIFESTYLE • FESTIVALS • CRAFTS

Fabulous Festivals

The Thais are always on the lookout for *sanuk* and lots of people having fun together is particularly *sanuk*, so Thailand is a land of festivals where people congregate in conviviality for a wide spectrum of reasons, religious and secular, seasonal and cultural, sporting and historical.

Some of the festivals are solemn, such as the important Buddhist holy days when the faithful go to their local or favourite temple to worship and make merit. These fall in February, May and July: *Makha Bucha*, *Visakha Bucha* and *Asakha Bucha*. Many are both religious and festive, such as the celebrations before and after Buddhist Lent, called *Khao Phansa* and *Ok Phansa*, which occur in July and October.

Others celebrate harvests of the premier local produce, such as the Mango Festival in Chachoengsao in April or the Rambutan Fair in Surat Thani in August. These are always very secular with lots of folk dancing and feasting and beauty contests to elect Miss Longan or Miss Banana.

Most of the festi-

Candle Festival preparations at Ubon Ratchathani, in the Northeast.

vals feature processions through the town which may involve the carrying of notable Buddha images and most likely include floral floats with heavily made-up beauties on top. In the area there will almost invariably be a grand open-air bazaar and funfair, offering all sorts of knick-knacks and foods, especially local produce, and various entertainments from movies to all-singing, all-dancing shows. Other festivals include those of ethnic minorities, mostly Chinese but also Indian and Muslim.

Practical Information

DATES. Many festivals and fairs are timed by the lunar calendar, thus the dates vary from year to year. In these cases, the approximate date is given. *Loy Krathong*, for instance, is held on the full moon night of the 12th lunar month, which falls around early November. For fixed date events, the precise calendar date is given. *Songkran*, the Thai New Year, for example, is celebrated on April 13th, and may splash on till the 15th in particularly festive places.

LOCATION. In the following listings, after the festival name and location, the province and region follows.

January

Chaiyaphum Elephant Round-Up, (Chaiyaphum, Northeast) January 10-12.

This is a colourful event that gathers together lots of working elephants from nearby forests at the provincial capital. The elephants demonstrate their prowess in a variety of skills, climaxing with a spectacular re-enactment of medieval warfare – until the Bangkok Period, kings rode to battle at the head of elephant-led armies.

<u>Access</u>: Chaiyaphum is in western Isan, around 120 km north of Nakhon Ratchasima (Korat). It is just 60 km northwest of Bua Yai on the upper northeast railway.

Bo Sang Umbrella Fair, (Chiang Mai, North) third weekend, Friday-Sunday.

Almost everyone in the village of Bo Sang makes a living from brightly-painted paper umbrellas. The annual Umbrella Fair is held in the high street to celebrate their traditional skill, inherited from medieval Chinese craftsmen. There are contests, exhibitions, and the election of Miss Bo Sang, the umbrella queen. The climax is a parade of bicycling umbrella-shaded maidens. Stalls sell handicrafts, especially paper umbrellas, of course.

<u>Access</u>: Bo Sang is just 10 km east of Chiang Mai.

Don Chedi Memorial Fair, (Suphanburi, Central) January 24-31.

In 1592 at Don Chedi, King Naresuan the Great won a famous duel on elephant-back with the leader of a Burmese army, thus saving the kingdom. This fair commemorates the momen-

Handicraft and Umbrella Fan Festival at Bo Sang, near Chiang Mai.

tous event with an elephant-back battle re-enactment, historical exhibitions and outdoor entertainments.

Access: Suphanburi town is about 130 km north-west of Bangkok and 50 km west of Ayutthaya; Don Chedi is a small town another 20 km north.

JANUARY/FEBRUARY

Dragon and Lion Parade, (Nakhon Sawan, Central) late January to early February (12 days).

Local residents of Chinese ancestry honour the dragon deity with thanks for his benevolence. Brightly costumed parades pass through town with elaborate dragon and lion dances, crashing cymbals and booming drums, plus marching bands and images of revered gods.
Access: Nakhon Sawan is 240 km north of Bangkok on Highway 1.

Straw Bird Fair, (Chai Nat, Central) late January to early February.

Straw is a plentiful by-product of rice farming and local villagers weave large bright straw birds modelled on the 90 odd species found in Chai Nat Bird Park. The straw birds are paraded at a fair featuring local handicrafts and foods.

Access: Chai Nat is 200 km north of Bangkok, close to Highway 1 and the northern railway (Ta Khli Station).

Phra Nakhon Khiri Fair, (Phetchaburi, Central/South) late January to early February.

On a wooded hill overlooking Phetchaburi town, King Mongkut built a palace, a monastery and an observatory. The City on the Mount Fair celebrates this monarch and his time (mid-19th century) with a highly atmospheric sound and light show upon the mount, whilst traditional music and puppet plays are performed in the tree-shaded grounds. The trees all over the mount are lit with a million little golden lights, whilst the fairground below is a bedlam of barkers and hucksters, blaring music and boxing matches, movie shows and noodle shops, and stalls, stalls, stalls selling every imaginable knick-knack.
Access: Phetchaburi is 120 km south-west of Bangkok on both the southern highway and railway.

FEBRUARY

Luang Wiang Lakon, (Lampang, North) first Friday and Saturday.

This is a great Lanna Thai festival

in which five important Buddha images are carried by serried ranks of bare-chested attendants in a procession including members of the northern royal families. Evening events include a traditional *khantok* (Northern Thai) dinner and dancing, and a sound-and-light historical show at Wat Lampang Luang.
Access: Lampang is 600 km north of Bangkok and 100 km south of Chiang Mai, on the northern railway.

Flower Festival, (Chiang Mai, North) first weekend, Friday-Sunday.

The north is noted for its rich variety of flowers, particularly temperate region types which are at their best in this cool month. Spectacular floral floats parade round the city streets, most sporting decorous beauty queens, and there are magnificent flower displays, plus handicraft selling and beauty contests. Chiang Mai is renowned throughout Thailand for the beauty of its women.
Access: Chiang Mai, 700 km north of Bangkok, has constant access by air, road and rail.

Chinese New Year, (nationwide in Chinese communities) early to mid-February (1st day of the 1st Chinese lunar month).

This is the only time of the year that most Chinese shops and small businesses shut, usually for three days. Chinese temples are full of worshippers, making prayers for good fortune, especially in Bangkok's Chinatown.

Makha Bucha, (nationwide) mid-February (full moon of 3rd lunar month).

This is an important Buddhist holy day. It marks the occasion when 1250 of Buddha's disciples gathered spontaneously to hear him preach. Most Thais make merit on this day by visiting a temple, particularly in the evening for *wian tian*, circling the main chapel in candlelight procession. The throng of devotees from all walks of life holding lighted candles and shuffling silently round is a beautiful and mesmerising sight.
Access: every Buddhist temple. In Bangkok, the ceremony is notable at Wat Bovornives and Wat Benjamobophit.

MARCH

Barred Ground Dove Festival, (Yala, South) first weekend (Saturday-Sunday).

Dove-fanciers from all over Thailand, plus Malaysia, Singapore and Indonesia, flock to Yala with their snowy pets. Rank upon rank of doves – over 1400 is the record – sit in cages perched on poles in a large field for a cooing contest. There's a bazaar of young prize doves and local products, plus sports contests.
Access: Yala is close to the Malaysian border.

Phra Buddhabat Fair, (Wat Phra Buddhabat, Saraburi, Central) early to mid-March.

The Shrine of the Holy Footprint is a

Mass monk ordination at the Poi Sang Long Festival in Mae Hong Son.

popular place of pilgrimage. It is an elaborate blue-and-bronze tiled pavilion set at the summit of a long stairway and perched beneath a rocky outcrop. The sanctuary and its surroundings host a week of festivities including drama and music, as well as the perennial stalls of varied merchandise and foods. Access: Wat Phra Buddhabat is 140 km north of Bangkok, on Highway 1 just before Lopburi and close to Nong Don station on the northern railway.

April

Poi Sang Long, (Mae Hong Son, North) first week, Thursday-Saturday.

One of Thailand's most picturesque celebrations, this is the ceremony of ordination of Buddhist novices of the Thai Yai tribal group. The boys are colourfully dressed and their faces rouged and made up. They hold ceremonial umbrellas, and they are carried on their fathers' shoulders in procession. There are also dances by performers in animal costumes. Friday is the procession day. Access: Mae Hong Son town is 120 km northwest of Chiang Mai as the crow or the commuter plane flies. The bus ride is long, circuitous and uncomfortable; the short flight is much preferable.

Songkran, (nationwide) April 13-15.

This is the most exuberant of national Thai festivals and it celebrates the traditional Thai New Year. [See box story, page 297.] April 13 is the main day and the only day of celebration in many places, but in others, notably Chiang Mai, it's a three-day splash. In Bangkok, celebration is muted; things get much wetter in nearby Ayutthaya.

MAY

Visakha Bucha, (nationwide) mid-May (full moon of 6th lunar month).

This is the holiest of Buddhist days and marks the birth, enlightenment and death of the Buddha (all reckoned to have happened on the same day). As on *Makha Bucha* in February, temples nationwide are crowded with the faithful listening to sermons by revered monks and, in the evening, forming solemn candlelit processions round the main chapel.

Royal Ploughing Ceremony, (Sanam Luang, Bangkok) May 11 (roughly 8-9am).

An ancient Brahman ritual, this celebrates the official start of the rice-planting season. Scarlet-clad handlers lead sacred oxen pulling ploughs, followed by the Minister of Agriculture who scatters consecrated rice seed. The colourful ceremony is presided over by the King and Brahman priests, with court and government officials participating. At the end, upcountry farmers leap the barriers and rush to dig up the auspicious seed in a grand melee.
Access: Sanam Luang is the large oval field north of the Temple of the Emerald Buddha.

Rocket Festival, (Yasothon, Northeast) second weekend, Saturday-Sunday.

This is a widespread custom in the north-east, most exuberant at Yasothon. Villagers build elaborate wooden rocket launchers and shoot huge squibs from them which go spluttering wildly across the fields. This takes place on the Sunday and is supposed to ensure plentiful rains for the imminent rice-planting season. On the Saturday, there are colourful parades of rockets and folk dancers, and the obligatory beauty contest.

Songkran

Songkran is the old Thai New Year's Day, April 13, and is the occasion for splashing a lot of water about, over Buddhas and people. On this day, household Buddha images are washed with scented water and in many places important temple images are paraded for the people to sprinkle with scented water.

The real fun of the occasion is to throw water over every person in sight. This is done with especial enthusiasm in places like Chiang Mai and Ayutthaya, where quite a few people go to the length of touring the streets in pick-ups with tanks of water from which to drench everybody.

No-one is immune, not even traffic cops and especially not tourists, who are considered very fair game. Even so, Thai politeness may still predominate. Foreigners are often asked for their permission prior to soaking or the water-thrower may at least say sorry before drenching you from head to toe.

Since this is the height of the hot season when temperatures can soar to 40C, nobody minds too much. If in Thailand on April 13th, or 14th and 15th for it tends to slosh on, dress down and join in!

Royal Ploughing Ceremony at Sanam Luang, Bangkok.

Much rice whisky is consumed and the men in particular get quite wild and very ribald – often costumed and caked in mud.

Access: Yasothon is 100 km northwest of Ubon Ratchathani in Isan. Frequent buses run from Ubon. Ubon has direct air, rail and road connections from Bangkok.

JUNE

Phi Ta Khon Festival, (Dan Sai, Loei, Northeast) three days decided by village shaman shortly in advance.

This curious festival's highlight is the prancing spirits – boys dressed in huge bizarre masks with long down-pointed noses who tease the celebrants in a kind of Thai Halloween.

The centrepiece is the parading of a sacred Buddha image with the goblins in attendance in their weird masks and colourful raggedy costumes. The first two days are lively, the third quiet. Though much of the festivity is animist in spirit, the core is a celebration of the Buddha-to-be, Prince Vessandorn, exemplar of kindness and generosity.

Access: Dan Sai is in northwest Isan, about 100 km north of Petchabun and 70 km west of Loei. There are flights to Loei.

JULY

Asakha Bucha, (nationwide) early to mid-July (full moon of the 8th lunar month).

This is an important holy day, the day on which the Buddha gave his first sermon and the day before the start of Buddhist Lent. Many young men choose to be ordinated on this day and such ceremonies can be observed in temples nationwide.

Candle Festival, (Ubon Ratchathani, Northeast) early to mid-July (the three days around Asakha Bucha).

This festival is a last bash before the holy period of the rains retreat or Buddhist Lent, and thus equivalent to the Catholic Mardi Gras. Beautifully carved beeswax candles, some several metres tall and accompanied by great wax birds and animals, are ceremonially paraded before being presented to local temples, where they may burn for the duration of Lent. There are also phalanxes of folk-dancers, beauty queens and contests, sales stalls and all the usual fun of the fair.

Access: Ubon is in the far southeast of Isan. It is served by road, rail and air.

Tak Bat Dok Mai, (Wat Phra Buddhabat, Saraburi, Central) early to mid-July (Asakha Bucha day).

This is the most dramatic *Asakha Bucha* celebration where a long file of monks is presented with flowers of a special local type plus incense, climaxing with their ascent of the steep stairway to the Holy Footprint Shrine (see March, *Phra Buddhabat Fair*, page 295).

Rocket Festival at Yasothon in the north-east, a call for plentiful rain.

Amidst shooting rockets, a 'costume' fair.

Phichit Boat Races on the River Nan, Central Plains.

This is preceded by parades of floats representing Saraburi's produce and history, with beauty queens, folk musicians and dancers, and marching bands. All the usual festival vendors are there with their wares too.

Access: see March, *Phra Buddhabat Fair*.

AUGUST

Longan Fair, (Lamphun, North) first weekend, Friday-Sunday (parade: Saturday morning).

This is a celebration of the longan harvest, the juicy little white-fleshed fruit (*lam yai* in Thai) for which Lamphun is famous. The Saturday morning parade features elaborate longan-themed floats sporting beauty queens, traditional costumes, folk dancers and musicians, not least of which are the drumming teams with their mighty *klong luang*. The rest of the day, there is a fierce drumming contest with great cannon-like drums at the fairground, plus many other entertainments and the usual bazaar.

Access: Lamphun town is just 25 km south of Chiang Mai.

SEPTEMBER

Phichit Boat Races, (Phichit, Central)

foods and gifts to monks. There are numerous cultural performances, especially of *nang thalung* shadow puppetry and *manohra* dancing. Contests, exhibitions and various entertainments are on offer.

Access: Nakhon Si Thammarat is on the Gulf coast. It is the terminus of a branch line of the southern railway (15 hours from Bangkok).

September/October

Kluai Khai Banana Festival, (Kamphaeng Phet, North) mid-September to early October (5 days, Wednesday-Sunday, parade: Thursday).

This festival celebrates the harvest of the short stubby 'egg banana', the province's premier produce for which it is renowned. The parade features gorgeously decorated floats with clusters of little green bananas and multi-coloured banana by-products – all this forming mythological beasts and the like. There is the obligatory beauty contest, a toffee-making contest and the usual fairground. Early Friday morning, there is a special alms-giving at the ancient temple ruins, with a huge *Tod Kathin* (see Box Story in Religion Chapter, page 262) ceremony there in the evening.

Access: Kamphaeng Phet is 360 km north of Bangkok on Highway 1.

Vegetarian Festival, (Phuket and Trang, South) late September to mid-October (nine days).

first weekend, Friday-Sunday.

A widespread traditional sport is races of longboats paddled furiously by twenty or thirty men each. One of the most noted events is held on the Nan River at Phichit. Nowadays there are female contests too.

Access: Phichit is on the Northern railway and just off Highway II, 334 km north of Bangkok.

Festival of the Tenth Lunar Month, (Nakhon Si Thammarat, South) mid to late September (15 days of the waning 10th moon).

This festival brings merit to the souls of ancestors; Buddhists offer a variety of

Mediums go into trances at the Vegetarian Festival, Phuket Island.

This festival originated among 19th century Chinese immigrants. Their descendents observe a nine-day vegetarian fast, wearing all-white clothes, and parade performing bloodless acts of self-mutilation such as the piercing of cheeks with spears. There is much cymbal-crashing and incense-burning, with ceremonies in Chinese temples.

Access: Phuket is reached by air and bus. Trang is the terminus of a southern railway branchline.

Wax Castle Festival, (Sakhon Nakhon, Northeast) late September to mid-October (*Ok Phansa*, end of Buddhist Lent, four days).

Celebrating the end of Buddhist Lent, this begins at the local lake with long-boat races, similar to Phichit's in September, and culminates in a beeswax candle procession, a smaller version of Ubon's in July.

Access: Sakhon Nakhon is in the far north-east; it has air services.

Illuminated Boat Procession, (Nakhon Phanom, Northeast) late September to mid-October (*Ok Phansa*, five days).

Celebrating the end of Buddhist Lent, people put little candle-lit boats on the Mekong River. The climax is a parade of elaborate illuminated boats of all sizes, some very large, representing temples and the like. There is also a temple fair by the riverside with dancing girls and singing shows, besides the usual bazaar.

Access: very close to Sakhon Nakhon (see preceding).

OCTOBER

Chak Phra Festival, (Surat Thani, South) early to mid-October (nine days).

Chak Phra means 'pulling a sacred image'; in this festival, Buddha images are placed on elaborate carriages and rope-hauled along the streets by local people. Even bigger ones are floated in procession along the town's river. Nearby there are all the usual entertainments and stalls.

Access: Surat Thani is 640 km south of Bangkok, on the main southern highway and railway, and has an airport too.

Chonburi Buffalo Races, (Chonburi, East) early October (one day).

Men ride water buffalos in hair-raising rodeo-like races, and they also pit themselves against the animals in contests of strength. Beauty contest and bazaar, as usual.

Access: Chonburi is 80 km southeast of Bangkok and about 60 km north of Pattaya.

Tak Bat Devo (Uthai Thani, Central) early to mid-October (day after *Ok Phansa*).

Tak Bat Devo means 'filling the bowls of the gods'; in this festival, a long file of monks descend the very long stairway to receive offerings from local people, as the Buddha is believed to have done after preaching to his mother in heaven. Folk theatre and other entertainment are on hand.

Access: Uthai Thani is 220 km north of Bangkok, just west of Highway 1.

OCTOBER/NOVEMBER

Golden Mount Fair, (Wat Saket, Bangkok) late October to mid-November (9 days around full moon).

This is the capital's premier temple fair and features all sorts of side-shows, like freak shows and ghost houses, monkey theatre and mini-zoos, besides the usual knick-knack and food stalls. Devotees pay homage to a large Buddha image at the foot of the mount by sticking gold leaf to it. The golden spire on the summit is swathed in a broad red cloth.

Access: the Golden Mount is just south of the junction of Rajadamnern Nok and Klang Avenues, on the edge of the old city.

NOVEMBER

Loy Krathong, (nationwide, [see box story, page 307] special events in Sukhothai, Chiang Mai, Bangkok) early to mid-November (full moon of the 12th lunar month).

This is Thailand's most picturesque national festival in which little candle-lit floral floats are placed on water. In

Bangkok, huge elaborate ones are floated on the ornamental lakes of Dusit Zoo.

In Chiang Mai, there is the *Yi Peng Loy Krathong* in which colourful hot air paper balloons are launched into the sky and beautiful lanterns are lit in homes and shops.

In Sukhothai, the celebration features an elaborate sound-and-light show with a historical pageant, fireworks and folk dancing.

Surin Elephant Round-Up, (Surin, Northeast) third weekend (Saturday-Sunday).

This pachyderm jamboree features over 100 trained elephants doing everything from the very silly to the most noble, from playing football to marching to medieval war. It includes hardwood-log-manoeuvring, tugs-of-war and wild elephant hunt simulation.

Access: Surin is in the lower northeast, and on the railway, 460 km from Bangkok.

River Kwai Bridge Week, (Kanchanaburi, Central) late November/early December.

This festival recreates the 1945 Allied bombing attack on the prisoner-of-war-built bridge in a dramatic sound and light show. There are also archaeological and historical exhibitions, and vintage train rides.

Access: Kanchanaburi is 130 km west of Bangkok on the western railway line from Thonburi (Bangkok Noi) Station.

DECEMBER

Trooping of the Colours, (Royal Plaza, Bangkok) December 3.

This is a ceremony of military allegiance to the monarch for his birthday (two days hence).

Squads of the Royal Guards march in brightly coloured uniforms – yellow, scarlet, purple, white, emerald, peacock blue, pink – with plummed helmets in a display of military precision and ceremonial pomp.

They march up Rajadamnern Nok Avenue and parade in the Royal Plaza before the King and Queen and past the equestrian statue of King Chulalongkorn.

Access: Royal Plaza is at the head of Rajadamnern Nok Avenue in front of the old National Assembly, Dusit district.

The King's Birthday Celebration, (nationwide, notable in Bangkok). December 5.

The King's birthday provides an annual occasion for public expression of the deep reverence and affection in which he is held.

On this national holiday, government buildings, businesses and homes nationwide are brightly decorated, usually with coloured lights and cardboard portraits.

In Bangkok, the historic area around Sanam Luang near the Grand Palace is spectacularly lit.

Loy Krathong

The prettiest of Thai national festivals takes place when the waters have reached their highest at the end of the rainy season, in late October or early November. On the full moon night of the 12th lunar month, Thais go down to the water – any water, pond, canal, river, lake or sea – and lay floating floral tributes lit by candles.

These are called *krathong* and they float, *loy*, hence the festival is called Loy Krathong. Historically, it is a thanksgiving to Mae Kong Ka, Mother Water, for her bounty and a plea for forgiveness for having used and polluted the water. Most people today believe it is to wash away the past year's sins and bring them luck for the future.

The first *krathong* is said to have been floated seven centuries ago at Sukhothai by Nang Noppamas, daughter of a Brahman priest who made a lotus flower *krathong* and presented it to the king. He lit the candle inside it and offered it to Mother Water. Loy Krathong is thus closely associated in the Thai mind with the birth of Thai nationhood at Sukhothai.

Today celebrations extend from cheap little banana leaf floats in slum ditches and pretty little *krathongs* on country canals, to the great plastic extravaganzas at Sukhothai Historical Park and Bangkok's Dusit Zoo with huge styrofoam creations holding beauty queens. Whatever and wherever, the thing to do is to watch your *krathong* till it floats out of sight and, if the candle is still burning, you will have luck in the coming year.

The frilliest of ladies at the prettiest of national festivals, Loy Krathong.

Son et Lumiere at the ruins of Sukhothai during Loy Krathong.

LIFESTYLE • FESTIVALS • CRAFTS

Handicrafts

by Kelvin Rugg

You don't need 20/20 vision to notice that Thailand is almost awash with examples of its citizens' prodigious artistic skill and craftsmanship. It is a talent that goes back a long way but even today the Thais do possess an almost unfair proportion of natural creativity and the means to express it – a high degree of manual dexterity. Examples abound of both traditional and modern adaptations of the Thai craftsmen's skills. The architecture itself for example. Even in modern reproductions the innate skill is clearly evident from the artistry of the basic structure to the craftsmanship displayed in woodcarving and decorative finishing.

Many of the traditional skills have been adapted and updated to cater for the real or imagined needs of that all important person, the tourist. Take a stroll along Bangkok's Silom Road for instance and you will see at least one of the 'Birdmen of Bangkok' giving impressive displays of their colourful flying paper models.

Even casual products like kites bear the mark of Thai craftsmanship.

311

Indigenous crafts like Thai silk have been revived and revitalised. The flourishing jewellery industry has drawn on those same nimble and creative talents to become a top exporting producer, the cutting skills of the Thai craftsmen are recognised throughout the world.

Every country has some tradition of folk arts and craft. In Thailand it has enriched the past and even as those concrete towers push ever more skywards, this creative skill of the people is surely to be admired and encouraged at every step.

For Thai silk, modern technology has yet to displace the drawing of single, unbroken strands from slumbering cocoons.

Thai Silk

Learning to weave was, in earlier times, part of the proper training of all young Thai women who would make all the household cloth and clothing. The introduction of silk-weaving to Thailand from China where the breeding of silkworms had begun around 3,000 BC was probably an early example of a major industrial espionage. Silk was then literally worth its weight in gold and stories tell of the seeds of the mulberry tree being smuggled out of China inside a bamboo pole by Syrian monks. In another version the precious seeds were smuggled out in the headdress of a Chinese princess.

Much patience and a lot of that traditional Thai skill is needed to produce a length of silk cloth. Fine strands from several cocoons are reeled together to form a single strand of the raw silk.

A single cocoon can produce around a thousand metres of filament-like strands but it takes over 20,000 cocoons to produce a kilogramme of silk thread. The skeins of raw silk are then bleached, dried and dyed in readiness for the weaving process.

Thai silk's unique quality owes much to the long tradition of hand-weaving which adds an individual character to each length of the finished fabric.

Mudmee which means "tied threads" is one kind of Thai silk which has greatly benefitted by the great interest shown by Her Majesty, Queen Sirikit through the SUPPORT Foundation and the Chitrlada shops to be found throughout the country.

Eggshell lacquerware, a process of painstaking craftsmanship.

The Thai silk industry as it is to day owes much of its prosperity to the renowned American Jim Thompson in whose name a business still thrives long after the founder's mysterious demise.

Many silk retailers are to be found in the Silom and Sukhumvit areas of Bangkok, some, such as Design Thai on Silom Road have introduced new processing technology which allows this lustrous material to be fashioned into elegant yet practical fashion wear, able even, to be washed and ironed – gently.

Lacquerware – *Lai Rot Nam*

During the Ayutthaya period of Thai history the art of decorative lacquer work found full expression. Furniture and artefacts and even a complete pavilion received the lacquer and gold leaf treatment of *Lai Rot Nam* – splash-water pattern. The basic technique, which like many ideas had come to Thailand from China, was quickly adapted to an unmistakeable Thai style. In contrast to the spatial Chinese landscapes, the Thai craftsmen produced designs of fine and intricate detail with an overall harmony achieved by the subtle juxtapositon of light and dark areas. Many fine examples of lacquerware cabinets and furniture of the 17th century can be seen in the National Museum. Originally, *Lai Rot Nam* was applied mainly to bookcases containing Buddhist scripts and to enrich door and window panels.

Although parts of the traditional

process have been speeded up in today's 'lacquerware villages' such as Ben Kern near Chiang Mai, the basic technique, then and now, is much the same. An undercoat or primer of a mixture called *samook*, whose ingredients read like a recipe for a magic potion, is first applied.

Ashes of rice-paddy husks or ground clay is then mixed with *rak*, the black lacquer to be obtained from a tree that grows in the northern hills. When the first application has thoroughly dried and the object polished, the whole *samook* process is repeated as many as fifteen times before a final polish with a rough leaf called *bai-nod* is applied. And that is just the first stage!

Nothing, it would seem, is easy in the time-consuming process of *Lai Rot Nam* and this is still a long way from the water part of the process. The pure black lacquer, the first coat of which is applied next, is derived from the milky sap of the Burmese varnish tree and it takes weeks of patient collecting before sufficient quantity can be accumulated.

With up to six layers and perhaps a couple of weeks of drying time between each application, it can take several months and a final polishing with water and powdered clay to achieve the gleaming, lacquered surface. And gilding has yet to be applied. Gilding takes a mere couple of days during which the yellow gum and the 'unwanted' gold leaf are given a thorough dousing with water, finally justifying that somewhat romantic description of what is essentially a tedious and painstaking process.

Yan Lipao – Basketry

Made from the stems of an abundant, southern forest vine, *Yan Lipao* is a particularly attractive form of basketware which like *Mudmee* silk, owes its revival to the support of Her Majesty Queen Sirikit. The art of transforming the humble vine into the boxes and bowls and even dishes of *Yan Lipao* basketware, dates back several hundred years but it was only popularised in the reign of King Rama V. Simple household utensils made from the vine were then embellished with gold or a copper and gold alloy called *naak*, for the ladies of the court.

Yan Lipao is a southern name, half Thai and half Malay, *yan* meaning vine in Thai and *lipao* from a Malay word which means lizard's foot, a description applied to the vine's leaves. The vine stems which are either naturally brown or black are cut and stripped at an early stage of growth as a precaution against the fibre breaking. Drawn through holes in a tin plate to ensure a uniform size, the stems are dipped in water for tough-

Khon Masks

Those fearsome looking masks, familiar to anybody who's seen a performance of a classical *Khon* dance are themselves the product of a small but highly specialised 'home' industry.

The *Khon* dance itself is the Thai version of the Ramayana, an ancient Sanskrit legend dealing with the battle between Rama and the evil King Totsakan who kidnapped Rama's wife, Sita. Rama is helped by his brother, Laksana and several monkey chieftains against Totsakan and his demon allies.

In the early days of the *Khon* the dancers simply painted their faces but by the reign of King Rama II masks were introduced. Today there are over one hundred different demon masks alone, all with appropriately devilish expressions. Masks are made from a plaster mould covered in several layers of *sa* paper coated with a paste derived from the **rak samu** tree, and then reinforced with leather and wire before being decorated with gold dust and pieces of glass.

The *Khon* can be a very energetic dance so why is it the masks do not fly off like unstrapped crash helmets? The answer is in the clenched teeth of the dancers biting firmly on a special wire grip!

ening before being threaded meticulously around a fine rattan framework. No dyes are used in the three month process which relies solely on the natural colour of the brown and black stems for the beauty of the finished item.

Yan Lipao can be bought in the SUPPORT Foundation shops and in several specialist stores in Bangkok.

Silverware

Thai silverware, like many of the country's handicraft, owes its origin to the adaptation of basic skills learnt from other countries. The techniques of silversmithing came to Thailand via Burma from India some two thousand years ago and flourished in the 13th century when immigrant Burmese craftsmen established Chiang Mai as the centre for silver work. The early Thai craftsmen, developing their own designs, were influenced not only by the Burmese but by the Portuguese in the 16th century. Intricate patterns and motifs of astrological signs and historical scenes were engraved on religious and household objects, very often on bowls and sword handles and scabbards. It was this Portuguese influence which resulted in the development of **nielloware**, the process of combining silver with a black, metallic alloy. Today Nakhon Si Thammarat in southern Thailand enjoys a considerable reputation for fine quality niello and silverware products.

But it's the silverware produced by the northern hilltribes which is catching the collector's eye. Although these colourful and essentially happy people are in danger of being caught in the inescapable spiral of self-interested exploitation, the silverware they produce for their own and commercial use is

Thai silverware, especially the hilltribe variety are highly collectable.

A vast range of highly decorative, yet functional table items are available at rather moderate prices.

uniquely different and highly collectable.

Betel-nut and opium containers and even beautiful silver opium pipes are some of the most popular items, all available in Bangkok. But there is much more; silver animals for instance, or if you're really lucky, an Akha tribal head-dress complete with silver rupees, a round silver pendant, a long flat neck- ring and a silver fish.

Jewellery

An ancient proverb asks, "Who can find a virtuous woman? For her price is far above rubies." If you're shopping for either in Bangkok today, you'll find that one is in far greater supply than the other. Amongst its many other distinctions, Thailand's captivating capital is gaining a well-deserved reputation for flawless beauties of a more durable kind.

The gems and jewellery business is now the rising star of the country's export industry employing an estimated million plus workers in the gemstone business alone. It has been the quality and cut of its coloured gemstones which has propelled the jewellery business to its pre-eminent position but Thailand's gold and silver jewellery, especially on the retail side, is also now widely acclaimed. Highly skilled gemstone and now diamond cutters have given Thailand's jewellers the edge over many of the world's traditional centres. Vast new jewellery trade centres are geared to attracting ever more business for the export market but there is a flourishing retail business too and bargains are still to be had.

For those interested in buying jewellery in Thailand caution and commonsense are prerequisites for getting a fair deal and three important rules for successful shopping should be followed: always shop around.

One method is to select your own centre stone after having it independently valued and then choose the small complimentary gemstones separately. With the help of an imaginative local jeweller you can then literally create your own piece. With gemstones it is the strength of colour, clarity and cut which

---

Palm Leaf Mobiles

The triangular-shaped native fish, the **tapian**, is perhaps the most common palm leaf mobiles to be seen on sale in shops and markets.

Originally designed to distract and soothe the sobbing infant, the gently- spinning figures, some with tiny bells that jingle in the breeze are now often bought by adults simply for decoration.

The fish shape is easily made from two palm leaves by an experienced worker, who shapes the fins with sharp scissors to prevent splitting. But the balancing of the complete mobile is more difficult.

It is not just fish, of course, which receive the palm leaf treatment. Crickets and grasshoppers, butterflies and birds are folded, plaited and painted by the Thai womenfolk of Tambon Hua Laem where making mobiles is a major occupation.

Unravelling a mobile which has been carelessly stowed away is, if you've ever had to do it, another major occupation.

determine their value.

In Bangkok, Silom again is the main jewellery area with a few important shops being located off Sukhumvit Road.

Wood-Carving

The earliest remaining pieces of Thai wood carving date from the 16th century. Many fine examples such as a collection of the mythical Thai mermaid, the *kinnaree* can be seen in the National Museum in Bangkok. There are countless examples too of traditional carving on temples, public buildings and as evidence that the craftsmen are as skilfull as ever, hotels, restaurants and even many houses are often decorated in the same manner.

Until its recent scarcity, teak has been the wood of choice but other hardwoods are used too especially in the cottage industries at Hang Dong near Chiang Mai where 'instant antiques' in the form of figures and animals are aged in the sun. Reproduction carvings are big business at Ban Thawai but it is also a place to view a renowned collection of genuine antiques, all examples of the wood carver's art.

Ceramics

Archaeological discoveries over the past few years point to a much earlier history of an indigenous Thai ceramic-making capability than was previously thought. The sensational discoveries in the mid-1960s at Ban Chiang in the northeast of Thailand provoked a radical reappraisal of the area's ceramic history. It now seems that the production of glazed stonewares probably began at Si Satchanalai as early as the 10th century.

The Si Satchanalai and Sukothai glazed stonewares of the 13th century were the precursors of the celebrated **Sawankhalok** celadons produced at Ban Ko Noi which represented a high point in early potting technology. The site at Si Satchanalai some 18 km from the town of **Sawankhalok** near Sukothai can still be visited and at least two shops sell pottery found in the original kilns.

Celadon is produced by the double-firing of common clay at very high temperaratures in combination with wood ash and other chemicals. Although occasionally found in blue and other colours, it is the pale, traditional apple green celadon which is still the most popular and which commands quite high prices.

The famed green-glazed pottery was to give rise to at least one curious superstition. In the middle ages, a court jester dressed in celadon green would be required to test suspect food for poison. The idea apparently was that it would show up on a celadon plate. A notion which adds a whole new dimension to the expression "turning green."

During the 17th and 19th centuries a special class of porcelain, made in China for exclusive export to Thailand

Thai pottery and ceramic-making has had a long history as evidenced in the Ban Chiang discoveries.

became known collectively as "Sino Thai Wares" and consisted of two main types of ceramics, *Benjarong* and *Lai Nam Thong*. *Benjarong*, literally "five colours" – red, yellow, white, black and green or blue being used most often with occasional introductions of pink, purple, orange and brown. *Lai Nam Thong* in addition used gold as a background and outline colour. Both *Benjarong* and *Lai Nam Thong* are produced today and even as modern reproductions can cost upwards of a few thousand dollars for a small bowl.

Parasols of Bo Sang.

Umbrellas Unlimited

Bo Sang, about nine kilometres from Chiang Mai, has been producing colourful paper umbrellas for the tourist and export market for the past 30 years. 'Umbrella village' is well established on the tourist circuit and its parade of parasols certainly presents irresistible photo opportunities.

Made from *sa* paper and bamboo the highly decorated umbrellas are often over two metres in diameter and in this form make ideal sunshades. A big attraction is the dramatic designs executed with exceptional artistic skill and flair. The *sa* paper is surprisingly robust and is given a coat of finishing varnish which makes the umbrellas shower-proof at least.

Although the best choice can be found in Bo Sang itself, the umbrellas are certainly available in Bangkok.

Mother-of-Pearl Inlay

Perhaps one of the most exacting and time-consuming of the decorative arts, mother-of-pearl work dates back in Thailand to around the 6th century AD The famed pink and green lustre of the Thai mother-of pearl, *hoi fai* comes from the curiously named 'turbo snail' indigenous to the Gulf of Thailand.

The curved, brittle shell is first cut into small pieces which are then filed until they are reasonably flat. These slices of shell are then glued to discs of wood for reinforcement before being shaped with a special curved saw. The pattern has already been traced in reverse on paper and after each piece has been pasted in position, the whole mosaic is pressed onto the freshly lacquered surface of the object to be decorated, and then, after a suitable drying period, the paper is washed off.

Traditionally the identations were filled with a mixture of ground charcoal and lacquer, a substance more in keeping with an ancient craft than the modern substitute of car-body filler. Perhaps the latter's introduction was inspired by the image of the 'turbo snail' itself. But the old methods prevail. Rubbing and polishing is finally completed with a dried banana leaf dipped in coconut oil.

Small, lined rectangular boxes are some of the most appealing mother-of-pearl objects which can be bought all over Thailand for a few thousand baht.

Miniature Clay Dolls

In the spacious compound of a temple some 20 km from Ayutthaya, housewives gather in their spare time to fashion tiny dolls of clay. Using the simplest of tools these ladies fill their spare time in a commendably productive and creative pursuit.

The *Bang Sadej* clay dolls, which are available in many of the traditional handicraft outlets, usually depict typical scenes of rural Thai life. Colourfully painted and often mounted on a cardboard base these creations of yet more Thai nimble fingers will certainly present no problems of transportation.

by Colin Piprell

Sports and Recreation

Imagine yourself sailing amidst the enchanted scenery of Phang Nga Bay. Or how about golfing in Hua Hin, where the surrounding hillsides are ornamented with Buddhist temples, grassy fairways traversed by orange-robed monks on their morning rounds? Perhaps you may rather try trekking in the north, swaying atop an elephant through rain forests.

Whatever the preferences, on land or water you will find activities to suit everyone all year round.

No lack of variety of sea sports in Pattaya.

TENNIS

Tennis facilities are often provided by first-class resorts around the country as well as by several of the deluxe Bangkok hotels.

Given Thailand's sweltering climate, many visitors from the more temperate zones may want to stay with the less-exhausting doubles game. Certainly, the December to late February season offers the most comfortable conditions for the sport.

Most courts are floodlit, however, and evening tennis is reasonably cool year-round.

Mornings and evenings are cooler, no doubt, while traffic in Bangkok is at its

lightest and one might think the pollution is then also at its most benign.

Not so, according to experts: wind conditions generally mean that it is healthier to play at midday, despite the pollution from traffic. To some people, this represents the choice of expiring from the heat in preference to asphyxiation.

A few Bangkok hotels with tennis:
Dusit Thani Hotel
Rama IV Road
Bangkok
Tel: 236-0450-8

Hilton Hotel
2 Wireless Road
Bangkok
Tel: 253-0123

Rama Garden Hotel
9/9 Vibhavadi Rangsit Road
Bangkok
Tel: 579-5400

GOLF

The single most popular past-time of the privileged Thai these days, golf is also rapidly becoming one of Thailand's biggest draws for tour groups and other travellers from abroad.

Why has the sport become so popular in this country? Consider, first of all, the physical beauty of the surroundings — the lush vegetation, the glimpses of traditional Thai architecture, the views of tropical seas. Secondly, facilities are still inexpensive, by international standards, with service of an incomparable standard. Caddie fees are so low that almost everyone takes at least two caddies (usually women, in Thailand) — one to look after the clubs and one to hold the parasol.

Still another advantage of golf in Thailand is that the courses are largely empty during the week, though on weekends they are packed, mostly with Thais, each player accompanied by an entourage commensurate with his or her status. Some hire caddies whose sole function is to keep running to the clubhouse for fresh drinks!

Golfing in the North

One advantage of golfing in the north during the winter months is that the weather is especially cool and dry. Play is pleasant and relaxed. In the summer, on the other hand, temperatures are often higher even than they are in Bangkok. This, of course, might slow down the golf fanatics but it would never discourage them, especially when there are caddies with parasols and clubhouses with cold drinks.

Lanna (7,174 yards, par 72): Nestled at the foot of Doi Suthep, Chiang Mai's famous mountain, the Lanna course presents an only moderately difficult challenge in lovely surroundings.

Contact **Lanna Golf Course**, Mae Rim Road, Chiang Mai 50000; tel. (053) 221-911.

Rose Garden golf course.

Bangkok & Pattaya Greens

Between 1988 and 1990, 30 new courses were opened in Bangkok and neighbouring provinces; still, new ones seem to be opening almost monthly.

Navatanee (6,241 yards, par 72): An hour from Bangkok, this course was designed by Robert Trent Jones for the 1975 World Cup. After playing in that tournament, Seve Ballesteros rated the Navatanee the best in Asia. Contact 22 Mu 1, Sukhaphiban 2 Road, Bang Kapi, Bangkok 10230; tel. (02) 374-6127.

Rose Garden (6,435 yards, par 72): Also an hour from Bangkok and like the Navatanee, beautifully designed and landscaped. This is one of Thailand's most popular courses. Contact 4/8 Sukhumvit Soi 3, Bangkok 10110; tel. (02) 253-0295-7.

Royal Thai Navy Golf Course (6,800 yards, par 72): Near the town of Sattaheep, 30 km south of Pattaya, this 36-hole course is rated by some to be the most difficult in Thailand. Great scenery; immaculate fairways and greens. Contact **Phlu Ta Luang Golf Course**, Sattaheep, Chonburi 20180; tel. (02) 466-1180, ext. 2217.

The following Bangkok hotels have driving ranges and putting greens:

Siam Intercontinental, 967 Srapatum Palace Property, Rama I Road, tel. 253-0355-7.

Oriental Hotel, 48 Oriental Ave., tel. 236-0400/0420.

Golfing in Phuket

The **Phuket Golf and Country Club** has an 18-hole course on the island. Set amidst wonderful scenery, it has been designed to provide lots of interesting challenges for the golfer.

Contact **Phuket Golf and Country Club**, Phuket; tel. (076) 213-388.

There are lots more 18-hole and 9-hole courses around the country, many of them of fine international standard.

See the following sources for more information:

1. *Golf Thailand: A Player's Guide to Golf in Asia's Most Exotic Land* (Bangkok: Asia Images, 1989; available at most bookshops and hotel kiosks in Thailand).
2. *Thailand: Golfing* (a pamphlet available at Tourist Authority of Thailand offices).

Caddies at many golf clubs are often women, with no loss of efficiency.

Shangri-La Hotel, 89 Soi Wat Suan Plu, tel. 236-7777.

Seaside Golf at Hua Hin

This charming seaside town is not nearly as developed as Pattaya which many consider its old style to be one of its chief attractions. The **Royal Hua Hin Golf Course** was the first 18-hole course in the country, established in 1922. At the time it was considered by many to be the best in Asia; and is certainly still one of the most charmingly scenic.

Contact **Royal Hua Hin Golf Course**, tel. (032) 511-099.

TREKKING

Since the 1970s, trekking Thailand's northern forests has increasingly become a 'must' for the tourist. Unfortunately, the very popularity of trekking itself has tended to spoil what most trekkers come to experience in the first place, so that subsequent travelers have to range further and further to find relatively unspoiled forests and hilltribe communities.

Ten years ago, Chiang Mai was the place to go to; but since then many of the villages in this province have become tourist institutions, purely and simply. Trekking agencies which wanted to provide the best value possible moved their operations further afield, thus into the hills around Chiang Rai, the next frontier. Within a shorter time still, however, given the ever-increasing popularity of trekking, the same thing has happened here as occurred in Chiang Mai. Now it is Mae Hong Son and the Burmese border area which tends to draw people who want 'the real thing'. One day there may be no new frontiers to move to.

The high season for tourism in the north is the winter, roughly from November-April, when the weather is cool and dry. But be warned the nights can be cold at this time, and you will need sweaters and sleeping bags unless you settle for the blankets provided by the tour operators. Mosquitoes are less troublesome in this season, as one consequence, though you are still advised to bring a good insect repellant — there is malaria in the area, especially as you approach the border with Burma. A pair of walking shoes should be comfortable, but it is not necessary to wear hiking boots, since it is not likely that you would walk for more than 4-5 hours in a day. The going is fairly easy, despite the hills (especially when you find yourself going elephant-back at some stage).

There is very little danger from wildlife in any season, but remember that it is jungle, after all, and precautions are in order. From your point of view, the first and most important precaution is selecting your trekking agency carefully. You want guides who are responsible, and who speak the necessary hilltribe dialects. But there is more at stake than personal security. It is also a good idea to deal with people who are conscious of the need for environmental and cultural conservation.

It is best to contact the following authorities for guidance and recommendations.

Chiang Mai:
Contact the **Tourism Authority of Thailand**
105/1 Chiang Mai-Lamphun Road
Amphoe Muang
Chiang Mai 50000
Tel: (053) 248-604/607
Fax (66 053) 248-605

Chiang Rai & Mae Hong Son:
Contact the **Chiang Rai Tourist Information Center**,
Singhakhlai Road
Chiang Mai 57000
Tel: (053) 711-313

Hiking, nature trails in other areas:
Thailand has more than 60 national parks, including marine parks, located all over the country. (Contact the Tourist Authority for detailed information.) You can plan hikes on cool, dry mountain plateaus where maple trees turn scarlet in October (**Phu Kradung National Park**, in Loei Province). Or you can walk the jungle trails on Phuket Island, and follow cascading streams through virgin rain forest (**Khao

Phra Thaeo Wildlife Park). Guides are available, sometimes for a nominal fee. If you plan to stay overnight, be advised that government accommodations are available in some parks, but you should book early:

National Parks Division
Royal Forestry Department
Phaholyothin Road, Bangkhen
Bangkok
Tel: (02) 579-0529
or, **Khao Yai National Park** (recommended, and not too far from Bangkok)
Tel: (02) 282-1143-7 (**The Tourist Authority of Thailand**)

For overnight trips, bring your rain gear, a small first-aid kit, some insect repellent, and a torch. Warm clothing is also recommended for treks in mountainous parks of the north, northeast, and central provinces. Check beforehand on the availability of food.

JOGGING

Modern Bangkok presents a fine contrast to the average jungle trail in Mae Hong Son or a white-sand beach in Krabi. Masses of wheezing, honking vehicles simmer and belch noxious fumes in traffic jams which will soon have no end, if things continue the way they are. Hardly a fitness fanatic's dream. Still, there is no reason not to keep fit while in Bangkok, all the better to enjoy your windsurfing or diving later, if you travel to the provinces.

Lumphini Park. This oasis is the green 'lung' of one of Bangkok's busiest and most congested commercial districts. Lots of trees and grass and cool ponds provide balm for eyes and soul as you join the throngs of other jogging enthusiasts, both local residents and visitors, who use the miles of tracks.

Sanam Luang. If you are staying in the Banglampoo area, you could join the many locals who jog the perimeter of the **Pramane Grounds**, the broad tree-lined park bounded on two sides by the Royal Palace, Thammasat University, and the National Museum. The only disadvantage: this is also a major nexus of the city's bus system, and the traffic exhaust can get a little dense.

If you want a longer run, you can expand the Sanam Luang circuit by also jogging around the walled compound containing the Temple of the Emerald Buddha and the Royal Palace.

Deluxe hotels nowadays incorporate jogging facilities, as well as swimming pools or tennis courts.

Hotels with jogging facilities:

** Siam Intercontinental Hotel
967 Srapatum Palace Property
Rama I Road
Tel: 253-0355-7

** Hilton Hotel
2 Wireless Road
Tel: 253-0123

* Rama Garden Hotel
9/9 Vibhavadi Rangsit Road
Tel: 579-5400

* **Oriental Hotel**
48 Oriental Ave
Tel: 236-0400/0420

* **Ambassador Hotel** (daily fee)
171 Sukhumvit Road
Tel: 254-0444/255-0444

Central Plaza Hotel
695 Phaholyothin Road
Tel.541-1234

(* outdoor and especially recommended
** also open to the public)

FITNESS CENTRES

Private clubs with local membership have fitness centres and gyms; however a visitor would almost have to rely on hotel facilities. The following may be places that one could try to make arrangements:

Private Fitness Clinic Health Club
16/15 Soi Somkhit Ploenchit
Tel. 02/251-0392.

For men and women. Day membership fees for use of the gym, sauna, or jacuzzi.

Most first-class hotels have fitness centers; those which follow are particularly well-equipped. (Those with an asterisk [*] have day memberships for non-guests).

Hilton Hotel
2 Wireless Road
Tel: 253-0123
Fax: 253-6509

* **Ambassador Hotel**
171 Sukhumvit Road
Tel: 254-0444/255-0444
Fax: 253-4123

Dusit Thani Hotel
Rama IV Road
Tel: 236-0450-9
Fax: 236-6400/7238

* **Landmark Hotel**
138 Sukhumvit Road
Tel: 254-0404/0424
Fax: 253-4259/254-0439

Oriental Hotel
48 Oriental Ave.
Tel: 236-0400/0420
Fax: 236-1939

OUTDOOR ACTIVITIES AT SEA AND ON WATERWAYS

Thailand has over 2,000 kilometres of coastline on two seas as well as thousands of kilometres of rivers and canals. Thais traditionally have built their communities on these seas and waterways, looking to them for food, travel, communication, and recreation. Travelling these routes today gives you glimpses of Thai life you might otherwise never get to see while, beyond that, you are led into some of the most spectacular scenery this country has to offer. From the seas and waterways, one may choose from a whole range of water sports and other recreations.

Boating in the North

One could take a relaxing cruise with overtones of adventure and tour the rivers of the Golden Triangle, or in the provinces of Chiang Mai and Chiang Rai, on rafts or in open longtail boats. One recommended trip would occupy you for six hours on the Mae Kok River as it wends its way through jungled hills, past hilltribe villages where colourfully costumed hilltribe people tend to their buffalo and children splash and wave as you go by. Occasionally, one of their simple dug-out canoes will shoot out from the bank to take a closer look at you.

A variety of interesting trips are organised from Chiang Rai.
For Mae Kok River longtail boat-rides, contact:
Mae Kok Villa,
Tel: (053) 711-786

For rafting on the Mae Kok, contact the **Chiang Rai Tourist Information Center**,
Singhakhlai Road
Chiang Mai 57000
Tel: (053) 711-313

For Mae Hong Son Pai River rafting:
Sam Mok Tour Co.
64 Khun Lum Prapat Road
Muang District
Tel: (053) 611-439
Tomas Tour Co.
6 Nivet Phisan Road
Muang District
Tel: (053) 611-313

Waterways around Bangkok

Overnight on cruisers and converted rice-barges to Bang Pa-In and Ayutthaya from Bangkok are highly recommended: **Mekhala I**, **II**, and **III** are three luxuriously appointed wooden rice barges which proceed at a pace permitting a

Boat trips on the rivers of the Golden Triangle such as the Mae Kok are interesting adventures through jungles and hills.

relaxed appreciation of all the diverse and colourful sights along the river. But Huckleberry Finn should only have had it so good — saloon bar on deck, dinner by candlelight, and all cabins complete with hot showers and air-conditioning. This is probably the single nicest thing you could do for yourself if you have just a couple of days to relax in Bangkok.

Contact: **Asia Voyages**,
1st Floor Charn Issara Tower
942/163 Rama IV Road
Bangkok 10500
Tel: (02) 235-4100-4
Fax: (02) 236-8094

Day boat cruises to Bang Pa-In and Ayutthaya are also recommended if you are short of time.

A number of comfortable, modern boats make daily trips to Bang Pa-In and Ayutthaya. A buffet lunch is normally served on board. You can either take the boat up the river and a coach back to the city, or else a coach up to Ayutthaya and a boat back to Bangkok.

The following contacts could help your plan such a journey up the Chao Phraya:

Oriental Queen I and **II**, leaving from the Oriental Pier, beside the Oriental Hotel Tel. (02) 236-0400-9, ext.3133.

Ayutthaya Princess, leaving from the River City Pier Diethelm Travel, Tel: (02) 255-9200-4.

River Sun Cruises, leaving from the River City Pier, Tel: (02) 237-0077-8, ext. 16.

Canal tours

The distinctive longtail taxis, with upswept prows and long trailing propellor shafts, loaded with passengers and huge baskets of produce, are to be seen everywhere on Bangkok's river and canals. Two popular places to hire your own longtail are the Tha Thien Pier, beside the Grand Palace, and the Oriental Pier. Prices by the hour, the half-day, or the day vary considerably, and depend in part on the customer's skill at bargaining. Tours along some of the canals on the Thonburi side of the Chao Phraya River offer fascinating glimpses of a colourful, sadly fast-disappearing life along the water. See Bangkok as it used to be.

(Read the chapter on River & Klong Life, page 93 for more details).

Pattaya Seasports

The Pattaya area has suitable conditions for sailing all year around, but some operators prefer to move their boats down to Phuket during the winter season (November-May).

For more details contact:

Thai Yachting
7th Floor, Rajadamri Arcade,
Rajadamri Road,
Bangkok 10330
Tel: (02) 253-1733-5, 253-3786-7
Fax: (02) 253-3788.

Crewed charters and 'bareboat' charters are available from June-October.

Dinghies and catamarans

Owing to severe pollution in Pattaya Bay, it is not recommended you sail there unless you are confident of staying dry. Jomtien Beach, just to the south, has yet to see the worst effects of pollution and therefore may be better. All around both Pattaya and Jomtien, you can hire 14-foot and 16-foot catamarans or Laser dinghies by the hour or the day. Jomtien gets particularly good winds.

Sailing on the winds of southern Thailand.

Sailing and Boating in the South

Phuket (and Samui, to a lesser extent) is enjoying a fast-growing popularity as both a cruising and a yacht-racing destination. The Phuket King's Cup Regatta, inaugurated in 1987, has already proven enormously successful with the international yachting fraternity, while the local yacht-charter business is booming.

Why should this be so? One reason is simply the incredible scenery, with tropical island paradises a dime a dozen. On the other hand, if desert isles should cloy, there are places such as Patong Beach right at hand, with a rollicking nightlife and numerous seafood restaurants. And there is the wonderful climate.

There are essentially two seasons in the south of Thailand — the northeast monsoon and the southwest monsoon. During the north-east monsoon (roughly November-April), the weather in the Phuket area beats anything you'll find even in the Mediterranean — consistently sunny and dry with calm seas, yet winds are perfect for sailing. During the southwest monsoon (March-October), on the other hand, similar conditions obtain on the Samui side, in the Gulf of Thailand. Yachting holidays are ill-advised when it is the off-season, but there is no 'off season' for Thailand as a whole — if it's the wrong time for Samui, go can go to Phuket, and vice versa. (Companies such as Asia Voyages simply move their sailboats from the Andaman Sea to the Gulf of Thailand, and back again, taking advantage of the best seasons in each area.) Sailors take note and plan your boating vacations accordingly.

It is also worth noting that crewed sailing charters let you choose: sit back and concentrate on the scenery, if that's what you prefer, or do as much of the sailing yourself as you like, always under expert guidance — if you've always wanted to learn to sail, this is a great opportunity to get hands-on training.

Dinghies and catamarans: the more developed beaches on both Phuket and Samui offer small sailing craft for hire on terms similar to those found on Pattaya and Jomtien Beaches. Patong Beach, on Phuket, is the single largest centre. Contact the following for more details:

Asia Voyages
Bangkok
1st Floor Charn Issara Tower
942/163 Rama IV Road
Bangkok 10500
Tel: (02) 235-4100-4
Fax: (02) 236-8094.

Asia Voyages
64/1 Rassada Center
Rassada Road
Phuket 83000
Tel: (076) 216-137/528
Fax: (076) 214-668.

Star Yachting
4th Floor Charn Issara Tower
924/126-7 Rama IV Road
Bangkok 10500
Tel: (02) 233-0232, 234-2209.

Thai Yachting
7th Floor Rajadamri Arcade
Rajadamri Road,
Bangkok 10330
Tel: (02) 253-1733-5, 253-3786-7
Fax: (02) 253-3788.

If you need servicing for your yacht, contact
Yacht Services Co. Ltd.
c/o Asia Voyages
64/1 Rassada Centre, Rassada Road
Phuket 83000
Tel: (076) 212-901, ext. 079, or (076) 216-137.

Motor Cruises

On the other hand, you might rather simply relax and enjoy the comfort and social life afforded by the big motorized cruise boats.

Andaman Princess
83 Mu 3
Thawiwong Road
Patong Beach
Phuket
Tel: (076) 321-322.

SeaTran Queen
1091/57 New Petchburi Road
Bangkok
Tel: (02) 251-8467.

Sea Canoeing

Here is something different — two-person inflatable canoes are a memorable way to explore the fantastic limestone islands and caves of Phangna Bay, off Phuket. Phangna Bay is sheltered from heavy seas in both the rough seasons, offering consistently calm seas ideal for canoeing all year round. Contact the following for more details:

Phuket Sea Canoe Centre
P.O. Box 276
Phuket 83000
Tel: (076) 212-848.

Phuket Tourist Centre
125/7 Phang Nga Road
Phuket
Tel: (076) 211-849.

DIVING AND SNORKELLING

Under Thailand's sparkling seas, just off her white-sand beaches, lies an experience more vivid than almost any other you could imagine on this planet. Crystal clear waters, sometimes affording more than 30 metres of visibility, present undersea vistas of breathtaking variety and colour. Over 200 species of hard coral help provide the foundation for an ecosystem which is home to literally hundreds of thousands of marine organisms. And these marvels are easily accessible to snorkellers as well as scuba divers.

Expert instruction at all levels from Beginner up to Master Instructor is readily available, should you want to learn scuba diving. Equipment either for hire or for sale is widely available, as well. Sailboats and motor launches set out regularly on dive cruises extending from one day to several — a surprisingly cheap and thoroughly memorable alternative to resort hotels.

Gulf of Thailand

Although the scenery here is not always as dramatic as some of that found in the Andaman Sea, it is still far more than just average. The quality of diving ranges from that found in Pattaya, which has the best dive facilities, entertainment, and accommodation in the region (but which has also experienced the degradation of the natural environment), to that of vast and almost wholly unspoiled groups of islands and reefs accessible only by boat (and requiring that you bring your own gear, including compressor or filled tanks).

Pattaya Area

Pattaya/Sattaheep/Samae San

Scuba-Diving For Beginners

Beginners and experienced divers alike will find first-rate scuba-diving courses in Thailand.

At one end of the scale, there are usually free introductory pool lessons where instructors let you try the basic equipment in the pool (usually at hotels with facilities), allowing you to judge whether or not you're going to enjoy the sport before investing any money in lessons.

The next step might be enrolling at a 'resort course'. These one-day courses often include a dive in the pool in the morning, and a dip in the sea after lunch. Should this whet your appetite further, you could then elect to do the Basic Open Water certification, either under the PADI (Professional Association of Diving Instructors) or the NAUI (National Association of Underwater Instructors) programme. In either case, count on clocking in around 40 hours of practical and theoretical instruction, plus exams, before you obtain your certificate. One could complete a continuously whole course in four or five days continous, or else stretch it out over a couple of weekends.

From there you might go on to the Advanced Open Water programme or onward and all the way to such courses as Dive Rescue, Dive Master, or Master Scuba Diver.

(year-round): at only a couple of hours from Bangkok, Pattaya is the oldest dive centre in Thailand, with some of the best dive shops and most expert instruction in the country. There is an abundance of recreational activities both on the sea and on land should you be tired of underwater sport, and prefer to try something else.

Unfortunately, siltation and pollution has largely destroyed the corals around the islands within an hour's boatride out from Pattaya. Just a day-trip away, however, in the islands around Sattaheep and Samae San, there is still good coral and, of great interest to scuba enthusiasts, two wrecks — the Bremen and the Hardeep, sunken freighters lying in 25 and 27 metres of water, respectively, provide homes to marine life of all sorts.

Great seascapes and even grander marvels below the sea.

Moorish idol fish off the Similan Isles, near Phuket.

The following may help you organise a diving trip:

Seafari
Royal Garden Resort
Beach Road
Pattaya
Tel:(038) 428-126, 428-127
Telex 85909 ROGADEN TH.

Mermaid's Sea-Sport Center
75/102 M 12 Nong Prue
Jomtien 20260, Chonburi
Tel: (038) 232-219
Fax: (038) 232-221.

Others in Pattaya:
Dave's Diver's Den
Max's Dive Shop
Pattaya International Diving Centre
Steven Dive Shop
Reef Dive Shop
Sea Sport Diving Centre

Chumphon

Chumphon (March-October):
Chumphon has become a favourite destination for local divers, offering good visibility and an interesting variety of corals in so far largely unspoiled surroundings.

Chumphon Cabana Resort
Chumphon
Tel: Bangkok (02) 224-1884/221-5263.

Samui

Samui (March-October):
Koh Samui, the largest of a group of about 80 islands, has some fine patches of live coral, but other islands, notably those just to the south, offer more. Koh Phangan, the second largest of the group, and only an hour north by boat, has some good reefs for snorkelling.

Koh Samui Divers
Ang Thong Road
Koh Samui
Tel: (077) 421-465
(Surat Thani Office)
Tel: (077) 421-386 (Chaweng Beach)

Swiss International Diving Centre
41 Na Amphoe Road
Koh Samui
Tel: (077) 421-538

Caesar Manelli
Malibou Bungalows, Chaweng Beach, Koh Samui

Koh Tao

Koh Tao (March-October): this island is better than Samui and, some would argue, better than Chumphon for scuba diving. Furthermore, there are basic dive facilities on the island itself. Three or four hours from Samui, Koh Tao is almost equally accessible from Chumphon by fast boat.

Andaman Sea

Experienced divers agree that the Andaman has some of the best dive sites in the world.

Surface conditions and underwater visibility are at their peak during the November-March season. Weather permitting, however, diving daytrips to islands such as Racha (about 1-1/2 hours by boat from Patong Beach) and Phi Phi (about 2 hours by boat) are possible all year round.

Excursions to all the islands here most often leave from Phuket, where all scuba facilities in the region are also based.

Phuket

On Phuket Island itself, the coral has suffered extensive damage from anchors, dynamite fishing, collectors, untreated sewage disposal, and tin-mining. But this is still the place to arrange for instruction, equipment, and excursions to the other islands in the Andaman.

Most recommended: **Surin Islands** (about 160 km from Patong Beach — 7 to 8 hours by motor launch — and about 60 km from the Similans); **Similan Islands** (about 85 km northwest of Phuket); **Koh Bon** (30 km north of the Similans).

The following may be useful:
Fantasea Divers
Patong Beach

Precautions for Snorkellers and Scuba Divers

1) The seas off Thailand are so warm you do not really need a wet-suit, but it is nevertheless a good idea to wear something while diving, even if it's only a T-shirt and an old pair of jeans. On the one hand, this can help protect you against stings and abrasions, and on the other hand, against sunburn particularly when snorkelling, as it is easy to forget that the sun burns even through some metres of water.

2) Gloves are always a good idea.

Even with gloves, never touch marine animals with which you are unfamiliar.

As importantly, do not put your hands into holes or crevices on the reef unless you have first checked to see that nothing untoward is lurking there.

3) If you are wading around corals and rocks, shuffle your feet. This should scare up any stingrays hidden in the sand; at the same time it will make it unlikely that you will step down on the poisonous dorsal spines of a stonefish. Such injuries are rare, but the simple precaution is nevertheless advisable, given the seriousness of a stonefish wound.

4) Wear foot protection, but don't rely on shoes or flippers to protect against stonefish wounds.

5) Check with locals before swimming or diving in unfamiliar waters: are there any dangerous currents to beware of; are there an unusual number of stinging jellyfish in the vicinity at that time?

There is very little danger if you do take these precautions. With scuba diving, however, the most important safety advice is this: do not go diving unless you have first been properly trained.

Dive facilities are plentiful both in the Gulf and Andaman.

Coral Reef Conservation

1. Do not collect corals, shells, or other marine organisms while on the reef. Given the current and growing popularity of diving, some species can rapidly be pushed to local extinction in this way.
2. Do not buy corals and shells from souvenir shops. This practice encourages commercial collectors, who can strip the reefs even faster than casual collectors.
3. Do not anchor boats directly over coral. A single anchoring on a virgin reef can destroy one square metre of coral.
4. Do not dump garbage on the reefs. Dispose of it properly. Not only does dumping at sea spoil the appearance of reefs and beaches, it can be harmful to marine animals.
5. Do not touch corals, if you can avoid it. When you disturb their mucus coating, you expose them to a range of algal and bacterial infection.

P.O.Box 74
Phuket
Tel:(076)321-309
Telex 69513 SHPSERV TH
Attn. FANTASEA.

South East Asia Yacht Charter
89/71 Thawiwong Road
Patong Beach
Phuket 83121
P.O.Box 199
Tel:(076)321-292
Telex 65542 SIMILAN TH.

Siam Diving Centre
Kata Karon Beach, P.O.Box 244,
Phuket 83000
Tel:(076)381-608
Telex 65542 SIMILAN TH
Attn. Siam Dive.

Others in Phuket:
Loan Island Resort
Phuket Travel and Tour
Sun and Sand Tour
Phuket Island Tour
Aloha Tours
Phuket Centre Tour.

WINDSURFING

An ever-increasing number of beaches all over Thailand are catering to this still new, yet phenomenally popular sport. Some of the more popular beaches have windsurf shacks all along their length, and many resort hotels have both equipment and instructors.

Crinoids and Damsel fish in shallow reef.

Winds are mostly dependable.

Hourly rates vary. Two-hourly, daily, and weekly rates are often negotiable. At the hotels, there is often no charge. If you do not know how to windsurf, it would be best to ask one of the attendants from the rental shack to provide a few tips. They should be willing to do so. Learning by trial and error can be enormously frustrating; simple awareness of a few basic principles, on the other hand, can make all the difference in getting started.

Jomtien Beach: good winds year-round; a several-kilometre-long beach with very little coral or rock.

Phuket: late November-February is the best season to windsurf — peak offshore winds on the west-coast beaches provide lots of action for the more adept, especially in the mornings; winds usually taper off to moderate breezes by early afternoon. In the April-October season, winds tend to be consistently moderate, but heavy seas roll in from the Indian Ocean and can present a hazard on some days.

Samui offers the north coast beaches of Mai Nam and Bophut, which have consistently good windsurfing throughout the year. The east coast beaches of Chaweng and Lamai, on the other hand, often have heavy seas from October till late January, making the sport ill-advised during this period.

DEEP-SEA FISHING

The best fishing to be had in Thailand is on the Andaman side. Marlin

> ### Refine Your Skills
>
> No matter how experienced you may be, there are always other courses you can take to refine and expand your scuba-diving skills. At least one dive shop (Seafari, in Pattaya), in fact, offers five-star PADI instruction all the way up to Master Instructor. And there are all the specialty courses — Night Diving, Wreck Diving, Search and Salvage, and lots more. One of these can often be completed in a day or two. What better souvenir of Thailand than a diploma certifying you as a trained Wreck Diver, something you can wave around as you regale the folks back home with tales of your adventures on the wreck of the Hardeep, a sunken freighter lying 27 metres deep, off Samae San.

and other much-sought-after big game species tend to be migratory, and the waters around Phuket are on the path of some prize-winners. Deep-sea fishing charters go out from one to five days at a time, trolling for everything from marlin to sailfish to tuna. Or you could try night-fishing for sharks.

This is one watersport in the Phuket area which, in many ways is best during the southwest monsoon (late April through November), when most sailors and divers have shifted their activities to the more protected waters of the Gulf of Thailand. This is because most of the best fish leave Phuket later in the high season (suggesting that some fish are smarter than they look), their instinctive annual itinerary taking them south until the following April.

It is probably because of these migratory patterns, the shallower waters (these resorts are simply not on the routes of the desirable fighting fish) as well as commercial over-fishing that you will not find sport of a similar calibre in the waters around Samui or Pattaya. Still, just as you may in Phuket during the winter season, you can also fish for sharks, barracuda, and lots more. In Pattaya, September-March is the best period, while October is the single best month. Sports fishing has not been developed to any extent in Samui and its surrounding area.

One of the highlights of the fishing season around Phuket is the Krabi Big Game Fishing Contest, in November, a time of year when sailfish and marlin are still caught in numbers sufficient to make this an exciting event.

The following may be useful in organising game–fishing:

Pattaya Game Fishing Club
Jenny's Hotel
325/34-36 Pattayaland Road 1
South Pattaya
Tel:(038) 429-645
(contact Martin Henniker)
Gamefishing, including sailfish.

Deutsche House Restaurant
54 Beach Road
North Pattaya
Tel: (038) 428-725
(contact D. Floeth)
Specializes in big sharks; organises larger groups on the boats.

Phuket Fishing Club
Hotel Neptuna
In front of the Paradise Complex
Patong Beach
Phuket
Tel: (076) 321-188.

Phuket Big Game Fishing Charter
82\25 Bangla Road
Patong Beach
Phuket 83121
Tel: (01) 723-0571
Fax: (076) 321-284.

Phuket Tourist Centre
125/7 Phangna Road
Phuket Town
Tel: (076) 211-849.

WATER-SKIING

In the peak tourist seasons on the major beaches around Phuket and Samui, year-round on Pattaya and Jomtien Beaches, water-skiing facilities are available.

On Phuket, there is very little to be had in the April-November season (one operator offers skiing off Coral Island, about 25 minutes from Chalong Beach). Patong and Kata/Karon are the big skiing beaches. Beginners should note that there is a starting platform moored off Nai Harn Beach, which can make learning a little easier.

On Samui, Bhoput and Mae Nam beaches on the north coast can provide suitable conditions throughout the year.

If one could be convinced, it could be quite a lot of fun.

PARASAILING

Parasailing is more a carnival ride than a sport, requiring very little skill and not much nerve, once you realise how easy it is. It should also be safe. Unfortunately, operators are not always as careful as they ought to be, and on Patong Beach (Phuket) for example, there have been several accidents due to congested boat traffic on the water and inexperienced boat drivers.

Once is fun, but once is usually enough.

WHAT TO DO / WHERE TO GO

by Kelvin Rugg

Eating Out

The aroma of Thai cooking, that all pervasive mixture of coriander and coconut milk, galanga and garlic and the peculiar pungency of fish sauce, can be a powerful stimulus to memories of more than just one country's cuisine.

Long after the traveller has returned to domestic shores and familiar surroundings, the very essence of Thailand and its people is evoked when the nostrils encounter any one of those provocative perfumes.

The provocative perfume of Thai cuisine is known to have beckoned many a visitor back.

Wherever you eat in Thailand the probability is that you will be offered well-cooked, fresh food. It is also highly likely that the Thai cook's most lethal weapon, the ubiquitous and for some, infamous, chilli, will be an integral and throat-searing part of one or more dishes. It is a fair assumption that if chilli-flavoured toothpaste is ever introduced it would have a ready market in this land of instant smiles and almost instant noodles.

Sheer availability of good food, almost any time of the day and late into the night removes the pressure from

one of life's constant demands – where and what are we going to eat today?

The Thai's predilection for sea food has resulted in a huge choice of specialist restaurants, many built around artificial lakes and featuring great tanks of live fish waiting for their number to be called. Meat too is favoured and flavoured with almost equal relish. Pork, 'buffalo' beef and chicken, all receive the Thai tenderising treatment and feature in a variety of dishes with tempting but tongue-twisting names.

Of the two temptations of the flesh for which Thailand is celebrated, it is probably still true that eating offers the best value for money. For the price of the one you can sample a double helping of the other in the form of a medium-priced dinner for two. And at the bottom end of the market (so to speak!) a bowl of noodles can be had for a handful of loose change.

Eating Out in Bangkok

Thai Restaurants

Tumnak Thai
131 Rajdapek Road
Telephone 277 3828.

Located in one of Bangkok's better known eating-out areas, this collection of landscaped Thai pavilions offers every kind of regional Thai dish under one roof. Or more accurately under several roofs. Tumnak Thai has been catering on the grand scale since 1985 when it was built at a cost of some 50 million baht.

Although the atmosphere is artfully contrived 'rural Thai' the scale of the operation has called for more metropolitan solutions to organisational problems. The 40 or so waiters and waitresses bedecked in traditional 'chongkrabane' costume rumble along the wooden walkways on roller skates, their customer's orders being relayed to the kitchen by computer.

Tumnak Thai is essentially a place for eating with friends. The menu offers over 300 different items covering selections from all the main regions of the country. Steamed catfish with Thai herbs, barbecued pork, fried chicken in pandanus leaves, and pumpkin and coconut soup are all reported favourites with the locals. The 'boiled serpent's head soup' is probably more an acquired taste.

Opening times: 11.00 am to 10.30 pm. with a Thai cultural dance show in the evening.

Prices: Dinner for two, around 350 baht.

Sala Rim Nam
Oriental Hotel
48 Oriental Avenue
Bangkok.
Telephone: 236 0400.

Literally 'Pavilion by the Water's Edge', the Oriental's Rim Nam offers a stylish opportunity to dine at what, in the long-standing opinion of at least one magazine, is 'The World's Best Hotel'. Getting to the restaurant is half the fun and evening is the best time to go. Diners are ferried from the hotel's twinkling terrace in true colonial style across the mighty Chao Phraya and led to the cavernous restaurant where first footwear is deposited on a silver tray. Tables are of the sunken-well variety and seating is very comfortable but considerable effort is required to get up. The kneeling position adopted by the waiters is borne of necessity rather than any special deference.

Evenings offer a set menu of Thai dishes and a polished programme of traditional dancing. The deep-fried honeyed chicken, *Gai Haw Bai Toey* in the ever popular pandanus leaf is almost as distracting as the glittering and graceful dancers.

An a\ la carte menu is available on the Rim Nam terrace where patrons can enjoy a meal there by the river, ignoring reports of pirana fish in the fast-flowing waters.

One wonders what those Danish sea captains Jarck and Salje who "commissioned to be built the modest Oriental Hotel" back in 1876, would make of it all today.

The food and service at the Sala Rim Nam reflect the impeccable standards of the hotel and although the hotel restaurant may be regarded expensive by some, costs generally are high, the Sala set menu is good value for money. It's worth the boat ride just for the stylish slice of culture and cuisine and the impressive souvenir menu.

Opening times: Buffet lunch from 12 noon. Dinner nightly from 7 pm.

Prices: Set menu 650 baht per person. A la carte for two, around 900 baht.

Lemongrass
5/1 Sukhumvit 24
Bangkok
Telephone 258 8637.

Often and highly praised for the quality and consistently high standards of cooking, the seven-year old Lemongrass is carefully supervised by partners Vorachoon and Narin. Antique-loving 'Choon' says their aim is to provide a true Thai atmosphere with the kind of food Thai people eat at home. The result of their endeavours is a comfortable, woody and cosy ambience which manages to appear completely uncontrived and a menu of traditional but sometimes uncommon dishes whose every ingredient has been carefully scrutinised for authenticity.

Emphasis is on regional Thai food, which itself is not all pure Thai, with many dishes originating from the south of the country.

Try the barbecued chicken, *Gai Yang Pak Panang* and the coconut in syrup. This dessert is common enough but the Lemongrass uses only the *Ma prow gatik* variety of coconut and the taste is lingeringly different.

One is assured well-cooked and charmingly presented food in a 'visiting

Hormoak – presentation often competes with deliciousness.

the grandparents' atmosphere. The Lemongrass is easily accessible off Bangkok's main Sukhumvit Road.
Opening hours: 11 am – 2 pm, 5.30 – 11 pm.
Prices: Dinner for two, around 350 baht.

Nipa
3rd Floor, Landmark Plaza
Sukhumvit Road
Telephone 254 0404.

The snappy Japanese sounding name notwithstanding, the Nipa is a classy but reasonably-priced restaurant which serves excellent Thai food. Khun Tukata, the suitably rotund lady chef, reassuringly presides over a kitchen which turns out an impressive choice of elegantly presented dishes. Seafood is especially good, for those who like it hot and spicy, and the wordy *Kaeng Som Sam Sad Yam Saeng Wa* will bring a definite sparkle to the eyes, perhaps even a few tears.

Grilled prawns with chilli, onion and lemon juice seasoning and served together with fried catfish in a pumpkin shell, provide a filling concoction.

Teak-panelled surroundings and well-timed service, the Nipa, named in fact after a former Miss Thailand, is part of the Landmark Hotel complex and is easy to find at the centrally-located hotel.

Opening times: 11.30 am–2.30 pm. 6.00 pm–10.30 pm.
Prices: Dinner for two, about 400 baht.

Kao Tom Kamlang Pai Nai
169/4-8 Radchadapisek
Hway Kwang
Telephone: 277-1275, 277-4009.

Whether or not you believe the claim implicit in the English rendering of this restaurant's name, that "rice soup provides vital *chi* energy", you'll need a fair amount, of energy that is, to take full advantage of the all-night opening hours.

The extrovert personality of the movie-maker owner is reflected in the general 'get up and go' atmosphere. Before you do just that, ensure your digestive system is sufficient at least for you to try the 'Special Red Rice' with pandanus leaves. There is also a good choice of seafood, duck, chicken and meat dishes.

Opening times: 5.00 pm to 6 am.
Prices: Dinner for two, around 450 baht.

Cabbages and Condoms
10 Sukhumvit
Sol 12.
Telephone: 252 7349.

Yes, there is a message in the name and it is nothing to do with cabbages. Aside from its crusading objectives, C&C does provide quite excellent Thai cooking.

The pleasant house-style restaurant was established by the Population and Community Development Association both as a means of generating profit for much-applauded charitable causes and as a useful focal point.

The food on offer is also a long way from cabbages. You will find an excellent selection for example, of traditional Thai curries, as tasty and as hot as they look. Roast duck with coconut milk is especially favoured by locals. And they should know. Not too difficult to find off the main Sukhumvit Road, this slightly self-conscious establishment provides perhaps the best value for money in town and encourages early dining from its patrons by operating appropriately conservative opening hours.

Opening times: 11 am to 10 pm.
Prices: Dinner for two around 150 baht.

Tea Rose
2nd Floor, Peninsula Plaza
Rachadamri Road
Telephone: 252 4528.

In the up-market atmosphere of one of Bangkok's smarter shopping com-

The Thai kitchen has been blessed with an abundance and variety of vegetables and fruits.

plexes, the Tea Rose is a stylish restaurant that offers much more than its name suggests.

Elegant and tasteful decor and panoramic views over a surprising amount of greenery makes this the sort of place you feel you have discovered all on your own.

The menu has been designed to be as interesting and as varied as possible. Crispy squid with mango or apple salad for example and ox tongue stew encourage further explorations.

A wide choice of coffees and over a dozen different blends of teas finally justify the restaurant's name, which sounds like this year's prize winner in a horticultural show.

The Tea Rose is the ideal place to drop in for an elegant respite from the rarified ramparts of marbled shopping malls.

Opening times: 10.30 am to 8 pm.
Prices: Dinner for two – about 450 baht.

The Whole Earth
93/3 Soi Lanngsuan
Pioenchit Road
Telephone: 252 5574.

The staff at the Whole Earth are reputedly required to meditate daily and this may explain the occasional slowness of service which however is generally very accommodating.

The Whole Earth is organised on two levels – tables and chairs and you can keep your shoes on, downstairs; upstairs it is a shoeless arrangement of low, knee-aching tables and back-aching cushions.

Essentially vegetarian, the menu nonetheless still caters for meat eaters with such temptations as charcoal broiled pork in honey sauce and sweet and sour with a choice of chicken or pork.

Vegetarians will probably enjoy the Thai style vegetarian curry with coconut milk or perhaps the seafood curry served in a guaranteed leak-proof banana leaf bowl.

Perhaps not for gourmets but a pleasant rendezvous with friends and if you elect to dine on the upper level, a useful prelude to yoga therapy.
Opening times: 11.30 am to 2 pm, 5.30 pm to midnight.
Prices: Dinner for two – about 400 baht.

Chinese Restaurants

Royal Seafood
50 Soi Lang Suan
Ploenchit Road
Telephone: 2513401.

Another name not entirely in keeping with the menu, the Royal Seafood, although providing a good selection of marine molluscs and fish, does in fact offer some delectable dim sum. Roast duck, protein-rich shark's fin soup and all the familiar favourites are cooked and presented in true Cantonese style. Fried pigeon with vegetables has its devotees as does the unusually tasty crab dim sum. On three floors, the Royal Seafood can accommodate very large private parties or provide intimate dining for two or more.

Refreshingly green dominated decor and over 100 dishes on an 11-page menu, the Royal Seafood is a pleasant alternative to the usually bustling and noisy atmosphere of most Chinese restaurants.
Opening times: 11.30 am – 2.30 pm. 6.30 pm – 11.00 pm.
Prices: 350 – 450 baht, dinner for two.

Lok Wah Hin
Novotel, Siam Square
Telephone: 255 6888.

Very inviting in its low-light mode when the individually spotlighted tables beckon alluringly in the plum red decor, the Lok Wah Hin is a crispy new addition to the Bangkok food scene. The restaurant hovers over the hotel lobby, affording diners a one-way view of the comings and goings. The food is essentially Cantonese and Szechuan, tailored slightly to local Thai tastes. Braised superior abalone in oyster sauce will appeal to those wishing to enrich the body fluid and balance the blood pressure.

The cost of a large portion however might well have the opposite effect! Presentation of the food is superb with a comprehensive menu offering several exotic and highly priced items; the service is discreet and attentive. Its location makes the Lok Wah Hin an excellent place to unwind after a shopping expedition in the nearby malls.

Opening times: 11.30 am–2.30 pm. 6.30 pm–11.00 pm.
Prices: Dinner for two, around 550 baht.

China Restaurant 231/3
Sol Sarasin
Rajdamri Road
Telephone: 2520737-8, 2526825, 2510227.

Living up admirably to its all-encompassing name, the China Restaurant has been providing a comprehensive range of regional dishes for over the past forty years.

Cantonese, Mandarin, Szechuan and Shanghai are all catered for in an authentic atmosphere enchanced by live music and unhurried dining encouraged by late night opening hours. The choice of food as in many Chinese restaurants is extremely varied and almost overwhelming.

Well worthy of consideration are some of the China Restaurant's specialities such as barbecued suckling pig, fillet steak Chinese style, steamed garoupa with soy sauce, Peking duck and stewed bean curd with shrimps in brown sauce.

There are four private function rooms where you can function in private and a reassuring selection of live seafood at which you can point and indicate your choice in suitably imperious tones.

Centrally located and with a long standing reputation for good food at a reasonable price, the China Restaurant will not disappoint.

Opening times: 11.30 am to 2 pm. 6.00 pm to 3.00 am.
Prices: Dinner for two – about 250 baht.

Regent Restaurant
4/4 Sukhumvit Road
Sol 20
Telephone: 2581410.

No clue is provided in its name but this decidedly Chinese restaurant is easily spotted by its decidedly un-Chinese entrance – a colourful contrivance of a fabricated and castellated windowed archway.

Being easily located is a prime requirement for any restaurant and the Regent, although bearing an indifferent name, will always be seen. It is also adjacent to the Windsor hotel, another useful local landmark.

The Chinese chefs here enjoy a well-deserved reputation for their treatment of a wide choice of dishes. Casserole of baked crab claws, baked pigeon stuffed with shark's fin and sauteed fresh abalone – reputed to "enrich the body fluid, balance the blood pressure and maintain a youthful appearance", steamed goby fish with chilli and garlic are all excellent examples of Chinese culinary skill on offer.

Five function rooms and a seating capacity of over 200 arranged in mostly circular Chinese style provide ample space should you decide to visit en masse.
Opening times: 11.00 am–2.00 pm, 5.00 pm–10.00 pm.
Prices: Dinner for two around 350 baht.

Fried fish cake.

Street-side dining

Bangkok's legendary street vendors are, without doubt, a breed apart. It does, after all, demand a particular tenacity, coupled with formidable dexterity to set up a fully-equipped kitchen on the pavement. Boiling super woks of oil and steaming saucepans produce an array of fiery fritters, fish ball and meat noodles alongside mobile satay grills and carts creating pancakes covered in copious amounts of condensed milk.

Night-time pavement restaurants abound and knowledgeable locals argue over their different merits. Some of the best require time and dedication to reach but the one at Pratunam at the intersection of Phetchaburi and Racha-

prarop Road is easily located and worth a visit.
Opening times: From early to very late evening. Prices: Minimal, no cover charge. Noodles for two, 40 baht.

BANG SAEN

Thai Seafood

Ban Talay
Beach Bay
Ban Saen
Telephone 038 3282441.

Well worth a visit if you are travelling the coast road to Pattaya or south. The Ban Talay is a fairly ordinary, wall-less restaurant with extraordinary views. Occupying a large part of a concrete jetty, the slightly windswept Ban Talay is so designed as to allow patrons to literally drive in and park alongside their table.

Once seated, one forgets to look at the menu, so mesmerising is the constant but slow changing view of seabirds plunging and swooping, and boats in the bay, silhouetted against the sparkling and dappled waters. Oh yes, the food is as poetic. Newly-shredded crab, grilled squid, steamed cotton fish, steamed garoupa with rare prawns, herbs and lemon and oyster omelette. Egon Ronay eat your heart out!
Opening times: 9 am - 10 pm.
Prices: Dinner for two, around 150 baht.

PATTAYA

Thai Restaurants

Thai Market Restaurant
Royal Cliff Beach Resort
Telephone: (038) 428513-5.

Although you can find good Thai food in downtown Pattaya the general ambience is not altogether conducive to carefree culinary adventures. Better perhaps to enjoy the reassuring surroundings of a good hotel.

The Thai Market Restaurant at the Royal Cliff Beach resort provides an opportunity to eat in a sort of sanitized arrangement of imitation market stalls and general orchestrated conviviality. A good opportunity to wander around and try anything from noodles to deep fried shrimp balls. It's a bit like being on the set of one of those very stagey operas. A band entertains somewhat noisily. The seafood section provides good local fare. A place to enjoy with a few friends in the evening. There is barbecue Mondays and Fridays, a Thai food market on Thursdays.
Opening times: 6.30 pm–11 pm.
Prices: Dinner for two – about 500 baht.

Somsak
436/24 M. 9 Soi 1
North Pattaya
Telephone: (038) 328987, 423284, 429869.

In a slightly less boisterous area on

the north side of the town, the Somsak provides an excellent range of Thai, Chinese and some European dishes.

Now in a modern Thai hybrid building in a garden setting, the Somsak can draw on over thirty years of experience of feeding the quality of the food and service.

Kai Hor Bai Toey for example is especially tasty. This Thai favourite is chicken wrapped and cooked in pandanus leaves.

The result is a delicious herbal impregnation that's quite addictive. The long pointed leaves of the pandanus plant also provide the green colouring in some Thai desserts.

Another Somsak special is *Mee Grob* – crispy rice noodles deep fried in a sugar and vinegar paste with pork, shrimp and a tomato sauce. A hotter alterative is the *Hor Mok Pla Shawn* a very spicy fish curry steamed in a whole coconut.

Service at the Somsak is cheerful and for a restaurant which is usually fairly full, quite fast.

Opening times: 11 am–1 am.
Prices: Dinner for two around 300 baht.

The Lobster Pot
228 Beach Road
Pattaya
Telephone: (038) 426-083, 424-389

You may just happen to find yourself downtown in the magic of the evening, innocently admiring the pretty coloured lights and being impressed with the remarkable conviviality of the locals and their efforts to foster international understanding. You may also be getting hungry and suddenly feel like eating a large, succulent lobster. You may even look like one but the Lobster Pot will provide you with the very best reason for being there in the first place.

A large, partly open-air restaurant beside, and over the sea, on the old fish wharf, the Lobster Pot exudes an atmosphere of cheerful abundance. All kinds of lobster dishes naturally and a good selection of other seafood and traditional Thai dishes, provide a menu best enjoyed by several persons. A special lunchtime menu has proven to be very popular.

Opening times: 11 am to around midnight.
Prices: Dinner for two around 300 baht.

Reun Thai Restaurant
Pattaya Sai 2
South Pattaya
Telephone: (038) 425911

A large garden-style restaurant designed to convince coach-loads of tourists that they are in Siam. Not a cosy rendezvous but for voyeurs of captured marine life, it has its own fascination. There is an excellent range of seafood fresh from the tank. Display of Thai dancing is staged at no extra charge.

The Reun Thai claims to be "very suitable as a venue for either cheerful or private parties." Sour-faced individuals, take note.

Opening times: 11am–midnight.

Artfully carved fruit and vegetables.

Prices: Dinner for two – about 400 baht.

Tam Nak Nam
252 Pattaya Central Road
Telephone: (038) 429059.

Not quite the 'Palace By The Water' as suggested by its Thai name, the Tam Nak Nam is more of a Thai pavillion style wooden building on concret piles erected over a man-made lake. But inspite of it having been inspired by the once burgeoning tourist industry, it does provide cool and pleasant surroundings in which to enjoy a vast selection of Thai, Chinese and even some European dishes.

The rather omninously name 'Black chicken with Chinese herbs' and 'Cherry duck' are specialities of the house or rather 'palace'. Seafood offerings such as 'Steamed crab with fresh milk' appeared to have been inspired by Thailand's recently acquired dairy industry and certainly would not have been a local dish when Pattaya was just an untainted fishing village. Baked squid comes with butter and live classical Thai dancing comes with live classical Thai folk music.
Opening times 11.00 am–2.00 am.
Prices: Dinner for two around 350 baht.

Nang Nual Seafood Restaurant
214/10 Beach Road
South Pattaya
Telephone: (038) 428177, 428708, 428478.

No doubt about what kind of food is on offer here, this specialist seafood establishment has a 15-year-old record of continued operation and for connoisseurs who have cause to be in Pattaya it is and opportunity to indulge uninterupted.

Fried baby clams with green onions, grilled sea bass in banana leaf, fried crabmeat with mushrooms are a few of the marine temptations at the Nang Nual. Others may by discerned disporting on the pleasure craft in the bay but they're not on the menu.

Dishes are reasonably priced and almost always well-cooked and quickly served. Spacious and well appointed. the Nang Nual is situated on both sides of the fairly narrow Beach Road.

Opening times: 10 am to 11.00 pm.
Prices: Around 200 baht, dinner for two.

Chinese Restaurants

Bua Thong Restaurant
Beach Road
Telephone: (038) 428487 /428066..

Chinese and Thai restaurants somehow manage to provide quite delicious food in the most unappetising surroundings. The Bua Thong in unappetising Beach Road is one such example. You could bring your elderly aunt here and she'd no doubt delight in the dim sum, the Peking duck and the suckling pig. When you leave the portals of the Bua Thong however, imaginative explanations will be called for to explain the

displays of another kind of local delicacy.
Opening times: 11.30 am–2.30 pm, 6.30 pm–11 pm.
Prices: Dinner for two - 350 to 400 baht.

PHUKET

Thai Restaurants

Khao Rang Restaurant
Rang Hill
Kho Sim Bi Road
Telephone: (076) 212789.

Located atop Rang Hill past the neatly named 'Fitness Park', the Kao Rang lets you play your private power games as you gaze down at the town. The whole, twinkling night-time vista can be yours for the price of a meal.
A comprehensive menu of Thai dishes with a good selection of seafood provides another good reason for making the uphill journey to the Khao Rang. Smilingly efficient service.
Opening times: 10 am–11 pm.
Prices: Dinner for two, 200 - 300 baht.

Malee's Seafood Village
94/4 Taweewong Road
Patong Beach, Phuket
Telephone: (076) 321205

Although situated in the 'verging on the vulgar' Patong Beach area, this long-established seafood restaurant has an almost European air of self-assured smartness. For Jaws fans with a taste for revenge the shark steak in green pepper sauce may well satisfy more than a seaside appetite. A shady spot on the garden terrace, a charcoal-grilled garoupa, a glass of cool local beer, and one might find dining companions becoming almost superfluous.
Opening times: 7 am - midnight.
Prices: Dinner for two, about 350 baht.

Ban Rim Pa
Patong Beach
Phuket
Telephone: (076) 7230786.

One of the small group of restaurants owned by international restaurateur Tom McNamara who operates in London and New York, the Ban Rim Pa must surely claim the most exotic sunsets of McNamara's illustrious band.
Seafood dominates the menu of this high class restaurant at the north end of Patong Beach. An air of quite confidence permeates the whole place. Service is polite and friendly in a restrained manner and the food very well cooked in the traditional manner but presented with a pleasing and, occasionally surprising, flair.
Opening times: 11 am–midnight.
Prices: Dinner for two about 450 baht.

Chinese Restaurants

Rooftop Chinese Restaurant
12th Floor, Pearl Hotel
Phuket town
Telephone: (076) 211044.

Chilli – the throat-searing and integral member of the Thai table.

Skyhigh mountain views, and excellent roast duck are reasons enough to take the lift to the Pearl Hotel's Rooftop Restaurant. This restaurant is very popular with the local business community who apparently take solace in the Cantonese style seafood.

Opening times: 10 am–11 pm.
Prices: Dinner for two, 450–500 baht.

Tien Kung Chinese Restaurant
Phuket Merlin Hotel
Phuket Town
Telephone: (2076) 2121866-70.

Another rooftop rendezvous, this time astride the Merlin Hotel. Once through the green bamboo entrance, diners may enjoy a wonderful Andaman Sea view, a crispy duck with plum sauce and Merlin-marinated chicken which sounds like it might have been created by the master magician himself. A pianist and singer provide background entertainment at lunchtimes and late evenings.

Opening times: 12.30 am–2.30 pm, 7 pm–10.30 pm.
Prices: Dinner for two, about 400 baht.

Lai-an
58 Rasada Road
Phuket Town
Telephone: (076) 211-245.

The Chinese, Thai and English neon sign of the Lai-an welcomes diners to the slightly cafeteria atmosphere of this restaurant which is to be found near the Laemthong Bank in Phuket town.

Before Chinese restaurants ventured more up-market, little attention was paid to the decor and much to the food. And this is still the appeal to afficionados from Soho to San Francisco. The Lai-an has a range of dishes, both Thai and Chinese, well cooked and presented.

The spring rolls as a starter are especially tasty.

Opening times: 11 am–2 pm, 5 pm–10 pm.
Prices: Dinner for two about 350 baht.

The Living Place
36/8 Sawadirak Road
Patong Beach
Phuket
Telephone: (076) 321-121.

Smartly stylish and serving mainly seafood, the Living Place is opposite Sai Nam Yan school. Apart from the general liveliness and willingness to oblige, displayed by the youngish staff, there's no real indication for the reason behind the restaurant's philosophical sounding name, apart from it being a part of an accommodation complex.

But you can spend a lifetime pondering the meaning of these curious names that often have no meaning at all. Better to get on with the business of eating and at the Living Place you could start with sauteed lobster in white wine.

The Durian

Delectable to some, the durian is distinguished by its appearance and unique pungency. Looking like an armour-plated American football, the spiky durian appears on the market stalls between May and August when it dominates the retail fruit scene.

Prized varieties such as *mon thong* – golden pillow, command high prices. Connoisseurs of the durian's yellow, fleshy meat pay as much as 200 baht for a good specimen.

The yellow flesh does in fact have a high sulphur content, which combined with the sweetness from the pure fructose probably accounts for its unique taste and its celebrated odour.

Normally eaten fresh, durian is also served cooked with sticky (glutinous) rice and coconut milk. Knowledgeable locals will also be wary of buying durians available after a rainy period. Although that formidable skin is waterproof, the fruit absorbs moisture through the tree, detracting from its freshness and desired taste.

Nantaburi, Chantaburi and latterly Rayong are all well-known durian districts, each having its adherents.

Handling this user-unfriendly fruit calls for self-protective measures even among the hardy Thais, who expertly cut and prepare the durian for sale.

Most wear at least one thick glove as they slice and remove the thick skin to expose the segmented yellow flesh.

Quick to take advantage of modern materials, the Thai fruit sellers now display their sample bisected durians in 'cling-wrap' plastic.

Left to its natural growing cycle, this 'king of oriental fruits' seems to be designed mainly for self-promulgation.

Durian, the king of fruit.

You could try the fried crab in a curry sauce with perhaps one of the special house salads. Oddly the wine list offers no less than four different kinds of champagne. In Phuket, perhaps that's what they mean by 'living'.
Opening times: 10.30 am to midnight.

HUA HIN

Thai Restaurants

Salathai Restaurant
Hotel Sofitel Central
Telephone: (032) 512021-40.

Set in the nostalgic surroundings of the recreated elegance of the magnificent Sofitel Central, the Salathai more than lives up to expectations. Rattan furniture and those great brass ceiling fans add to the nostalgia. A comprehensive menu of regional Thai foods, excellent service and surprisingly reasonable prices combine to let the Salathai at Hua Hin compete with the best in the country.
Opening times: 6.30 pm–11.00 pm.
Prices: Very reasonable - dinner for two around 300 baht.

Sang Thai Seafood Restaurant
Naresdamri Road
Telephone: (032) 512144.

Next to the fishing jetty, the Sang Thai is about as close as any restaurant will get to its main supplier. Its slightly gaudy and open-air style belies the excellent and friendly service. *Tom Yam*,. lobster with garlic and pepper, fried garoupa with chilli and tamarind sauce and grilled prawns in a bean sauce are all local favourites. A genuinely local restaurant with a history of over fifty years, the Sang Thai provides seafood dining at its freshest.
Opening times: 10 am–11 pm.
Prices: Dinner for two – about 400 baht.

Ban Tappikaew
7 Naebkhehat Road.
Telephone: (032) 512210.

A little way out from the town centre, the Ban Tappikaew is a delightful garden restaurant centred around an old Thai-style house. The Mercedes and BMWs in the car park reflect the worldly wealth of the Tappikaew's local clientele who like to be seen at the best places. The food is traditionally classic Thai, beautifully presented and served by well trained staff.
Opening times: 11.30 am–11pm.
Prices: Dinner for two – around 500 baht.

CHIANG MAI

Thai-Chinese Restaurants

Feung Fah Restaurant
The Novotel Suriwongse
110 Changlan Road
Telephone: (053) 251051-4.

This is another restaurant that has been around for a fair time and which has earned itself a reputation for consistently excellent food. Located within the highly-acclaimed Novotel hotel, the Feung Fah offers Thai and Chinese cuisine, cooked and served to the highest standards. It has a comfortable ambience and gives excellent value for money. Curiously, the Feung Fah closes only between 3 am and 6 am, hours during which the restaurant and kitchens must be subjected to a minor cleaning frenzy.

Opening times: 6 am–3 am
Prices: Dinner for two from around 400 baht.

Nang Nual Seafood Restaurant
27/2 Koalklang Road
Chiang Mai
Telephone: (053) 241274, 2411771, 243946.

An expansive building on the banks of that lovely old river, the Ping, the Nang Nual also encompasses Chiang Mai's first Japanese restaurant.

The Nang Nual itself provides a vast menu of Thai, Chinese and European dishes and is definitely to be visited *en group* in order to justify the perfect riverside setting and take maximum advantage of the extensive menu. Good service and even better value.

Opening times: 10 am - 10 pm.
Prices: Dinner for two, around 200 baht.

Thai European Restaurants

The Riverside
9-11 Charoenrat Road
Telephone: (053) 243239.

Still literally, down by the riverside, this is a place for eating, drinking and listening, above the noisy chatter, to a variety of country, blues, flok and even classical music.

Stunning views of the river, a friendly atmosphere and surprisingly good northern Thai food, supplemented where necessary by a selection of Western style steaks.

An excellent place at which to spend the entire evening or at which to wind up the day.

Opening times: 10 am–2 am.
Prices: Dinner for two, about 250 baht.

The Whole Earth – Thai Vegetarian
88 Sridonchai Road
Telephone (053) 232463.

A modern, Thai-style house is the setting of the Whole Earth whose name immediately signals its vegetarian pretensions.

The Thai and local content of the menu is interspersed with a near Indian curry. Vietnamese spring rolls are also offered on the menu. If you believe eating can be a spiritual experience and that you are what you eat, then this is the place to enrich your soul at the risk of looking like an egg plant covered in

Dip of fermented soy bean paste.

coconut milk.

Opening times: 11.30 am - 10.30 pm.
Prices: Dinner for two, about 300 baht.

Chinese Cuisine

The White Orchid
The Diamond Hotel
33/10 Charoenprated Road
Telephone: (053) 234153-55.

One of the most highly-acclaimed restaurants in the North, the White Orchid at the Diamond Hotel sits proudly and almost nonchalantly on the banks of the wonderfully-named River Ping. The vast menu of well over 200 Chinese dishes, including a tremendous seafood selection, matches the restaurant's general air of confidence.

Superb food and service at very reasonable prices.

Opening times: 10 am–midnight.
Prices: Dinner for two–around 300 baht.

WHAT TO DO / WHERE TO GO

Off the Beaten Track

This guide has covered the most obvious places of touristic interest in each of the regions but Thailand is full of interesting little sights, or perhaps spectacular ones, if you wander a little off the beaten track. This section is designed just to give you a few examples of what you can find if you stray a little. There are thousands of pleasant surprises in Thailand. Find them by following your instinct, surmising from a map, word of mouth, or just asking the locals where they go for *thiaw* – for having a good time.

Jim Thompson's house from the other side of the klong.

Quiet Locales in Bangkok

Bangkok may seem like an endless cacophony of busy roads and commerce but off the main streets it is often a city of quiet lanes and alleys, rich and poor. For example one typical low-income area is right in the centre near a prime tourist attraction, Jim Thompson's House, Soi Kasemsan 2, north off Rama I Road. At the end of this lane, a 1-baht punt ferry takes you across the canal to a district of wooden houses,

canal-side walkways and narrow alleys characteristic of many poorer areas of the city.

A wander around here will be in sharp contrast to the hustle and bustle of the modern metropolis that Bangkok has become, but you will be surprised that off the main streets many do still live in such less affluent surroundings.

Upmarket Garden Retreat

If you prefer an upmarket escape from the capital's pressures, try the luxury hotel gardens. The most spacious in the whole city are those of the Siam Inter-Continental, also just north of Rama I Road, downtown. Another very pleasant garden environment is that of the Hilton at Nailert Park, at the north end of Withayu (Wireless) Road, beyond the British Embassy.

It is big, noisy and sprawling, beyond Bangkok, but the outskirts soon give way to peaceful rural and provincial life, at least if you take the train. There are two minor lines out of the city which will quickly deliver you into countryside and interesting destinations. One is the Eastern Line, destination Chachoengsao, departing Hua Lampong Station at 6.00, 7.00, 8.05, 9.40, 11.25, and 13.10. This train gets you out into the eastern ricefields to an area where people still travel a lot by canal. About 50 minutes out of Bangkok and you will begin to see boats waiting by little stations. Jump out and hire one,

Bamboo forests, off the beaten track.

first checking the times of return trains. You will see traditional waterborne and waterside Thai life in the rice-growing river basin.

Departing from the little-known Wongwian Yai Station in Thonburi, a commuter line runs down southwestwards to a rivermouth town. Trains leave frequently and soon get out into rural fields, passing little farming communities. After about 40 minutes, the train pulls into Samut Sakhon. This small but thriving town has a fascinating general and fish market between the narrow pedestrian-dominated main street and a river creek. Walking westward, you come to the broad Tha Chin River winding down to the Gulf of Thailand, busy with criss-crossing ferries, fishing trawlers and freighters. At a scenic promontory, there is a large two-storey seafood restaurant, serving very good food at most reasonable prices.

Up Country

The best way to get off the beaten track upcountry is always under your own steam, by car, motorcycle or bicycle, or just on foot. The next best thing to do is to hire a driver, whether he has a taxi, a pick-up, a *tuk-tuk,* a trishaw, or a boat. It is you who should decide where to go. Alternatively the third choice is to hop on and off buses and trains at will, as the whim takes you.

The following are some examples of what you can find and experience.

Lopburi Waterways, Central Plains

Everybody goes to Lopburi to see the interesting 17th century ruins of King Narai's palace. However, if you wander up to the north-west end of town, to the river confluence, you will find boats taking local people to their houses in the network of waterways to the north. Hire one and you will see traditional water life of the Central Plains.

Railway Viaduct Walk

Most people go just to the bridge River Kwai, or all the way to the end of the railway line, passing the dramatic wooden viaduct in a couple of minutes. Yet there is a stop there, plus restaurants and bungalows, and you can walk all along the viaduct when the train is not there (99% of the time). Why not get off?

Deserted Beaches of the South

There are many well-publicised beaches in the south but far more that are little-known and little-frequented. For example, both north and south of Prachuap Khiri Khan, wonderful deserted beaches stretch for miles and miles. The northern one is great for walking in the cool season. Koh Samui:

hiring yourself a motorbike will enable you to search out hidden pockets such as the northeastern and southwestern capes. These promontories are avoided by the island ring road; they have dirt-tracks by which to explore access to little coves and secluded beaches.

Elephant training in the North

Many of the north's finest sights are well off the beaten track – the densely-forested mountains, for example. The train passes through such an area between Lampang and Chiang Mai and makes a stop. Why not get off? Lampang province offers an interesting out-of-the-way insight into the Asian elephant, the Young Elephant Training Centre. It is 54 km northeast of Lampang town on Highway 1 at Ban Pang La, near the 656km marker, a mile up a dirt road to the left. Buses ply this main route.

The centre genuinely trains young elephants for work in government teak forests. Around twenty of them go through their paces for visitors' pleasure in the mornings up to 11am, except from March to May, and on public and Buddhist holidays. Entrance is free!

Nightlife

Thais are great nightclub-goers and the whole country is sprinkled with night spots from the most basic to the highly elaborate. Despite the quality difference, the format is remarkably uniform: live musicians and rotating singers, Thai and Western pop music, both food and drink served. Give them a try – the music may be syrupy and out of tune, but you will be made welcome and observe the Thais letting their hair down. The most fun kind are the *ramwong* dance clubs where you can hire a female dance partner – the venerable Oriental tradition of the taxi-dancer. Thais add charm to the tradition by the system of payment: you buy flower garlands from a waiter for about 6 baht each, choose your partner, and put one round the young lady's neck before each dance. (She receives 1-1/2 baht for each). The music is usually played by a shaky ten-piece band and goes the whole gamut through disco, rock'n'roll, ballroom, Latin, and, of course, *ramwong*, the graceful Thai folk dance. Two Bangkok examples are Club 16 under the Washington Cinema on Sukhumvit Road near Soi 22. Here the girls sport mini-mini-skirts; and Hennessy Nightclub, Pradipat Road, Saphankwai, where the ladies wear formal evening clothes and dance rather expertly.

D. I. Y.

These have been just a few hints of what lies off the tourist trail in Thailand. Take the cue and strike out for yourself – you should have some nice surprises.

L A O S

Beyond Thailand

Thailand is bordered by Burma to the west, Laos to the northeast, Cambodia to the east and Malaysia to the south. The Thais share with the Burmese the practice of Theravada Buddhism and some important geographical features, such as broad rice-growing flood plains. With the Cambodians, they also have a common religion and some shared cultural heritage, such as in classical dance. With Malaysia, Thailand is roughly equal in socio-economic development, approaching industrialised status. By contrast, in the key factors of race and language, Burma, Cambodia and Malaysia are quite distinct from Thailand.

Of all Thailand's neighbours, only one country is a cousin, and that is Laos. The Thai and Lao peoples share origins in China, speak closely related languages, practise the same religion and follow many similar customs. Laos is also currently the easiest to visit of the northern neighbours, with individual tourist visas being more easily obtainable, unlike for Burma and Cambodia. Thailand is often a popular jumping-

Silhouettes against the Mekong from Pak Ou cave.

off point for visits to neighbouring Indo-China areas and for all these reasons, we include a compact guide to Laos.

The Lao People

The most important thing to understand about Laos is that it is a nation in which the dominant ethnic group, the Lao, forms only half the population. The present government considers there to be 68 different peoples amongst the population, though it has never listed them. In practice, the most useful way to describe Laos' heterogeneous population is to classify it in three groups on the combined basis of cultural, linguistic and geographical criteria.

This divides the diverse inhabitants, estimated at four million in total, into the peoples of the mountain summits, **Lao Soung**, speaking Tibeto-Burman languages (approaching 10%); the peoples of the mountain slopes, **Lao Theung**, speaking Mon-Khmer languages (perhaps 35%); and the peoples of the mountains and plains, **Lao Loum**, speaking T'ai languages (around 55%).

Of these three, it is the lowland group of the Lao Loum, about one-third of Laos' citizens, who dominate culturally, economically and politically. To put it simply, the ethnic Lao who live along the Mekong valley run the country virtually, whilst a hugely diverse range of people goes about its business elsewhere. It is only a slight exaggeration to say that Laos is a nation of hill-tribes fronted by some riverine farmers.

Geography

The second most important thing to understand about Laos is that it is largely mountainous and the bulk of the people live in isolated hill and river valley villages. Laos snakes 1000 km down from China in the north to Cambodia in the south, separated from Thailand to the west most of the way by the River Mekong and from Vietnam to the east by the Annamite Cordillera. The north and east are particularly mountainous, whilst the Mekong is its most important natural asset, winding the whole length of the country and serving as the major transport channel. Landlocked and hemmed in by mountains to north and east, river rapids hindering waterborne access from Cambodia, Laos is only easily accessible through the flat northeast Thailand.

Economy

All the above factors have hindered trade and development, particularly in modern times, with the result that Laos is rated one of the world's least developed countries (LDC) by United Nations criteria. Statistics are lacking but Laotians were generally reckoned to earn less than US$200 per capita in the mid-'80s. Railways are non-existent, air connections sparse, and metalled roads rare.

Casting for fish in the Nam Khan, Luang Prabang, Laos.

School is never more than a walk away, even in the isolated hills.

Agriculture is the almost universal occupation; industry hardly exists.

Significant development is not expected any time soon: the cash is simply not available, though Western aid is increasing as Soviet bloc aid falls off. With the meager surplus income they may acquire, Laotians are neither savers nor investors: to the despair of the government, they prefer to spend it on a party, a *boun* or a *baci!*

History

The history of Laos as a state is not the same as that of the Lao as a people. As already mentioned, 45% of Laotian citizens are not ethnic Lao, whilst many times more ethnic Lao live in Thailand than in Laos. Nevertheless, the Laotian state is a creation of the ethnic Lao and they are central to the country's history.

Originating in southern China as one of the T'ai people, the Lao migrated southwards along with their cousins, the Thais and the Shans, from the 8th to the 13th centuries. Whilst the Shan filtered into upper Burma and the Thais into the Ping and Chao Phraya river valleys that now form north and central Thailand, the Lao settled in the Mekong valley. In doing so, and farming rice, they ousted the Lao Theung peoples who took to the hills and slash-and-burn agriculture.

In coming into contact with the Mon and Khmer peoples located to the south, the Lao eventually adopted their Theravada Buddhism and facets of their

Hindu culture. Their first kingdom was established on the northern Mekong at Luang Prabang by Prince Fa Ngum, who achieved the remarkable feat, as the Khmer empire crumbled, of subjugating the whole of present-day Laos plus most of Isan. In 1353 he declared himself King of Muang Lane Xang Hom Khao, the "Land of the Million Elephants and the White Parasol".

Lane Xang

Luang Prabang remained the centre of the Lao state, usually called Lane Xang, for 200 years and was the cradle of the institutions, ceremonies and beliefs which were to shape the traditional Lao-Buddhist state for the next six centuries, right up to the mid-1970s. Fa Ngum installed a sacred golden Buddha image from Angkor as the symbol of the kingdom, the Phra Bang; it became the focal point of ceremonies honouring Buddhist truth and kingly rule in which the nobles pledged loyalty.

The Buddhist monkhood, or *sangha*, and the monarchy formed the mutually reinforcing cement of Lao society. The Lao people, scattered in hundreds of almost autonomous and self-sufficient communities, acceded to the monarchy through their popular Buddhism mixed with mythic folk beliefs. Despite this order, authority was spread amongst petty princelings and the king's continuing supremacy rested on their perceptions of his strength.

Splendour of Laos

For three and a half centuries, Laos held firm as a major power in Southeast Asia, competitive with Siam, Vietnam and Burma. After both the Siamese and Burmese had invaded and were later repulsed, King Setthathirat moved the capital in 1563 to Vientiane, which was more easily defensible and more centrally located. The city was beautified with fine new temples, notably Wat Phra Keo and Wat That Luang.

The 17th century was the height of Lao power, under the long rule of King Souligna Vongsa (1637-94), who controlled an area exceeding 400,000 sq km, Vientiane was a splendid city and a

King Sisavangvong, one of the last kings who died in 1960.

renowned centre of Buddhist learning, yet upon his death quarrels of dynastic succession split the kingdom in three and brought about rapid decline. Luang Prabang, Vientiane and Champassak vied in vain for control, and eventually fell prey to the ploys of powerful Vietnam and Siam.

Sacking of Vientiane

The most destructive event in this decline was the Siamese sacking of Vientiane in 1827, leaving only Wat Sisaket intact. Territorially, Isan was lost to Siam, cutting off most ethnic Lao from their mother country. At the same time, the Lao Soung hill-tribe peoples, such as the Hmong and Yao, began filtering into the northern mountains from China in a process that continues to this day, forming possibly 10% of the population.

Colonisation

The culmination was French colonisation in the closing years of the 19th century. Laos became developed to suit French interests, with roads, telegraph lines, port facilities and so on, paid for largely by taxes on the people. Large numbers of energetic Vietnamese were brought in to fill menial, clerical and commercial tasks. Strangely, the ethnic Lao acquiesced, leaving rebellion to the hill-tribes, but by 1920 resistance had been eliminated. A French-educated elite grew up.

Only with the Second World War and Japanese hegemony over the French did Lao nationalism stir, resulting in a 1945 declaration of independence, repudiated by the returning French, determined to re-establish control. In 1950, a Lao resistance government was formed in Vietnam supported by the Viet Minh nationalists. Along with Vietnam, Laos achieved independence in 1954 under a royalist regime, but the dissatisfied Lao left wing, known as the Pathet Lao, took to arms parallel with the Viet Cong in Vietnam and eventually achieved victory in 1975. During the Vietnam War, Laos was heavily bombed by the USA, particularly in the northeastern Plain of Jars, and a quarter of the population was displaced. Vientiane, however, was a place of wartime deals and pleasures.

In 1959, about halfway through the Indochinese Wars, a French major, quoted by Norman Lewis in *The Changing Sky*, had said: "As for the future, you might say it's a toss-up between the strip-tease and the political lecture". In the event, Laos was thought to have passed into a long-drawn politicising process.

The Lao People's Democratic Republic was declared in December 1975, and the last king then abdicated his Luang Prabang throne, later to be exiled to the northern forests. About 300,000 people fled the country, including most high officials, professionals and business people, creating a dearth

Colonialists have departed but fresh French bread still turns up at the markets.

of expertise. Power passed to a new class of communist cadres drawn from the Pathet Lao fighters and their non-combatant supporters. Opponents were sent to re-education camps and 40,000 Vietnamese troops became stationed in the country. The new Laos established close relations with Vietnam and the USSR and became closed to Westerners.

The central roles of the monarchy and Buddhism were replaced with that of the party and Marxism, with entry into monkhood being drastically curtailed. Nationalisation of businesses and

Rice is nice.

collectivisation of agriculture ensued, with varying completeness, until in the mid-1980s liberalisation measures began to decentralise the economy and encourage the return of private enterprise and foreign investment. In 1988, the Vietnamese troops departed and Laos re-opened its doors to tourism. Still, the old revolutionary guard of the Pathet Lao under Kaysone Phoumivane remained in power.

Making a Living

Most Laotians are subsistence farmers working on family farms, as they always have been even during the period of collectivisation in the early communist years. Nevertheless, of Laos's 236,800 sq km, only 4% is cultivated. Rice is the main crop, grown either on the irrigated lowland plains or in slash-and-burn hill cultivation. In normal years, Laos is self-sufficient in rice. Timber production is second in importance, particularly of hardwoods for export.

Coffee, cotton, corn, and tobacco are supplementary crops, especially in the southern Bolovens Plateau. Last but far from least, hill-farm opium poppy production is said to be the largest single source of foreign exchange, courtesy of the international heroin trade. Another big earner is the export of hydro-electric power to Thailand.

Other manufacturing industries are almost non-existent, and not very likely in the near future.

VIENTIANE

Vientiane is an old Lao settlement and princely seat that was raised to primary importance in 1563 when the king moved his capital there from Luang Prabang. At that time, when the Lao kingdom included the bulk of Isan (modern northeast Thailand), the "Sandalwood City" was central to the realm and situated amidst the major rice-growing plain. King Setthatirat fortified it, built himself a palace, and raised two major temples, Wat That Luang and Wat Phra Keo. In the early 18th century, the kingdom was split in three, with Vientiane as one of the capitals. The city prospered despite growing Siamese interference until 1827 when Siam sacked it and destroyed all the great buildings except Wat Sisaket.

In the early 20th century, the French imperialists set about restoring it and creating a workable colonial capital. Many government offices and the grand boulevards testify to this epoch. In the 1960s, a second surge of construction occurred out of the American money that poured in to support the right wing politico-military forces: the market-halls, the premier hotel (the Lane Xang) and the massive Monument Aux Morts all date from this period.

The city's Vietnam War era was summed up by the American author Paul Theroux in this way: "Vientiane is exceptional, but inconvenient. The brothels are cleaner than the hotels,

Monumental Monument Aux Morts.

marijuana is cheaper than pipe tobacco, and opium easier to find than a glass of cold beer." Pumped with American funds, Vientiane thrived as never before or since.

Today Vientiane counts around 300,000 citizens yet hardly musters more profile than a provincial market town. Traffic is thin and mostly two-wheeled; the typical citizen is a cyclist. Most of the city has single-storey wooden housing, often raised on stilts in the traditional style, and even the central commercial districts rarely rise above three floors. Buildings are rundown and activity is desultory. Commerce, located largely around Samsenthai Street, is rising from the grave after long years of suppression, with the effect that spruce new shops and hotels are popping up amongst the general dilapidation.

Old-style Grandeur

Despite this, the city does have some grandeur. Its axis is the broad Lane Xang Avenue which runs northeast from the old royal palace by the river to the seat of government in mid-town. Vientiane's inescapable number one sight stands amid a huge roundabout frequented mostly by bicycles at the head of Lane Xang Avenue. It is the truly monumental Monument Aux Morts, a four-square *arc de triomphe* with four arches and a fanciful oriental castle on top.

The monument was built in the 1960s by the neutralist regime to commemorate the dead of the preceding civil wars. Appropriately and amusingly, it was constructed out of USAID concrete expressly donated for the extension of the airport runway to accommodate B-52 bombers, hence its nickname, "the Vertical Runway".

It can be ascended by internal stairways for a small fee. The top platform has elaborate turrets at each corner, whilst a central tower rises further, affording splendid views over the whole city, whose low density amidst much greenery can be well observed.

Beneath is a small cafe serving soft drinks and cakes. From here, the colourful stucco central ceiling can be appreciated, depicting mythological scenes. The building to the northwest is the Supreme

Wat That Luang

Assembly, the equivalent of a parliament in the Laotian system.

Wat That Luang

The avenue forking roughly eastwards from the Monument Aux Morts sweeps up to Vientiane's grandest temple and Laos's principal religious site, Wat That Luang. On a rise above the city and set amongst pastures, it features a great golden stupa protected behind fortifications and a golden facaded chapel set in grassland. The ensemble is quietly majestic.

The original stupa is said to date from 307BC, built by the founder of Vientiane and five monks ordained in India who together interred a rib of the Buddha inside it. Its present glory was created in 1566 by King Settathirat who built a much larger stupa over the old one soon after establishing his capital at Vientiane. Damaged in the Siamese sacking of 1827 and by the Ho bandit attack of 1873, it was restored by the French in 1900 and remodelled in the early '30s and late '70s by Lao authorities.

In traditional Lao style, the tall stupa is four-sided and curves vertically to a point. It is clad in gold leaf and surrounded by a square platform along which are ranged 30 much smaller gold stupas of "perfection". Below this is a lower terrace lined with 323 leaf motifs which mark off the sacred space. Central to each of the four sides is a pavilion for offerings. Around this sacred inner shrine is a grass courtyard protected by four outer walls with a gateway in the centre of each. Entrance is by the western gateway which faces a statue of the seated King Settathirat looking towards the city. (Open Tuesday to Sunday, 8.00-11.30am and 2.00-4.30pm; fee, minimal).

To the north, Wat That Luang's chapel presents a glittering golden facade from its high-pointed wooden roof. West of that lies the Buddhist High School of Vientiane, one of Laos's few notable academic institutions, where novice monks gain a broad education. It fronts upon an extensive parade ground which only truly comes alive in mid-November during the That Luang Temple Fair. The northern end of this plaza is marked by the tall spire of the Monument to the Unknown Soldier, also called the Pathet Lao War Memorial.

Presidential Palace

From this rise, Phon Khong Avenue leads straight back to the Monument Aux Morts and beyond this Lane Xang Avenue ends at the Presidential Palace, Vientiane's sole grand residence, formerly the Royal Palace.

A grey stucco *belle epoque* mansion set behind a formal French garden, the Presidential Palace is used as a venue for state functions involving important foreign visitors, for whom it is also a guest house.

BEYOND THAILAND

387

Once the residence of the Emerald Buddha, Wat Phra Keo's formal gardens have become somewhat of a casual grazing ground.

Wat Sisaket, Vientiane's oldest building whose loveliness survived the Thai invaders in 1827.

The Emerald Buddha

In the same block to the southeast stands Laos's second most important temple, Wat Phra Keo, the Temple of the Emerald Buddha. For almost three centuries, this royal chapel housed the sacred Emerald Buddha image that symbolised regional power. When the Thais sacked and looted the city and destroyed almost all its buildings in 1827, their greatest prize was this jadeite image which they carted off to Bangkok to symbolise their new supremacy.

The French restored the temple in the 1930s and the revolutionary government made it a museum. Set in a formal garden, it gives an impression of great height due to three main features: it is raised on a platform approached by flights of steps; it is surrounded by a tall colonnaded gallery; and it has a pointed, three-tiered roof. Inside are kept the city's religious art treasures gathered for safekeeping, as well as fine pieces from around the country.

There are not only notable pieces of Lao sculpture such as the standing Buddha, exhibit No.4, but also of Khmer art (a 13th century head of Vishnu, No.456) and of Burmese-influenced work, like the gold lacquer Buddha, No.345. At the back, there is furthermore a wooden door with erotic carved panels of Indian influence; these come from Savannakhet and date from the 16th century. Glass cases contain various works in gold and silver.

Outside, along the inner gallery walls are lined with bronze sitting Buddhas in the Lao style. One of these bronzes (No.3) is a Buddha calling for rain. The grounds and the museum are open Tuesday to Sunday, 8.00-11.30pm and 2.00-4.30pm.

Wat Sisaket

Opposite Wat Phra Keo across Setthathirat Street at the end of Lane Xang Avenue stands Vientiane's oldest original building, Wat Sisaket, built in 1818. It is the seat of Laos' Supreme Patriarch. The main chapel stands amid a terracotta paved courtyard surrounded by a rectangular cloister. The chapel, or *viharn*, has yellow-ochre colonnaded galleries all around it. Inside, the walls have faded murals of fine artistry depicting scenes from the Buddha's life, while above there is a superb lotus-flowered ceiling. The cloisters contain many Buddha images characteristic of the 15th to 19th centuries.

A short walk southeast down Setthathirat Street past Wat Phra Keo, stands Wat Simuang on the left. Its *viharn* houses the city pillar, Lak Muang, a kind of foundation stone regarded as the shelter of the city's guardian spirit. In provenance, it is actually a Khmer city limit marker. The Buddha in front of the pillar's altar is much revered for its magic protective powers.

At the southeast point of the temple precinct stands Vientiane's most strik-

Samsenthai Street, Vientiane.

ing statue, a standing figure of the penultimate king, Sisavangvong, who died in 1960. His grim grey crew-cut stance confronts all visitors arriving by road from the south and from Thailand.

From here, Samsenthai Street leads back into the city centre. Shortly after crossing Lane Xang Avenue, this street becomes the main commercial thoroughfare, lined with shops, hotels, cafes and travel agents, though none have a great deal to offer and few look attractive. The first on the left is a terrace cafe offering a good French breakfast; the first on the right is the Aeroflot office.

Up a side street from Aeroflot stands a notable monument known as the Thai Dam. This is an overgrown stupa said to harbour a sleeping dragon which rises up to protect the city whenever Thai invaders threaten. The other notable sight on Samsenthai Street lies a few hundred metres along on the right, the Museum of the Revolution. Aesthetically, the exterior is best, having a long mellow facade. Inside it contains large rooms exhibiting black-and-white photographs depicting the course of the revolutionary struggle. Some pictures are fascinating but unfortunately the captions are all in Lao. Other exhibits include weaponry. Theoretically, it is open during office hours, 8.00-11.30pm and 2.00-4.30pm.

LUANG PRABANG

Luang Prabang is the old royal city of northern Laos, first capital of the Kingdom of Lane Xang founded in 1353. It is an ancient settlement sited on a tongue of land where the River Nam Khan flows into the Mekong. It is named after the Phra Bang, the fine gold Buddha image which was the kingdom's symbol. After 1563, Vientiane assumed primary importance as capital, whilst from 1720 to 1946 it was capital of one of the three kingdoms into which Laos split. Finally, from 1946 to 1975, its king became monarch of all Laos once more until the declaration of the People's Republic.

The Royal Palace, dating from early this century, is one of the principal sights. Set between Mount Phousi and the Mekong, it is now a museum displaying valuable artifacts in the ground floor audience and throne rooms. The latter is particularly impressive, with its golden throne, red walls encrusted with glass mosaic scenes, and displays of royal ceremonial clothing and jewelry. A copy of the Phra Bang stands in the right wing, the original being kept in the national bank vaults. To visit the palace, a permit must first be obtained from the Lao Tourism office at the Luang Prabang Hotel.

At the palace main gates, steps rise up Mount Phousi, surmounted by a Buddhist shrine, from which there are very fine views in all directions. The "Marvellous Mount", 150 metres high, once hosted many monasteries, and three temples still cling to its slopes.

Immediately south of the Royal Palace is Wat May, the royal chapel and residence of the Supreme Patriarch. Its front porch is a riot of gold, the facade being a gold stucco bas-relief and the pillars of gold patterns stencilled on black. In the courtyard, there is a red post for tying up the royal elephants.

Luang Prabang's crowning glory lies near the tip of the tongue of land around which the Nam Khan winds into the Mekong. Wat Xieng Thong was where kings were crowned and cremated, where the monarch descended to the river down broad flights of steps for official journeys, and where important guests were welcomed. It is also the "cathedral" of the province and the temple of the river port.

Buddha and local legends depicted in gold leaf on black at Wat Xieng Thong.

One of the two deep pink-walled pavilions at Wat Xieng Thong.

Exquisite Luang Prabang decoration.

Its extensive grounds feature a broad paved plaza from which rise several chapels, pavilions and shrines. The *viharn* is a gem of the pure Luang Prabang style, with multi-tiered roof and a rear wall richly decorated with a symbolic representation of the Thong tree. The interior walls are black with gold stencil images depicting the legend of King Chanthaphanith, the predecessor of Fa Ngum who founded the kingdom of Lane Xang in 1353.

Behind the main chapel stand two deep pink pavilions, the smaller being a library and the larger a shrine to the reclining Buddha, an image in bronze as old as the temple. The Red Chapel, as it is called, has exquisite exterior walls encrusted with multi-coloured glass mosaic images relating a local legend. This was executed in 1957 in honour of the Buddha's 2,500th anniversary. The technique is the most distinctive feature of Luang Prabang decoration and dates back at least to the 16th century.

Across the plaza in the eastern corner stands the golden garage of the funerary chariot. This astonishing vehicle of gilded wood features a prow of multi-headed *naga* serpents and carries the twelve-sided funerary urn of the penultimate king encircled by the eight-sided urns of his wives. King Sisavang Vong received in 1960 the last of the enormously elaborate cremation rites traditionally accorded the monarch.

A jar-shaped stone from the Plain of Jars.

Luang Prabang is a quiet town of less than 20,000 people. Strolling its quiet streets (the best way to get around) the visitor can discover at least 40 more temples of widely varying character. Some call it "the last Shangri-la" and "the last paradise in Asia" but such encomiums are misleading and may one day, God forbid, lead it astray. Suffice it to say that it is a relaxed place of great beauty whose chief asset is not the temples or the palace, not the green mountains or the majestic Mekong, but its lack of self-consciousness.

Plain of Jars

The most noted prehistoric sight in Laos is the Plain of Jars in Xieng Khouang province in the north-east. This area was so devastated by American bombing in the Vietnam War that Laotians renamed it the Mountain of Steel. It is a cattle-raising plateau with numbers greatly reduced from the pre-war total. Its name derives from the thousands of large jar-shaped stones scattered across it, the largest weighing six tons with most being from 600 kilos to one ton. Their significance is still debated by archeologists and they give a unique air of mystery to the region, which also has a large hill-tribe population. One quarter (40,000) of the inhabitants are Hmong.

In the far south lies the old kingdom of Champassak whose last king, Chao Boun Oum, renounced his throne in 1964 in the interests of national unity. Its principal site, Wat Phu, attests to the ancient history of the area with stone inscriptions dating from the 5th century. This sanctuary probably originated under the Champa empire; most of its remains are from 11th to 13th centuries, the Khmer period. It takes the form of several temples standing at different levels on a hillside, the highest at 1200 metres.

Laos is not over-endowed with touristic sights. Luang Prabang and Vientiane are the only two towns of great interest. The country's greatest assets otherwise are the vast and completely untouristed hill country, ideal for wild trekking, but this is officially still off-limits to foreigners at the time of writing; and the Mekong River, which

Luang Prabang, a quiet town.

can be cruised uncomfortably amidst goats and chickens in the old wooden riverboats that ply most of its course.

TRAVEL TIPS

Most visitors go to Laos on package tours arranged either in their own countries or in Bangkok. Wherever the agent selected to help you with a trip to Laos, all tours are controlled by the state body, Lao Tourism, and almost all of them start by air from Bangkok. Furthermore, most tours are either organised by or very similar to those offered by the principal agent for travel in Laos, Diethelm Travel of Bangkok.

Diethelm offers two varieties of tours, twice-monthly from Bangkok:

1) 3 days in Vientiane and surroundings; at US$590 per person, US$45 single supplement.

2) 6 days in Vientiane and Luang Prabang, with 3 nights in Luang Prabang; at US$1050 per person, US$155 single supplement.

These prices include all flights, taxes, and visa fees; transfers and tours with English/French speaking Laotian guides; accommodation and all meals. They are thus fully comprehensive but nevertheless expensive for the quality of amenities provided, which are adequate

Boy monks with angelic smiles at Wat Nak, Vientiane.

but far from luxurious. The tour guides, though, are excellent.

Alternatively, you can get a visa for individual travel. Visas are difficult and probably quite impossible to get except through certain travel agents in Bangkok. The best location is Khaosan Road, the budget travel centre, where some agents offer a visa service for around US$100, which in current circumstances is a bargain. (CSC Travel is consistent and reasonable.)

This gets you a 15-day visa for the Vientiane area only; and once there, you must apply to the Immigration Department for a permit to travel elsewhere, e.g. Luang Prabang. If you wish to fly to Luang Prabang (US$80 return), a permit is essential. If you should wish to rough it overland by bus, please note that this is not the practice. It is also possible, but lengthy, to return from Luang Prabang to Vientiane by riverboat, making several changes.

The flight takes 40 minutes, but the plane may well be significantly late, or may take off early (so if you are told to turn up two hours ahead, do it!). The bus and truck trip can (masochistically) be done in 24 hours in the dry season (November to April) or probably not at all in the wet season (May to October). The route is also subject to occasional bandit attack. By contrast, the river trip is quickest in the wet season when the water is high.

However, since all travel is officially controlled, individual travellers should be prepared for bureaucratic restrictions controlling their movement. In Laos, successful individual travel is a matter of pot luck and personal ingenuity. The one sure way to get to Luang Prabang without paying Bangkok prices is to buy a tour ex-Vientiane. In 1989, Lao Tourism was offering two nights including flights for about US$210 ($40 single supplement).

Land and river transport is very cheap. Hotels in Vientiane range from the Mekong Guest House at $6 per day to the Lane Xang Hotel at around $100 per day. There are several newly renovated tourist hotels at around $30 per day, such as the Ambassador and the Muang Vilai. Adequate meals can be had for $2 or $3 dollars, whilst there are a few excellent French restaurants at higher prices.

From Bangkok, there are daily flights to Vientiane operated by Thai Airways and Lao Aviation and the flying time is 65 minutes at a return fare of 4,335 baht. There are numerous buses from the Northern Bus Terminal to Nong Khai on the River Mekong close to Vientiane. There is also a night sleeper train to Nong Khai from Hua Lampong Station, departing at 8.30pm and arriving at 7.30am, a second class berth costing around 350 baht one-way. From Nong Khai, a ferry continually crosses to Tha Deua in Laos up to 4pm daily. From there, it is a 25km taxi ride to Vientiane.

Banking facilities are very sparse. Credit cards are unusable, travellers cheques only cashable in Vientiane. Visitors are strongly advised to carry only cash in Thai baht and US dollars; baht are preferable, being known and accepted everywhere at a roughly uniform and advantageous rate.

Hmong lady in Luang Prabang.

TRAV TIPS

COMING & GOING

AIR TRAVEL
Bangkok is at the hub of international air travel, rivalling Singapore in the Southeast Asian region. At the crossroads of both regional and intercontinental traffic (particularly between Europe/Middle East and the Far East/Australasia), Thailand is also the major tourist destination of Asia.

Dozens of airlines operate in Bangkok which works to benefit the traveller who can choose from a vast away of cut-price tickets available both within and outside Bangkok. But remember, wherever you are shop around for the best offer.

From Europe, the Eastern European airlines offer good value, like LOT of Poland and Interflug of Germany that are thought to be upgrading their equipment.

In Bangkok, use your discretion to source for reliable discount travel agents.

ARRIVAL
Thailand has four international airports, at Bangkok (Don Muang), Chiang Mai, Phuket and Pattaya (U-Tapao). The latter three are small and relatively easy to pass through.

Bangkok's Don Muang Airport has a new international terminal. The arrival floor is extremely roomy and offers 24-hour cafés, banks and a hotel agency (see Being There/Accommodation, page 400). It also offers a confusing plethora of transport services to the city. The prices are as follows:-

    limousine – 300 baht
    minibus – 100 baht per person (serves most hotels)
    taxi from inside desk – 200 baht upwards
    taxi from outside desk – 100 baht upwards

Shop around and be aware that the minibus might take a much longer time to reach your destination. If your hotel is last on the list and there is a traffic jam (there usually is), it could even take longer than your flight into Bangkok! All these services operate on a pre-paid ticket basis.

Bus and rail services are available outside the airport. Access is not that convenient as you have to turn right outside the terminal and struggle onto the main road (about 50 metres out) where buses screech to a halt at any point. A good bet is to scramble on a number 4, 10 or 29 air-conditioned bus. (Even better, first buy a bus-route map at a newsstand inside the terminal). All three of these bus-routes will take you into the town centre.

For the railway, you will have to cross the overhead footbridge and turn left for the station. (Note: The footbridge from the terminal only goes to the airport hotel, even though it passes over the station, totally ignoring mass transit users). Train services are erratic, but during the day you can probably get on one within 20 minutes and arrive downtown within another 40 minutes.

Travelling time by road to downtown Bangkok and vice-versa can take anything from 30 minutes (late at night) to two hours at rush-hours.

IMMIGRATION & VISAS
There are three categories of visa for tourists: short-stay, tourist and non-immigrant. Your passport needs to be valid for at least six months.

Short-stay 15-day visas (free) are issued on arrival to those with onward tickets and sufficient funds (officially US$125 per person).

Tourist visas of 60 days' duration are issued in Thai consulates abroad for a fee of roughly US$12. They can be extended within the country for another 30 days at a fee of 500 baht.

Non-immigrant visas last 90 days and are issued in Thai consulates abroad at a fee of about

US$20. Usually you need a good reason, such as business or study requirements, to obtain one; it varies from one consulate to another.

If you overstay your visa, you will be fined 100 baht for every extra day payable upon departure, whether by air, rail or road. Extensions and any other visa problems are dealt with at the Immigration Department offices located in every provincial capital. The Bangkok office is in Soi Suan Plu, off Sathorn Tai Road. Hours for applications are 8.30-12pm and 1-3.30pm. A nasty little catch awaits those who stay more than 90 days in one calendar year, either consecutively or in total, or those on a non-immigrant "B" (business) who stay more than 14 days. In these cases, you must get a tax clearance from the Revenue Department in Chakraphong Road, off Sanam Luang, Bangkok, or from some provincial revenue offices such as those in Chiang Mai and Hat Yai.

HEALTH REGULATIONS

The only entry restrictions imposed are against those who have been in yellow fever endemic areas within the previous six days. Visitors from these areas must be vaccinated before entry into Thailand, and AIDS carriers, who are barred. Neither rule is likely to be enforced, unless you mention it yourself.

CUSTOMS & EXCISE

Entry: All the usual prohibitions apply – no firearms, non-prescription drugs, pornography, and so on. Regarding electronic and luxury goods, if you carry any of these in duplicate or in large quantities, you may be suspected of harbouring the intention to sell them within the country and therefore be charged duty. Use your discretion; the customs officers will too. Any amount of currency exceeding US$10,000 must be declared.
Departure: Antiques and art objects need an export licence, though the ruling is flexible except for Buddha images, which are rarely permitted for export. If in doubt, go to the Department of Fine Arts for a ruling.

DEPARTURE

Check-in time is 2 hours before take-off time. It is wise to heed this in Bangkok because of the constant city traffic jams.

The downtown taxi fare to Don Muang Airport should be in the 150 to 200 baht range, possibly more during the rushhour.

The journey time is rarely less than an hour and may take more than two hours during a traffic congestion.

Airport tax is 200 baht for international and 20 baht for domestic flights.

BEING THERE

ACCOMMODATION

A wide range of accommodation is available in most town and city centres, a fair choice in most towns, and some kind of hostelry just about everywhere, certainly in every place of touristic interest. Thai people are renowned for their hospitality, thus fittingly enough Thais are adept hoteliers. As in anywhere else in the world, you get what you pay for, but the price/quality ratio is especially favourable in Thailand.

The widest range of accomodation can naturally be found in Bangkok, from The Oriental, regularly voted the world's best hotel with rooms starting at around 4,000 baht, down to a dormitory bed in Khaosan Road for 40 baht. In both cases, good value is offered.

If you wish to book a hotel room from Bangkok Airport, you can do so via a hotel agency called THA (Thai Hotels Association) which is located on the international arrivals floor (ground level). This service is especially good for booking rooms for 300 baht upwards.

If you are looking for budget accommodation, you should head straight for Khaosan Road in Banglampu district near the Grand Palace. This area teems with guest houses and dormitories available in the 40 to 200 baht price range. Do not forget to shop around!

If you wish to stay at slightly more expensive "digs" say within the 200 to 1,000 baht range, *Soi* (=lanes) off it offer a wide choice. Five hundred or 600 baht will get you a decent air-conditioned room with reasonable service. One could try the Federal Hotel, Sukhumvit Soi 11 (which offers good amenities and value).

If you want to stay in a big first-class or luxury hotel, most of which are located in the central business districts of Ploenchit Road/Rajdamri Road/Silom Road area – you can expect to pay from 1,200 to 2,500 baht upwards. Many of these hotels are operated or managed by major international chains and are of 5-star standard.

In the provinces, Chiang Mai, Pattaya and Phuket offer a similar range. However with the tourist boom in Thailand, many towns and resorts now offer a smorgasbord of hotels – ie a few world class hotels and a variety of less expensive ones to cater for all and any budget. But they share one thing in common good value and a range of amenities. Every town with a minimum population of 5,000 has at least one cheap Chinese hotel which may or may not be pleasant — it's pot luck but the prices are competitive and start with 70 baht a room.

Any tourist beach or island has chalet or hut accommodation, usually of very good value. Always called 'bungalows' by the Thais, for 40 baht they are basic (small and rudimentary). A 100 baht can get you a decent fan-cooled double bed with attached bathroom in most places, except in the high season (November-March). Places with constant demand such as Koh Samet to the east charge higher prices – 300 baht for a decent fan-cooled room.

BANKS & MONEY

Normal banking hours are 8.30am-3.30pm, Monday-Friday. Exchange bureaux located in tourist-frequented areas open from 8am-8pm. These bureaux are all operated by banks, no money-changers are available. Some of the major hotels exchange foreign currency for their guests. Automatic banking machines (ATM) operate daily from 7am-10pm.

BANKS

Thai banks offer the full range of foreign exchange facilities: travellers' cheque cashing and selling, currency exchange, cash advances on credit cards, telegraphic transfer, and so on. In tourist areas, you can easily find a bank familiar with such transactions. Elsewhere, you may have to shop around for a bank that specialises in foreign exchange. The following banks give cash advances: Visa – Thai Farmers', Siam Commercial, Thai Military and Bangkok Banks; MasterCard – Thai Farmers', Siam Commercial. American Express provide their usual encashment/travellers cheques facilities.

EXCHANGES

The exchange bureaux change cash and travellers cheques in all recognised international currencies. Some give cash advances on Visa and MasterCard (as above).

The ATM machines of the above-named banks give Visa cash advances up to 10,000 baht daily.

CREDIT CARDS

Practically all major international credit cards are accepted throughout the main town centres and cities for hotels, shopping, restaurants and travel services.

CURRENCY

The Thai baht is closely linked to the US dollar. For several years now, it has fluctuated only slightly remaining between 25 and 26 baht to the dollar. There is no black market exchange in Thailand. However it will be wise to check the latest rates prior to transaction.

Banknotes come in these denominations: 500, 100, 50, 20 and 10. Coins come in these denominations: 10, 5, 2, 1, 50 satang (1/2 baht) and 25 satang (1/4 baht).

The banknotes are easy to distinguish in daylight by their colour and value, but in dim light one has to be careful in separating the 50, 20 and 10 baht notes and especially the 500 and 100 baht notes.

The coins are can be confusing no matter what time of day it is! The 10 baht coin is no problem because it is silver with a brass centre, and the little brass 50 and 25 satang coins are also easily identifiable. However, the rest of the coins can be confusing muddle. There are three types of 5 baht coin and three types of 1 baht coin, while the 2 baht is a rare joker that pops up now and again to really confound you. The best advice we can give is good luck!

BUSINESS HOURS

The business week is usually five days long lasting from Monday to Friday, the hours are 8am-5pm. Government office hours are usually 8.30am-4.30pm, closed for lunch from 12pm-1pm and often after 3.30pm. Some business houses work Saturday mornings too. Most shops are open every day from 9am to 8 pm. All department stores are usually open at from 10am-8pm.

CLIMATE

Thailand has three seasons: dry and cool (November-February), dry and hot (February-May), and rainy and warm (May-November). This pattern holds true for the whole country, with slight regional variations throughout the country except for the southern peninsula, where rain is more extensive. The breaks between the seasons are not sudden and vary slightly from year to year. See Geography chapter, page 33 for more details.

CLOTHING

Light cotton clothing is the best choice throughout the year, except for the cool season (November-February) in the north when sweaters and jackets are necessary at night in the town of Chiang Mai town and in the hills.

Visitors should bear in mind that once away from the beach skimpy clothing is regarded as impolite, particularly when worn in temples. Never wear shorts, singlets or other revealing clothes when visiting a temple – it is considered offensive.

Business dress: a suit is rarely necessary, a simple shirt and tie is adequate, or a safari suit, women should exercise a similar formality. In most cases, a well-pressed shirt and trousers or dress is adequate; this is especially advisable for tourists when visiting government offices.

Evening dress: neither formal nor skimpy is a good rule if visiting a medium-to-upper range restaurant, a theatre or social function.

NB: a collapsible umbrella is handy any time of year, it gives good protection from downpours in the rainy season and can be a sunshade on hot, sunny days. They can be bought cheaply in Thailand for 100 baht.

COSTS

Thailand is very good value for money, unless you are looking for electrical goods and cameras, in which case you should go on to Hong Kong or Singapore.

The essentials of travel – food, accommodation and transport – are all very reasonable and of good quality. At the bottom end, you can catch a bus from Bangkok to Chiang Mai for 150 baht, eat three square meals for 100 baht, and sleep anywhere from Bangkok to Chiang Mai for 50 baht a night – ie 350 baht (US$14) for 700 km and 36 hours and be well fed and well-rested. The same trip in the mid-range – second class train, hotels and restaurants – would cost about 1,000 baht or US$40.

The same route by air with first class hotels and restaurants would cost at least 5,000 baht (US$200). In other words the closer you get to top standards, the closer the prices resemble international levels. The real bargains are in the mid-to-lower range.

DRUGS

Thailand is widely known for its marijuana, opium and heroin. All of these are illegal and possessors are subject to heavy fines or long jail sentences.

ELECTRICITY

The current is 220 volt, 50 cycle. Sockets receive flat two-pin plugs only. Power cuts are rare in Bangkok, and infrequent upcountry. The better hotels provide transformers for 110 volt appliances.

EMBASSIES & CONSULATES

Every major and middle-ranking country enjoys diplomatic representation in Bangkok. Addresses and phone numbers can be found in the English telephone directory.

ETIQUETTE

Thais place great emphasis on politeness and good appearance; substance is of secondary importance. What you appear to be is usually taken as what you are. Thais are generally well-mannered and neatly-dressed, whatever their background. They speak softly and they do not show extremes of emotion. Affection between the sexes is shown very subtly in public. People of the same gender, by contrast, often hold hands and show affection, especially amongst women.

All these are Thai cultural characteristics and visitors should not step too far outside these norms themselves unless they wish to give offence or to be frowned upon. Avoid dirty or dishevelled dress whenever possible – difficult if you are trekking or doing long distance travelling, but quite easy otherwise, especially given the abundance of water and cheap laundering.

Do not show anger – it is regarded as both ill-mannered and a sign of weakness. This may be difficult in some situations and for certain personalities, but bear in mind that you will achieve your aim much better with patience, reasoning, and a smile. Polite determination goes much further than loud bluster in Thailand, and also gains you respect. This is a Buddhist country and that for better or worse is the Thai way.

Similarly, loud speech is frowned upon and public kissing is completely out of line. Public displays of affection are more relaxed in Thai male-female relationships but as yet only limited to public hand-holding which can mostly be seen only in Bangkok.

Two very specific taboos are: showing the soles of your feet or pointing your feet towards others, at least those people you are talking to or accompanying; touching someone else's head, even a child's. No hair-tousling, please! The explanation is that in Thai culture, the head is spiritually high whilst the feet are spiritually low.

All that said, you are hardly likely to get jumped upon for transgressing these rules and norms, for Thais are tolerant and averse to disturbing other people's equilibrium, even if you have upset theirs.

The only two areas which should definitely be treated with caution are the monarchy and religion.

The king is held in the highest regard and should not on any account be criticised – even abstract discussions of monarchy are risky. The Buddha is even more revered, so no Buddha images should be treated with disrespect, which includes putting your arms round one for a photo. These things are not just custom, they are law.

Temple etiquette is therefore important. Go to temples neatly dressed and reasonably well covered. Take your shoes off when entering temple buildings. Women should never touch a monk.

After all this, you will find that Thais can quite easily offend you. They will ask you all sorts of personal questions about your age, your salary, how much your shirt cost, and so on. To you, this is nosiness; to them, it is friendly interest and they would ask the same of another Thai. In part, they are also gauging your relative status so they can ascertain whether they are superior or inferior to you – Thai society is so hierarchical that Thais are not comfortable with strangers until they know where to position themselves in relation to them. You should just grin and bear it! Or you could have fun thinking up all sorts of personal questions of your own.....

Lastly, two everyday customs. When entering a house, take off your shoes. When meeting somebody, if they hold their hands together in a prayer-like gesture before their face or chest, do likewise in return. It is nicer anyway than shaking hands, which most Thais are neither accustomed to nor fond of, especially women.

HEALTH & HYGIENE

Thais are very clean and this makes for a rather clean and hygienic country in Third World terms. Nevertheless, as always in a new country, visitors will encounter new bacteria and may succumb to Bangkok Belly or a provincial version, but these are the day-to-day handicaps of travelling. If you are prone to upset stomachs, then avoid street food, salads, peeled fruit, crushed ice and unbottled drinks. If you are adventurous, just make a decision on an eating place by the way it looks – if it is clean, it is probably safe. The serious health hazards are malaria and AIDS. Malaria is present in the far-flung north and west, and is generally on the increase, but cases are still quite rare amongst travellers. Get advice in your home country if you want to take prophylactic protection: there is much controversy about effective methods. A recent BBC broadcast seemed to say "go back to quinine".

In any event, the malaria mosquito only bites at night; rub-on repellents such as Autan or the local Skeetolene are effective deterrents, as are airsprays, burning coils and mosquito nets slung over beds. All are widely and cheaply available in Thailand.

As for AIDS, you ought to know by now: if you are having casual sex, use a condom.

If you feel ill, and you know (more or less) your ailment and what medicine you need, do what the Thais do: go to a pharmacy and ask directly for it. Most proprietary drugs are sold without prescription in Thailand. Indeed, the pharmacists are professional prescribers, so if you want to trust their advice, just tell them your symptoms and take what they sell you. Again, that is what most Thais do.

All visitors can afford average Thai doctor's fees and most visitors can afford the best. Health care in Thailand is like hotels and restaurants – the price/quality ratio is very favourable. Do the same as you would for the latter: choose a clinic or a hospital on recommendation or by appearance. Clinics proliferate the whole of Thailand including small towns and even provincial capitals have their own hospitals. Expertise is heavily concentrated in Bangkok. All doctors speak a smattering of English and many speak excellent English, having been trained abroad, especially in the USA. Another point in favour of Thai medicine is that it is the most highly regarded profession to which most brilliant young people gravitate.

HOLIDAYS

The following are Thailand's public holidays.

January 1 – New Year's Day.

Mid-February – Makha Bucha (Buddhist Holy Day).

April 6 – Chakri Day (anniversary of founding of current royal dynasty).

April 13 - Songkran (Thai New Year's Day).

May 1 – National Labour Day.

May 5 – Coronation Day (anniversary of King Bhumiphol's coronation).

Mid-May – Visakha Bucha (Buddhist Holy

Day).
Mid-July – Asalha Bucha (Buddhist Holy Day)
August 12 – Queen's Birthday.
October 23 – Chulalongkorn Day (anniversary of King Rama V's death).
December 5 – King's Birthday.
December 10 – Constitution Day (anniversary of the promulgation of the constitution).
December 31 – New Year's Eve.

NEWSPAPERS & MAGAZINES

A wide range of European, North American, Australasian and Asian newspapers and magazines are on sale in Bangkok in hotels, bookshops and department stores. Luxury hotels are the best place to buy newspapers and Central Department Stores for magazines. In the provinces, availability is limited by the size and affluence of the touristic population, so your best bet is in Phuket, Chiang Mai and Pattaya.

Much more widely available are Thailand's two English language daily newspapers, the *Bangkok Post* and *The Nation*. The *Post* is the old-timer, dating from 1946, and has more cachet, whilst *The Nation* is younger and more crusading. Both have very high journalistic standards. For practical information, the *Post* is a superior in touristic events, while *The Nation* is possibly ahead for cultural events, cinema, TV and radio listings.

Both newspapers are generous and extensive users of the wire services thus providing a good international news service. Both also employ large teams of local reporters who divulge more about the state of the nation than is permissible in nearly the whole of Asia. That said, you still have to do a lot of reading between the lines to know what is really happening amongst Thailand's political bigwigs. The nitty-gritty and the rumours are conveyed by word-of-mouth.

It is interesting to note that Thailand is probably one of the few countries in the world whose prestigious newspapers are not found in the national language. Few Thai language newspapers have as high a reputation as the two mentioned above.

Well-produced local magazines in English are also available. The two best tourist-oriented ones are *Accent Thai* and *Phuket* magazine, the first is national, the second is limited to the Phuket region, apart from which there are numerous give-away magazines and news sheet of varying value. On the business front, *Manager* and "Business In Thailand" are leaders. Both include useful social and leisure information. Several gem and jewellery magazines are also published.

PHOTOGRAPHY/FILM/PROCESSING

Film of all kind is widely available, especially in Bangkok. These days, it is not surprising to find photo shops within a village. That said, most shops stock mainly popular colour print film, plus Ektachrome and Fujichrome 100 slide film. Kodachrome is hard to come by, but Kodachrome 64 is usually available in Bangkok's Chinatown (Charoen Krung), around Khaosan Road, Banglampu, in Siam Center, Rama I Road, and along Silom Road. Although, Agfa, Ilford and Konica film is sold in some shops Kodak and Fuji have the lion's share of the film market.

Prices are low, e.g. Fujichrome/Ektachrome 100 is between 130 to 150 baht (maximum US$6), expiry date is usually long, and film is mostly well-kept, so it is best to buy film in the country unless you use something outlandish.

The standard of developing is rapid and good, with film processors seemingly found on every corner, even in Nakhon Nowhere, that mythical back-of-beyond town. Beware instant slide film processing, however – it is better to go to the "ready tomorrow" shop.

POSTAL SERVICES

The Royal Thai Mail is consistently reliable and efficient, certainly by developing country standards. It would surprise you to know that mail to and from Europe rarely takes more than a week at least for Bangkok! Most post offices are open Monday-Friday, 8am-5.30pm, and Saturday, 8-12pm, but some principal ones open on Sunday mornings too, while some minor ones shut at 4pm.

Bangkok's Poste Restante is at the General Post Office in New Road (Charoen Krung) near the bottom of Suriwong Road.

RADIO & TV

Thailand has five television channels, some of which provide English soundtrack on FM radio for the evening news and imported series, movies and documentaries. Check the English newspapers for more programme information. The FM bands are:
Channel 3 – 105.5 MHz.
Channel 7 – 103.5 MHz.
Channel 9 –107 MHz.
Channel 11 - 88 MHz.

The best news channel is 5, which begins transmission from 10-11pm on weekdays, relaying CNN and BBC broadcasts, with direct English sound or subtitles. Most other programmes are typically Thai soap operas, Hong Kong kung fu, and American cops and robbers.

Thai radio is at times rather like US trends with 95% music and advertising. There are 41 FM and 35 AM stations in Bangkok alone and more than 400 stations nationwide. Virtually the only programming is Thai pop music and almost the only interruption is government-presented news in the early morning, at mid-day, and in the early evening, which is transmitted over all stations.

The exception lies with the three English language FM stations in Bangkok, plus some English broadcasting in Chiang Mai and Phuket. The Bangkok stations are 95.5 and 107 MHz for music and 97 MHz for music and information. The music is completely Western, ranging from commercial pop through easy listening to light jazz. 97 MHz is Radio Thailand, which specialises in news interspersed with muzak.

SECURITY & DIRTY TRICKS

Fraud and theft can be widespread. Take note of these areas:

Hotels: wherever a hotel offers some form of safekeeping for valuables and money, use it, whether it is a safe box, a safe or just safekeeping. However, always carry your credit cards with you – the practice of "borrowing" cards from safe deposits for fraudulent use or even copying is becoming epidemic.

Shops: if paying by credit card, try not to let the card out of your sight; if that's not possible, allow a two-minute maximum. Reason: same as above.

Long distance travel: keep a constant eye on luggage wherever possible.

City buses: hold bags in front of you, not behind or at the side, so as to forestall bag-slashers.

City streets: the same, so as to forestall bag-snatchers.

Anywhere: beware of friendly people who offer to take you on free boat-trips, to play cards, to give you huge discounts on gems, seductive female couples with strange voices, etc. There are many tricksters preying on tourists, especially in Bangkok. Some are very plausible, and violent if you refuse to cough up the huge boat fare or gambling debt or whatever it is you have got yourself into. There are many innocently friendly people too, so use your head: if in any doubt, firmly say "No thank you" and walk away.

If in need of assistance in a tourist centre, your best bet is usually the Tourist Police, who specialise in tourists' problems and speak English.

TELECOMMUNICATIONS

Telephone: Long distance calls may be made either by direct dialling or through the operator. Direct dialling is largely limited to private subscribers, though most international standard hotels offer this service to their guests. Generally speaking, all hotels priced above 300 baht a room will provide operator-controlled international service on a 3-minute minimum with a surcharge. All provincial capitals and larger towns have a Post and Telegraph office with long distance telephone facilities, again on a 3-minute minimum but without surcharge.

Cost examples for 3 minutes station-to-station at a P&T office are:

USA, Canada, UK, Germany, Australia – 240 baht (US$9); France, Sweden, Italy – 270 baht (US$10); Hong Kong, Japan – 210 baht (US$8); Singapore – 135 baht (US$5).

Fax and telex services are provided by the better hotels for their guests and sometimes for non-guests, especially if they have a "business centre", as at the Ambassador Hotel, Sukhumvit Road, Bangkok. Some travel agents provide fax and telex services. Specialist phone and fax service businesses are now sprouting in all well-touristed areas.

Domestic phone service: public phone booths have red push-button phones that take the new small 1 baht coin. Instructions for use:
· Lift the receiver.
· Insert the coin.
· Wait for the dialling tone (continuous).
· Dial the number.

You get about 3 minutes for 1 baht and you cannot extend the call by inserting more money. Shortly before the end of your time-limit, you will hear a long bleep, then the line is cut off. To continue the call, you must repeat the process. Many restaurants and some shops for example pharmacies have big red pay-phones at the cashier's counter. These cost 5 baht and the time limit is about 5 minutes. They operate as above except that when your correspondent answers, a steel button on the front of the phone has to be pressed in order to be heard.

If you do not get through for any reason,

TIME

Thailand is 7 hours ahead of GMT. Some broad guidelines for the time differences are as follows:

UK is 7 hours behind in winter, 6 hours in summer. New York is 11 hours behind, Los Angeles is 14 hours behind. Singapore is 1 hour ahead, Sydney is 3 hours ahead.

Being close to the equator, Thailand has almost equal daytime and nighttime. Dawn is around 6am, dusk around 6pm. Being in the northern hemisphere, the country gets its longest days in June and the shortest ones in Deecember, but the difference is less than one hour at both dawn and dusk.

TIPPING

Tipping is less widespread than in the West and less generous, though of course it is up to the individual. Generally speaking, the more expensive the restaurant or hotel, the greater the chance that a tip is expected. About 5% of the total bill is normal. In noodle shops and the like, nobody tips. Taxi-drivers do not expect a tip unless they have done some special service like carrying luggage.

TOURIST INFORMATION

Travel agents abound in all tourist areas. The government has a promotion organisation: the Tourist Authority of Thailand (TAT). TAT has offices within Thailand in Bangkok, Chiang Mai, Phitsanulok, Korat, Ubon, Pattaya, Kanchanaburi, Surat Thani, Phuket and Hat Yai.

Abroad, it has offices in London, Paris, Frankfurt, Rome, New York, Los Angeles, Sydney, Singapore, Kuala Lumpur, Hong Kong and Tokyo.

All the branches provide brochures and information. The Bangkok office is located in Ratchadamnern Nok Avenue (between the Golden Mount and the National Assembly).

GETTING AROUND

BANGKOK

Nearly all Bangkok transport is by road, with a small percentage by river and canal, and even less by rail. In 1990, three separate rail mass transit projects seemed to be geared for completion in the mid-90s, but time will tell if such sorely needed systems actually make it.

By road, you have the choice of limousine, taxi, *tuk-tuk*, motorcycle or bicycle-cart; air-con bus, ordinary bus, mini-bus and pick-up. Bangkok is highly flexible in its modes of road transport; the bad news is that traffic is increasingly congested. Your choice should depend on your priority: speed, price or comfort.

The quickest way to get around is to hire a motorcycle chauffeur; they usually wear outer waistcoats with writing on the back and hang around where side roads meet main roads. This is the only way to beat the jams – motorcyclists are adept at weaving in and out of stalled vehicles and getting to the front of the lights. They charge 5 baht upwards; if you really want to get across the city in a hurry, eg from the Eastern Bus Terminal to the Southern, 50 or 60 baht might do it.

The cheapest way to get around is on a minibus or ordinary bus – 2 baht per journey. The green minibuses suit small people who can tolerate reckless driving (the Thais, it seems). The big blue and white ones are safer and roomier, the big red and white ones (3 baht a journey) are somewhat more so. The air-con buses (blue and white, charge 5-15 baht according to the distance travelled) are best if not crowded but excruciatingly uncomfortable if packed and you are forced to stand; they are also potential death-traps when packed, having only one door with all the windows sealed shut.

All these buses have highly unpredictable stopping patterns, pulling up where and when they feel like it, within vague distance of an official bus stop. For routes, buy one of the several city bus maps available in tourist-type shops; none is complete or fully accurate but close enough. Buses can be quicker than any other form of transport if you want to go along a contra-flow such as Sukhumvit Road eastwards or Rajaprarop/Rajdamri Road southwards; otherwise they are the slowest mode of transportation.

The most comfortable way to get around, unless you get a real rattletrap, is by taxi. These take three forms – limousines, cabs and *samlors*. The most expensive being limousines can be hired from hotels and come with a fixed tariff. Cabs and *samlors* cruise the streets for customers and do not have meters – fares must be negotiated.

Cab fares were rapidly increasing at the time

of writing. Midtown trips of 5 km were usually 70-80 baht. Fares start at 30 baht for under 1 km on a clear road and rise to 150 baht to cross town in the rush hour. Drivers usually accept up to six passengers, even if the cabs are made for three-and-a-half. Cab quality varies from the pristine to the junkheap, yet they all try to charge the same fare!

Most cab-drivers cannot speak any English or can only manage a rudimentary variety. The best way for non-Thai speakers to hire a cab is to show the driver your destination written in Thai. All hotel receptionists and many shop assistants will oblige with this. If the driver is being fair, he will quote a figure just 10 baht above what he wants, holding up 6 fingers for 60 baht and so on, so you should show him 5 fingers back for 50 baht, etc. If he is out for real money, he will quote some outrageous figure, in which case you should just walk away – there is usually another taxi lurking somewhere behind.

Samlors, better known as *tuk-tuks* on account of their engine sound, are three-wheeled open-sided scooter-taxis seating three Westerners or a complete Thai family. Noisy, dirty, smelly, dangerous, uncomfortable and difficult to see out of, they are still loved by tourists – a veritable piece of local colour. The drill is the same as for cabs - bargain; fares are roughly 20 baht lower across the board, starting at 10 baht.

For river and canal transport, see Bangkok: River & Klong Life, page 93.

UPCOUNTRY TOWNS

Most provincial towns have neither cabs nor *tuk-tuks*; the staples are twin-bench pick-ups (*song taew*) and trishaws (bicycle rickshaws). Trishaw fares start at 5 baht and pick-ups at 20 baht; NB: NEGOTIATE. Urban bus services are usually provided by communal pick-ups with cheap fares.

INTER-CITY

There is a choice of bus, train and plane. Buses are the most widespread, trains are the best value, and planes are, naturally, the quickest.

BUS

Most Thais travel by bus, since even the back-of-beyond has bus services and all big towns have frequent connections. There is far too much to detail here; let some general advice suffice.

Bus types vary in comfort and price from tiny-seated ordinary buses, through comfortable air-conditioned reclining seat buses, to VIP overnight sleeper buses. The advantages of bus travel are frequency, ubiquity, and cheapness. The disadvantages are discomfort, dangerous driving, small seats, shot suspensions and maniac drivers who all-in-all add up to a nightmare journey. Be warned that head-on crashes with ten-wheel trucks are a regular feature of inter-city bus transport. Buses leave Bangkok throughout the day from any of the three terminals:

• Northern Bus Terminal on Phaholyothin Road for the North and Northeast.

• Eastern Bus Terminal on Sukhumvit Road for the East (Pattaya, Koh Samet, Chanthaburi).

• Southern Bus Terminal on Charan Sanitwong Road in Thonburi for the South (including Kanchanaburi).

TRAIN

By contrast, rail transport is one of the best in the world especially considering the prices charged. The one disadvantage are the limited routes offered. There are three major lines: Northern which goes to Chiang Mai and northeast to Ubon and the Southern line which goes to both the Malaysian east and west coasts, (the latter line goes right to Singapore). There is also a short Eastern line to the Cambodian border at Aranyaprathet. The Southern line has branches to Kanchanaburi, Nakhon Si Thammarat and Trang.

Almost all the trains start their journey from Hua Lampong Station in Bangkok; this is the place to go for the latest timetables in English and for advance booking. The advance booking office is open weekdays 8.30am-6pm and weekends and holidays 8.30am-12pm. When travelling for long distances, the second class overnight sleeper is highly recommended. Fares vary according to the type of train, air-conditioned or fan-cooled carriage, and upper or lower berth, but a fair example is a 500 baht average Bangkok-Chiang Mai. For this price, you can get a clean and comfortable bed, restaurant service right to your seat, reasonable toilets and washrooms, and no head-on crashes with trucks. Go for it – trains may be slightly slower than buses but they are a hell of a lot more civilised. NB: book sleepers well ahead, especially around New Year and from March to April the usual Thai holiday time.

PLANE

Air travel connects most of the big cities with Bangkok and some with each other. Places cur-

rently served are:
- North – Mae Hong Son, Chiang Mai, Chiang Rai, Nan, Phrae, Lampang, Mae Sot, Tak, Phitsanulok.
- Northeast – Loei, Udon Thani, Khon Kaen, Sakhon Nakhon, Ubon Ratchathani.
- South – Koh Samui, Surat Thani, Nakhon Si Thammarat, Phuket, Trang, Hat Yai, Narathiwat.

BY SEA

Sea travel is rapidly growing, with new ferry and hydrofoil services connecting Bangkok with Pattaya, Hua Hin and Koh Samui. Most sea services connects Surat Thani with Koh Samui, and Krabi and Phuket with Phi Phi Island. These southern routes offer a variety of frequent services.

SELF-DRIVE

Car hire is available in most cities, car, jeep and motorcycle hire in tourist resorts. Car and jeep hire starts at around 800 baht (US$32) a day and usually necessitates an International Driving Licence and leaving a deposit or your credit card. Motorcycle hire is usually 150-200 baht (US$6-8) a day and you normally have to deposit your passport. A licence is usually irrelevant.

Thais drive on the left, most of the time. At first, visitors may think that there are no rules of the road at all, but gradually it will become clear that it is all a question of ebb and flow, as if the Thais were still waterborne, it represents a kind of weaving in and out in a constant stream like canal and river boats. Join the flow, not too fast, and you should survive.

If there is any principle, it is to fill the space ahead. Thai drivers abhor a vacuum and rush to fill any gap, the worst effect is that it is impossible to keep a safe distance from the vehicle in front when cruising because some fool will always overtake and plug the gap.

Amazingly, the law does stress right of way very much like everywhere else – the main road over side roads, traffic keeping in lane over traffic cutting into a lane, and so on. If you have a scrape, the drill is to stop right there as evidence, discuss and settle responsibility and compensation with the other driver; if there is no agreement, you call the police, still not moving unless there's a massive traffic jam in consequence. If there is a serious accident – may God forbid! – and the other driver is at fault and fit, he may "flee the scene", a time-honoured phrase in local road accident reports. In Thai culture, this is not cowardice but avoidance of conflict and shame.

DIRECTORY

AIRLINES

Aeroflot
7 Silom Road
Bangkok
Telephone: (02) 233 6965

Air Canada
1053 New Road
Bangkok
Telephone: (02) 233 5900

Air France
3 Patpong Road
Bangkok
Telephone: (02) 236 9279

Air India
287 Silom Road
Bangkok
Telephone: (02) 233 8950

Air Lanka
1 Patpong Road
Bangkok
Telephone: (02) 236 9292

Air Pacific
3rd Floor
Chongkolnee Building
56 Suriwong Road
Bangkok
Telephone: (02) 234 0300

Alfa Royal Jordanian Airlines
Yada Building
56 Silom Road
Bangkok
Telephone: (02) 235 3970

Alitalia
138 Silom Road
Bangkok
Telephone: (02) 233 4000

Bangladesh Biman
Ground Floor
Chongkolnee Building
56 Suriwong Road
Bangkok
Telephone: (02) 233 6178

British Airways
2nd Floor
Chan Issara Tower
Rama IV Road
Bangkok
Telephone: (02) 236 8655

Burma Airways
208 Suriwong Road
bangkok
Telephone: (02) 234 9692

Canadian Airlines
89/12 bangkok bazaar
Rajdamri Road
bangkok
Telephone: (02) 251 0063

Cathay Pacific Airways
109 Suriwong Road
Bangkok
Telephone: (02) 235 6022

China Airlines
Siam Centre
Rama I Road
Bangkok
Telephone: (02) 251 9656

CAAC
134/1 Rama IV Road
Bangkok
Telephone: (02) 235 6510

Continental Airlines
5th Floor
Dusit Thani Building
Rama IV Road
Bangkok
Telephone: (02) 233 0566

Egypt Air
120 Silom Road
Bangkok
Telephone: (02) 233 7601

Fiji Air
3rd Floor
Chongkolnee Building
56 Suwiwong Road
Bangkok
Telephone: (02) 234 0300

Garuda
944/19 Rama IV Road
Telephone: (02) 233 3873

Gulf Air
9 Dejo Road
Bangkok
Telephone: (02) 234 5605

Indian Airlines
2/1 Dejo Road
Bangkok
Telephone: (02) 233 3890

Iraqi Airlines
29/3 Soi Saladaeng I

Silom Road
Bangkok
Telephone: (02) 233 3271

Japan Air Lines
1 Patpong Road
Bangkok
Telephone: (02) 234 9105

KLM Royal Dutch Airlines
2 Patpong Road
Bangkok
Telephone: (02) 235 5150

Korean Airlines
Dusit Thani Hotel
Rama IV Road
Bangkok 10500
Telephone: (02) 234 9283

Kuwait Airways
159 Rajdamri Road
Bangkok
Telephone: (02) 251 5854

Lao Aviation
3rd Floor Chongkolnee Building
56 Suriwong Road
Bangkok
Telephone: (02) 234 0300

Lot Polish Airlines
485/11 Silom Road
Bangkok
Telephone: (02) 234 2223

Lufthansa
331/1 Silom Road
Bangkok
Telephone: (02) 234 1350

Malaysian Airlines
98 Suriwong Road
Bangkok
Telephone: (02) 234 9790

Northwest Airlines
965 Rama I Road
Bangkok
Telephone: (02) 251 9652

Pakistan International Airlines
Thai Style Building

Suriwong Road
Bangkok
Telephone: (02) 234 2961

Pan American
Maneeya Building
518 Ploenchit Road
Bangkok
Telephone: (02) 252 7309

Philippine Airlines
Chongkolnee Building
56 Suriwong Road
Bangkok
Telephone: (02) 233 2350

Qantas
14-8 Patpong Road
Bangkok
Telephone: (02) 234 0102

Royal Nepal Airlines
1/4 Convent Road
Bangkok
Telephone: (02) 233 3921

Sabena Belgian Airlines
CCT Building
109 Suriwong Road
Bangkok
Telephone: (02) 233 5940

Saudi Arabian Airlines
Ground Floor
CCT Building
109 Suriwong Road
Bangkok
Telephone: (02) 234 7930

Scandinavian Airlines System
312 Rama I Road
Bangkok
Telephone: (02) 253 5309

Singapore Airlines
12th Floor
Silom Centre Building
2 Silom Road
Bangkok
Telephone: (02) 236 0303

Tarom Romanian Air Transport
Zuellig Building

1-7 Silom Road
Bangkok
Telephone: (02) 235 2668

Thai Airways (Domestic)
Thai Airways Building
6 Larn Luang Road
Bangkok
Telephone: (02) 282 7600

Thai Airways International
89 Vipavadi Rangsit Road
Bangkok
Telephone: (02) 234 3100

UTA French Airlines
3 Patpong Road
Bangkok
Telephone: (02) 233 7100

United Airlines
183 Rajdamri Road
Bangkok
Telephone: (02) 251 6006

Vietnam Airlines
83/1 Wireless Road
Bangkok
Telephone: (02) 251 7202

Western Airlines
501 Dusit Thani Building
Rama IV Road
Bangkok
Telephone: (02) 233 0566

BANKS

Asia Trust Bank
80-82 Anuwong Road
Bangkok
Telephone: (02) 222 2171

Bangkok Bank
333 Silom Road
Bangkok
Telephone: (02) 234 3333

Bangkok Bank of Commerce
171 Suriwong Road
Bangkok
Telephone: (02) 234 2930

Bangkok Metropolitan Bank
Yukol 2 Road
Bangkok
Telephone: (02) 282 3281

Bank of Agriculture
Mansion 1
Rajadamnoen Klang Avenue
Bangkok
Telephone: (02) 281 3622

Bank of America
2/2 Wireless Road
Bangkok
Telephone: (02) 251 6333

Bank of Asia for Industry & Commerce
Samyek Charoen Krung
601 New Road
Bangkok
Telephone: (02) 222 5111

Bank of Ayudhya
550 Ploenchit Road
Bangkok
Telephone: (02) 252 8171

Bank of Canton
197/1 Silom Road
Bangkok
Telephone: (02) 234 7030

Bank of Korea
16 Soi 20
Sukhumvit
Bangkok
Telephone: (02) 391 8605

Bank of Thailand
Bangkhunprom
Bangkok
Telephone: (02) 282 3322

Bank of Tokyo
Thaniya Building
62 Silom Road
Bangkok
Telephone: (02) 233 0790

Banque de l' Indochine et de Suez
142 Wireless Road
Bangkok
telephone: (02) 252 2111

Bharat Overseas Bank
221 Rajawong Road
Bangkok
Telephone: (02) 221 8181

Chase Manhattan Bank
Siam Centre
965 Rama I Road
Bangkok
Telephone: (02) 242 1141

Four Seas Communications Bank
231 Rajawong Road
Bangkok
Telephone: (02) 222 2161

Government Housing Bank
77 Rajdamnoen Avenue
Bangkokg
Telephone: (02) 2815155

Hongkong & Shanghai Banking Corporation
64 Silom Road
Bangkok
Telephone: (02) 233 5996

International Commercial Bank of China
95 Suapa Road
Bangkok
Telephone: (02) 221 8121

Krung Thai Bank
53 Sukhumvit Road
Bangkok
Telephone: (02) 241 2032

Mercantile Bank
63 Silom road
Bangkok
Telephone: (02) 233 5996

Mitsui Bank
Boon Mit Building
138 Silom Road
Bangkok
Telephone: (02) 234 3841

Siam City Bank
1101 New Petchaburi Road
Bangkok
Telephone: (02) 252 4425

Siam Commerical Bank
1060 New Petchaburi Road
Bangkok
Telephone: (02) 2519111

Standard Chartered Bank
Saladaeng Circle
Rama IV Road
Bangkok
Telephone: (02) 234 0821

Thai Danu Bak
393 Silom Road
Bangkok
Telephone: (02) 233 9160

Thai Development Bank
20 Yukol 2 Road
Bangkok
Telephone: (02) 281 3533

Thai Farmers Bank
400 Paholyothin Road
Bangkok
Telephone: (02) 270 1122

Thai Military Bank
34 Phayathai Road
Bangkok
Telephone: (02) 282 2727

Union Bank of Bangkok
634 Yawaraj Road
Bangkok
Telephone: (02) 233 4740

United Malayan Banking Corporation
3rd Floor
Hua Kee Building
107 Suapa Road
Bangkok
Telephone: (02) 221 9191

Wanglee Bank
1st Floor
Cathay Trust Building
1016 Rama IV Road
Bangkok
Telephone: (02) 233 2111

FOREIGN MISSIONS

Argentina
20/85 Sukhumvit Soi 49
Bangkok
Telephone: (02) 259 0401

Australia
37 South Sathorn Road
Bangkok
Telephone: (02) 286 0411

Bangladesh
6 Sukhumvit Soi 63
Bangkok
Telephone: (02) 391 8069

Belgium
44 Soi Phya Pipat
Silom Road
Bangkok
Telephone: (02) 233 0840

Brazil
PIM Building
8/1 Sukhumvit Soi 15
Bangkok
Telephone: (02) 251 6043

Britain
1031 Wireless Road
Bangkok
Telephone: (02) 253 0191

Brunei
26/50 Orakarn Building
Soi Chitlom
Ploenchit Road
Bangkok
Telephone: (02) 250 1483

Bulgaria
11 Soi Lampetch
Huamark
Bangkok
Telephone: (02) 314 3056

Burma
132 North Sathorn Road
Bangkok
Telephone: (02) 233 2237

Canada
11th Floor
Boonmitr Building
138 Silom Road
Bangkok
Telephone: (02) 234 1561

Chile
15 Sukhumvit Soi 51
Bangkok
Telephone: (02) 391 8443

China
57 Rajadapisek Road
Bangkok
Telephone: (02) 245 7030

Czechoslovakia
7th Floor
Silom Building
197/1 Silom Road
Bangkok
Telephone: (02) 234 1922

Denmark
10 Soi Attakarn Prasit
South Sathorn Road
Bangkok
Telephone: (02) 286 3930

Dominican Republic
92/6 Changwattana Road
Laksee
Bangkaen
Bangkok
Telephone: (02) 579 1130

Egypt
49 Soi Ruam Rudee
Ploenchit Road
Bangkok
Telephone: (02) 252 6139

Finland
3rd Floor
Vithayu Place
89/17 Wireless Road
Bangkok
Telephone: (02) 252 8636

France
35 Customs House Lane
New Road
Bangkok
Telephone: (02) 234 0950

Germany
9 South Sathorn Road
Bangkok
Telephone: (02) 286 4223

Greece
1977 New Petchaburi Road
Bangkok
Telephone: (02) 314 7333

Hungary
28 Soi Sukchai
42 Sukhumvit Road
Bangkok
Telephone: (02) 391 7906

India
46 Soi Prasarnmit
23 Sukhumvit Road
Bangkok
Telephone: (02) 258 0300

Indonesia
600 Petchaburi Road
Bangkok
Telephone: (02) 252 3135

Iran
9th Floor
Shell House
140 Wireless Road
Bangkok
Telephone: (02) 251 4925

Iraq
47 Pradipat Road
Bangkok
Telephone: (02) 278 5335

Israel
31 Soi Langsuan
Ploenchit Road
Bangkok
Telephone: (02) 252 3131

Italy
399 Nang Linchee Road
Bangkok
Telephone: (02) 286 4844

Japan
1674 Ne Petchaburi Road
Bangkok
Telephone: (02) 252 6151

Jordan
47 Sukhumvit Soi 63
Bangkok
Telephone: (02) 391 7142

Korea, Republic
28/1 Surasak Road
Bangkok
Telephone: (02) 234 0723

Laos
19 South Sathorn Road
Bangkok
Telephone: (02) 286 0100

Malaysia
35 South Sathorn Road
Bangkok
Telephone: (02) 286 1390

Monaco
3rd Floor
Nailert Building
888 Petchaburi Road
Bangkok
Telephone: (02) 252 8106

Nepal
189 Soi Phuengsuk
71 Sukhumvit Road
Bangkok
Telephone: (02) 391 7240

Netherlands
106 Wireless Road
Bangkok
Telephone: (02) 252 6103

New Zealand
93 Wireless Road
Bangkok
Telephone: (02) 251 8165

Norway
20th Floor
Chockchai Building
690 Sukhumvit Road
Bangkok
Telephone: (02) 251 8165

Oman
134/1 Silom Road
Bangkok
Telephone: (02) 235 8868

Pakistan
31 Soi Nana Nua
3 Sukhumvit road
Bangkok
Telephone: (02) 253 0288

Peru
723 Siphya Road
Bangkok
Telephone: (02) 233 5910

Philippines
760 Sukhumvit Road
Bangkok
Telephone: (02) 390 0993

Poland
61 Sukhumvit Soi 23
Bangkok
Telephone: (02) 258 4112

Portugal
26 Bush Lane
New Road
Bangkok
Telephone: (02) 234 0372

Romania
39 Sukhumvit Soi 10
Bangkok
Telephone: (02) 252 8515

Saudi Arabia
10th Floor
Boonmitr Building
138 Silom Road
Bangkok
Telephone: (02) 233 7941

Singapore
129 South Sathorn Road
Bangkok
Telephone: (02) 286 2111

Spain
104 Wirelesss Road
Bangkok
Telephone: (02) 252 6112

Sri Lanka
7th Floor
Nailert Building
87 Sukhumvit Soi 5
Bangkok
Telephone: 902) 251 8534

Sweden
11th Floor
Boonmitr Building
138 Silom Road
Bangkok
Telephone: (02) 234 3891

Switzerland
35 Wirelss Road
Bangkok
Telephone: (02) 252 8992

Taiwan
Chiengnuan Building
140 Wireless Road
Bangkok
telephone: (02) 251 9274

Turkey
153/2 Soi Majadlekluang
Rajdamri Road
Bangkok
Telephone: (02) 251 2987

USA
95 Wireless Road
Bangkok
Telephone: (02) 252 5040

USSR
108 North Sathorn Road
Bangkok
Telephone: (02) 234 9824

Vatican
217 South Sathorn Road
Bangkok
Telephone: (02) 233 9109

Vietnam
83/1 Wireless Road
Bangkok
Telephone: (02) 251 7201

Yugoslavia
28 Sukhumvit Soi 61
Bangkok
Telephone: (02) 391 9090

HOTELS

BANGKOK

Airport
333 Choet Wudhakat Road
Bangkok 10210
Telephone: (02) 566 1020
Fax: (662) 566 1941
300 rooms
Single: Bt1,600
Double: Bt1,700

Ambassador
171 Sukhumvit Soi 11
Bangkok 10110
Telephone: (02) 254 0444
1,050 rooms
Single or Double: Bt1,200

Ariston
19 Sukhumvit Soi 24
Bangkok 10110
Telephone: (02) 259 0960
Fax: (662) 259 0970
152 rooms

Asia
296 Phyathai Road
Bangkok 10400
Telephone: (02) 215 0808
Fax: 9662) 215 4360
640 rooms
Single: Bt1,600
Double: Bt1,800

Bangkok Centre
328 Rama IV Road
Bangkok 10500
Telephone: (02) 235 1780
Fax: (662) 236 1862
650 rooms
Single: Bt1,200
Double: Bt1,400

Century
9 Rajprarob Road
Bangkok 10400
Telephone: (02) 245 3271
89 rooms
Single: Bt540
Double: Bt660

Continental
971/16 Patholyothin Road
Bangkok 10400
Telephone: (02) 278 1385
113 rooms
Single: Bt550
Double: Bt695

Dorchester
21 Soi Kotoey
Pratipat
Bangkok
Telephone: (02) 279 2641

Dusit Thani
946 Rama IV Road
Bangkok 10500
Telephone: (02) 233 1130
Fax: (662) 236 6400
525 rooms
Single: Bt2,340
Double: Bt2,730

Erawan
494 Rajdamri Road
Bangkok
Telephone: (02) 252 9100
250 rooms
Single or Double: Bt1,450

Federal
27 Sukhumvit Soi 11
Bangkok 10110
Telephone: (02) 253 0175
75 rooms
Single or Double: Bt450

First
2 Petchaburi Road
Bangkok 10400
telephone: (02) 245 3221
107 rooms
Single: Bt500
Double: Bt600

Fortuna
19 Sukhumvit Soi 5
Bangkok 10110
Telephone: (02) 251 5121

Golden Dragon
20 Ngam Wong Warn Road
Bangkok 11000
Telephone: (02) 589 5141

Fax: (662) 598 8305
114 rooms
Single: Bt600
Double: Bt710

Golden Horse
5/1-2 Damrongrak Road
Bangkok 10200
Telephone: (02) 281 6909
130 rooms
Single: Bt700
Double: Bt800

Grace
12 Nana North Soi 3
Sukhumvit Road
Bangkok 10110
Telephone: (02) 253 0651
550 rooms
Single or Double: Bt675

Hilton
2 Wireless Road
Bangkok 10500
Telephone: (02) 253 0123
Fax: (662) 253 6509
389 rooms
Single: Bt2,270
Double: Bt2,380

Honey
31 Sukhumvit Soi 19
Bangkok 10110
Telephone: (02) 252 7111

Hyatt Central Plaza
1695 Patholyothin Road
Bangkok 10900
Telephone: (02) 541 1234
Fax: (662) 541 1087
607 rooms
Single: Bt1,700
Double: Bt2,000

Imperial
Wireless Road
Bangkok 10500
Telephone: (02) 254 0023
Fax: (662) 253 3190
400 rooms
Single: Bt2,210
Double: Bt2,470

Indra Regent
Rajprarob Road
Bangkok 10400
Telephone: (02) 252 1111
Fax: (662) 253 3849
438 rooms
Single: Bt1,800
Double: Bt2,100

Landmark
138 Sukhumvit Road
Bangkok 10110
Telephone: (02) 252 3819
Fax: (662) 254 0404
415 rooms
Single: Bt1,800
Double: Bt2,000

Liberty
215 Pradipat Road
Bangkok 10400
Telephone: (02) 271 0150
Fax: (662) 271 0945
200 rooms
Single: Bt390
Double: Bt460

Majestic
97 Rajdamnoen Avenue
Bangkok 10200
Telephone: (02) 281 5000
66 rooms
Single: Bt460
Double: Bt580

Malaysia
54 Ngan Duplee
Rama IV Road
Bangkok 10120
Telephone: (02) 286 3582
Fax: (662) 249 3120

Mandarin
662 Rama IV Road
Bangkok 10500
Telephone: (02) 233 4980
Fax: (662) 234 1390
343 rooms
Single: Bt1,000
Double: Bt1,200

Manhattan
13 Sukhumvit Soi 15
Bangkok 10110
Telephone: (02) 252 7141
Fax: (662) 255 3481
210 rooms
Single: Bt600
Double: Bt700

Manohra
412 Suriwong Road
Bangkok 10120
Telephone: (02) 234 5070
230 rooms
Single: Bt1,110
Double: Bt1,300

Menam
2074 New Road
Yanawa
Bangkok 10120
Telephone: (02) 289 3814
Fax: (662) 291 1048
727 rooms
Single: Bt1,500
Double: Bt1,700

Meridien President
135/26 Gaysorn Road
Bangkok 10500
Telephone: (02) 253 0444
Fax: (662) 253 7565
400 rooms
Single: Bt1,480
Double: Bt1,700

Metro
1902 New Petchaburi Road
Bangkok
Telephone: (02) 391 1736

Miami
2 Sukhumvit Soi 13
Bangkok 10110
Telephone: (02) 253 5611
123 rooms
Single: Bt165
Double: Bt210

Mido
222 Pradiopat Road
bangkok 10400
Telephone: (02) 279 4560
215 rooms
Single: Bt695

Montien
54 Suriwong Road
Bangkok 1050
Telephone: (02) 234 8060
Fax: (662) 236 5219
600 rooms
Single: Bt1,800
Double: Bt2,200

Morakot
2802 New Petchaburi Road
Bangkok 10400
Telephone: (02) 314 0761
121 rooms
Single: Bt350
Double: Bt400

Nana
4 Soi Nana Tai
Sukhumbit Road
Bangkok 10110
Telephone: (02) 252 0121
Fax: (662) 255 1769
334 rooms
Single: Bt550
Double: Bt590

Narai
222 Silom Road
Bangkok 10500
Telephone: (02) 233 3350
Fax: (662) 236 7161
500 rooms
Single: Bt1,400
Double: Bt1,600

New Empire
572 Yawaraj Road
Bangkok 10500
Telephone: (02) 234 6990
140 rooms
Single: Bt250
Double: Bt350

New Fuji
299 Suriwong Road
Bangkok 10500
Telephone: (02) 234 5364
Fax: (662) 236 5526
66 rooms
Single: Bt600
Double: Bt700

New Peninsula
295/3 Suriwong Road
Bangkok 10500
Telephone: (02) 234 3910
Fax: (662) 236 5526
120 rooms
Single: Bt560
Double: Bt610

New Trocadero
343 Suriwong Road
Bangkok 10500
Telephone: (02) 234 3910
Fax: (662) 236 5526
130 rooms
Single: Bt611
Double: Bt699

Oriental
48 Oriental Avenue
Bangkok 10500
Telephone: (02) 236 0400
Fax: (662) 2361936
398 rooms
Single: Bt3,100
Double: Bt3,400

Park
6 Sukhumvit Soi 7
bangkok 10110
Telephone: (02) 252 5110
128 rooms
Sinlge: Bt400
Double: Bt480

Parliament
402 Visutkasart Road
Bangkok 10200
Telephone: (02) 281 7237
93 rooms
Single: Bt360
Double: Bt440

Plaza
178 Suriwong Road
Bangkok 10500
Telephone: (02) 235 1760
Fax: (662) 235 1779
160 rooms
Single: Bt900
Double: Bt1,000

President
135/26 Gaysorn Road
Bangkok 10500
Telephone: (02) 252 9880

Prince
1537/1 New Petchaburi Road
Bangkok 10310
Telephone: (02) 251 3318
200 rooms
Single: Bt390
Double: Bt460

Princess
269 Larn Luang Road
Pomprab
Bangkok 10200
telphone: (02) 218 3088
142 rooms
Single: Bt620
Double: Bt760

Rajah
18 Sukhumvit Soi 4
Bangkok 10100
Telephone: (02) 251 8563
435 rooms
Single: Bt800
Double: Bt900

Rama Gardens
9/9 Vibhavadi Rangsit Road
Bangkok 10210
Telephone: (02) 579 5400
Fax: (662) 561 1025
372 rooms
Single: Bt1,300
Double: Bt1,450

Ramada
1169 New Road
Bangkok 10500
Telephone: (02) 234 8971
48 rooms
Single: Bt330
Double: Bt400

Regent
155 Rajdamri Road
bangkok 10500
Telephone: (02) 251 6127
Fax: (662) 253 9195
410 rooms
Single or double: Bt2,700

Reno
40 Soi Kasemsan 1
Rama I Road
Bangkok 10500
Telephone: (02) 252 6121

Rex
762/1 Sukhumvit Soi 32
Bangkok 10110
Telephone: (02) 259 0106
Fax: (662) 253 9195
135 rooms
Single: Bt494
Double: Bt598

Rich
136/14 Sukhumvit Road
Bangkok 10110
Telephone: (02) 252 9174

Rose
118 Suriwong Road
Bangkok 10500
Telephone: (02) 233 7695
100 rooms
Single: Bt460
Double: Bt580

Royal
2 Rajdamnoen Avenue
Bangkok 10200
Telephone: (02) 222 9111
Fax: (662) 236 8320
300 rooms
Single: Bt506
Double: Bt570

Royal Orchid Sheraton
2 Captain Bush Lane
Bangkok 10500
Telephone: (02) 234 5599
Fax: (662) 236 8320
780 rooms
Single: Bt1,800
Double: Bt2,100

Royal Plaza
30 Naret Road
Bangkok
Telephone: (02) 234 3091
320 rooms
Single: Bt290
Double: Bt400

Royal River
670/805 Charnsanitwong Road
Bangplad
Bangkok 10700
Telephone: (02) 433 0300
Fax: (662) 433 5880
404 rooms
Single: Bt1,400
Double: Bt1m60

Sakol
Soi 2
Phyathai Road
Bangkok 10400
Telephone: (02) 252 8161

Shangri-La
89 Soi Wat Suan Plu
New Road
Bangkok 10500
Telephone: (02) 236 7777
Fax: (662) 236 8579
697 rooms
Single: Bt2,250
Double: Bt2,550

Siam
1777 New Petchaburi Road
bangkok 10310
Telephone: (02) 252 5081
120 rooms
Single: Bt666
Double: Bt766

Siam Intercontinental
967 Rama I Road
bangkok 10500
telephone: (02) 253 0355]
Fax: (662) 253 2275
400 rooms
Single: Bt2,400
Double: Bt2,600

Silom Plaza
320 Silom Road
Bangkok 10500
Telephone: (02) 236 8441
Fax: (662) 236 7567
209 rooms
Single: Bt1,100
Double: Bt1,300

Suriwong
31/1 Suriwong Road
Bangkok 10500
Telephone: (02) 233 3223

Swan
31 Custom House Lane
Bangkok
Telephone: (02) 234 8594
72 rooms
Single or Double: Bt290

Tara
18/1 Sukhumvit Soi 26
Prakanong
Bangkok 10110
Telephone: (02) 259 2900
196 rooms

Tawana Ramada
80 Suriwong Road
Bangkok 10500
telephone: (02) 236 0361
Fax: (662) 236 3738
265 rooms
Single: Bt1,700
Double: Bt1,800

Thai
78 Prajathipatai Road
Bangkok 10500
Telephone: (02) 282 2831
100 rooms
Single: Bt430
Double: Bt512

Tower Inn
533 Silom Road
Bangkok 10500
Telephone: (02) 234 4051
120 rooms
Single or Double: Bt600

Victory
322 Silom Road
Bangkok 10500
Telephone: (02) 233 9060
Fax: (662) 236 7161
122 rooms
Single: Bt580
Double: Bt680

Viengtai
42 Tanee Road
Bangkumpoo
Bangkok 10200
Telephone: (02) 281 5788
240 rooms
Single: Bt520
Double: Bt620

Windsor
8 Sukhumvit Soi 20
Bangkok 10110
Telephone: (02) 258 0160
Fax: (662) 258 1491
362 rooms
Single: Bt1,000
Double: Bt1,100

World
1996 New Petchaburi Road
Bangkok 10400
Telephone: (02) 314 4340
90 rooms
Single: Bt280
Double: Bt320

YMCA
27 Sathon Tai Road
Bangkok 10120
Telephone: (02) 287 2727
189 rooms
Single: Bt500
Double: Bt600

CENTRAL REGION

Asia
Pattaya Beach
Pattaya City 20260
Telephone: (038) 428 602
320 rooms
Single: Bt860
Double: Bt1,000

Bangsaen Beach
55-150 Tambon Saensuk
Chonburi
Telephone: (038) 376 675
128 rooms
Single or Double: Bt521

Cosy Beach
400 Cliff Beach Road
Pattaya City 20260
Telephone: (038) 429 344

Diamond Beach
Pattaya Beach Resort
Pattaya City 20260
Telephone: (038) 428 071
126 rooms
Single or Double: Bt500

Dusit Resort
240 Pattaya Beach Road
Pattaya City 20260
Telephone: (038) 428541

Eastern
899 Thachalaep Road
Muang District
Chanthaburi
Telephone: (039) 312 218
142 rooms
Single or Double: Bt320

Grand Palace
Pattaya Beach
Pattaya City 20260
Telephone: (038) 418 319
500 rooms
Single: Bt1,039
Double: Bt1,196

Hilton
41/210 Raksakchamun Road
Muang District
Chanthaburi
Telephone: (039) 311064
68 rooms
Single or Double: Bt250

Island View
401 Cliff Beach Road
Pattaya City 20260
Telephone: (038) 428 818
147 rooms
Single: Bt759
Double: Bt886

Merlin
Pattaya Beach Resort
Pattaya City Resort
Telephone: (038) 428 755
360 rooms
Single: Bt700
Double: Bt800

Montien
Pattaya Beach Road

Pattaya City 20260
Telephone: (038) 428 155
320 rooms
Single: Bt1,300
Double: Bt1,400

Nakhon Inn
55 Rajavithi Road
Nakhon Pathom
Telephone: (034) 251 152
70 rooms
Single: Bt300
Double: Bt350

Nipa Lodge
Pattaya Beach Road
Pattaya City 20260
Telephone: (038) 428 195
150 rooms
Single: bt900
Double: Bt1,000

Novotel Tropicana
98 Mu 9
Pattaya Beach Road
Pattaya City 20260
Telephone: (038) 428 566
200 rooms
Single: Bt715
Double: Bt786

Ocean View
382 Pattaya Beach Resort
Pattaya City 20260
Telephone: (038) 428 084
115 rooms
Single or Double: Bt660

Orchid Lodge
Pattaya Beach Resort
Pattaya City 20260
Telephone: (038) 428 161
243 rooms
Single: Bt,1000
Double: Bt1,100

Palace
Pattaya Beach Resort
Pattaya City 20260
Telephone: (038) 428 542
261 rooms
Single or Double: Bt920

Pattaya Inn
380 Sukhabhibarn Road
Pattaya City 20260
Telephone: (038) 418 400

Pranburi Beach Resort
9 Paknam Pranburi
Prachuap Khiri Khan
Telephone: 621 701
60 rooms
Single: Bt1,570
Double: Bt1,690

Prima Villa
Na Klua Soi 18
Pattaya City 20260
Telephone: (038) 429 398
72 rooms
Single or Double: Bt759

Rama of the River Kwai
284/3-16 Saeng Chuto Road
Kanchanaburi
telephone: (034) 511 184
131 rooms
Single: Bt450
Double: Bt530

Rayong Resort
Laem Than
Ban Phe
Rayong
Telephone: (01) 211 0855
50 rooms
Single: Bt1,300
Double: Bt1,700

Regent
849/21 Cha Am Beach
Petchaburi
Telephone: (032) 471 483
550 rooms
Single or Double: Bt,1000

Regent Marina
463/31 North Pattaya Beach Road
Pattaya City 20260
Telephone: (038) 428 015
220 rooms
Single: Bt900
Double: Bt1,000

Rose Garden
21 Mu 2 Phetkasem Rpad
Nakhon Pathom
Telephone: (034) 311 171
120 rooms
Single: Bt500
Double: Bt800

Royal Cliff
359 Mu 12
Pattaya Beach resort
Pattaya City 20260
Telephone: (038) 428 511
700 rooms
Single: Bt1,600
Double: Bt2,000

Royal Garden
218 Pattaya Beach Road
Pattaya City 20260
Telephone: (038) 428 122
210 rooms
Single: Bt1,089
Double: Bt1,331

Royal Garden Resort
107/1 Phetkasem Beach Road
Hua Hin
Prachuap Khiri Khan
Telephone: (032) 511 881
220 rooms
Single: Bt1,500
Double: Bt1,600

Sailom
Hua Hin Beach
Phetkasem Road
Prachuap Khiri Khan
Telephone: (032) 511 890
66 rooms
Single: Bt660
Double: Bt860

Seaview
Na Klua Soi Wong Amat
Pattaya City 20260
Telephone: (038) 429 317
219 rooms
Single: Bt700
Double: Bt800

Siam Bayshore
599 Mu 10
Pattaya Beach
Pattaya City 20260
Telephone: (038) 428 677
275 rooms
Single: Bt800
Double: Bt1,000

Siam Bayview
Pattaya Beach Resort
Pattaya City 20260
Telephone: (038) 428 728
302 rooms
Single: Bt1,200
Double: Bt1,800

Sofitel
1 Damnoen Kasem Road
Hua Hin
Prachuao Khiri Khan
Telephone: (032) 511 012
150 rooms
Single: Bt1,800
Double: Bt2,170

Thanaporn
Bangkamung
Pattaya City 20260
Telephone: (038) 418 690
100 rooms

Travel Lodge
14 Raksakchamun Road
Muang District
Chanthaburi
Telephone: (039) 311 531
212 rooms
Single or Double: Bt250

Weekender
Soi 2
Pattaya Beach Road
Pattaya City 20260
Telephone: (038) 418 400
120 rooms

Wong Amat
Pattaya Beach Resort
Pattaya City 20260
Telephone: (038) 428 118
207 rooms
Single: Bt900
Double: Bt2,700

NORTHEASTERN REGION

Charoen
549 Pho Si Road
Udon Thani
Telephone: (042) 221 331
120 rooms
Single or Double: Bt300

Chom Surang
2701 Mahat Thai Road
Nakhon Ratchasima
Telephone: (044) 242 940
119 rooms
Single: Bt400
Double: Bt500

Kaen Inn
56 Klang Muang Road
Muang District
Khon Kaen
Telephone: (043) 237 744
160 rooms
Single: Bt306
Double: Bt450

Khai Yai Motor Lodge
Amphoe Pakchong
Nakhon Ratchasima
48 rooms
Single or Double: Bt380

Khon Kaen
43/2 Phimphasut Road
Khon Kaen
Telephone: (043) 237 711
140 rooms
Single: Bt300
Double: Bt400

Kosa Khon Kaen
250 Sichan Road
Khon Kaen
Telephone: (043) 225 014
120 rooms
Single: Bt375
Double: Bt436

Lert Nimit
447 Niwetrak Road
Chaiyaphum
Telephone: (044) 811 522
98 rooms

Single: Bt225
Double: Bt245

Muang Mai Korat
4014/1 Atsadang Road
Nakhon Ratchasima
Telephone: (044) 242 444
119 rooms
Single: Bt230
Double: Bt300

Nakhon Phanom
528/39 Aphiban Bancha Road
Nakhon Phanom
Telephone: (042) 511 455
57 rooms
Single: Bt220
Double: Bt300

Pathumrat
173 Chayangkun Road
Ubon Ratchathani
Telephone: (045) 241 501
120 rooms
Single: Bt400
Double: Bt500

Petchkasem
104 Chitbamrung Road
Surin
Telephone: (045) 511 274
162 rooms
Single: Bt350
Double: Bt450

Rosesukon
1/10 Klang Muang Road
Muang District
Khon Kaen
Telephone: (043) 237 797
82 rooms
Single: Bt363
Double: Bt424

Sri Pattana
3571/5 Suranari Road
Nakhon Ratchasima
Telephone: (044) 242 944
183 rooms
Single: Bt250
Double: Bt300

NORTHERN REGION

Amarintr Nakorn
3/1 Chao Phya Road
Phitsanulok
Telephone: (055) 258 588
130 rooms
Single: Bt260
Double: Bt320

Anodad
57 Rajmaraka Road
Chiang Mai 50000
Telephone: (053) 235 353
150 rooms

Asia
299 Bunyawat Road
Muang District
Lampang
Telephone: (054) 217 844
72 rooms
Single: Bt300
Double: Bt370

Chang Puak
133 Chotana Road
Telephone: (053) 221755
60 rooms
Single or Double: Bt300

Chiang Come
7/35 Mu 3
Suthep Road
Chiang Mai 50000
Telephone: (053) 211 020
150 rooms
Single: Bt300
Double: Bt500

Chiang Dao Hill Resort
28 Mu 6
Chiang Dao District
Chiang Mai 50000
Telephone: (053) 236 995
63 rooms
Single: Bt700
Double: Bt900

Chiang Inn
100 Changklan Road
Chiang Mai 50000
Telephone: (053) 235 655
175 rooms

Single: Bt900
Double: Bt1,000

Chiang Rai Island Resort
1129 Singhaklai Road
Muang District
Chiang Rai
Telephone: (053) 711 865
22 rooms
Single: Bt300
Double: Bt500

Ckakrungrao
123/1 Thesa Road
Kamphaeng Phet
Telephone: (055) 711 326
116 rooms
Single: Bt220
Double: Bt260

Dhevaraj
466 Sumon Thewarat Road
Nan
Telephone: (054) 710 094
154 rooms
Single: Bt400
Double: Bt500

Diamond
33/10 Charoen Prated Road
Chiang Mai 50000
Telephone: (053) 234 153
145 rooms
Single: Bt520
Double: Bt930

Dusit Inn
112 Changklan Road
Chiang Mai 50000
Telephone: (053) 251 034
Fax: (053) 251 037
200 rooms
Single: Bt940
Double: Bt1,000

Erawan Resort
149/10 Changklan Road
Chiang Mai 50000
Telephone: (053) 232 450
51 rooms
Single or Double: Bt750

Hills
18 Huay Kaew Road

Chiang Mai 50000
Telephone: (053) 221 255
120 rooms
Single: Bt600
Double: Bt700

Iyara
126 Chotana Road
Chiang Mai 50000
Telephone: (053) 222 723
102 rooms
Single: Bt450
Double: Bt550

Klissada Doi
14 Hang Dong Samoeng Road
Chiang Mai 50000
Telephone: (053) 251 191
20 rooms
Single: Bt750
Double: Bt1,400

Mae Ping
Sridonchai Road
Chiang Mai 50000
Telephone: (053) 251 060
416 rooms
Single: Bt1,000
Double: Bt2,000

Maesod Hill
100 Asia Highway
Mae Sot
Tak
Telephone: (055) 532 601
120 rooms
Single: Bt550
Double: Bt630

Muang Mai
502 Huay Kaew Road
Chiang Mai 50000
Telephone: (053) 221 392
155 rooms

Nanchao
242 Baromtrilokanat Road
Phitsanulok
Telephone: (055) 259 511
115 rooms
Single: Bt242
Double: Bt700

Navarat
2 Soi Prapan
Thesa Road
Kamphaeng Phet
Telephone: (055) 711 211
78 rooms
Single: Bt200
Double: Bt300

New Asia
55 Soi Tadmai
Rajawong Road
Chiang Mai 50000
Telephone: (053) 235 288
204 rooms
Single: Bt420
Double: Bt480

Northern Inn
234/18 Maninopharat Road
Chiang Mai 50000
Telephone: (053) 210 002
90 rooms
Single: Bt420
Double: Bt530

Orchid
100 Huay Kaew Road
Chiang Mai 50000
Telephone: (053) 221 625
267 rooms
Single or Double: Bt1,000

Phailin
38 Baromtrilokanat Road
Phitsanulok
Telephone: (055) 252 411
175 rooms
Single: Bt600
Double: Bt1,200

Phet
99 Wichit Soi 3
Kamphaeng Phet
Telephone: (055) 712 810
234 rooms
Single: Bt360
Double: Bt440

Phucome
21 Huay Kaew Road
Chiang Mai 50000
Telephone: (053) 211 026
150 rooms

Single: Bt500
Double: Bt880

Plaza
92 Sridonchai Road
Chiang Mai 50000
Telephone: (053) 252 050

Pornping Tower
46 Charoen Prated Road
Chiang Mai 50000
Telephone: (053) 235 099
Fax: (053) 249 136
320 rooms
Single: Bt650
Double: Bt759

Poy Luang
146 Superhighway
Chiang Mai 50000
Telephone: (053) 242 633
228 rooms
Single: Bt968
Double: Bt1,089

President
226 Witchayanon Road
Chiang Mai 50000
Telephone: (053) 251025
150 rooms
Single or Double: Bt700

Prince
3 Taiwang Road
Chiang Mai 50000
Telephone: (053) 236 306
121 rooms
Single: Bt440
Double: Bt541

Railway
471 Charoen Muang Road
Chiang Mai 50000
Telephone: (053) 236 463
76 rooms

Rajapruk
99/9 Phraong Dam Road
Phitsanulok
telephone: (055) 258 477
100 rooms
Single or Double: Bt300

Rincome
301 Huay Kaew Road
Chiang Mai 50000
Telephone: (053) 221 044
158 rooms
Single: Bt1,210
Double: Bt1,331

Rintr
99/9 Huay Kaew Road
Chiang Mai 50000
Telephone: (053) 221 750
138 rooms
Single: Bt450
Double: Bt500

Royal Park
471 Charoen Muang Road
Chiang Mai 50000
Telephone: (053) 245 124
80 rooms
Single: Bt500
Double: Bt600

Sri Tokyo
63 Changklan Road
Chiang Mai 50000
Telephone: (053) 213 899
111 rooms
Single: Bt250
Double: Bt680

Sumit
198 Rajpakinai Road
Chiang Mai 50000
Telephone: (053) 235 996
165 rooms

Suriwong
110 Changklan road
Chiang Mai 50000
Telephone: (053) 236 891
170 rooms
Single: Bt1,089
Double: Bt1,210

Thepnakorn
43/1 Sitham Traipnidok Road
Phitsanulok
Telephone: (055) 258 507
150 rooms
Single: Bt300
Double: Bt400

Tipchang Garnet
54/22 Takrao Noi
Soptui
Lampang
Telephone: (054) 218078
125 rooms
Single: Bt400
Double: Bt500

Wangcome
869/96 Pemaviphak road
Chiang Rai
Telephone: (054) 711 800
221 rooms
Single: Bt500
Double: Bt600

Wiang Inn
893 Phahonyothin Road
Chiang Rai
Telephone: (054) 711 543
260 rooms
Single: Bt424
Double: Bt508

Wiang Tak
25/3 Mahatthai Bamrung Road
Tak
Telephone: (055) 511 910
100 rooms
Single: Bt390
Double: Bt500

Wieng Kaew
7 Huay Kaew Road
Chiang Mai 50000
50 rooms
Single: Bt220
Double: Bt450

SOUTHERN REGION

Amanpuri Resort
Surin Beach
Phuket
Telephone: (076) 216 545
40 rooms
Single or DOuble: Bt1,331

Ambassador
23 Phadungphakdi Road
Hat Yai
Songkhla
Telephone: (074) 246 665
170 rooms
Single: Bt340
Double: Bt400

Arcadia
41/25 Montri Road
Karon Beach
Phuket 83130
Telephone: (076) 214 840
255 rooms
Single: Bt2,118
Double: Bt2,360

Asian
55 Niphat Uthit 3 Road
Hat Yai
Songkhla
Telephone: (074) 245 455
104 rooms
Single or Double: Bt532o

Banthai Beach Resort
89/71 Mu 4
Thawiwong Road
Patong Beach
Phuket 83121
Telephone: (076) 321 328
128 rooms
Single: Bt1,210
Double: Bt3,509

Cape Panwa
Phuket
Telephone: (076) 213 563
122 rooms
Single or Double: Bt2,300

Chumphon Cabana
Mu 8
Thung Wau Laen Beach
Tambon Saphli Amphoe Pathiu
Chumphon
Telephone: (077) 511 885
26 rooms
Single: Bt200
Double: Bt400

Club Andaman
77/1 Thawiwong Road
Patong Beach
Phuket 83121
Telephone: (076) 321 361
107 rooms

Single or Double: Bt500

Club Med
Kata Beach
Phuket 83000
Telephone: (076) 212 901
300 rooms
Single or Double: Bt1,600

Cora1 Bay Resort
Samui Island
Surat Thani
Telephone: (077) 272 222
42 rooms
Single or Double: Bt500

Coral Beach
104 Mu 4
Patong Beach
Phuket 83121
Telephone: (076) 321 106
200 rooms
Single: Bt980
Double: Bt1,080

Diamond Cliff
61/9 Kalin Beach
Phuket 83121
Telephone: (076) 321 501
Fax: (076) 321 507
140 rooms
Single: Bt2,100
Double: Bt2,300

Dusit Laguna
390 Srisoontorn Road
Bang Thao Bay
Phuket 83110
Telephone: (076) 311 320
Fax: ()76) 311 174
240 rooms
Single: Bt1,500
Double: Bt1,700

Emperor
1 Tanrattanakon Road
Hat Yai
Songkhla
Telephone: (074) 245 166
108 rooms
Single or Double: Bt630

Family
20 Chunmakkha Road

Amphoe Sungai Kolok
Narathiwat
Telephone: (073) 611 397
148 rooms
Single: Bt320
Double: Bt420

Grand Garden
104 Arif Makkha Road
Narathiwat
Telephone: (073) 611 219
129 rooms
Single: Bt450
Double: Bt500

Holiday
1 Sanchanuson Road
Hat Yai
Songkhla
Telephone: (074) 243 881
106 rooms
Single or Double: Bt620

Holiday Inn
86/11 Thawiwong Road
Patong Beach
Phuket 83000
Telephone: (076) 321 020
280 rooms
Single: Bt1,815
Double: Bt2,057

Holiday Resort
Patong Beach
Phuket 83000
Telephone: (076) 321 101
100 rooms
Single: Bt450
Double: Bt900

Indra
Hat Yai
Songkhla
Telephone: (074) 243 277
90 rooms
Single or Double: Bt506

Inter Tower
160 Prachawiwat Road
Narathiwat
Telephone: (073) 611 192
80 rooms
Single or Double: Bt396

International
42 Niphat Uthit 3 Road
Hat Yai
Songkhla
Telephone: (074) 244 744
210 rooms
Single or Double: Bt440

Jansom Thara
2/10 Phetchakasem Road
Bang Rin District
Ranong
Telephone: (077) 811 510
230 rooms
Single or Double: Bt500

Karon Villa
36/4 Karon Beach
Phuket 83130
Telephone: (076) 212 709
150 rooms
Single or Double: Bt1,936

Kata Thani
62/4 Rasda Road
Kata Beach
Phuket 83000
Teephone: (076) 214 824
212 rooms
Single: Bt1,700
Double: Bt1,936

Kosit
Niphat Uthit 2 Road
Hat Yai
Songkhla
Telephone: (074) 244 711
182 rooms
Single or Double: Bt506

Lee Gardens
1 Lee Phatthana Road
Hat Yai
Songkhla
Telephone: (074) 245 888
122 rooms
Single or Double: Bt751

Lilla
28 Saritwong Road
Narathiwat
Telephone: (073) 611 039
72 rooms

Single: Bt180
Double: Bt220

Meridien
Karon Beach
Phuket 83000
Telephone: (076) 321 480
470 rooms
Single: Bt2,300
Double: Bt,2541

Merlin
158/1 Yawaraj Road
Phuket 83000
Telephone: (076) 211 618
180 rooms
Single: Bt660
Double: Bt780

Montien
120 Niphat Uthit 1 Road
Hat Yai
Songkhla
Telephone: (074) 246 968
180 rooms
Single or Double: Bt506

My House
600 Phetchakasem Road
Hat Yai
Songkhla
Telephone: (074) 246 372
137 rooms
Single or Double: Bt560

Nara Lodge
Bophui Beach
Samui Island
Surat Thani
Telephone: (077) 272 2222
30 rooms
Single or Double: Bt380

New World
144 Niphat Uthit 2
Hat Yai
Songkhla
Telephone: (074) 246 993
133 rooms
Single or Double: Bt605

Nora
216 Thammanum Withi Road
Hat Yai

Songkhla
Telephone: (074) 244 944
168 rooms
Single or Double: Bt506

Pansea
118 Mu 3
Pansea Beach
Phuket 83000
Telephone: (076) 216 137
101 rooms
Single: Bt1,610
Double: Bt1,800

Patong Beach
Phuket 83000
Telephone: (076) 321 301
120 rooms
Single: Bt480
Double: Bt560

Patong Merlin
23/5 Patong Beach
Phuket 83000
Telephone: (076) 321 070
137 rooms
Single: Bt1,452
Double: Bt1,694

Patong Resort
94/2 Rajuthit Road
Patong Beach
Phuket 83000
Telephone: (076) 321 333
213 rooms
Single: Bt700
Double: Bt800

Pearl Village
Nai Yang Beach
Phuket 83000
Telephone: (076) 311 338
185 rooms
Single: Bt1,815
Double: Bt2,057

Phangnga Bay Resort
Tha Dan
Phangnga
Telephone: (076) 411 067
90 rooms
Single: Bt666
Double: Bt786

Pharadorn Inn
180/12 Pharadorn Road
Muang District
Chumphon
Telephone: ()77) 511 500
106 rooms
Single or Double: Bt466

Phi Phi Island Cabana
201/3-4 Utarakit Road
Krabi
Telephone: (075) 611 496
40 rooms
Single or Double: Bt100

Phi Phi Village
Phi Phi Island
Krabi
Telephone: (075) 611 188
60 rooms
Single or Double: Bt600

Phuket Cabana
Patong Beach
Phuket 83000
Telephone: (076) 321 138
77 rooms
Single or Double: Bt1,000

Phuket Island Resort
73/1 Rasda Road
Phuket 83000
Telephone: ()76) 215 950
Fax: (076) 215 956
231 rooms
Single: Bt847
Double: Bt1,150

Phuket Yacht Club
23/3 Vises Road
Nai Harn Beach
Phuket 83130
Telephone: (076) 214 020
108 rooms
Single: Bt2,775
Double: Bt3,219

Plaza
2 Thetpathom
Narathiwat
Telephone: (073) 611 035
94 rooms
Single: Bt420
Double: Bt450

Porn Sawan
Pharadonraphap Beach
Chumphon
Telephone: (077) 521 031
75 rooms
Single: Bt400
Double: Bt550

Rama President
420 Phetchakasem Road
Hat Yai
Songkhla
Telephone: (074) 244 477
110 rooms
Single: Bt430
Double: Bt480

Rawai Resort
22 Vises Road
Rawai Beach
Phuket 83000
Telephone: (076) 212 943

Regency
23 Prachathipat Road
Hat Yai
Songkhla
Telephone: (074) 245 454
189 rooms
Single: Bt500
Double: Bt550

Samila
Rajadamnoen Road
hat Yai
Songkhla
Telephone: (074) 311 310
70 rooms
Single: Bt600
Double: BT700

Samui Ferry Inn
Thong Yang Beacn
Samui Island
Surat Thani
Telephone: (077) 273 130
25 rooms
Single or Double: Bt400

Siam Thani
180 Surat Phunphin Road
Surat Thani
Telephone: (077) 273 081
172 rooms
Single or double: Bt480

Siam Thara
1/144 Donnok Road
Muang District
Surat Thani
Telephone: (077) 273 740
172 rooms
Single or Double: Bt480

Sintawee
89 Phangnga Road
Phuket
Telephone: (076) 211 186
137 rooms
Single: Bt150
Double: Bt250

Sukhontha
26 Sanehanuson Road
Hat Yai
Songkhla
Telephone: (074) 243 999
205 rooms
Single or Double: Bt702

Tan Yong
16/1 Sophaphisai Road
Narathiwat
Telephone: (073) 511 477
83 rooms
Single: Bt342
Double: Bt586

Thai
1373 Rajdamnoen Road
Muang District
Nakhon Si Thammarat
Telephone: (075) 356 451
210 rooms
Single: Bt300
Double: Bt350

Thara Patong
81 Thaweewong Road
Patong Beach
Phuket 83121
Telephone: (076) 321 135
43 rooms
Single or Double: Bt390

Thavorn
Rasada Road
Phuket
Telephone: (076) 211 333
200 rooms
Single: Bt380
Double: Bt480

Thavorn Bay Resort
6/5 Mu 5
Nakalay-Potong Beach
Phuket 83120
Telephone: (076) 321 486
30 rooms
Single: Bt1,500
Double: Bt1,700

Thavorn Palm Beach
Karon Beach
Phuket
Telephone: ()76) 214 835
210 rooms
Single: Bt1,500
Double: Bt1,700

Wang Tai
1 Talat Mai Road
Muang District
Surat Thani
Telephone: (077) 273 410
230 rooms
Single or Double: Bt600

Yala Rama
21 Sibamnung Road
Yala
Telephone: (073) 212 815
133 rooms
Single: Bt292
Double: Bt576

NIGHTSPOTS IN BANGKOK

Abbots
(hostess nightclub)
Sukhumvit Soi 33

Admakers
(Western music club)
Soi Lang Suan

Ballroom
(hostess nightclub)
Sukhumvit Soi 33

Bobby's Arms
(pub)
Patpong Road
Bangkok

Brown Sugar
(Western music club)
SOi Sarasin
Bangkok

Bubbles
(discotheque)
Dusit Thani Hotel
946 Rama IV Road
Bangkok 10500

Burgundy
(Western music club)
Soi Sarasin
Bangkok

Chamois
(hostess nightclub)
Soi Lang Suan
Bangkok

Diana's
(discotheque)
Oriental Hotel
48 Oriental Avenue
Bangkok 10500

King's Castle
(go-go bar)
Patpong Road
Bangkok

Manet
(hostess pub)
Sukhumvit Soi 33
Bangkok

MGM
(discotheque)
Asoke Road
bangkok

Old West
(Western music club)
Soi Sarasin
Bangkok

Palace
(discotheque)
Superhighway
Bangkok

Pegasus
(hostess nightclub)
Sukhumvit Soi 23
Bangkok

Peppermint
(go-go bar)
Patpong Road
Bangkok

Renoir
(hostess pub)
Sukhumvit Soi 33
Bangkok

Round Midnight
(Western music club)
Soi Lang Suan
Bangkok

Saxophone
(Western music club)
Victory Monument
Bangkok

Superstar
(go-go bar)
Patpong Road
bangkok

Talk of the Town
(discotheque)
Shangri-La Hotel
89 Soi Wat Suan Plu
New Road
Bangkok 10500

Toby Jug
(pub)
Silom Road
Bangkok

Van Gogh
(hostess pub)
Sukhumvit Soi 33
Bangkok

Witch's Tavern
(pub)
Sukhumvit Soi 55
Bangkok

RESTAURANTS IN BANGKOK

AMERICAN

Bourban Street
Sukhmvit Soi 22
Bangkok
Telephone: (02) 259 0328

Hamilton's
Dusit Thani Hotel
946 Rama IV Road
Bangkok 10500
Telephone: (02) 236 0450

BURMESE

Mandalay
Sukhumvit Soi 11
Bangkok
Telephone: (02) 250 1220

CHINESE

Golden Dragon
Sukhumvit Soi 2
Bangkok
Telephone: (02) 252 7412

Grand Shangarilla
Thaniya Road
Bangkok
Telephone: (02) 234 2045

Hoi Thien Lao
Suapa Road
Bangkok
Telephone: (02) 437 1121

Mayflower
Dusit Thani Hotel
946 Rama IV Road
Bangkok 10500
Telephone: (02) 236 0450

Shangri-La
Soi Pipat
Bangkok
Telephone: (02) 235 5118

FRENCH

La Brasserie
Regent Hotel
155 Rajdamri Road
Bangkok 10500
Telephone: (02) 251 6127

Le Banyan
Sukhumvit Soi 8
Bangkok
Telephone: (02) 253 5556

Le Bistro
Soi Ruam Rudee
Bangkok
Telephone: (02) 251 2525

Ma Maison
Hilton Hotel
2 Wireless Road
Bangkok 10500
Telephone: (02) 251 7111

Metropolitan
135/6 Gaysorn Road
Bangkok
Telephone: (02) 252 8364

Normandie Grill
Oriental Hotel
48 Oriental Avenue
Bangkok 10500
Telephone: (02) 236 0400

GERMAN

Bierstube
Sukhumvit Soi 31
bangkok
Telephone: (02) 258 9303

By Otto
Sukhumvit Soi 14
Bangkok
Teleophone: (02) 252 6836

Singha Bierhaus
Asoke Road
Bangkok
Telephone: (02) 391 7501

HUNGARIAN

Nick's
1 Sukhumvit Soi 16
Bangkok
Telephone: 902) 259 4717

INDIAN

Cafe India
460/8 Suriwong Road
Bangkok
Telephone: (02) 233 0419

Himali Cha Cha
1229/11 New Road
Bangkok
Telephone: (02) 235 1569

Nawab
New Road
Bangkok
Telephone: (02) 233 2503

Italian Pavilion
Sukhumvit Soi 4
Bangkok
Telephone: 902) 250 1550

L'Opera
Sukhumvit Soi 39
Bangkok
Telephone: (02) 258 5606

JAPANESE

Bengkay
Royal Orchid Sheraton Hotel
2 Captain Bush Lane
Bangkok 10500
Telephone: (02) 234 5599

Hanaya
Siphya Road
Bangkok
Telephone: (02) 234 8095

Shogun
Dusit Thani Hotel
946 Rama IV Road
Bangkok 10500
Telephone: (02) 236 0450

Tokugawa
Ambassador Hotel
171 Sukhumvit Road
Bangkok
Telephone: (02) 251 0404

KOREAN

Arirang
Silom Road
Bangkok
Telephone: (02) 234 7869

Koreana
Siam Square
Bangkok
Telephone: (02) 252 9398

SCANDINAVIAN

Two Vikings
Sukhumvit Soi 37
Bangkok
Telephone: (02) 258 8843

SEAFOOD

Seafood Market
Sukhumvit Soi 16
Bangkok
Telephone: (02) 258 0218

Seafood Restaurant
New Petchaburi Road
Bangkok
Telephone: (02) 314 4312

THAI

Bean Thai
Sukhumvit Soi 32
Bangkok
Telephone: (02) 258 5403

Bussaracum
35 Soi Pipat 2
Convent Road
Bangkok
Telephone: (02) 235 8915

D'Jit Pochana
Sukhumvit Soi 20
Bangok
Telephone: (02) 258 1597

Dusit Bussaracum
Dusit Thani Hotel
946 Rama IV Road
Bangkok 10500
Telephone: (02) 236 0450

Khum Luang
Asoke Dindaeng Road
Bangkok
Telephone: (02) 245 6605

Krua Tow
Sukhumvit Soi 39
Bangkok
Telephone: (02) 392 8273

Lemongrass
5/1 Sukhumvit Soi 24
Bangkok
Telephone: (02) 258 7866

Sala Rim Naam
Oriental Hotel
48 Oriental Avenue
bangkok 10500
Telephone: (02) 236 0400

Silom Village
Silom Road
Bangkok
Telephone: (02) 234 4448

Spice Market
Regent Hotel
155 Rajdamri Road
Bangkok 10500
Telephone: (02) 251 6127

Toll gate
245/2 Sukhumvit Soi 31
Bangkok
Telephone: (02) 391 3947

Tum Nak Thai
Rajadapisek Road
Bangkok
Telephone: (02) 276 1810

VEGETARIAN

Whole Earth Cafe
93/3 Soi Lang Suan
Ploenchit Road
Bangkok
Telephone: (02) 257 5574

VIETNAMESE

Le Danang
Hyatt Central Plaza Hotel
1695 Paholyothin Road
Bangkok 10900
Telephone: (02) 541 1234

Thien Duong
Dusit Thani Hotel
946 Rama IV Hotel
Bangkok 10500
Telephone: (02) 236 0450

TOURIST INFORMATION

Headquarters
Tourism Authority of Thailand
Rajdamnoen Nok Avenue
Bangkok 10100
Telephone: (02) 282 1143
Fax: (662) 280 1744

Central Region
Tourism Authority of Thailand
Saeng Chuto Road
Amphoe Muang
Kanchanaburi 71000
Telephone: (034) 511 200

Central Region
Tourism Authority of Thailand
382/1 Chaihat Road
South Pattaya 20260
Telephone: (038) 428 750

Northeastern Region
Tourism Authority of Thailand
2102 Mittraphap Road
Tambon Nai Muang
Amphoe Muang
Nakhon Ratchasima 30000
Telephone: (044) 243 427

Northeastern Region
Tourism Authority of Thailand
Sala Prachakhom
Si Naron Road
Amphoe Muang
Ubon Ratchathani 34000
Telephone: (054) 255 603

Northern Region
Tourism Authority of Thailand
135 Praisani Road
Amphoe Muang
Chiang Mai 50000
Telephone: (053) 235 334

Northern Region
Tourism Authority of Thailand
209/7-8 Surasi Trade Cenre
Boromtrailokanat Road
Amphoe Muang
Phitsanulok 65000
Telephone: (055) 252 742

Southern Region
Tourism Authority of Thailand
1/1 Soi 2
Niphat Uthit 3 Road
Hat Yai
Songkhla 90110
Telephone: (074) 243 747

Southern Region
Tourism Authority of Thailand
73 Phuket Road
Amphoe Muang
Phuket 83000
Telephone: (076) 212 213

Southern Region
Tourism Authority of Thailand
5 Talat Mai Road
Ban Don
Amphoe Muang
Surat Thani 84000
Telephone: (077) 282 828

Australia
Tourism Authority of Thailand
12th Floor
Royal Exchange Building
56 Pitt Street
Sydney
New South Wales 2000
Australia

Telephone: (02) 277 549
Fax: (612) 251 2465

England
Tourism Authority of Thailand
49 Albemarle Street
London W1X 3FE
England
Telephone: (071) 499 7670

France
Office Nationale du Tourisme
de Thailande
90 Avenue des Champs Elysees
75008 Paris
France
Telephone: 456 28656
Fax: 9331) 456 37888

Germany
Thailandisches
Fremdenverkehrsburo
Bethmannstrasse 58/4
D6000 Frankfurt am Main
Germany
Telephone: (069) 295 704
Fax: (4969) 284 468

Hong Kong
Tourism Authority of Thailand
Room 401
Fairmont House
8 Cotton Tree Drive
Hong Kong
Telephone: 868 0732
Fax: 868 4585

Italy
Ente Nazionale peril Turismo
Thailandese
Via Barberini 50
00187 Rome
Italy
Telephone: (06) 474 7410
Fax: (396) 474 7660

Japan
Tourism Authority of Thailand
5th Floor Hirano-machi
Yachiko Building
2-8-1 Hirano-machi
Higashi-ku
Osaka 541
Japan

Telephone: (06) 231 4434
Fax: (816) 231 4337

Japan
Tourism Authority of Thailand
Hibiya Mitsui Building
1-2 Yurakucho 1-chome
Chiyoda-ku
Tokyo 100
Japan
Telephone: (03) 580 6776
Fax: (813) 508 7808

Malaysia
Tourism Authority of Thailand
c/o Royal Thai Embassy
206 Jalan Ampang
Kuala Lumpur
Malaysia
Telephone: 248 0958

Singapore
Tourism Authority of Thailand
c/o Royal Thai Embassy
370 Orchard Road
Singapore 0923
Telephone: 235 7901
Fax: (65) 733 5653

USA
Tourism Authority of Thailand
Suite 1101
3440 Wilshore Boulevard
Los Angeles
California 90010
USA
Telephone: (213) 382 2353
Fax: (213) 380 6476

USA
Tourism Authority of Thailand
Suite 2449
5 World Trade Center
New York
NY 10048
USA
Telephone: (212) 432 0533
Fax: (212) 912 0920

USEFUL TELEPHONE NUMBERS

Ambulance
(02) 281 1544

American Express
(02) 251 4862

Fire
(02) 281 6666

Immigration
(02) 286 7013

International Calls
100
Local Calls
13

Long Distance Calls
101
within Thailand

Police
(02) 281 0372

Post Office
(02) 233 1050

Tourism Authority of Thailand
(02) 282 1143

USEFUL PHRASES

Hello	Sawatdi krap (when said by a male) Sawatchi ka (when said by a female)	One	Nung
		Two	Sorng
Goodbye	Sawatdi krap (male) Sawatchi ka (female)	Three	Sam
How are you?	Sabai di ru?	Four	Si
I am fine	Sabi di krap (male) Sabidi ka (female)	Five	Ha
Thank you	Kawphum krap (male) Kawpkun ka (female)	Six	Hok
Yes	krap (male) Ka (female)	Seven	Chet
No	Mai	Eight	Paet
Excuse me	Kaw thot		
Never mind	Mai pen rai	Nine	Kow
I cannot speak Thai	Phut Thai mai dai	Ten	Sip
May I know your name?	Kun chu arai krap? (male) Kun chu arai ka? (female)		
Where is ...?	You nai...?	Monday	Wan chan
I want to go to	Yak ja pai...	Tuesday	Wan angkan
How much does this cost?	Ni raka towrai?	Wednesday	Wan phut
Hotel	Rongram	Thursday	Wan paruhat
Restaurant	Ran ahan	Friday	Wan suk
Police Station	Sat hani tamruat	Saturday	Wan sao
Embassy	Sat han thot	Sunday	Wan athi
Airport	Sanam bin		
Bus station	Sat hani rotmeh		
Railway station	Sat hani rotfai		

INDEX

A

agriculture, 27
ahaan, 119
Aisawan Tiphaya-art, 131, *132*
Ajarn Cha, 183
ajarns, 263
Akha, 155, *155*, 243, 248, 317
Alaungpaya, 12
albino, 156
Aloha Tours, 340
Amanpuri hotels, 222
Amarin Plaza, 87
Ambassador Hotel, 107, 109, 329, 397
Amnat Charoen district, 183
amulets, 258
Ananta Samakom Throne Hall, 53, 66
Anantanagaraj, 69
Ancient City, 76
Andaman, 220
Andaman Princess, 334
Andaman Sea, 11, 219, 225-227, 334, 335, 338-339, 342, 363,
Ang Thong archipelago, 139, 231
Angkor Wat, 177-180
Angkor, 10, 135, 166, 177, 179-*181*, 267
animism, 154, 248, 257, 259-160, 264
Annamite Cordillera, 376
Annual Fair, 210
Ao Baw Mao, 219
Ao Cho, 202
Ao Manao, Lime Bay, 218
Ao Nang Beach, 226-227
Ao Noi, Little Bay, 217

Ao Phanang Tak, 219
Ao Thung Wua Laen, 219
Ao Wai, 202
Ao Wong Deuan, 202
Aphonphimo Prasat, 131
Aporn Phimok Prasat, 61
Aquarium of the Scientific Marine Centre, 196, 225
Aranyaprathet, 205
architecture, 270
art & antiques, 83
art shows, 276
artifacts, 135
artistic culture, 268
Arunthip, 212
Asakha Bucha, 291, 300
Asia Voyages, 331, 334
Asia, *140*
Asian, 69, *70*, 122-123
Assam, 245
Auditorium, 73
Austro-Asiatic, 147
Austro-Thai, 154
autocracy, 10
Ayutthaya Historical Study Centre, 127
Ayutthaya Princess, 102, 332
Ayutthaya, 1, 10-14, 16-17, 48, 52, 67, 77, 101-102, 118, 122, 124, 127-131, 135-136, 138-139145-146, *167*, 168, 179, 245, 269, 269, 270, 273, 284, 294, 297, 313, 330-332

B

Buddhist monkhood, 379
Baan Khun Luang, 108
Baan Thai, 106

bai-nod, 314
Bakhon Pathom, 8
Balinese, 278
bamboo forests, 371
bamboo, 321
Bamrungmuang Road, 50, 64
Ban Baht, 50, 52
Ban Cheun, 205
Ban Chiang pottery, 8, 70, 186, 188, 318-319
Ban Kok Lao, 189
Ban Pang La, 373
Ban Phe, 202
Ban Rim Pa, 361
Ban Talay, 357
Ban Tappikaew, 365
Ban Thawai, 318
banded kraits, 45
Bang Chiang, 16
Bang Pa-In Palace, 77, 102, 130-131, 134-135, 225, 273, 278, 330,
Bang Pu, 216
Bang Sadej, 321
Bang Saen, 195, 196, 200, 357
Bang Sai district, 135
Bang Sai Folk Arts & Crafts Centre, 135
Bang Tao Bay, 222
Bangkok Airport, 40
Bangkok Bank, 253
Bangkok period, 14, 99, 101
Bangkok's City Pillar, 278
Bangkok's Dusit Zoo, 307
Bangkok's Weekend Market, 45
Bangkok, 3, 7, 22, 29, 41, 47-56, 55-57, *56*, 59-77, *63*, 63-64, 66, 77, 79-80, 84, 87, 90, 94, 107, 117-120,

431

123, 126, 131, 135, 145, 147, 149, 155, 156, 195-198, 209, 231, 253, 263, 269, 270, 273, 275, 276, 283, 284, 294-295, 304-305, 321, 323, 370, 389, 395
Bangkokians, 196, 197
Banglampoo, 65, 91, 107, 328
Bangrak Market, 74
banteng, 41
Barred Ground Dove Festival, 295
basketware, 85, 314
Bayon, 179
bear, 41, 138
beauty contests, 291
Beeswax Candle Procession, 304
Ben Kern, 314
Bencharong, 82, 318-319
Beung Wai International Forest Monastery, 183
Bhumiphol, 4, 18, *19, 21*, 25, 66
Big Buddha, 228, 231
Big Channel, 205
birdlife, 41, 138
birth control programme, 246
Black Buddha, 129
Black Scene, 114
blue and white, 82
Blue Moon, 114
Blues Jazz Pub, 114
Bo Paw, Bo Mae and Bo Luk, 220
Bo Phut, 228
Bo Sang Umbrella Fair, 292
Bo Sang, 157, 292-293, 320-321
boar, 41, 138
Bolovens Plateau, 383
Bophut, 341
Boromakot, 12
bot, 101, 272, 276
Boy's Secondary School, 234
Brahma, 137, 260, 297
Brahmin priests, 50
Brahmin shrines, 259, 260
Brahminism, 65, 257, 260
brass, 82
Bremen, 336
British-influence, 17
British, 121

bronze age, 135
bronze technology, 8
Brown Sugar, 113
Bua Thong Restaurant, 360
Bua Yai, 292
Bubbles, 109
Buddha image, 76, 169, 233, 300, 305, 389, 391,
Buddha Phra Singh, 149
Buddha statuary, 269
Buddha Uthayan, 183
Buddha, 52, 64, 101, 129, 137, 139, 164, 166, 168, *169, 171, 182*-183, 260, *268*, 272, 275, 295, 379, 389, 393
Buddhadasa, 151
Buddhism, 4, 5, 7, 118, 152, 154, 175, 262, 264, 276, 248, 255, 257, 260, 263, 304, 381
Buddhist civilisation, *145*, 166
Buddhist High School, 386
Buddhist Lent, 68, 197, 291, 300, 304
Buddhist mythology, 275
Buddhist novices, 296
Buddhist temples, *189*, 323
Buddhist-inspired, 83, 268
Buenos Aires, 119
buffalo, 37
Bura, 154
Buri Ram, 179
Burma, 8, 11, 12, 17, 33-34, 120, 122-123, 126, 146, 159, 166, 209, 248, 254, 283, 285, 315, 327, 375, 378-379
Burmese and Lanna architecture, 164
Burmese-influences, 148, 159, 272, 389
Burmese kings, 122
Burmese occupation, 14
Burmese temples, 164
Burmese vassal, 11
Burmese, 1, 12, 33-34, 48, 83, 126, 130-131, 137, 146, 147, 164-*165*, 211, 245, 246, 268, 327, 379,
butterfly, 112, 138

C

Cabbages and Condoms, 349

cabinet, 24
Caesar Manelli, 338
Calypso Cabaret, 113
Cambodia, 13, 17, 34, 50, 137, 176, 177, 179, 180, *181*, 182, 204, 205, 243, 246, 278, 283, 285, 375, 376
canal system, 93, 130
candle dance, *247*
Candle Festival, 183, 291, 300
Cantonese food, 352
Casablanca, 109
Cat Island (Koh Nu), 236
catamarans, 334
cattle, 41
Cattleya, 40
Celadon pottery, 82, 318
Central Department Store, 88
Central Isan, 190
Central Kingdom, 268
Central Plains, 3, 34, 38, *117*-143, 118, 126, 138, 139, *140*, 146, 164, 179, 246, 253, 268, 269, 273, 372
Central Plaza Hotel, 329
ceramics, 82, 318
Cha-am, 198, 211
Chachoengsao, 102, 291
Chai Nat Bird Park, 294
Chainat, 139
Chaiyaphum, 190, 292
Chak Phra Festival, 234, 305
Chakrapetch Street, 234
Chakravat Phaichayon Hall, 129
Chakri dynasty, 14, 17, 48, 60
Chakri Maha Prasad, 61
Chalermchai Kositpipat, 276
Chalong Beach, 343
chameleons, *39*
Champa empire, 394
Champassak, 380, 394
Chan Kasem Palace, 127
Chandrakasem Palace, 130
Chang Klan Road, 152
Chanthaphanith, 393
Chanthaburi provinces, 205
Chanthaburi, 11, 13, 28, 202, 204, 205, 364
Chanthara Phisan, 135
Chao Boun Oum, 394
Chao Phraya River, 7, 10, 12, 14, 33, 48, *54*, 59, 93, 95, 94, 98, 101, 108, 128, 130, 131, 135, 197, 332, 347, 379

Chao Phraya valley, 8, 9
Chao Phraya Wichayen Residence, 137
Chao Phya Chakri, 14
Chao Sam Phraya Museum, 127
Chapel Royal, 60
charity, 261
Charoen Krung, 74, 91
Chatuchak Park, 90, 91
Chaweng Beach, 228, 342
Chedi Luang, 149
Chedi Sao, 164
chedi, 52, 64, 98, 99, 118, 129, 137, 145, 150, 152, 164, 168, 170, 185, 204, 210, 217, 233, *268*, 272
Chenla, 179
Chiang Dao, *156*
Chiang Khan, 184, 188
Chiang Mai Cultural Centre, 152
Chiang Mai Night Market, 152, 154
Chiang Mai realm, 10
Chiang Mai, 12, 16, 34, 37, 40, 145, 146, *147*, 147, *148*, 149, 151, 154, 155, 157, 159, 164, 234, 245, *247*, 248, 268, 272, 273, 292, 293, 295, 296, 297, 302, 314, 318, 321, 324, 326, 327, 330, 366, 373
Chiang Rai province, 155
Chiang Rai Tourist Information Centre, 327, 330
Chiang Rai, 145, 146, 157, *160*, 330, 327
Chiang Saen, 9, 16, 33, 159, 146, 268, 270
Chitrlada, 312
Chilli, 362
China Restaurant, 353
China, 2, 9, 48, 146, 154, 245, 248, 260, 267, 283, 285, 313, 376
Chinatown, 54, 73, 74, *86*, 88, 91, 295
Chinese businesses, 253
Chinese cuisine, 366, 367
Chinese immigrants, 246, 253
Chinese language schools, 253
Chinese merchants, 48
Chinese New Year, 295
Chinese Restaurants, 352
Chinese, 7, 8, 134, 135, 139,
147, 154, 185, 243, 245, 253, 254, 264, 267
ching, 285
Chitralada Palace, 53, 66, 67
chongkrabane costume, 346
Chonburi Buffalo Races, 305
Chonburi, 197, *277*, 305
Christians, 154, 203, 248, 264
Chulalongkorn (Rama V), 9, 17, 18, 66, 67, 129, 131, 134, 197, 204, 216, 306
Chulalongkorn University, 72, 283
Chumphon Cabana Resort, 219, 337
Chumphon Gate, 177
Chumphon, 34, 209, 210, 218, 219, 254, 337, 338
circumcision, 250
City Pillar, 62, 149
classic style, 275
classical dance, 267
Clay Dolls, 321
climate, 34
clothing, 79
club, 16, 373
Club Aldiana, 213
Club Mediterranee, 224
colonisation, 380
commerce, 27, 254
Constantine Phaulkon, 121, 137
constitutional monarchy, 17
contemporary art scene, 276
Coral Islands, 198, 227, 343
Coral Reef, 340
corals, 335, 336
court culture, 267, 284, 260
Court of Siam, *13*
crafts, 267
craftsmanship, 249, 311
Crocodile Farm, 76
crocodiles, 44
crops, 37
crows, 44
Crystal Buddha, 149
Crystal Sand Beach, 200
cultural conservation, 327
culture, 145, 267-289
customs, 145

D

Damnernkasem Road, 213
Damnoen Saduak, 120, 139
Dan Sai, 300

dance drama, 82, 278-283
Dan Sai, Loei, 300
Dawn of Happiness, *167*
Death Railway, 121, 122
deep-sea fishing, 342
deer, 138, 190
deet, 41
dek wat, 263
Democracy Monument, 65, 76
democracy, 21
dendrobium, 40
Design Thai, 313
Deutsche House Restaurant, 342
Diana, 109
Diethelm Travel of Bangkok, 395
Din Daeng, 109
dinghies and catamarans, 332, 334
dinner cruises, 107
diplomacy, 135
diplomatic facilities, 15
disco, 108
divine kingship, 179
Divine Seat of Personal Freedom, 131
diving trips, 335, 337
Dixieland Jazz Club, 114
Doi Khun Tan Park, 164
Doi Suthep, 146, 147, 151, 152, 272, 324
Don Chedi Memorial Fair, 139, 292
Done Rek mountains, 34, 176, 179-180
Donsak, 228, 231
down, 154
Dragon and Lion Parade, 294
drama, 267
dry season, 117, 397
dug-out canoes, 330
durian, 364
Dusit district, 53
Dusit Laguna Resort, 222
Dusit Maha Prasad, 61
Dusit Thani Hotel, 109, 324, 329
Dusit Zoo, 66, 306
Dusit, 54, 66, 306
Dutch, 12
Dvaravati kingdom, 118, 135
Dvaravati, 8, 16, 267, 268

INDEX

E

East Asiatic, 98
East, *196*, 268
Eastern Seaboard Project, 195
Eating, 345-367
economic growth, 17
economy, 27-31, 376
Egg Banana Festival, 170
egrets, 44
Eightfold Path, 263
Ekatat, 12
electronics, 29
elephant camp, 157
elephant, 37, 38, 130, 138, 156, 190, 373
Emerald Buddha, 14, 15, 48, 60, 157, 164, 270, 387, 389
English, 255
enviromental conservation, 327
Erawan Falls, 126
Erawan Hotel, 71, 87, 260
Erawan Park, 126
Erawan Shrine, 71, 87, 108, 257, 259, 278, 284
ethnic Lao, 378
ethnic, 380
etiquette, 260
Europe, 136
evil spirits, 258, 259
exporters, 117
exports, 29
Express Boat, 95

F

Fa Ngum, 379, 393
fabrics, 79
faith, 257
fakery, 85
Fantasea Divers, 338
Far From Worries Palace, 212
farang, 201
farming, 119, 253, 254
Father, Mother and Child Springs, 220
Festival of the Tenth Lunar Month, 303
festivals, 267, 291-309
Feung Fah Restaurant, 366
Firecat, 111
fish cake, 356
fish farming, 28, *31*, 254
fishing port, 212, 217
Fitness Park, 361
fitness centre, 329

Flamingo, 109
floating hotel resorts, 126
Floating Market, 100, 120, 76
flora, 37
Flora & Fauna, 37-45
flower garlands, 75
Flower Festival, 295
Flower Garden Temple, 150
flying lizards, 41
folk arts and crafts, 312
folk dance, 152
folk tales, 284
folk theatre, 305
foreign exchange, 28, 29
foreign trade, 12
France, 136
frangipani, 38
Freak In, 109
Freak Out, 109
French Embassy, 98
French influence, 17
French rule, 204
French, 13, 136, 380, 386, 389
Friendship Highway, 188
frogs, 41
Funan, 8
furniture, 85

G

Gai Haw Bai Toey, 347
Gai Yang Pak Panang, 347
gai yang, 252
Galeries Lafayette, 87
garments, 79
Gaysorn intersection, 89, 259
General Taksin, 48
Geography, 33-35
Germany, 40
Giacometti Buddhas, 170
Giant Swing, 50, 64, 65
gibbons, 41
gin khao, 119
glassware, 82
GNP, 27
gold, 81
Golden Buddha, 73
Golden Mount Fair, 305
Golden Mount, 52, *53*, 64, 305
Golden Palace, 129
Golden Triangle, 159, *160*, 330, 331
Goldfingers, 112
Golf Thailand, 326
golf, 139, 324

Government, 21-25
Government House, 54
government service, 29, 253
Grand Palace Complex, 59, 61
Grand Palace, 47, 50, 53, 60, 75, 91, 93, 98, 129, 306, 332
Grand Prix, 112
Grandmother and Grandfather Rocks, 228
Greater Bangkok, 195
Greek influence, 269
growth rate, 246
guardians, 259
Gulf of Thailand, *30*, 102, 209, 321, 334, 335, 342, 372
Gulf, 236, 339
gyms, 329

H

Ha Yai, 236
Hainan Island, 245
Hall of Mirrors, 136
Han Chinese, 245
handicrafts, 135, 234, 311-321
Hang Dong, 318
Hanuman, 278
Hardeep, 336, 342
Haripunchai, 8, 9, 145, 146, 159, 164
Harrie's Bar, 113
Hat Chao Samran, 211
Hat Lek, 205
Hat Simila, 236
Hat Yai, 210, 236, 236, 236, 237
Hennessey Nightclub, 373
Heo Narok, 138
Heo Suwat Waterfall, 138
herons, 126, 44
hiking, 327
hill tribe (handicraft), 157
hill tribes, 147, 154, 157, *244*, 152, 248, 316, 330
hill-tribe Hindus, 264
Hilton Hotel, 324, 328, 329, 370
Hindu-influence, *175*, *189*
Hindu, 136, 179
Hindu–Buddhist art, 268, 267
history, 7-19, 48, 145
Hmong, 152, 154, 243, 248, 380, 394, 397
Ho, (bandit attack), 386

Ho Withun Thasana, 135
hoi fai, 321
Holy Footprint Shrine, 300
Holy Footprint, 137, 138
Holy Rosary Church, 98
Hong Kong, 27
hoon, 283
Hor Mok Pla Shawn, 358
horankang, 273
Hormoak, 348
hot mineral water, 220
Hotel Sofitel Central, 213
hotrai, 273
house gecko, 45
Hua Hin, 31, 211, 212, 213, 214, 323, 326, 365
Hua Lampong Station, 73, 102, 120, 397
Huay Kaew area, 147
Huay Khamin, 126
Hyatt Erawan Hotel, 71

I

Illuminated Boat Procession, 304
Immigration Department, 396
India, 183, 245, 269, 283, 285, 315, 386, 389
Indian Buddhists, 118, 269
Indian culture, 7
Indian Devanagari system, 255
Indian elephant, 156
Indian-influence, 150, 232, 246
Indian Ocean, 341
Indian, 243, 245, 264, 267, 282
Indianised, 8, 255
Indochina, 122, 123, 267
Indochinese wars, 246
Indra Arcade, 86
industrialisation, 17, 4, 27
industry, 176
infrastructure, 29
Inner Palace, 134, 135
instrumentation, 283
inter-marriage, 253
investment, 27, 147
irrigation, *117, 140*
Isan Rocket Festivals, 191, *192*
Isan, 11, 17, 34, *175*-193, 177, *181*, 182, 184, 185, 188, 189, 190, 191, 193, 252, 268, 292, 300, 379, 380
Islam, 264
Italy, 40

ivory, 82

J

Jade, 82
Jamnian Srithaipahan, 284
Jansom Thara Hotel, 220
Japan, 17, 40
Japanese investment, 18
Japanese, 121, 122, 380
Jataka Buddhist, 232, 278
Java, 231, 283, 285
Javanese, 278
Jayavaraman VII, 178, 179
Jayavarman VI, 178
jazz clubs, 113
jazz, 115
JEATH Museum, 122, 123
Jim Thompson house, 69, *70*, 369
Jim Thompson, 70
jogging, 328
Jomtien Beach, 332, 334, 341, 343

K

Kaeng Krachan Dam and National Park, 211
Kaeng Saphue, 183
Kaeng Som Sam Sad Yam Saeng Wa, 348
Kaeng Tana, 183
Kai Hor Bai Toey, 358
Kalasin, 190, 191
Kamala Beach, 222
Kamphaeng Phet, 10, 128, 145, 168, *169, 170*, 171, 262, 262, 303, 304
Kamthieng House, 70, 72
Kanchanaburi Cemeteries, 122
Kanchanaburi, 28, 38, 40, 77, 120, 122, 123, 126, 154, 248, 306
Kangdadan, 284
Kao Tom Kamlang Pai Nai, 349
Karen, 154, 211, 243, 248
karma, 47, 258, 260,
Karon Bay, 224
Kata Bay, 224
Kata Beach, 223
Kata/Karon, 343
kating, 41
Kaysone Phoumivane, 383
khaen, 191, 252
Khanom, 228, 231

khantok, 295
Khao Chamao National Park, 202
Khao Chong Krajok, 216
Khao Krachom, 213
Khao Laem, 139
Khao Lom Muak, 216
Khao Luang Cave, 211
Khao Mong Rai, 217
khao nio, 119, 236
Khao Ok Thalu, 234
Khao Phansa, 291
Khao Phra Thaeo Wildlife Park, 328
Khao Ploi Waen, 203
Khao Rang Restaurant, 361
Khao Sam Roi Yod, 213
Khao Soi Dao Tai National Park, 204
khao suay, 119
Khao Wang Palace Mount, 210
Khao Yai National Park, 138, 328
Khao Yai, 41, 156
khao, 119
Khaosan Road, 396
Khlong Yai, 205
Khmer architecture, 137, 177, *178*
Khmer art, 180, 389
Khmer carved-stone, 179
Khmer city, 177
Khmer civilisation, 179, 246
Khmer culture, 178, 268
Khmer empire, 135, 166, 178, 179, 394, 379
Khmer irrigation system, 166-168
Khmer Lopburi style, 136/137
Khmer people, 378
Khmer period, 394
Khmer power, 16, 179
Khmer ruins, 177
Khmer sites, 180, 181
Khmer temple, 177
Khmer, 9, 10, 69, *70*, 118, 136, 164, 166, *175*, 176, 178, *179*, 245, 246, 253, 255, 389
Khmer-style, 10, 129
Khmer-influenced art, 268
Khno, 315
Khon Kaen, 190, 191
khon, 82, *267*, 276, 278, *280*,

282, 285, 287, 315
Khong Chiam, 184
khong wong yai, 284, 285
Khorakhopura, 177
Khuk Khee Kai, 204
Khun Klang, 10
Khun Muang, 10
Khun Na, 10
Khun Tukata, 348
Khun Wang, 10
Khunying Mo, 177
king cobras, 45
King's Lounge, 109
Keu Na, 152
King Narai's palace, 273, 372
King Naresuan, 16, 139, 292
King of Ayutthaya, 16
King of Muang, 379
King of Sukhothai, 16
King Prasat Thong, 131
King's Corner, 112
King's Castle, 1, 112
King's Hawaii Cabaret, 113
King's Lounge, 109
King, 24
Kingdom of Lane Xang, 391
Kingdom of Siam, 126
kingfishers, 44, 126
kinship, 246
kinnaree, *274*, 318
kinnari, 232
Kitchakut National Park, 204
kitchen, 350
Klai Kangwon "Far From Worries" Palace, 212
Klang Avenues, 305
Klong Bang Khung Si, 101
Klong Bangkhunthien, 100
Klong Bangkok Noi, 69, 101
Klong Bangkok Yai, 99, 100
Klong Banglamphu, 50
Klong Damnoensaduak, 96
Klong Dan, 100
Klong Lawd, 48, 64
klong life, 94
klong luang, 302
Klong Mahanak, 50, 52
Klong Ong Ang, 50
Klong Phasi Jaroen, 100
Klong Sanam Chai, 100
Klong Toey, 102
klong, 55, 94, *101*, 102, 285
Kluai Khai Banana Festival, 303
kluai khai, 170

Ko Lang Kachiu, 218
Ko Samui, 240
Ko Siray, 225
Koh Bon, 338
Koh Chang, 204
Koh Faan Bay, 230
Koh Kradat, 205
Koh Kut, 204
Koh Larn, 198, 227, 228
Koh Nok, 227
Koh Pannyi, 265
Koh Phangan, 231, 338
Koh Phi Phi, 209, 226, 227
Koh Samet, 200
Koh Samui Divers, 338
Koh Saui, 209, 210, 227, 228, 338, 372
Koh Si Chang, 196, 197
Koh Tao, 338
Kok River, 157
Korat, 11, 16, 177, 178, 183
Krab Big Game Fishing Contest, 342
Krabi, 225, 226, 227, 328
krabok, 283
krathong, 307
Krating Waterfall, 204
kruang sai, 285
Krung Thep Bridge, 95
Krungthep, 48
Krungthon Bridge, 108
Kuang River, 164
kuti, 273
Kwae Noi, 123, 138, 138

L

lacquerware, 69, 82, 313
Laem Chabang, 195
Laem Mae Phim, 202
Laem Ngop, 204
Laemthong Bank in Phuket, 363
Lahu, 155, *155*, 243, 248
Lai Nam Thong, 318-319
Lai Roi Nam, 313, 314
Lai-an, 363
Lak Muang, 48, 62, 389
lakorn jati, 232, 278, 282, 283, 285, 287
Lakshman, 278
Lamai, 228, 342
Lamphun, 164
Lampang, 8, 9, 145, 159, 165, 245, 276, 295, 373, 302
Lan Na Thai, 146

Lan Xang Hom Khao, 379
Landmark Hotel complex, 329, 349
Lane Xang Avenue, 385, 386, 389, 390
Lane Xang Hotel, 397
Lane Xang, 11, 12, 383, 393
language, 254
Lanna dynasty, 10, 149, 324
Lanna Golf Course, 324
Lanna royal family, 151
Lanna Thai architecture, *165*
Lanna Thai, 9, 11, 16, 146, 248, 249, 270, 146
Lanna tradition, 164
Lao authorities, 386
Lao Aviation, 397
Lao dialect, 252
Lao-influence, 175, 268, 389
lao khao, 119
Lao Loum people, 8
Lao Loum, 376
Lao nationalism, 380
Lao People's Democratic Republic, 380
Lao people, 379
Lao resistance government, 380
Lao society, 379
Lao Soung hill-tribe peoples, 380
Lao Soung, 376
Lao state, 379
Lao Theung peoples, 378
Lao Theung, 376
Lao Tourism office, 391, 395, 397
Lao's Supreme Patriarch, 389
Lao, *175*, 184, 375, 376, 378, 380, 383, 386, 389, 391
Lao-Buddhist state, 379
Lao-style, 185
Laos, 17, 34, 154, 159, 166, 176, 182, 183, 184, 185, 188, 242, 245, 252, 254, 375-397, 376, 379, 380, 381, 383, 391, 395
Laotian armies, 177
Laotian guides, 395
Laotian handicrafts, 188, 147, 246, 155, 184, 185, 386
Laotian border, 154
Lavo, 8
Lawa Cave, 126
Le Meridien Hotel, 222-224

Le Meridien President Hotel, 87, 114
leeches, 138
lemongrass, 347
lemurs, 41
leopard, 41
library, 61
Ligor, 231
likay, 232, 282, 285
Limelight, 112
lingam, 179
Lipstick, 111
Lisu, 155, 155, 243, 248
Little Beach, 205
lizards, 44, 45
Loan Island Resort, 340
Local Government, 10
Lod Cave, 159
Loei province, 190, 327
Loei, *180, 182*, 184, 188, 190, 300
Lohaprasad, 65
Lok Wah Hin, 352
London, 119, 276
Long-boat racing, *190*
Longan Fair, 302
longan harvest, 302
longtail boats, 126
longtail taxis, 332
Lookout Tower, 135
Lopburi Palace, 136
Lopburi Waterways, 372
Lopburi, 8, 119, 135, 137, 179, 268, 270, 273, 296
lotus flower offerings, 7
lotus, 38
Louis XIV, 136
Loy Krathong festival, 168, *255*
Loy Krathong, 292, 305, 307, 308
loy, 307
Luang Prabang Hotel, 391
Luang Prabang throne, 380
Luang Prabang, 391, 245, 379, 380, 383, 391, 393, 394, 395, 396, 397
Luang Wiang Lakon, Lampang, 294
Luang, 394
lucky charm, 258
luk tung, 282
lukmoh, 45
Lumpini Park, 71, 77, 113, 328

M

ma prow gatik, 347
macaques, 41
mae chi, 261
Mae Hong Son, 159, 162, 171, 296, 327, 328
Mae Kok River, 330
Mae Kok Villa, 330
Mae Kok, 331
Mae Kong Ka, 307
Mae Nam Khong, 184
Mae Nam, 102, 228, 343
Mae Rim Road, 324
Mae Rim Valley, 40
Mae Rim, 157
Mae Sa Valley, 157
Mae Sai, 159
Mae Salong, *153*
Magic Land, 77
magpies, 44
Maha Sarakham, 190
Mhabodhi of Bodh Gaya, 183
Mahanak, 52
Maharat Pier, 74
Mahayana Buddhism, 178, 179, 264
mahori, 284, 285
mahouts, 156
Mai Khao Beach, 221
Mai Nam, 341
main crop, 383
maize, 28, 37
Makha Bucha, 152, 291, 295, 297
Malay Peninsula, 10, 123, 231
Malay sultanantes, 254
Malay, 243, 245, 254, 264, 282
Malaya, 17, 122, 283, 285
Malaysia border, 227
Malaysia, 3, 264
Malee's Seafood Village, 361
Manchuria, 254
Maneeya Lotus Room, 106
Mango Festival, 291
mangrove forests, 38
Manhra & Nang Thalung, 232
Manohra, 232, 234, 285, 303
manufacturing, 28, 383
Marble Temple, 53, 67, *68, 69*
Marine National Park, 231
Market of Yesteryear, 76
markets, 130
Mars Party House, 109
Marxism, 381

Mechai, 246
meditation hall, *257*
Mee Grob, 358
Mekhala I, II, III, 330
Mekong Guest House, 3397
Mekong river, 159, 177, 183, 248, 304, 394
Mekong valley, 245, 376
Mekong, 183, 184, 185, 188, 267, 268, 375, 378, 391, 394
Members of Parliament, 24
Memorial Bridge, 54, 98
Menam Beach Samui, 230
Menam Hotel, 197
Mengrai, 9, 16, 146, 147, 148, 149, 157
Meo Village, 152
Meo, 154, 154, *244*, 248
Mergui, 16
merit, 152, 258, 261, 262
Merlin Hotel, 363
Metal Mansion, 65
metallurgy, 8
metalware, 81
Midnite Bar, 113
mien, 155
Mieng Kham, 234
migratory fowl, 44
Miss Bo Sang, 292
Mon civilisation, 246
Mon culture, 268
Mon people, 378
Mon state, 159
Mon, 8, 9, 10, 50, 118, 122, 145, 159, 164, 166, 243, 245, 246, 255
Mon-Khmer Buddhist civilisation, 8
Mon-Khmer kingdom, 8, 175
Mon-Khmer languages, 376
mon thong, 364
monarchist, 4
monarchy, 4, 260
monasteries, 262
monastic discipline, 261
mondop, 273
Mongkut, *13*, 17, 53, 65, 135, 202, 210, 294
Mongkut (Rama IV), 17, 272
Mongols, 9
mongooses, 138
monkeys, 41, 138
monkhood (social structure),

263-264
monkhood, 2, 261, 381
monks, 130, 183, 197, 257, 259, 262, 263
monsoon, 333
Montien Hotel, 283
Montien, 199
Montientong Theatre, 283
Montine Hotel, 109
Monument Aux Morts, 383, 384, 385, 386
Monument to the Unknown Soldier, 386
Mon–Khmer civilisation, 255
Moon Shadow, 114
mosque, 98
mosquitoes, 45, 327
Most Exalted Order of the White Elephant, 156
mother-of-pearl inlay, 82, 321
Moulmein, 11
Mount Meru, 68, 168
Mount Phousi, 391
Mountain of Steel, 394
mousedeer, 41
Mouse Island (Koh Meo), 236
Mrabri tribe, 171
Mu Koh Chang National Park, 204
Muang Boran, 76
Muang Vilai, 397
Muay Thai, 67
mudmee, 80, 312
Mukdahan, 184
Mun River, 178, 183
Mun, 184
murals, 149, 275, 276
Museum of the Revolution, 391
music (influences), 283
music, 267, 283-284
musical instruments, 83, 285
musical style, 252
Muslim, 50, 220, 227, *254*, 265
mynahs, 44
mythical Thai mermaid, 318

N

Na Dan, 202
Na Phralan Road, 99
Na Thon, 228
naak, 314
naga, 69, 232, *271*, 393
naga-flanked, 152
Nagara Sri Dharmaraja, 231

nagas, *153*, 180
Nai Harn Bay, 224
Nai Yang Beach, 221, 343
Nailert Park, 370
Nakhon In Tha Chang Road, 234
Nakhon Kasem, 91
Nakhon Nayok, 138
Nakhon Pathom, 8, 77, 118, 120, 184, 185, 272, 273,
Nakhon Ratchasima, 177, 292
Nakhon Sawan, 139, 294
Nakhon Si Thammarat, 16, 149, 231, 232, 233, 234, 237, 245, 254, 303, 315
NamKhan, Luang Prabang, 377
Nam Khna, 391
Nam Tok, 122 123-126
Namgkok, 332
Nan River, 303
Nan, 171
Nana Plaza, 112
Nanchao, 8, 245
Nang Chi, 100
Nang Noppamas, 307
Nag Nuai Seafood Restaurant, 360, 366
Nang Nual, 360
nang talung, 283
nang thalung, 233, 234, 285, 287, 303
nang yai, 283
Nantaburi, 364
Narai, 12, 16, 99, 129, 135, 136, 137
Narathiwat, 237, 254, 264
Naresuan the Great, 11
Nasa Spacedrome, 109
National Assembly, 22, 54, 66, 306
National Gallery, 62, 276
National Museum, 62, 168, 233, 237, 313, 318
National Park, 156, 213, 216
National Parks Division, 328
National Theatre, 62, 283
Navatanee, 325
neo-classicism, 275
neo-Gothic, 275
neolithic, 135
New Road, 53, 74, 90, 91
New World Department, 91
NIC (Newly Industrialised Country), 27

nielloware, 234, 315
night bazaar, 107
nightlife, 105-115, 373
nights, 327
Nipa, 348, 349
Nirvana, 64, 261
Nok, 305
Nong Don station, 296
Nong Khai, 184, 185, 188, 189, 397, 397
Nong Mol, 196
Nonthaburi, 95
north, 145-173
north (population), 248
North America, 40
north-east, 41
north-western Laos, 245
Northeast, 291
Northeastern plateau, 138
Northeasterners, 252
Northern Bus Terminal, 91, 397
northern Laos, 8
northern Nan, 255
Northern Terminal, 131
northern Thai food, 366
Northern Thai Hamlet, 76
northern Thailand, 37, *39*, 245
northern, 38
northern-eastern, 38
nothern Mekong, 379
Nun's Temple, 100

O

Ocean World, 196
oil, *30*
Ok Phansa, 262, 291, 304
old town, 146
opium poppy, 248
orchid, 38, 40
Oriental Hotel, 53, 74, 90, 95, 99, 106, 218, 325, 329, 329
Oriental Lane, 74
Oriental old wing, 98
Oriental Pier, 95, 332
Oriental Plaza, 90, 109
Oriental Queen I, II, 102, 332
ornamental wood carving, 85
Outer Palace, 134

P

Pa Sak River, 128
Padaung, *159*
PADI instruction, 342
Paduang, 159

pagoda, 135
pah, 45
Pahurat Market, 73
Pai River, 159
painting, 268, 275-278
Pak Chong, 138, 139
Pak Klong Market, 74
Pak Klong, 98
Pak Nam River Mouth, 102, 219
Pak On Cave, 375
Pali, 255
Pansea, 222
Pantip Plaza, 87
Panya Vijinthanasarn, 276
Paphiopedilum, 40
papier-mache, 85
parasailing, 343
park, 139, 327
parliamentary system, 21, 24
Paruhat Market, 91, 264
Pasak River, 130
Pasteur Institute, 72
Pathet Lao fighters, 381
Patheet Lao War Memorial, 386
Pathet Lao, 380
Patong Beach, 222, 224, 225, 333, 334, 338, 343, 361
Patong, 106, 107, 109, 112, 222, 239, 343,
Patpong 1, 111
Patpong 2, 111, 112
Patpong 3, 113
Pattani, 16, 237, 254, 264
Pattani, Yala, Narathiwat, 237
Pattaya Bay, 332
Pataya Game Fishing Club, 342
Pattaya, *195*, 197, 198, 198, 201, 202, 213, 227, 305, 323, 325, 332, 334, 335, 336, 342, 343, 357, 360
Payao, 9, 16
Pearl Village resort, 222
pearls, 82
Chinese food, 353
Peninsula Plaza, 87
People, 243-255
People's Republic, 391
Peppermint Bistro, 109
Persians, 136
Petchabun Mountains, 190, 300
Petchburi, 55, 87
pewterware, 81
Pha Taem, 184
Phaholyothin Road, 91

Phalaenoposis, 40
Phang-nga, 220, 323
Phangan Island, 231
Phangnga bay, 225, 335
Phanwa, 225
Phattalung, 44, 234
Phayao, 146
Phetumiroj Hall of the Khao Wang, 210
Phetburi Province, 211
Phetburi River, 210
Phetburi, 210, 211
Phetchabun province, 191
Phetchaburi Road, 356
Phetchaburi, 292, 294
Phi Island, 225
Phi Ta Khon Festival, 300
Phi-Phi Island, 226, 227, 338
Phichit Boat Races, 302, 303
Phichit, 303
Phimai, 177, 179
Phiman Mongkut, 135
Phitsanulok, 171
Phlu Ta Luang Golf Course, 325
Phom Phet Fortress, 130
Phra Aphaimani, 202
Phra Bang, 379, 391
Phra Buddhabat Fair, 295, 302
Phra Buddhabat shrine, 273
Phra Isawara Sumrit, 169
Phra Mongkol Ming Muang, 183
Phra Nakhon Cave, 216
Phra Nakhon Khiri Fair, 294
Phra Nakhon Khiri, 210
Phra Narai Raja Nivet, 135
Phra Pathom Chedi, 118
Phra Pinklao Bridge, 98
Phra Putthabat, 137
Phra Setag Khamani, 149
Phra Sila, 149
Phra Singh Buddha, 234
Phra Singh, 149
Phra Sumane, 98
Phra Taew National Park, 225
Phra Thinang Uthayan Phumisathian, 134
Phra Thinang, 131, *132*, 134
Phra Tinang Wehat Chamrun, 134
Phrae, 171
Phu Kradung National Park, 189, 327
Phu Kradung, 189, 190
Phu Phaan Mountains, 191

Phu Phaan National Park, 191
Phuket Big Game Fishing Charter, 343
Phuket Centre Tour, 340
Phuket Fishing Club, 343
Phuket Golf and Country Club, 326
Phuket Island Tour, 340
Phuket Island, *31*, 220, 327, 338
Phuket King's Cup Regatta, 333
Phuket Sea Canoe Centre, 335
Phuket Tourist Centre, 343, 335
Phuket town, 225
Phuket Travel and Tour, 340
Phuket Yacht Club, 224
Phuket, 28, 44, 209, 210, 213, 220, 221, 223, 224, 225, 227, 238, 326, 332, 333, 334, 335, 337, 338, 341, 342, 343, 361, 365
Phuping Palace, 152
Phya Chakri, 48
Phya Taksin, 13
Phya Valleys 267
Phyathai Road, 72
pi nai, 285
pi phat, 284
Pi Sua Samut, 202
Piman, 106
pineapple, 28
Ping River, 146, 168, 169, 245, 366, 378
Pink Panther, 113
piphat, 282, 285
Plain of Jars, 394
pleng rua, 93
Pliu Waterfall, 204
Ploenchit Road, 71, 87, 88, 89, 106, 259
poetry, 267
Poi Sang Long, 296
pop music, 284
poppy harvest, 39, *160*
popular culture, 267
Population Control, 246
porcelain, 134, 318
porcupines, 138
Portuguese, 12, 315
Portuguese Embassy, 98
Portuguese-influence, 315
Pra Nang Beach, 221
Prachuab Khiri Khan, 209
Prachuap Bay, 217, 218

Prachuap Khiri Khan, 216, 217, 218, 372
Pradipat Road, 373
Prakhon Chai, 179
Pramane Ground, 62, 328
Pranburi, 213
Pranburi Beach Resort, 213
Prang Khaek, 136
Prang Sam Yod, 136, 137
prang, 68, 128, 129, 136, 137, 171, 273, 284, 272
Pransiri Hotel, 213
Prasad Phra Thepidon, 60/61
Prasat Hall, 136
Prasat Hin Phimai, 177, 178
Prasat Hin, 178
Prasat Khao Phra Viharn, 180
Prasat Muang Tam, 180
Prasat Phanom Rung, *176*, 178, 179, 180
Prasat Phanom, 179
Prasat, 283
Pratu Chai, 177
Pratunam Market, 74, 86, 87
Pratunam, 107, 356
prayer, 260
pre-Bangkok literature, 284
pre-history, 7, 8
precious stones, 82
presidential palace, 386
Prince Fa Ngum, 379
Prince of Burma, 139
Prince of U Thong, 10
Prince Rama, 278
Prince Vessandorn, 300
Princess Sita, 278
private clubs, 329
Private Fitness Clinic Health Club, 329
Promthep Cape, 224
props, 82
Province Hall, 168
Pu Island, 224
Pussy Galore/Alive, 111
pythons, 45

Q

Queen Sirikit, 314
Queen, 135

R

Racha, 338
Rachaprarop Road, 356
Radamnern Avenue, 53

Raging Bulls, 237
rainfall, 117
rainforests, 38
rainy season, 117, 118
Raja Orot, 100
Rajadamnern Nok Avenue, 306
Rajadamnern Road, 233
Rajadamnern, 305
Rajadamnoen Klang Avenue, 91
Rajadamnoen Klang, 65
Rajadamnoen Nok, 66
Rajadamnoen Stadium, 66
Rajdamri Arcade, 87
Rajdamri Road, 71, 87, 90, 259
rak samu, 315
rak, 314
Rama Garden Hotel, 324, 328
Rama I Road, 90, 369, 370
Rama IV Road, 71
Rama I, 14, 17, 48, 99
Rama VI, 134, 135, 212
Ramahibodi, 10
Ramesuan, 129
Ramkhamhaeng, 7, 9, 11, 16, 146, 166, 231, 255
Rama II, 15, 17, 202, 315
Rama III, 15, 17, 52, 64, 100
Rama IV, 17, 18, 52, 72, 73
Rama Park, 128
Rama V, 18, 73, 134, 210, 314
Rama VII, 18
Rama, 315
Ramakien, 60, 61, 278, *280*, 284, 287
Ramayana, 278, 287
Rambutan Fair, 291
Ramkhamhaeng National Museum, 168
Ramkhamhaeng, 10
ramwong, 225, 252, 373
ranat, 285
Rang Hill, 361
Rangsit Canal, 94
Ranong, 34, 219, 220
Ratchadamnoen Klang, 65
Ratchburi, 139
Rattanakosin architecture, 101, 131, *132*
Rattanakosin era, 14, 50
Rattanakosin Island, 14, 48, 62, 64
Ravana, 278
Rawai Beach, 224, 225
Rayong, 195, 200, 200, 364

Reclining Buddha, 170
recreational activities, 336
Red Dragon, 197
Regent Cha-am, 212
Regent Hotel, 87, 106
Regent Restaurant, 353
regional culture, 8
Relax Bay, 222
Religion, 257-265
religious art, 267-268
religious practice, 243
Renaissance style, 134
restaurant, 139
Reun Thai Restaurant, 358
Reun Thai, 358
rhododendron, 38
rice barge, 102, 330
rice exporter, 119
rice, 27, 37, 117, 119, 139, *140*, 175
rice-bowl, 117
ricefields, 37
Rim Nam terrace, 347
Rim Nam, 346
River Bridge Week, 306
River Chao Phraya, 67, 129
River City, 90, 108
River Kok, *158*
River Kwai Noi, 122
River Kwai, 44, 77, 120, *121*, 122, 123, 372
River Mekong, 33, 176, 184, 376, 397
River Nam Khan, 391
River Nan, Central Plains, 302
River Ping, 367
River Sun Cruises, 332
River Sun, 102, 332
roads, 55
Robert Trent Jones, 325
Robinson, 87, 90, 113
Rock Pubs, 113
Rocket Festival, 297, 301
Roi Et, 190, 191
Rome Club, 109, 113
Rooftop Chinese Restaurant, 363
Rose Garden, 76, 325
Rotchana Road, 127
Round Midnight, 114
Royal Banquet Hall, 136
Royal Barge Museum, 169, 01
Royal Barge Procession, 69
Royal Boat House, 98

Royal Cliff Beach, 199
Royal Cliff Resort, 357
Royal Family, 211
Royal Fine Arts Department, 100, 178, 180
Royal Garden Resort, 213
Royal Garden, 199
Royal Hua Hin Golf Course, 326
Royal Residence of Heavenly Light, 134
Royal Orchid Holidays, 40
Royal Orchid Sheraton Hotel, 40, 90
Royal Palace, 129, 328, 386, 391
Royal Palace, Thammasat University, 328
Royal Plaza, 22, 306
Royal Ploughing Ceremony, 119, 297, 298
Royal Residence of the Garden of the Secured Land, 134
Royal Seafood, 352
Royal Thai Navy Golf Course, 325
rua duan, 95
rua mai, 99
ruah hang yao, 99
rubber plantations, 28, 37
rubies, 82, 203
Ruen Thep, 106

S

sa, 315, 321
Safari World, 77
Safari, 112
Sai Nam Yan School, 363
Sai Yok Nai Falls, 123, 126
sailing craft, 334
sailing, 333
Sakhon Nakhon, 190, 191, 304, 305
Sakorn Sin, 108
Sala Rim Naam, 106, 346
Sala Thai, 106
sala, 272
Salathai Restaurant, 365
salt, 28
Sam Mok Tour Co., 330
Sam Roi Yod Three Hundred Peaks, 216
Samae San, 335, 336, 342
sambar, 41

samook, 314
Sampeng Lane, 73, 91
Samsenthai Street, 385, 390, 391
Samui Bhoput, 343
Samui Island, 227, 230
Samui, 231, 333, 334, 338, 341, 342, 343
Samut Prakarn, 76
Samut Sakhon, 372
San Kamphaeng, 157
Sanam Luang, 62, 91, 119, 276, 297, 298, 306, 328
Sang Thai Seafood Restaurant, 365
Sanphet Prasat, 129
Sanphet Road, 127
Sanskrit, 255
Santa Cruz church, 98
sanuk, 5, 291
Sao Chaliang, 184
Saphankwai, 373
Sapphire Ring Hill, 203
sapphires, 82, 203
Sarabrui, 137, 138, 273, 302
Sarasin Bridge, 220
Sarika Waterfall, 138
Sathorn Road, 53
Sattaheep, 325, 335, 336
Sattahip, 200
Satun, 227, 254, 264
Savannakhet, 389
Sawankhalok, 171, 318
Saxophone, 114
scuba-diving, 336
sculpture, 168, 268, 269
Sea Gypsies, 225
sea sports, 329
Sea Tran Queen, 335
sea turtles, 44, 221
seafari, 342
Seafood, 348
Second World War, 380
secular architecture, 273
Sema, 177, 275
services, 27, 102
Settathirat, 383, 386, 379, 389
Seve Ballesteros, 325
Shan Mountains, 159
Shan people, 8, 159, 378
Shangri-La Hotel, 326
Sheraton Hotel, 108
Shiva, 50, 65, 136, 137, 169, 179

Shopping, 79-91
Shrine of the Holy Footprint, 295
Si Phya Pier, 108
Si Racha, 196
Si Sa Ket, 182
Si Satchanalai, 10, 171, 318
Siam Cement, 253
Siam Center, 90
Siam Diving Centre, 340
Siam Inter-continental, 106, 325, 370
Siam International Hotel, 328
Siam Park, 77
Siam Society, 70, *72*
Siam Square, 89, 102
Siam, 16, 126, 128, 136, 175, 379, 380
Siamese court, 12
Siamese Fighting Fish, 45
Siamese, 175, 249, 379
Sikhs, 264
silk-weaving, 312
silk, *79, 80*
Silom Plaza, 109
Silom Road, 53, 55, *80*, 90, 106, 107, 109, 113, 154, 264, 311, 313
Silom Village, 90, 106
Silom, 90, 313, 317
Silpa Bhirasri, 276
Silpakorn University, 62, 276
silver, 81
silver rupees, 317
silverware, 315, 316
Simila Hotel, 236
Similan Islands, 338
Similan Isles, 337
Singapore, 27
Singtoh Island, 213
Sino Thai Wares, 318
Sino-Portuguese influences, 225
Sino-Tibetan languages, 254
Sino-Tibetan, 147
Siray, 225
Sirindhorn Dam, 183
Sisavangvong, 379, 390, 393
slash–and–burn agriculture, 248
snake-blood drinking, 236
Snake Farm, 72
snakes, 44
snorkelling, 335, 339
Sogo Department Store, 87

Soi, 24, 26, 55, 113, 114
Soi Asoke, 83
Soi Charoen Suk, 114
Soi Cowboy, 112, 113
Soi Langsuan, 114
Soi Sarasin, 113
som tam, 252
Sompop Budtarad, 276
Somsak, 357, 358
song thaew, 225
Songai Golok, 33
Songkran, 292
Songkhla, 5, *30*, 236, 237, 292, 297
sonng thaew, 228
Sop Ruak, 159
Sorasak Road, 136
Souligna Vongsa, 379
South East Asia Yacht Centre, 340
South Korea, 27
South, 241, *254*
Southeast Asia, 2, 29, 196, 379
southern China, 155
Southern Thailand, 34, *265*, 333
Southerners, 254
Special Red Rice, 349
spirit house, 259
Spirits of the Yellow Leaves, 171, 255
Sports fishing, 342
sports and recreation, 323-343
squirrels, 41
Sri Ayutthaya Road, 69
Sri Lanka, 149
Sri Lankan tradition, 10
Sri Lankan, 150
Sri Nakharin Dam, 126
Sri Nakharin Lake, 126
Sri Satchanalai Historical Park, 168
Sri Satchanalai, *166*, 168
Sri Suphannahongse, 69
Sri Thammarat, 9
Srivijaya Empire, 231, 236
Srivijaya, 231, 267, 268
standard Central Thai, 255
staple food, 252
Star Yachting, 334
Station, 306
Straw Bird Fair, 294
Street-side dining, 353
Study Centre, 129
stupa, 136, 148, 152

Suan Moke, 151
Suan Pakkad, 69
Suan Sida, 138
Suang Kong Kaew, 138
sugar cane, 37
Sugar, 28
Sukhothai Buddha sculpture, 270
Sukhothai girl, *255*
Sukhothai Historical Park, 168, 307
Sukhothai kingdom, 270
Sukhothai period, 260
Sukhothai style, 270
Sukhothai, 9, 10, 16, 145, 146, 164, *166*, *167*, 168, 170, 231, 245, 255, 268, 270, 273, 306, 307, 308, 318
Sukhumvit Road, 88, 102, 107, 195, 318, 349, 373
Sukhumvit Soi, 112, 106
Sukhumvit, 55, 89, 313
Sukthothai, Chiang Mai, Bangkok, 305
Sumatra, 231
Sumatran rhinoceros, 38
Summer Palace, *136*
Sun and Sand Tour, 340
Sunni Muslims, 264
Sunthorn Phu, 200, 202
Supergirls, 111
Superhighway, 109, 150
supersition, 257
Superstar, 109, 112
Suphanburi town, 294
Suphanburi, 139
SUPPORT Foundation, 315
supremacy, 60
Supreme Patriarch, 391
Supreme, 385
Surat Thani port, 231
Surat Thani province, 151, 227
Surat Thani, 119, 210, 228, 229, 291, 305
Surin Beach, 222
Surin Elephant Round-Up, 306
Surin Islands, 338
Surin, *259*, 306
Suriwong Road, 112, 113
Suriyas Amarin Hall, 129
Suryavarman II, 179
Suthep Road, 151
Swiss International Diving Centre, 338

Sydney, 119
Szechuan food, 352

T

T'ai people, 8, 9, 252, 378
Ta Khli Station, 294
Tad Tone Waterfall, 184
Taiwan, 27
Tak Bat Devo, 305
Tak Bat Dok Mai, 300
Tak, 38, 171
Taksin, 14, 17, 99
Talad Nakhon Kasem, 73
TAM Dance Company, 283
Tam Nak Nam, 360
Tambon Hua Laem, 317
Tambralinga, 231
Taoist beliefs, 154
taphon, 285
tapian, 317
tapioca, 28, 37
tapir, 41
Tarutao island, 227
Tarutao Marine National Park, 227
Tasaneeya Nava, 108
TAT Duty Free Store, 88
tattoos, 258
Tea Rose, 349
teak, 37, 85
telephone system, 29
temple architecture, 268, 273
temple mural painting, 275
temple murals, 287
Temple of the Dawn, *49*, 68, 98, 99
Temple of the Emerald Buddha, 14, 50, 59, 129, 273, 297, 328
Temple of the Reclining Buddha, 64, 287
temple roof, *271*
Tenasserim Mountains, 122
tennis, 323
Tewan Sapsanyakorn, 284
Tewes, 98
Textiles, 79
Tha Chin River, 372
Tha Deua, 397
Tha Orienten, 99
Tha Thien Pier, 332
thaan khao, 119
Thai Airways, 40, 397
Thai architecture, 324

Thai art, 83, 145
Thai Boxing, 67
Thai Buddhist tradition, 253, 261
Thai civilisation, 260
Thai cuisine, 345, 366
Thai cultural dance ahow, 346
Thai culture, 260, 287
Thai Daimaru, 87
Thai Dam (Black Thai), 245, 390
Thai ethnic, *72*
Thai European Restaurants, 366
Thai family, 245
Thai invaders, 388
Thai kingdoms, 267, 268
Thai Market Restaurant, 357
Thai monarchy, 131
Thai nation, 10
Thai nationhood, 10
Thai New Year, 296
Thai Night, 106
Thai people, 8
Thai principalities, 159
Thai Red Cross, 72
Thai Rodeo, 197
Thai Silk, 312
Thai society, 154
Thai style, 270
Thai Vegetarian, 366
Thai Village, 106
Thai vocabulary, 255
Thai woman, 258
Thai writing system, 10, 255
Thai Yachting, 332, 334
Thai Yai (Greater Thai), 245
Thai Yai tribal group, 296
Thai, 3, 4, 17, 69, *70*, 122, 135, 145, 146,159, 179, 184, 282, 375
Thai-Buddhist civilisation, 145
Thai-Buddhist culture, 1, 4
Thai-speaking, 8
Thai-style,131
Thailand Cultural Centre, 283
Thailand, 4, 8, 118, 122, 126, 131, 146, 147, 152, 159, 179, 180, 180, 185, 254, 376, 378
Thais (southern), 254
Thais, 2, 5, 7, 10, 118, 122, 146, 166, 184, 243, 378
Thale Noi Waterbird Sanctuary, 236

Thale Noi, 44
Thale Sap, 236
thalung, 233
tham ngaan, 119
Thammasat University, 62
Thao Suranari, 177
That Luang Temple Fair, 386
That Phanom, 184, 185
That, 278
The East, 195-207
The Grand Palace, *275*
The King's Birthday Celebration, 306
The Living Place, 363
The Lobster Pot, 358
The Mall, 87
The Palace, 109
The Red Chapel, 393
The Riverside, 366
The South, 209-241
The Theque, 109
The White Orchid, 367
The Whole Earth, 351
Theatrical costumes, 82
Theravada Buddhism, 10, 268, 375, 378
Thervada Buddhist, 264
Thewes Market, 74
thiaw, 369
Thieves Market, 73, 91
Thigh Bar, 112
Thiparet Road, 152
Thoburi, 273, 276, *277*, 279
Thon-Lamai, 228
Thonburi Bangkok Noi, 306
Thonburi temple, 202
Thonburi, 14, 48, 50, 54, 55, 67, 69, 94, 99, 102, 332, 372
Thonburi, Thong tree, 393
Thong Yang Beach, 228
Three Hundred Peaks, 213
Three Pagodas Pass, 33, 122
Thumnakthai, *109*
Thung Wua Laen Beach, 219
Tibet, 154, 254
Tibetan people, 155
Tibeto-Burman, 154, 376
Tien Kung Chinese Restaurant, 363
tiger, 38, 138, 190
Tilokaraj, 12, 147, 149
tin deposits, 28
tine mine, *31*

tobacco, 37
Tod Kathin, 262, 303
Tom McNamara, 361
Tomas Tour Co., 330
Ton Sai, 225
Tongsai Bay, 228
Tortoises, 44,
Tosakan, 315
Tourism Authority of Thailand, 68, 327
tourism, 29, 176, 327
tourist expenditure, 29
Tourist Police, 111
tourist season, 176
trade, 15, 48, 98
traditional painting, 275
Trailok of Ayutthaya, 16
train, 370
Trang & Satun, 227
Trang, 227, 304
transvestite, 113
Trat Road, 204
Trat, 195, 204, 205
trees, 38
trekking, 157, 326
tribal people, 243
Trimuk, 129
tripatka, 61
tripitaka, 273
Trok Chang, 203
Trooping of the Colours, 306
tuk-tuk, 128, 372
Tumnak Thai, 346
Tung Ming, 231
turbo snail, 321
twin-sitting Buddhas, 170

U

U-Tapao, 195
U-Thong, 129, 139, 245, 268
Ubon Ratchathani in Isan, 300
Ubon Ratchathani railway, 179
Ubon Ratchathani, 33, 177, 182, 183, 291, 300
Ubon, 183, 184, 188
ubosot, 99, 100
Udon Thani, 8, 185, 188
Umbrella Fair, 292
Umbrella Fan Festival, 293
Umbrellas, 321
underwater sport, 336
United Nations, 376
US base, 17
USAID, 385

USSR, 381
Uthai Thani, 305

V

valleys, 268
vanda cerulea, 40
Vegetarian Festival, 304
vegetarians, 352
Versailles, 136
Vichai Prasit Fort, 99
Victory Gate, 177
Victory Monument, 109, 114
Vientiane, 14, 379, 380, 383, 386, 394, 395, 396, 397
Viet Cong, 380
Viet Minh, 380
Vietnam War, 17, 112, 154, 177, 183, 380, 383, 394
Vietnam, 17, 55, 203, 245, 375, 379, 380, 381
Vietnamese troops, 381, 383
Vietnamese, 50, 185, 204, 243, 245, 246, 264
Vietnamese-French influence, 203
Viharn Laikam, 149
Viharn Luang, 233
Viharn Somdet, 129
viharn, 64, 100, 148, 149, 164, 257, 272, 276, 389, 393
Vimarnmek Palace, 61, 66, 69, 273
Visakha Bucha, 152, 291, 297
Vishnu, 137, 389
Visual Dhamma Gallery, 83

W

wai, 257
Wan Fah, 108
Wang Bang Pa-In, 131
Wang Kaew, 202
Wang Luang, 129
Wang Takrai Botanical garden, 138
Warin Chamrap, 183
Warophat Piman, 134
Washington Cinema, 373
Wat Arun, 48, 49, 50, 68, 98, 99, 273
Wat Benjamabopit, 67, *68*, 295
Wat Bovornives, 65, 91, 295
Wat Buddhapadipa, 276
Wat Bupparam, 152, 153
Wat Chang Rop, 170

Wat Chedi Luang, 149
Wat Chet Yod, 150
Wat Chiang Man, *148*
Wat Chom Khiri Nak Phrot, 139
Wat Dusit Daram, 279
Wat Haripunchai, 165
Wat Intharam, 99, *277*
Wat Jong Kham, 159
Wat Jong Klang, 159
Wat Lampang Luang, 295
Wat Lokaya Sutha, 129
Wat Mahathat, 62, 128, 168, 171
Wat Maheyong, 234
Wat Mani Cholakhan, 137
Wat May, 391
Wat Nak, Vientiane, 396
Wat Nivet Dhammaprawat, 135
Wat Nong Bua, 183
Wat Nong Pa Pong, 183
Wat Pa Mok, 139
Wat Pak Nam, 100
Wat Palelai, 139
Wat Phai Lom, 102
Wat Phra Buddhabat Saraburi, 295, 296, 300
Wat Phra Buddhabat, 296
Wat Phra Kaew Don Tao, 164
Wat Phra Kaew, 15, 59, 62/64, 157, 262, 272, 276
Wat Phra Keo the Temple, 389
Wat Phra Keo, 379, 383, 389
Wat Phra Mahthat, 233, 234
Wat Phra Mongkol Bophit, 129
Wat Phra Ram, 129
Wat Phra Si Atana Mahathat, 137
Wat Phra Si Iriyabot, 170
Wat Phra Si Sanphet, 129
Wat Phra Singh, 149
Wat Phra That Doi Tung, 157
Wat Phra That Sadet, 164
Wat Phra, 64
Wat Phrathat Doi Suthep, 152
Wat Phrathat Haripunchai, 145, 164, 276
Wat Phrathat Lampang Luang, 164
Wat Phrathat, 170
Wat Phu, 394
Wat Po Temple, *63*
Wat Po, 62, 98
Wat Pra Kaew, 169, 170
Wat Prakeu, 164

Wat Raj Burana, 127, 129
Wat Rajanada, 74
Wat Saket, 305
Wat Si Sanphet, 128
Wat Simuang, 389
Wat Singh, 170
Wat Sisaket, 380, 383, 388, 389
Wat Sri Chum, 164, 168
Wat Sri Rong Muang, 164
Wat Suan Dok, 150, 151
Wat Suthat, 50, 64, 65, 276
Wat Suvarnaram, 101, 276
Wat Tapotharam, 220
Wat Tham Malai, 234
Wat Thammamum, 139
Wat Thammikaram, 216
Wat That Luang, 379, 383, 385, 386
Wat That Phanom, 185
Wat Traimitr, 73
Wat Trapang Thong, 168
Wat Umong, 151
Wat Xieng Thong, 392, 393
Wat Xieng, 391
Wat Yai Suwannaram, 211
water birds, 44
water buffalo, 126, 156, 197
water lily, *42*
water market, 120
water sports, 329
waterways around Bangkok, 330
waterways, 329
water-skiing, 343
Wax Castle Festival, 304
wedding ceremony, 260
Weekend Market, 74, 91
Western imperialists, 17
Western tradition, 276
Westerners, 122, 123
Westernisation, 246
wet season, 397
Whole Earth, 366
wian tian, 295
Wichayen Road, 136, 137
Wimbledon, 276
Witch's Tavern, 114
Withayu, 370
wizard–monks, 263
Wong Deuan Beach, 201
Wongwian Yai Station, 372
wood-carving, 318
woodwork, 85
World Trade Centre, 87, 259

World War II, 17
World War, *121*, 122
worship, 260

X
Xieng Khouang, 394

Y
Yacht Services Co. Ltd., 334
Yala, 237, 254, 264, 295
Yan Libu, 314
yan lipao, 234, 314
Yao, 154, *154*, 243, 248, 380
Yaowaraj, 74
Yasothon, 190, 191, 192, 297, 300, 301
Yi Peng Loy Krathong, 306
Young Elephant Training Centre, 373
Yunnan, 8, 245

Z
Zen department store, 87

PHOTO CREDITS

Terry Andrews : 41, 218/219
Rita Ariyoshi : 100, 101
Marcus Brooke : xiv, 31 top right, 44/45, 98, 125, 154 top, 154 centre, 154 bottom, 155 left, 155 top right, 155 bottom right, 156, 160 top, 166, 167, 178, 179, 194, 196, 200/201, 220, 222, 224, 225, 244, 245, 248/249, 250, 254, 264, 265, 277 bottom, 282, 319, 322, 325, 326, 333, 336, 341, 343
Mary Connors : 393 right, 394, 396, 397
Wendy Chan : vi top, xi top left, 52, 60/61, 116, 320
Jean Leo Dugast : 6, 26, 28, 31 bottom right, 94, 95, 128, 232, 251, 256, 263, 271, 273, 285, 301 bottom, 302, 304, 307
Design Thai : 78, 80
Alain Evrard : Back cover top left, back cover top right, vi bottom left, vi/vii centre, viii bottom left, 5, 49, 63, 82, 83, 109, 110, 112/113, 159, 203, 230 top, 242, 255, 289, 293, 296, 308/309, 370/371
Peter Friedrich : 39 bottom, 42/43, 313, 364
Marlene Guelden : 20, 252, 277 top, 279
James Huchison/Margo Pfeiff : 45 bottom right
Joe Lynch : vii right, 118/119, 189, 229, 259, end-paper front
Aileen Lau : 72
Doug McMillan : End-paper back
John May : 39 top
Keith Mundy : viii/ix centre, xiii centre, 22/23, 24, 25, 46, 53,54, 55, 71, 75, 77, 104, 108, 111, 115, 120/121, 122/123, 123, 130/131, 132/133, 134, 136, 138/139, 147, 152, 153 top, 153 bottom, 158, 160 bottom, 165, 169, 170, 174, 180, 182, 183, 184, 185, 190, 192, 193, 216, 217, 262, 301 top, 330/331, 374, 377, 378, 379, 381, 382, 384, 385, 387, 388, 390, 392, 393 left, 395
Gilles Massot : ix top right, x, xi bottom centre, xii top right, 35, 36, 58, 61 bottom right, 70, 84 top, 84 bottom, 86, 87, 91, 205, 211, 212, 269, 272, 274, 368
RCA Nichols : 68, 69, 88/89, 124 top, 124 bottom, 127, 208, 221, 226/227
Fiona Nichols : ix bottom right, 181, 316 top, 337, 339, 340
Allan Seiden : 312
Tony & Nok : 348, 356, 367
Mathias Tugores : xii bottom left, 290
Luca Invernizzi Tettoni : Cover, back cover bottom, 2/3, 9, 13, 19, 30, 56/57, 92, 96/97, 106/107, 140, 144, 148/149, 150/151, 162/163, 186/187, 198/199, 214/215, 223, 247, 266, 280/281, 286/287, 298/299, 310, 344, 350/351, 354/355, 359, 362
Eric Yeo : 90, 171, 230 bottom, 268, 275, 316 bottom
Julia Wilkison : 176, 188

NOTES

NOTES